Race in American Sports

Race in American Sports

Essays

Edited by
JAMES L. CONYERS, JR.

McFarland & Company, Inc., Publishers
Jefferson, North Carolina

The essay by N. Jeremi Duru originally appeared in *Virginia Sports Entertainment Law Journal*, vol. 7, no. 2 (Spring 2008): 179–197.

LIBRARY OF CONGRESS CATALOGUING-IN-PUBLICATION DATA

Race in American sports : essays / edited by James L. Conyers, Jr.
    p.   cm.
    Includes bibliographical references and index.

    ISBN 978-0-7864-7319-9 (softcover : acid free paper) ∞
    ISBN 978-1-4766-1584-4 (ebook)

    1. Racism in sports—United States.   I. Conyers, James L.
GV706.32R3 2014
796.089'96073—dc23   2014012474

BRITISH LIBRARY CATALOGUING DATA ARE AVAILABLE

On the cover: (left to right) Jackie Robinson (Library of Congress); Jeremy Lin (Nicholas La); Kirk Cousins (Mobilus)

Printed in the United States of America

McFarland & Company, Inc., Publishers
  Box 611, Jefferson, North Carolina 28640
    www.mcfarlandpub.com

Table of Contents

Introduction

This volume's essays look at race and sports from an interdisciplinary perspective. Researchers locate how race and sport directly and indirectly enhance the conversations surrounding social inequities, racism, and the creation of subordinate group status. Simply put, sport is a form of entertainment, but it is also a million-dollar business which allows the display of men's and women's athletic prowess to be exhibited in an arena of competition, on the collegiate and professional levels.

There is more at play than just the winners or losers of a Sunday football game or weeknight baseball game. Americans employ race and sport as tools to interlink our world-view about politics, economics, history, literature, education and modern events.

The lineup begins with Rita Liberti's "'As Girls See It': Writing Sport on the Margins of the Black Press." Her essay describes the writings of three women in the pages of the *Baltimore Afro-American* of the 1930s, illustrating the solid space female athleticism held in the community and on the pages of the black press. The columns take on greater significance as a window through which to examine broader issues related to racial and gendered politics of the period.

Billy Hawkins, Joseph N. Cooper and Ashley Baker, in "The Modern Day Black Sporting Experience: A Dialogue on Race," examine current popular black athletes and the sports media commentary around them to show how notions of race are created, reinforced or reproduced. Historically, black athletes have been used to construct certain ideas about race; for males, physicality or bruteness, while the female was either asexual or hypersexualized.

What little is known about the experiences of today's black female college athletes is that these experiences have been marked by racial and gender stereotypes, social isolation and alienation, silencing, a thirst for mentorship, and the on-going development of coping mechanisms within their daily environment. In "An Ethic of Care: Black Female College Athletes and Development,"

Akilah R. Carter-Francique explores these issues surrounding the development of black female college athletes who attend predominantly white institutions of higher education and programmatic benefits of fostering social development.

When Jackie Robinson joined the major leagues in 1947, what took place in Brooklyn was perceived by many as unthinkable, inconceivable, unconscionable and un–American. But the event provided the impetus for the questioning of civil liberties, and ultimately social change in America. Demetrius W. Pearson focuses on what happened in the city in "Right Place, Right Time: The Galvanization of Brooklyn During the Robinson Years."

Earl Smith argues that the primary mechanism that drives the exploitation of student athletes is "The Athletic Industrial Complex." The AIC is an institution embedded in both higher education and the global sports economy and as such it has the power to shape hegemonic ideology and collude with other institutions in the enterprise of sports. His essay focuses on conference realignment, race and Title IX.

Too few fans, educators, alumni, policy makers and pundits have had to come to terms with the conditions that continue to use Indian mascots and make such imagery and rituals pleasurable, powerful and profitable. Discussing these issues is C. Richard King in "Encountering the Undead: An Open Letter on the Persistent Problem of Native American Mascots."

J. Kenyatta Cavil reviews the possibilities of moving one institution to another athletic conference in "The Case for Tennessee State as an Expansion Member of the SWAC: Economic Impact." It's a question of maximizing potential.

One Chicago baseball team was also known for its skating rink, dance hall, bowling alley and a movie theater. Michael E. Lomax writes about "The Leland Giants Baseball and Amusement Association: A Symbol of Race Pride Through Self-Help, 1907–1911." His essay explains how the Leland Giants emerged as the premier black semiprofessional club in the Midwest; how the association maintained its relationship with white semiprofessional teams and its attempt to exploit Chicago's growing black consumer market; and how it collapsed.

David J. Leonard looks at "Linsanity" in "A Fantasy in the Garden, a Fantasy America Wants to Believe: Jeremy Lin, the NBA and Race Culture." The Asian American basketball player's ascendance meant something not simply because it propelled the New York Knicks back into the playoffs, but because he represents or embodies a larger narrative; he signifies larger debates and sources of tension.

In "Institutional Barriers and Self-Handicapping Behaviors of Black Male Student-Athletes: Catalysts for Underperformance in the Classroom," Gary

A. Sailes and Rebecca Milton Allen examine what contributes to underachievement in the classroom for black male student-athletes. Black student athletes are among the poorest academic performers compared to all student athlete groups and have the lowest graduation percentages. Black athletes receive more attention from university officials and the media when they get into trouble, exacerbating the stereotype that black athletes are "gangstas" and emanate from undisciplined environments where few rules exist to restrict their behavior.

Ray V. Robertson asks "Why Do I Get Hit in the Face?" It is because he stepped into the ring to learn more about the myriad constructions of masculinity of a young African American professional boxer.

N. Jeremi Duru looks at the history of racial exclusion in the NFL, the barriers minority coaches seeking NFL head coaching positions have faced, and the changes in "The Fritz Pollard Alliance, the Rooney Rule and the Quest to Level the Playing Field in the NFL."

How do we nurture future athletes, mind, body and soul, to prepare them to embrace the joys and challenges that are inherent when one possesses out-of-the-ordinary athletic talent? Edward "Will" Thomas gets down to basics in "Does Race Matter? Core Character Matters."

The concept of race and sport in America is vexing. James L. Conyers, Jr., offers "Sacrifice, Modality, Inspiration and Triumph: An Afrocentric Analysis of Race and Sport in America."

Drew Brown uses Fanonian analysis in "Race, Colonization and the NFL Draft: A Fanonian Analysis of the Interviewing of Black NFL Prospects" to tackle the ways in which language, criminal stereotypes and inferiority as characteristics of colonization exist in interviews during the NFL drafting process by NFL hiring agents and black NFL players.

These essays make a contribution to the ongoing discussions centered on race and sports in America.

"As Girls See It":
Writing Sport on the
Margins of the Black Press

Rita Liberti

In a six-year period beginning in 1928, Ivora (Ike) King, Olga Bowers, and Faith Woodson wrote a total of nearly four dozen columns published on the sports pages of the *Baltimore Afro-American*. Under headings such as "As Girls See It," "Women in Sports," "Coed Sports Chatter," and "Just Between Sportswomen" King, Bowers, and Woodson penned articles about the status of physical education, recreation, and athletic programs for girls and women in Baltimore and beyond.[1] The mere presence of a sports column authored by a woman that detailed the experiences of female participants at all levels of athletic activity was an anomaly, as women's events and achievements remained on the margins (albeit a respected place on the margins) within the black community and press.[2] Nonetheless, King, Bowers, and Woodson's columns illustrate the small, yet solid space female athleticism held in the community and on the pages of the black press. Given the marginalized position of women's sport, the columns take on greater significance as we are afforded a unique and potentially valuable window through which to examine broader issues related to racial and gendered politics of the period. At their core, the columns give voice to African American women and at least a small glimpse of their perspectives on a range of issues and topics. In many ways King, Bowers, and Woodson's columns take on the same attributes of the black press more generally as they worked to challenge dominant discourses, by acknowledging and asserting girls' and women's place in sport and physical activity.

Writing from their location on the margins of the black press King, Bowers, and Woodson gave voice to African American female perspectives on sport

5

related topics, often asserting, what they deemed, women's rightful place in the athletic arena. In writing about African American journalists, more generally, historian Jean Marie Lutes argues women in the profession served to challenge dominant discourses by defining themselves and the black community more generally, rather than being defined by whites. Lutes concludes, African American female journalists, "acted as conduits for and representatives of a black counterpublic."[3] In this essay, I argue that King, Bowers, and Woodson fulfilled a similar function as they made their voices heard in engaging issues of gender, sport, and physicality. The notion of a "counterpublic" discussed in depth by theorist Nancy Fraser and used here by Lutes offers, I think, a useful way of reading the columns and the writers.[4]

The concept of a "counterpublic" is in some ways a response to the construction and conceptualization of the "bourgeois public sphere" as advanced Jurgen Habermas, a contemporary sociologist and philosopher, who was eager to examine and make sense of the changing political landscape of eighteenth century Europe. Habermas concluded that the public sphere emerged during the 1700s, a period in which individuals began to come together in a variety of locations, beyond the bounds of the church or the state, to openly identify, discuss, and debate societal problems and issues. Thus, coffeehouses, salons, and even exchanges in newspapers, outside of the home yet not under direct control of the state, became important spaces to discuss, debate, and at times influence political processes in a liberal democracy.[5] Several subsequent scholars, including Nancy Fraser, have taken Habermas to task, arguing that there was/is not a single, bourgeois public sphere, but many public spheres. Fraser notes that there were many alternative publics or as she claims "subaltern counterpublics," through which marginalized groups in society gathered to voice and challenge the specific and unique realities of their oppression.[6]

Fraser is quick to caution, however, that counterpublics are not monolithic, nor necessarily always virtuous. Tensions, contradictions, and exclusions can emerge within already marginalized counterpublic spaces. In this chapter, I argue the themes brought to the fore in King, Bowers, and Woodson's columns expose ways in which sport was used as a tool in advancing the place of black women as strong, capable partners in the struggle against injustice. Simultaneously, their writings afford us a valuable perspective on the multiple narratives within a counterpublic filled with diverse and sometimes competing values, giving rise to tensions and debates over women, physicality, and sporting participation.[7]

The black press joined with a host of other black institutions to create counterpublic spaces. Historically black colleges and universities, churches, music, sororities, fraternities, and other volunteer associations created as Fraser argues, "parallel discursive arena where members of subordinated social groups invent and circulate counterdiscourses to formulate oppositional interpretations of their identities, interests and needs."[8] Borne out of systemized and formal exclusion from dominant sites of public discourse these sites, including the black press, are invaluable forms of communication in and to a democracy. As Catherine Squires concludes, black public spheres have been a "bulwark against the collective amnesia some would impose on historical consciousness."[9] In this instance the black press was far from a space where African American writers simply reacted to and contested dominant narratives promoted by white society. Rather, the black press, acting as a counterpublic, functioned to expand discursive space by promoting self-expression and self-definition among black Americans.

For nearly two centuries the black press has worked to promote the achievements of African Americans as well as throw into sharp relief racial injustices that privilege whites while disenfranchising black Americans.[10] As the result of having no voice, or an exceedingly misrepresented one, African Americans created and built the black press as part of a much more expansive black public sphere. They desperately needed to as the white press ignored "the Negro almost completely, except to play him up as a criminal or a clown," according to Vishnu V. Oak in 1948.[11] Said another way, blacks rarely found themselves on the pages of the white press and when they did it was not good. It would be misguided to cast counterpublic spaces in solely defensive ways, as a "response to" racism, however. It may have been an element of the organization's origination, yet hardly speaks to the dynamic potential of the space for African American agency. Writing, in 1922, of the black press' power and place Frederick G. Detweiler notes that the press "supported by the Negro comes in this way to be a means for making his life significant to himself." Years of slavery left the "impression that the black man did not count in the real world. But now, on the printed page, only does a man's name appear before his fellows, but the whole race seems to become articulate to mankind."[12]

From its initial publication, *Freedom's Journal* in 1827 forward through much of the twentieth century, the orientation of the black press was much more than a "feel good" read, a place where African Americans could turn for the triumphs among them. It was that, no doubt, but the starkly politicized pages of text left no question as to the publications' greater aim and focus. Radical calls for justice ran across the published pages of text and were taken in, discussed, debated and acted upon by the community. Publishers were keenly aware, according to Roberts and Klibanoff, that readers wanted "racial inequities in America examined and denounced" and the black press met that demand.[13] Increases in literacy rates and purchasing power among African Americans in the late nineteenth and early decades of the twentieth century led to a jump in circulation numbers. Moreover the size of the black press grew in post–World War I America as large numbers of African Americans migrated north creating large readerships across more cities. So much so that in 1920, Robert Kerlin opined, "the Negro seems to have newly discovered ... the extraordinary power of his press. Into every town and village of the land, and into many a log cabin in the mountains, come the colored papers."[14] Large city newspapers, like the *Atlanta Daily World, Pittsburgh Courier, Baltimore Afro-American, the Chicago Defender,* and others reached hundreds of thousands of black Americans. By mid-twentieth century nearly 200 black newspapers remained in circulation, doing what the press had done for over a century, providing an important location for its readers to contest the dominant white narrative—refashioning it to suit their needs and perspectives. By the time King, Bowers, and Woodson's columns began appearing in the late 1920s on the pages of the *Baltimore Afro-American*, the paper's circulation rates were among the highest in the nation.[15]

Among other major themes, achievement featured prominently on the pages of the *Baltimore Afro-American,* as it did across much of the African American press. Since its inception in the late decade of the nineteenth century the newspaper was eager to report on the successes of African American citizens across Baltimore, as well as the entire nation. With an eye on dismantling racism and empowering those who read from its pages, the newspaper grew more radical in its calls against injustice and demands for equality into the 1920s and 1930s. Editors of the *Baltimore Afro-American* were determined to see and to help create a strong black community, free from the oppressiveness of white domination. According to *Afro-American* officials, fashioning an independent, powerful populace rested with the "respectable" middle and upper classes whose job it was to lead the lower classes toward that end.[16] African American elites thus defined what values were to be sought after, as they claimed monopoly status on them. Not surprisingly, "uplift" ideologies that stressed self-help and racial solidarity are sprinkled throughout the pages of the *Baltimore Afro-American* during the 1920s and 1930s and were clearly visible in the writings of King, Bowers, and Woodson.[17] Each urged for greater opportunities that enabled recreational and athletic expression among girls and women because each believed those activities to foster individual strength and competence, which ultimately served the greater good of all African Americans.

The tone of King, Bowers, and Woodson's columns reflect and reinforce a bit of the energy among African Americans in the 1920s who were eager to assault enduring racial inequalities in post–World War I America. Girls and women in the black community matched these bold strides toward eradicating racism in the period with their own sense of purpose as they moved, with an increasing sense of entitlement, into the male preserve of sport. In describing the hopeful mood of the period, Ivora King declares, "there is more independence and more freedom allowed women today than ever before and women ... have taken advantage of these privileges and just as they vote and conduct successful business enterprises, so are they entering more successfully in athletic ventures."[18] Despite this encroachment, or possibly because of it, tensions arose around athleticism, physicality, and constructions of femininity—these tensions and competing discourses got played out on the pages of the black press and within the writings of King, Bowers, and Woodson. Seemingly undaunted by numerous constraints playing upon girls' and women's efforts to participate, King, Bowers, and Woodson's desire to see girls' and women's athletic opportunities continued. "Regardless of the few appropriate recreational centers, lack of available leaders, poor equipment, and other drawbacks to physical and athletic activities" wrote Ivora King in 1931, "the girls of our group ... seem to be forging ahead in the athletic world." She concludes, "girls ... in school and out are finding suitable athletic activities to use up their surplus energy."[19] King's observations allude to the myriad constraints upon African American girls and women's athletic involvement, while they underscore a persistent optimism and sense of resourcefulness amid impediments to full and unfettered participation.

The columnists' desire to see more serious attention and additional resources devoted to the quality and quantity female athletic endeavors often came in the form of pointed criticisms directed at the white power structure of Baltimore, as well as African Americans within the city. "What are we doing toward helping the athletically inclined women of Baltimore to express themselves?" queried Olga Bowers in 1933. "The answer is obvious," she concluded, "nothing."[20] Columnists King, Bowers, and Woodson were not alone in their criticisms of the lack of recreational opportunities for African American youth in the city of Baltimore. In 1928, African Americans were prohibited from entering any of Baltimore parks except for a small section of Druid Hill Park. Public school facilities were woefully inadequate as well. As a result, playgrounds and schoolyards could accommodate less than three percent of the city's 25,000 African American children. Editors at the *Baltimore Afro-American* were straightforward and persistent in their disapproval of the abysmal conditions, calling the city's recreation director "Baltimore's worst enemy," in 1929.[21]

King and Woodson wrote routinely of the enthusiasm among young girls at Playground Athletic League (P.A.L) events and were as critical of those within the African American community as they were of Baltimore's white establishment in meeting this interest with financial support and attention. "Baltimore athletics are neglecting its girls in the outdoor sports," Woodson noted in 1928, to which she added, "it is with a great deal of expectation that the boys look forward to their annual track meet." Why then she asked, given the number of great female athletes in the area, could the city not do the same for girls?[22] In a column three years later, King continued the questioning, as she offered up her perspective on the importance of such events for African American girls in Baltimore. King noted that the white press was filled with stories anticipating the P.A.L.'s sponsorship of a winter carnival for white girls within the city. Hinting at the realities of racist public policy, the solution for King lay in self-help, "we cannot expect ... members of the other race to back such a meet for us, but why isn't it possible for a group in our race to sponsor such a meet?"[23] She reminded readers of the potential far reaching positive merits yielded by athletic participation, including better health, sportsmanship, and fair play.

King added that the carnival held other benefits for some participants, namely that the event involved girls from various parts of the city and in *that* fact rested the greatest value. The carnival would attract those girls "used to the better things in life" according to King, as well as those "who need to know more about the wholesome things in life."[24] King's remarks provide us with a glimpse surrounding the tensions of uplift ideology throughout the period. In response to a profoundly racist society, black upper classes worked to position themselves as those best able to impart notions of respectable behavior upon the black masses. King believed that athletic events, such as a winter carnival, provided a unique and potentially powerful arena in which to support the diffusion of moral behavior. "All of the social work in the world, lectures on right and wrong, punishment and other corrective measures are not going to offer these girls half as much as being face to face with the right things and the privilege of mingling with the people who have the right ideas about life."[25]

Several of Ivora King's columns from February of 1931 to February of 1932 underscore still other tensions surrounding women's involvement in competitive sport, namely constructions of athleticism and femininity. As a former basketball star at Morgan College, King at times speaks with great passion in favor of women's participation in sports. Although King continued to support that position, she did so within a context that increasingly highlighted limits to female athletic participation, parameters that constructed and policed a narrowly conceptualized and defined notion of femininity. "Competition and rivalry bring out the best that we have in us," King concluded as she advocated for a girls' basketball league in Baltimore in one of her first columns, published in February 1931.[26] She extended her position months later, in August 1931, by advocating the creation of an intercollegiate athletic organization for women, similar to the Colored Intercollegiate Athletic Association (CIAA) for men (CIAA was established by HBCUs as a result of their exclusion from the National Collegiate Athletic Association—NCAA). King's unequivocal support of competitive opportunities for women is clear: "there is nothing wrong with intramural activities," she says, "I know of nothing better for children in the elementary schools and some of the secondary schools, but when one reaches college it is time for a more serious attitude to be taken toward athletics."[27] Sports provided a laboratory of sorts, according to King in which larger life lessons and skills could be learned and honed. Intercollegiate competition enabled participants to prepare for the "hard knocks, rivalry and other problems of everyday life."[28] For African American women this was especially pivotal, as they needed to employ the fullest set of strategies in use against sexism and racism.

One month later, on September 19, King's previous unconditional advancement of women's involvement in athletics was tempered with the concern that if the female athlete were not careful, she ran the risk of becoming something other than a "real" woman. "You have seen them as well as I," King argues, "girls who walk with the stride of a man, dress mannishly even to wearing neckties and collars and low heeled, broad toed shoes, just because they are superior to some of their sisters in sports." King stops short of condemning all sport activity for women while clearly equating athleticism with mannishness and deviance. "Beside clothing they [female athletes] have tried to assume the air of a man, independence, worldliness and a certain amount of braggadocia" [sic].[29] In part, King's conclusions run counter to earlier columns in which she implied that the confidence and assertive behavior that athletics inspired was not only suitable but desirable qualities for African American women.

Tellingly, King's reservations surrounding women's athletics followed by one week a column in which she introduced and praised Maryrose Reeves Allen, the director of physical education for women at Howard University. Allen, who was near the start of her three decade long tenure at the University, would go on to be one the most influential female physical educators of the twentieth century. Allen clearly approved of physical activity for women, but maintained that it emphasize "light" games and activities, including dancing, archery, and badminton. However, she frowned upon women's engagement in "heavier" sports (like basketball for example), arguing that such activities did not "develop in women the qualities of poise, beauty, and femininity." For Allen, competitive athletics did not foster an "atmosphere of dignity, courtesy, and refinement," and thus were unsuitable for young African American girls and women.[30] King encouraged those women interested in physical education to attend Howard where students will find Allen to be "one of the loveliest and most radiant persons ... in [the] field," a person with whom students feel comfortable "confess[ing] little intimacies."[31]

Following this column in which she pays homage to Allen, King's writings shift to more moderate endorsements of female athleticism. Far from idiosyncratic positions, Allen's views reflect broader strains and tensions upon women's place in sport and multiple, sometimes competing constructions of femininity and womanhood. Fears that athletic involvement promoted "mannish" tendencies in women were constant themes around which unease was woven. Moreover, the notion that sport masculinized women forged with the view that athleticism threatened woman's established nature, or so it was thought.[32] "Then there is the question of children," King observes, "too strenuous participation in athletics is not good for a woman, since her structure is vastly different from that of her brothers, the odds are all against her when it comes to athletics. Too much shock and strain to the nervous system may injure her for life or certainly shorten her life."[33] Such biological determinist arguments rested on assumptions of female frailty and weakness, and were the antithesis of physical realities embodying the everyday experiences of many African American women whose livelihoods rested on corporeal exertion. "I am not trying to discourage girls from participating in athletics," acknowledges King. "At the same time" she counters, "I think that they should be modified and confined to those chiefly created for women."[34]

This rhetoric is indistinguishable from philosophies touted by white female physical educators throughout the 1920s and 1930s, who promoted an agenda that stressed moderate, non-competitive physical activity under the guidance of woman-only mentorship.[35] Maryrose Reeves Allen subscribed, at least in part, to the basic tenets of the platform promoted by white female physical education professionals and thus it is not surprising that King writes this ambivalence into her column shortly after her meeting with Allen. "Many of our college women believe that an intercollegiate league of any kind, would encourage our girls to follow too seriously the path of the athlete," according to King, "but at the same time they are of the opinion that some form of athletic competition is necessary, as well as useful in carrying out their programs to the greatest extent." De-emphasizing competition, though not eliminating it entirely from a school or college athletic program rested with a solution known as a "play-day." The fact that play-days were "carried out in many of the large eastern universities" lent them even more credibility in King's view. Aimed at promoting a "spirit of play ... better social contacts ... and encouraging friendly relationships between colleges" play-days enabled women to be physically active, yet within well-regulated boundaries that limited the scope and extent of competition and physicality. These events were "very gala affairs" according to King, who hoped that local schools and colleges would work toward organizing events at their institutions.[36]

For some, play-days might also minimize what Faith Woodson saw as the "greatest drawback" to women's competitive athletic activities, specifically the "unsportsmanlike conduct ... and unnecessary roughness" between girls' and women's teams.[37] Thought to promote moral behavior, not disrupt it, athletic competitions among African Americans were frequently offered up as locations were highly regarded behaviors such as self-control and discipline could be honed. Against the continually harsh barrage of racist stereotypes of African Americans as wild and unrestrained, athletics, with its demands around rule bound behavior seemed especially suited to cultivate desired characteristics. However, constructions of sports that privileged physicality and aggressiveness created an activity that potentially had double-edged consequences. "I have witnessed games [basketball] where the girls did so much fighting, talking back to the referee, etc., as to render themselves absolutely unfit for anything but a straight jacket," noted Woodson.[38] Rather than the "wholesome pep" Ivora King hoped sports promoted, she instead witnessed and scorned those who exhibited behavior that departed from civility and fair play. "Poor sports" she commented, promoted "animal-like desire" among participants. It is "essential" concluded King, "for girls to know how to play fair and square."[39] Indeed the display of sportsmanship was essential, as dominant cultural constructions worked to dehumanize African Americans, making moral strength and self-control in the face of challenges on the court vital in preparing for those obstacles encountered off the court.

Broader tensions surrounding constructions of femininity and athleticism manifested themselves no more clearly than in the debate over five versus six player basketball that unfolded on the pages of the black press and in the wider community. The game soared in popularity among many throughout the United States in the early twentieth century. Within African American communities, basketball became the winter sport of choice, as it needed little in terms of space and resources. By the mid–1920s the game's popularity grew on the tiny courts of urban community centers in the north as well as wide-open, outdoor courts in the south, creating a fair amount of community interest and media coverage.[40]

Just a decade after the game's inception in the early 1890s however, white female physical educators, including Senda Berenson, of Smith College, unnerved by the game's physical and rowdy play, developed a different version of basketball for girls and women that sought to place limits on movement and physical contact between players. While a variety of more restrictive versions of the game were popularized in the first few decades of the twentieth century, two forms took hold, each with six players per team. The first divided the six players on three quadrants of the court, the second version separated the six teammates by a centerline. Regardless of whether the court was divided in halve or into thirds, players were prohibited from running beyond the boundaries of their prescribed section of the court. The game's new rules disallowed body contact, while restricting players' movements across the court and thus better suited the Victorian sensibilities of some, who feared five player (full court) basketball endangered the physical and emotional well-being of female participants.[41]

Ivora King's perspective on the debate over basketball rules for girls and women in the African American community was clear, although her view was one among many, as a host of competing narratives circulated among observers. "At best," according to King, "a game where boys' rules are used is merely a scramble [that] resembles a disorganized football game more than anything else."[42] While there certainly wasn't consensus on this issue, King's arguments and those of others who were in favor of the six-player game for girls and women, won out as many African American schools and colleges abandoned the five-player game by the mid–1930s, preferring instead the more restrictive rules. Many of the basketball players with whom I have spoken conceptualized femininity in such a way that did not preclude participation in rigorous athletics and thus they disapproved of rules which sought to restrict movement on the court. Annie Bowers, who played for Shaw University from 1934 to 1937, disliked the move to six-player basketball. Bowers recalls that the five player game "gave us a chance to take in the whole floor, [in] that six business" she said, "you would go up to the middle of the floor and have to give the ball up and stand there and watch."[43] For William Mae Bailey, who played for North Carolina College during the 1937 season, the transition to the six player version of the game seemed illogical and disconnected from the realities of hers and other women's life experiences and expectations. "They told us that our hips wasn't geared for that kind of strong activity," she then adds, "but it was a foolish idea, because I think all the girls that played with me have children and if you don't think havin' a youngster is tough ... basketball was [in comparison] pie!"[44] This sampling of diverse discourses surrounding female basketball rules symbolizes the ongoing negotiation over definitions and understandings of African American womanhood throughout the 1920s and 1930s. For Annie Bowers and William Mae Bailey their athleticism blended seamlessly with their constructions of themselves as women. For others, including Ivora King, a female participant risked her "womanly dignity" by engaging in five-player basketball. Grounded in notions of essential and natural difference between men and women, King concludes, "Woman being a physically different animal from man, should follow the rules and regulations that have been set aside for her ... why then should girls' basketball teams try to imitate men in their playing?"[45]

Women's dress, including athletic apparel, became another contested site within the black press and elsewhere where larger struggles over identity and values took place. The New Negro and New Woman movements that marked the period ushered in alternative visions of black womanhood that sought to reclaim stereotypes by extolling black female beauty and sensuality, rather than denigrating it. The rapidly expanding place and role of consumption helped to drive attitudes and representations of female sexuality, including those in fashion. Shorter sleeves and hemlines symbolized broader trends toward greater female independence and expressiveness. These changes did not come with ease however as some, including this observer, feared the broader cultural trends harmed not just individual African American women, but the entire race. "The woman who worships at the shrine of fashion loses her bearings, she has not time to read good books, no time to cultivate those things that minister to the refinement and beauty of her home, and no time or inclination to contribute ... to the uplift of those around her."[46] Rather than blurring boundaries between the sexes, dress reform both on and off the court in the 1920s, seemed to do just the opposite as it accentuated female difference and distinctiveness, playing up new images of women as sensual and independent. Women's athletics, in the 1920s, provided a cultural setting for expanding freedoms and increasingly eroticized femininity to play out, as teams transitioned from bloomers and long sleeved shirts to tank tops and shorts.[47] In the late 1920s Faith Woodson was hopeful that local teams would cease play in "despicable black bloomers" noting that shorts were "proper" and permitted "freedom of action."[48] Others, including *Baltimore Afro-American* male sports columnist Bill Gibson, also endorsed the fashion revolution in the name of freedom. It was not common for Gibson to comment on women's athletics, but the move from bloomers to shorts gave him cause. "In the old style baggy bloomers," Gibson offered, "a girl would run around for fifteen minutes and never get out of a certain spot. She was moving fast enough, but the balloon-like pantalets were standing still."[49] Hinting at other benefits, Woodson noted, the "Washington Y[WCA] girls drew many admiring glances with their neatly fitting suits, when they played here."[50] For others as well, the change in fashion highlighted and celebrated players' beauty and physical attractiveness. J.H. Drawborne, a North Carolina girls' basketball coach, was quoted in Woodson's column, "sure my girls' team looks hot" he said, "but girls naturally do their best when they know they look good, so I just dressed 'em up. Look 'em over when they begin to play."[51] Though steeped in patriarchal conceptualizations of gender, the erotic tone of the narrative positions black womanhood and comeliness as the attraction, thus departing from dominant white representations that often sought to do otherwise. Increasingly in this era, women's athletic successes and their bodies were exhibited for public consumption as Victorian conventions about sexuality and the body began to give way to a culture of relatively greater openness. For some within the African American community, hinting at the sensuousness of athletic female bodies underscored the beauty of black womanhood, and represented a source of race pride.

Using sport as a tool to promote racial pride was certainly nothing new to African American men, who throughout the inter-war years in the United States used athletics in this way. For some in the community sport was long seen as a foundational piece of African American manhood and thus provided a setting on which to advance notions of honor and self-respect.[52] Despite the tensions around womanhood and athleticism, it is clear as well that at least for some in the black community, including Faith Woodson and Ivora King, female athletes could form the basis around which pride was conceived. "While we are paying tribute to the great [Ralph] Metcalfe and [Eddie] Tolan," King extolled, "I wonder why there was no woman to share the honors of the recent Olympiad along with them?"[53] As the historian Patrick Miller has noted, the African American press used the Metcalfe's and Tolan's accomplishments on the athletic field in the 1932 Games to illustrate possibility and achievement. Moreover, feats of athletic greatness, it was hoped, might lead whites to reexamine their attitudes toward African Americans—easing the confines around which racism sustained itself.[54]

Support of female athletics among *Baltimore Afro-American* columnists illustrates their belief that accomplishments on the fields and courts was cause for pride, although they supply no evidence of the transformative potential of such successes on race relations, as they did for men. In one of his rare discussions about the place and possibility of women's sport, Bill Gibson asks, "why is it that there are no outstanding women athletes being developed among the race? Is it possible that ... athletic competition is looked upon as being too ROUGH? We look forward to the day when we will have some of which to be proud."[55] Gibson hints at some of the ambivalence around female athleticism within the African American community only to dismiss it.

Ivora King and Faith Woodson were emphatic in their support of Olympic level female competitors of which the race could be proud. However, they were mindful of the many inequities that stood in the way of such a scenario from occurring. "Boys are getting the better of the deal athletically," according to Woodson in 1928," who added, "future Olympic entries from our race need more than dodge ball and flag relays."[56] King too underscored the need for early training and quality athletic competition for girls and women to advance themselves and the race. King admonished readers that unless qualified coaches were willing to train and develop young talent, the female athlete will "still be in obscurity and some member of the other race will be enjoying a title that might have been hers."[57]

Six months later in August 1932 in what would be the final column she wrote for the *Baltimore Afro-American*, Ivora King restated, with even more emphasis, her desire to see female athletes excel in Baltimore and across the country. Commenting on the single-handed dominance of Babe Didrikson among female athletes, King noted, "I cannot and will not be convinced that there are no one woman track teams among our women." Talented women athletes according to King, needed "athletic organizations, constant practice, confidence in one's ability and constant competition."[58] In a telling final statement, King concluded that the men's 100 meter dash in the 1932 Olympics was a race between two African American champions [Metcalfe and Tolan] as other competitors, she said, "were hardly in it." She added, "we want to develop talent like that. We want our girls to be far superior to the others, for it is the only way for them to get a decent break."[59] One wonders if King was speaking only to the place of African American women in sport or the broader society as well.

Ivora King, Faith Woodson, and Olga Bowers' written words across the pages of the *Baltimore Afro-American* in the late 1920s and early 1930s provide us with a valuable position from which to better understand ongoing issues around gender, race, and class. In many ways they clearly argued for progressive change that would bring about greater and more competitive opportunities for African American girls and women in sport and recreation. In the words of Woodson, each was eager to put girls' athletics "on the map."[60] Indeed the columnists, "[p]roduced by and through the black counterpublic, represented the very possibility of making oneself heard."[61] Their narratives are not seamless however, as there are disruptions across the pages of text. Though they often speak forcefully in favor of female athleticism, they do so amid the constraints of racism, gender conventions, and class expectations. The multiple and sometimes competing perspectives on issues related to African American women in sport represent and reinforce the diverseness within a counterpublic space. The varying standpoints remain far from neat, static, or routine as the columnists contest and reconstruct notions of gender, race, and class. Thus, their columns, situated figuratively and quite literally on the margins of the *Baltimore Afro-American*, give us, I believe, an invaluable site to examine the complexities of African American womanhood during the period.

Notes

1. I have been unable to locate biographical information about King, Bowers, and Woodson. However, based upon late 1920s articles in the *Baltimore Afro-American* is it clear that King played basketball for Morgan College in the city. See, for example: "Will They Wear the Crown," *Baltimore Afro-American*, April 14, 1928, p. 13.

2. Susan Cahn, *Coming On Strong: Gender and Sexuality in Twentieth-Century Women's Sport* (New York: Free Press, 1994), 39.

3. Jean Marie Lutes, *Front Page Girls: Women Journalists in American Culture and Fiction, 1880–1930* (Ithaca, NY: Cornell University Press, 2006), 43.

4. Nancy Fraser, "Rethinking the Public Sphere: A Contribution to the Critique of Actually Existing Democracy," *Social Text* 25/26 (1990): 67.

5. See, for example, Robert Asen and Daniel C. Brouwer, "Introduction: Reconfigurations of the Public Sphere," in *Counterpublics and the State*, eds., Robert Asen and Daniel C. Brouwer (Albany: State University of New York Press, 2001), 7; Robert N. Jacobs, *Race, Media and the Crisis of Civil Society: From Watts to Rodney King* (Cambridge, UK: Cambridge University Press, 2000), 2; Craig Calhoun, "Introduction: Habermas and the Public Sphere," in *Habermas and the Public Sphere*, ed., Craig Calhoun (Cambridge, MA: MIT Press, 1992), 1–48.

6. Fraser, "Rethinking the Public Sphere," 67.

7. Ibid.

8. Ibid. On the concept of the black public sphere and counterpublics, see, for example, Deborah Elizabeth Whaley, *Disciplining Women: Alpha Kappa Alpha, Black Counterpublics, and the Cultural Politics of Black Sororities* (Albany: State University of New York Press, 2010); Melissa Victoria Harris-Lacewell, *Barbershops, Bibles, and BET: Everyday Talk and Black Political Thought* (Princeton, NJ: Princeton University Press, 2004); Taeker Lee, *Mobilizing Public Opinion: Black Insurgency and Racial Attitudes in the Civil Rights Era* (Chicago: University of Chicago Press, 2002); Thomas C. Holt, "Afterword: Mapping the Black Public Sphere," in *The Black Public Sphere Collective: A Public Culture Book*, ed., The Black Public Sphere Collective (Chicago: University of Chicago Press, 1995), 325–328; Houston A. Baker, Jr., "Critical Memory and the Black Public Sphere," in *The Black Public Sphere Collective*, 13–23; Michael C. Dawson, "A Black Counterpublic? Economic Earthquakes, Racial Agenda(s), and Black Politics," in *The Black Public Sphere Collective*, 201–204.

9. Catherine R. Squires, "Rethinking the Black Public Sphere: An Alternative Vocabulary for Multiple Public Spheres," *Communication Theory* 12 (2002): 455.

10. Todd Vogel, "Introduction," in *The Black Press: New Literary and Historical Essays* (New Brunswick, NJ: Rutgers University Press, 2001), 1.

11. Vishnu V. Oak, *The Negro Newspaper* (Westport, CT: Negro Universities Press, 1948), 36.

12. Frederick G. Detweiler, *The Negro Press in the United States* (Chicago: University of Chicago Press, 1922; College Park, MD: McGrath, 1968), 268. Citation refers to the McGrath edition.

13. Gene Roberts and Hank Klibanoff, *The Race Beat: The Press, the Civil Rights Struggle, and the Awakening of a Nation* (New York: Alfred A. Knopf, 2006), 13.

14. Robert Kerlin, quoted in Catherine Squires, "The Black Press and the State: Attracting Unwanted (?) Attention," in Asen and Brouwer, eds., *Counterpublics and the State*, 117–118.

15. Oak, *The Negro Newspaper*, 126–163.

16. Hayward Farrar, *The Baltimore Afro-American, 1892–1950* (Westport, CT: Greenwood, 1998), 131–135.

17. For a thoughtful examination of "uplift" see: Kevin K. Gaines, *Uplifting the Race: Black Leadership, Politics, and Culture in the Twentieth Century* (Chapel Hill: University of North Carolina Press, 1996).

18. Ivora King, "Women in Sports: Are Women Losing?" *Baltimore Afro-American,* March 12, 1932, p. 15.

19. Ivora King, "Co-Ed Sport Chatter," *Baltimore Afro-American,* January 24, 1931, p. 14.

20. Olga H. Bowers, "Just Between Sportswomen," *Baltimore Afro-American,* February 18, 1933, p. 16.

21. Farrar, *The Baltimore Afro-American*, 184.

22. Faith Woodson, "As Girls See It," *Baltimore Afro-American,* April 14, 1928, p. 13.

23. Ivora King, "Co-ed Sport Chatter," *Baltimore Afro-American,* February 28, 1931, p. 14.

24. Ibid.

25. Ibid.

26. Ivora King, "Co-ed Sport Chatter," *Baltimore Afro-American,* February 14, 1931, p. 14.

27. Ivora King, "Co-ed Sport Chatter," *Baltimore Afro-American,* August 22, 1931, p. 13.

28. Ibid.

29. Ivora King, "Women in Sports: Feminine Yet Athletic," *Baltimore Afro-American,* September 19, 1931, p. 13.

30. Maryrose Reeves Allen, "The Development of Beauty in College Women Through Health and Physical Education," archived in the Maryrose Reeves Allen Papers, Box 160–4 (folder 4), Moorland-Spingarn Research Center, Howard University, Washington, DC.

31. Ivora King, "Women in Sports," *Baltimore Afro-American*, September 12, 1931, p. 13.

32. Cahn, *Coming On Strong*, 2–5.

33. Ivora King, "Women in Sports," *Baltimore Afro-American*, September 19, 1931, p. 13.

34. Ibid.

35. Cahn, *Coming On Strong*, 55–82.

36. Ivora King, "Women in Sports," *Baltimore Afro-American*, December 26, 1931, p. 15.

37. Faith Woodson, "As Girls See It," *Baltimore Afro-American*, January 18, 1930, p. 15.

38. Faith Woodson, "As Girls See It," *Baltimore Afro-American*, April 12, 1930, p. 15.

39. Ivora King, "Co-ed Sport Chatter," *Baltimore Afro-American*, February 7, 1931, p. 15.

40. On the growth of women's basketball in the black community during this period, see Pamela Grundy and Susan Shackelford, *Shattering the Glass: The Remarkable History of Women's Basketball* (New York: New Press, 2005), 61–84.

41. Cahn, *Coming on Strong,* 85–86.

42. Ivora King, "Women in Sports," *Baltimore Afro-American,* February 27, 1932, p. 15.

43. Annie Bowers interview with author, (Charlotte, NC), July 18, 1996.

44. William Mae Turner Bailey (Durham, NC), September 2, 1995.

45. King, February 27, 1932, p. 15.

46. Fannie Barrier Williams, quoted in Noliwe M. Rooks. *Ladies' Pages: African American Women's Magazines and the Culture That Made Them* (New Brunswick, NJ: Rutgers University Press, 2004), 65.

47. Pamela Grundy, "Bloomers and Beyond: North Carolina Women's Basketball Uniforms, 1901–1907," *Southern Cultures* 3 (1997): 57–58.

48. Faith Woodson, "As Girls See It," *Baltimore Afro-American*, January 19, 1929, p. 13.

49. Bill Gibson, "Hear Me Talkin' to Ya," *Baltimore Afro-American*, March 15, 1930, p. 15.

50. Faith Woodson, "As Girls See It," *Baltimore Afro-American*, April 21, 1928, p. 13.

51. J.H. Drawborne quoted in Faith Woodson, "Carolina H.S. Coach Trained Girls and Made Uniforms Too," *Baltimore Afro-American*, February 9, 1929, p. 11.

52. David K. Wiggins and Patrick B. Miller, *The Unlevel Playing Field: A Documentary History of the African American Experience in Sport* (Urbana: University of Illinois Press, 2003), 206.

53. Ivora King, "Women in Sports," *Baltimore Afro-American*, August 27, 1932, p. 17.

54. Wiggins and Miller, *The Unlevel Playing Field,* 154–157.

55. "Sport Editorial," *Baltimore Afro-American*, April 14, 1928, p. 13

56. Faith Woodson, "As Girls See It," *Baltimore Afro-American*, May 19, 1929, p. 13

57. Ivora King, "Women in Sports," *Baltimore Afro-American*, March 19, 1932, p. 15.

58. Ivora King, "Women in Sports," *Baltimore Afro-American*, August 27, 1932, p. 17.

59. Ibid.

60. Faith Woodson, "As Girls See It," *Baltimore Afro-American*, April 14, 1928, p. 13.

61. Lutes, *Front-Page Girls,* 46.

References

Asen, Robert, and Daniel C. Brouwer. "Introduction: Reconfigurations of the Public Sphere." In *Counterpublics and the State,* edited by Robert Asen and Danield C. Brouwer, 1–34. Albany: State University of New York Press, 2001.

Baker, Houston A., Jr. "Critical Memory and the Black Public Sphere." In *The Black Public Sphere: A Public Culture Book,* edited by the Black Public Sphere Collective, 5–38. Chicago: University of Chicago Press, 1995.

Cahn, Susan. *Coming on Strong: Gender and Sexuality in Twentieth-Century Women's Sport.* New York: Free Press, 1994.

Calhoun, Craig. "Introduction: Habermas and the Public Sphere." In *Habermas and the Public Sphere,* edited by Craig Calhoun, 1–48. Cambridge, MA: MIT Press, 1992.

Dawson, Michael C. "A Black Counterpublic? Economic Earthquakes, Racial Agenda(s), and Black Politics." In *The Black Public Sphere: A Public Culture Book,* edited by the Black Public Sphere Collective, 199–228. Chicago: University of Chicago Press, 1995.

Farrar Hayward. *The Baltimore Afro-American, 1892–1950.* Westport, CT: Greenwood, 1998.

Fraser, Nancy. "Rethinking the Public Sphere: A Contribution to the Critique of Actually Existing Democracy." *Social Text* 25 (1990): 56–80.

Grundy, Pamela. "Bloomers and Beyond: North Carolina Women's Basketball Uniforms, 1901–1907." *Southern Cultures* 3 (1997): 52–67.

_____, and Susan Shackelford. *Shattering the Glass: The Remarkable History of Women's Basketball.* New York: New Press, 2005.

Harris-Lacewell, Melissa Victoria. *Barbershops, Bibles, and BET: Everyday Talk and Black Political Thought.* Princeton, NJ: Princeton University Press, 2004.

Holt, Thomas C. "Afterword: Mapping the Black Public Sphere." In *The Black Public Sphere: A Public Culture Book,* edited by the Black Public Sphere Collective, 325–328. Chicago: University of Chicago Press, 1995.

Jacobs, Robert N. *Race, Media, and the Crisis of Civil Society: From Watts to Rodney King.* Cambridge, UK: Cambridge University Press, 2000.

Lee, Taeker. *Mobilizing Public Opinion: Black Insurgency and Racial Attitudes in the Civil Rights Era.* Chicago: University of Chicago Press, 2002.

Lutes, Jean Marie. *Front Page Girls: Women Journalists in American Culture and Fiction.* Ithaca, NY: Cornell University Press, 2006.

Oak, Vishnu V. *The Negro Newspaper.* Westport, CT: Negro Universities Press, 1948.

Roberts, Gene, and Hank Klibanoff. *The Race Beat: The Press, The Civil Rights Struggle, and the Awakening of a Nation.* New York: Alfred A. Knopf, 2006.

Squires, Catherine R. "Rethinking the Black Public Sphere: An Alternative Vocabulary for Multiple Public Spheres." *Communication Theory* 12 (2002): 446–448.

Vogel, Todd. *The Black Press: New Literary and Historical Essays.* New Brunswick, NJ: Rutgers University Press, 2001.

Whaley, Deborah Elizabeth. *Disciplining Women: Alpha Kappa Alpha, Black Counterpublics, and the Cultural Politics of Black Sororities.* Albany: State University of New York Press, 2010.

Wiggins, David K., and Patrick B. Miller. *The Unlevel Playing Field: A Documentary History of the African American Experience in Sport.* Urbana: University of Illinois Press, 2003.

The Modern Day Black Sporting Experience: A Dialogue on Race

Billy Hawkins, Joseph N. Cooper and *Ashley Baker*

Introduction

Race prevails as a social construct in this country. This country's preoccupation with the concept of race prevents it from fading way uneventfully despite the post-racial rhetoric. Thus, we can extend W.E.B. Du Bois' statement that "the problem of the Twentieth Century is the problem of the color line," to include the twenty-first century (1961, p. 19). Furthermore, stated more bluntly, race matters, as the title of Dr. Cornel West's seminal piece poignantly denotes.

It has been pervasive as a divisive social descriptor throughout the history of this country. When Europeans came in contact with the indigenous people (also referred to as Indians or Native Americans) that inhabited this country, race was a divisive social descriptor. During the slave trade and the practice of slavery in this country, which provided the economic foundation for this country's growth and development into a world power, race prevailed as a divisive social descriptor. Race continues to matter, despite the progress we have made as a nation in electing our first multiracial president, Barack Obama. He undoubtedly is grounded in blackness by first lady Michelle Obama, and he is reminded of his blackness by the guardians of whiteness or white privilege: e.g., Tea Partiers and the likes of Representative Joe Wilson and Governor Jan Brewer, etc. These guardians of whiteness are determined to provide President

Obama with having a black experience. Thus, they have used a national public platform to remind the president of the United States of America that he is still black, regardless of his mother's matrilineal heritage. This further informs us that regardless of how high blacks climb in this country they will still encounter episodes of having a black experience. Consequently, race and furthermore blackness continues to serve as a divisive social descriptor in this country.

Regardless, according to the late Dr. Manning Marable, the request of young African Americans during the sixties of "wanting a black face in a high place," (1998, p. 76) has been honored. However, with the revival of white supremacist organizations and the residual effects of white privilege, I am prone to agree with the late professor Derrick Bell that, "We have made progress in everything, yet, nothing has changed" (1989, p. 10). U.S. institutions persist in constructing and reinforcing stereotypical notions about race.

Sport[1] is a socially constructed institution that works to inform our racial practices and beliefs. As a microcosm of our society, sport reproduce, reflect, and reinforce dominant ideologies that are pervasive in this country. As a social construction, it is created, organized, played, and changed, if necessary, to meet the needs and provide cultural meaning for individuals with cultural similarities within a given society. For example, football is a favorite pastime for many U.S. citizens; it is a cultural practice that creates meaning, a sense of community, a sense of identity, and belonging for millions in this country, while soccer, what the rest of the world refer to as futbol, or football, provides similar benefits for citizens of many European, South American, African, and Caribbean citizens. Thus, different nations construct sport differently to serve the needs of their citizens and with different meaning. Therefore, the same social and cultural benefits some Americans obtain from American football other countries

This essay will explore how sports, by way of sport images and commentary (i.e., sport media content), work to reinforce dominant ideas about race, and more specifically about blacks. Historically, black athletes have been used to construct certain ideas about race; for example: Jack Johnson reinforced ideas of black physicality or bruteness in the public discourse, Muhammad Ali reinforced ideas of black rebelliousness and militancy, while the black female athlete was either asexual or hypersexualized. This chapter will examine current popular black athletes and the commentary around these athletes to show how notions of race are created, reinforced, and/or reproduced.

It is important to note that a critical examination of the mass media and mediate messages will be a part of this exploration. The mass media have, unknowingly at times, been the means by which images and messages have been disseminated that construct and reinforce ideas about race; "unknowingly at times" because often it is the reporting on an issue and the amount of coverage they give to particularly topics that makes the media effective in constructing or reinforcing ideas about race. Furthermore, as an ideological state apparatus, the mass media have tremendous power through constitutional protection, accessibility, and corporate support to construct and reinforce dominant ideologies. Therefore, we will use a critical analysis of these mediated images and/or commentary to illustrate how ideas regarding race are reproduced and reinforced.

Black Female Athletes

In general, black women have had to confront issues of racism and sexism. Their experiences have been labeled as a double burden (St. Jean and Feagin, 1998), double jeopardy (Giddings, 1984), and multiple jeopardies (King, 1988). In the context of sport, black female athletes have had to face similar "isms," including classism (Carter, 2008; Carter-Francique, 2011; Staurowsky, 2011). Furthermore, the mass media has reinforced the stereotypes of black female athletes through sport images and commentary. These stereotypical depictions have provided a framework for individuals to construct ideas of black females' athletic appearance, behavior and performance. The images of these athletes have reinforced the idea that there is a deviance from traditional standards of beauty that idealize whiteness. Additionally, these images reiterate ideas that black female athletes are not only racially different, but physically and sexually different than white female athletes.

Historically, the commentary on black female athletes has focused on power, strength, and "natural" athletic talent and very little has been said about their effort, hard work, intelligence or mental skill. Furthermore, black female bodies have been described as masculine, aggressive, and overpowering with the exclusion of characteristics that describe their beauty, sex appeal, or intellectual ability. One example of a modern day black female athlete that has been used to reinforce dominant racial ideologies is Serena Williams. In 1999, Serena won the U.S. Open title and at the end of 2002 she was ranked as the number one top female player in the world, the same spot which was held one year prior, by her sister Venus. This was the beginning of what have become a very successful career and an abundance of media attention.

Some believe that over the course of her career, Serena has become a representative of black female athletes. While she has been described as powerful, intense, and intimidating her integrity, character, and work ethic have all been called into question by the media. For example, former players such as Martina Navratilova and Chris Evert have been very critical of Serena's involvement in her off-court activities and have expressed that these commitments distract from her responsibility to playing tennis (Douglas, 2012). Evert's open letter to Serena, in a 2005 issue of *Tennis Magazine* stated:

> In the short term you may be happy with the various things going on in your life, but I wonder whether 20 years from now you might reflect on your career and regret not putting 100 percent of yourself into tennis. Because whether you want to admit it or not, these distractions are tarnishing your legacy [Evert, 2006, p.1].

Another criticism occurred at the 2012 London Olympic Games. To note what occurred one has to preface the context of the criticism by stating that the Williams family is originally from Compton, California, which has been generally labeled as the "ghetto." Consequently, much of the criticism of her behavior is that she reinforces public opinion about "ghetto behavior." After defeating Maria Sharapova in the singles match and winning the gold Serena broke into a Crip Walk dance. The media did not respond favorably to what Serena considered a moment that she had not pre-planned and found herself overwhelmed with joy and began celebrating her victory. One reporter described Serena's behavior as "immature and classless" (Sieczkowski, 2012, p. 1). Another reporter stated:

> and there was Serena—the tennis legend, the winner of 14 individual Grand Slams, the best player of her generation, the American girl being crowned at the All-England Club as the queen of tennis—Crip-Walking all over the most lily-white place in the world....You couldn't help but shake your head. It was as if Serena just couldn't seem to avoid dipping into waters of controversy even as she'd ascended to the top of her sport [Sieczkowski, 2012, p. 1].

It is believed that because of the controversial origin of the dance and the already questionable behavior identified by the media, Serena's celebration was considered inappropriate, relaying a bad message and mistake made during a very public moment. Several headlines read "Serena Deserves the Criticism," "Serena's Crip Walk Dance: Fun Celebration or Bad Message?"; and "Serena Williams SLAMMED for Glamourizing Gang Culture with Crip Walk Dance After Olympic Win."

Although the criticism was predicated on Serena's decision to do the Crip-Walk dance, her celebratory act informs of the cultural and racial gaps between Serena's assumptions and that of the avid tennis fan. Her naïveté or blatant disregard for exhibiting cultural expressions that is a departure from "white norms" is duly noted in these criticisms. Thus, any expression affiliated with the black culture, hip hop, gangsta rap, positive or negative, warrants heavy criticism in this predominantly white preserve. Maybe her status and performance clouded her judgment and distorted her perception of being fully accepted into the domain as a black female from Compton, California; Crip Walk dance included.

It is important to note however, that celebratory dances are not uncommon in sports, and certainly not during the 2012 Olympic Games. After scoring in the 25th minute of what would become a 1–0 victory over North Korea for the predominately white, United States National Women's Soccer Team (USWNT), Abby Wambach led her teammates in a preplanned and choreographed celebratory dance routine. The team held hands, then did a consecutive arm wave. After the last player finished the team pointed to midfield where goalkeeper Hope Solo and team captain Christie Rampone were on the ground doing the Worm. Some of the headlines regarding the USWNT celebrations during the Olympics were "U.S. Women's Soccer Team Annoys Some Foes with Goal Celebrations," "U.S. Team's Goal Celebration Choreography Annoys New Zealand Coach," and the "U.S. Soccer Team's Cartwheel Celebration Annoys Opponent." These headlines are in stark contrast to the personal attacks after Serena's celebration.

In contrast, to the negative commentaries of Serena in many predominantly white-controlled mainstream media, she has appeared on a number of magazines that portray her in a more positive manner, many of which target black audiences. In 2005, she was listed in *Essence* magazine as one of the 35 "most remarkable and beautiful black women" in the world (Johnson, P. 2005, p. 198). At the age of 28, Serena was chosen to be in the 2009 *ESPN The Magazine*'s "Body Issue," because her passion was matched by her body's ability to channel it. In 2012, Serena and her sister Venus were portrayed on the cover of the *New York Times Magazine*, which featured the cover story "Venus and Serena Against the World." The cover image shows the women standing tall next to one another, holding hands while confidently displaying their rock solid abs while the story details the sisters' reflections on their careers having to face scrutiny, racism, defeat and success.

Gabrielle "Gabby" Douglas is another modern day black female athlete the media has used to reinforce dominant racial ideologies. Gabby, a native of Virginia Beach, Virginia, began taking formal gymnastics classes at the age of 6. Within 2 years she was named a Virginia State Gymnastics Champion. In 2010 Natalie Hawkins, Douglas' mother, made the decision to send her 14-year-old daughter to Iowa to train with the 2008 United States Olympic women's gymnastics coach Liang Chow. The decision was made to afford Gabby the opportunity to work with renowned coach Chow, as well as attempt to escape the self-reported bullying and racism experienced at the Virginia Beach gymnasium where she had been training.

According to a 2007 diversity study commissioned by USA Gymnastics, it was reported that just 6.6 percent of the American participants in gymnastics were black, while 74.4 percent were Caucasian (Holcomb, 2007). The low participation of black girls in gymnastics may be attributed to the lack of access to training facilities, the high cost for participation and the increased amount of time commitment that is required at the elite level. Each of these barriers can shape a young black girls experience if they do choose to participate in what some consider a "country club sport."

Early in her career Gabby, like many other young black girls in gymnastics, she experienced isolation. Even after moving to Iowa to train with Coach Liang Chow, Douglas still faced the all too familiar white world of gymnastics. Her host family was white; they lived in a nearly all-white community and at most of her meets she was the only black competitor. Due to homesickness and the feelings of isolation, her mother stated that Gabby often expressed the desire to return home. Although she struggled with being away from home, she excelled under Coach Chow's direction and was selected to compete with the U.S. Olympic women's gymnastics team for the 2012 Summer Olympics in London, England. It was in London, where Gabby at the age of 16, became the first African American to win a gold medal in the individual all-around competition. Just days before, she and her four U.S. teammates, Aly Raisman, Mckayla Maroney, Kyla Ross and Jordyn Wieber, outscored Russia and Romania in the women's gymnastics team finals to win the gold medal.

However, the celebration of athletic success has not gone without criticism from various forms of media. As Douglas was making history as a U.S. Olympian, headlines surfaced about her personal life, specifically her family's financial woes and her relationship with her father. All too often positive commentary of black athletes' accomplishments tend to be overshadowed by the negative narratives of hardships and struggles, along with increased attention on those who come from broken homes. While Gabby's family was not the only family with reports of financial trouble, limited attention was given to other white Olympians whose families were in similar financial trouble and the primary focus remained on their performance in the Olympic events.

The traditional narrative of the black athlete, the "absent black father" and the "single black mother" is consistently reproduced in the media. In Douglas' case the narrative remains the same. Timothy Douglas, Gabby's father, has been reported as abandoning his wife and their children. Her mother has been regularly referred to as Natalie Hawkins, single mother of four. Much of the media coverage has reported the negative details of the family's relationship with Timothy and the struggles Natalie faced raising their children alone, in Virginia, while her husband was deployed for military service. Although the media has praised Gabby for reaching Olympic success, despite such difficult family circumstances overcoming difficult obstacles, it has incessantly reinforced the negative images of her black family.

In addition to the commentary of her family background, while Douglas and her teammates were celebrating her accomplishments as a gymnast, multiple social-media outlets began producing critical commentary on her "unkempt" hair. During her Olympic competitions she wore her chemically straightened hair, pulled into a ponytail with barrettes and gel, which matched her four Caucasian teammates. Much of the criticism she received focused on her lack of "representing" black females by wearing a hairstyle that looked disheveled.

Despite these misrepresentations, Gabby's recent achievement of being named Sportswoman of the Year by the Women's Sports Foundation is an amazing accomplishment that provides a counter narrative to the multiple jeopardies she encounters a black female athlete. The context of sport has often presented contradicting images of the black female athlete: asexualized to hypersexualized. The challenge for sport media content will reside in embracing the complexities among black female athletes and discarding the former script that negatively racialized their experiences.

Black Male Athletes

Historically, prevailing stereotypes of black males have been reinforced through mass media coverage of black male athletes. These stereotypes are deeply rooted in a white supremacist ideology, which views black males as intellectually inferior, yet physically superior. Under this belief, the preponderance of black males in sports such as football, basketball, and track and field was accepted only because it reinforced these racist beliefs. Within each of the aforementioned sports, the power structure provided white owners with control over the black athletes who were, and remain, commodities for athletic revenue generation. Therefore, the mass media hegemony in the U.S. has normalized the racist coverage of black male athletes and perpetuated the status quo of white supremacy.

A prime of example a modern day black star athlete that has been used by the mass media to reinforce dominant racial ideologies is LeBron James. LeBron was touted as the most heralded high school basketball player ever. He grew up in poor neighborhood in Akron, Ohio, and was raised his single mother, Gloria James. Ever since LeBron was an adolescent, he was placed on the conveyor belt (Rhoden, 2006). According to Rhoden (2006), the conveyor belt is a socialization process whereby talented athletes are granted certain implicit and explicit privileges in society based on their athletic potential. Once the national media caught wind of this new phenomenon, LeBron-mania ensued. As a high school junior, he became the first high school athlete since the 1960s to appear on the coveted *Sports Illustrated* cover (Powell, 2008). The controversial title of the cover was "The Chosen One," which LeBron would later have tattooed across his back. This cover page and title reflected the mainstream media's perception of him as the heir apparent to Michael Jordan, even though he had to yet to play a game in the National Basketball Association (NBA). At six feet eight inches and two hundred and forty pounds as high school senior, he was labeled as a once in a generation athlete. During both his junior and senior years, many of his high school games were nationally televised on the Entertainment and Sports Programming Network (ESPN). In addition, global sponsors like Nike were eager to acquire his endorsement. At the age of seventeen, he signed a $90 million contract with Nike before he was even drafted into the NBA (Coakley, 2009).

Several years later, after successful seasons with the NBA's Cleveland Cavaliers, the media's admiration of LeBron reached an all-time high, where he was heralded as the "savior" of, not only his hometown team, but also the entire NBA. Nike capitalized off this moniker by marketing T-shirts that read "We Are All Witnesses." All of this attention at such a young age was a reflection of the media's infatuation with the commodification of young talented black athletes. In concert with the agenda of commercialized sports, LeBron was portrayed as hero or superhuman based on his physical talents. The media viewed LeBron similar to how they view all black star athletes as targeted commodities whose sole purpose is to generate revenue for white owners and their businesses. Thus, as long as LeBron acted within the social parameters set by these white corporate sponsors, the mass media would continue to market him in a positive light. Therefore, the interest convergence of this relationship provided benefits to LeBron only when it served the interests of those in power (e.g., white-controlled corporations) (Bell, 1992; Ladson-Billings and Tate, 1995). Similar to Michael Jordan and Tiger Woods, LeBron has displayed his unwavering commitment to his corporate sponsors and remained largely apolitical when it came to championing broader social issues that affected the black community. Even the few times he has displayed acts of social activism (e.g., in wake of the Trayvon Martin case he galvanized his team to wear hoodies to represent solidarity with Trayvon and the black community), the mass media provided very little coverage to these instances. Therefore, by not being considered a social justice activist (e.g., like Muhammad Ali, Arthur Ashe, Jackie Robinson, Jim Brown, and Bill Russell), the white capitalist driven media can continue to promote positive images of LeBron and reward his complicity, while simultaneously generating a profit.

Furthermore, LeBron embodies every characteristic of the modern day black athlete. He is celebrated for his phenomenal athletic prowess, selfless play on the court, and his business acumen. All of these characteristics reinforce dominant race ideologies of black male athletes. Similar to his black star athlete predecessors (e.g., Jack Johnson, Muhammad Ali, Michael Jordan, etc.) his black body has been revered, eroticized, and commodified by the white-controlled media. His physical talents reflect the dominant race logic that views black males as athletically superior and therefore justifies their overrepresentation in sports and underrepresentation in areas such as higher education and upper level leadership positions in society. The selfless characteristic resembles the Sambo stereotype of black males whereby they are viewed as careless, content, and subservient individuals for white power holders (Hawkins, 1998).

Although on the surface his business acumen seems contradictory to the dominant race logic that views blacks as intellectually inferior, a critical examination of this portrayal reveals that the white controlled media celebrate LeBron only when it benefits their bottom line of profit generation. Hence, the interest convergence of LeBron's celebrated business acumen fulfills the purpose of reinforcing the dominant U.S. ideology of meritocracy. In other words, LeBron is successful because he worked hard and if any aspiring black male wants to be in his position they must work hard too. The problem with this media narrative is that it ignores various socio-structural inequalities in society and the minuscule probability of attaining LeBron's level of success regardless of athletic ability (Edwards, 2000). This distorted media coverage, which overemphasizes meritocratic athletic rewards results in what Edwards (2000) called the institutionalized triple tragedy[2] for the black community. Essentially, these tragedies result in the holistic underdevelopment of black males.

Contrary to these positive images of LeBron, he has also been vilified for his perceived acts of arrogance and selfishness. One of his all-time low experiences came on July 8, 2010, when he announced to the world the infamous "decision" that he was taking his talents to South Beach to play with Dwayne Wade and Chris Bosh and the Miami Heat. In addition to the controversial decision, Cleveland Cavaliers owner Dan Gilbert intensified the racial undertones of the media coverage when he wrote a scathing open letter to Cleveland Cavaliers supporters about LeBron to Cleveland fans. Gilbert described LeBron and his actions as "narcissistic," "cowardly betrayal," "self-titled former king" and "taking the curse with him down south" (Gilbert, 2010).

According to the Rev. Jesse Jackson, "He [Gilbert] speaks as an owner of LeBron and not the owner of the Cleveland Cavaliers. His feelings of betrayal personify a slave master mentality. He sees LeBron as a 'runaway slave'" (Jackson Sr., 2010). Although the manner in which LeBron made his decision is definitely worthy of criticism, the bottom line is he simply chose to relocate his place of employment like many Americans do all the time. Thus, as Jackson purports, "This is an owner employee relationship—between business partners—and LeBron honored his contract" (Jackson Sr., 2010).

The significant amount of mass media coverage on both LeBron's "decision" and Gilbert's response reflected the media's indirect reproduction of the dominant racial ideology of white supremacy. In this case, the white owner, Gilbert, was simply putting his former employee or laborer, LeBron, in his place and the media reinforced this notion through massive coverage. Several media's outlets justified Gilbert's response and condemned LeBron's decision and manner in which he made the decision. More importantly, since the motive of these mass media outlets is to attract audiences and increase TV ratings, the media's negative coverage of him had less to do with his character, but more to do with the entertainment and economic value of the story. By depicting him as the villain, the media reinforced the dominant race logic that black males are erratic and unworthy of being trusted. He was excessively scrutinized by the media simply because he exercised his right as a free agent to relocate his place of employment. More specifically, this harsh media coverage reinforced the idea that black athletes are selfish, arrogant, and out of touch with the average American. Yet after two years with the Miami Heat, LeBron had arguably one of greatest single season performances in NBA history. In the 2011–2012 season, he claimed his first NBA championship, third regular season NBA MVP, first NBA Finals MVP, and second Olympic Gold medal.

Another modern day black star athlete that has been used to reinforce dominant racial ideology is Michael Vick. Growing in a low-income community in Newport News, Virginia, Michael's athletic success epitomized black athlete rags to riches story. From an early age, Michael used his athletic talents as source for economic mobility not only for himself, but also for his family. Like many black males, Michael viewed a professional career in sports as his best option for improving his living conditions. Fortunately, his talents met the right opportunity and he was able to play Division I football at Virginia Tech where he starred at quarterback. The highlight of his college career came in 1999 when he led Virginia Tech to the Bowl Championship Series (BCS) National Championship game. In the same year, he finished third in the Heisman Trophy (an award given to the best college football player) voting. In 2001, he became the first overall pick in the NFL draft by the Atlanta Falcons. While a quarterback for the Atlanta Falcons, he became the highest paid quarterback in the National Football League (NFL). His exceptional athletic ability was described as a once in a generation talent. His ability to elude defenders with his feet and execute difficult throws in the pocket with effortless finesse led fans to adore his performances. Michael's exceptional talent had taken him out of the substandard living conditions of his childhood into the luxurious lifestyle of a professional athlete.

Consequently, Michael was labeled by the mass media as a thug for his hip-hop style of dress, hairstyle, and overall demeanor. The media's coverage of Michael used coded racist language like "trouble man," "violent," and "deviant." All of these terms are consistent with the brute stereotype of black males, which suggests black males are innately animalistic, violent, and defiant (Hawkins, 1998). Thus, this depiction of Michael and other black males persuades the general society to view them as threats who must be controlled by any means necessary (e.g., economic exploitation, imprisonment, etc.).

The media's coverage of his dogfighting scandal was a prime opportunity to reinforce ideas about the deviant black male persona. On December 11, 2007, Michael Vick was convicted for operating a dog fighting ring and sentenced to 23 months in federal prison (18 of which he served). As a result, he lost an estimated $100 million in future income including salary, bonuses, and endorsement money (Myers, 2007). Off the field, he portrayed a different image. To the black community, he was viewed as symbol of hope, resistance, and perseverance. Everything from his dark skin to the cornrows to the confident swagger reflected what Nelson George referred to in his book *Elevating the Game* as the black aesthetic or what Richard Majors and Janet Mancini Billson referred to as "cool pose" in *Cool Pose: The Dilemmas of Black Manhood in America*. As a star athlete in one of the major urban centers in the United States, Atlanta, further intensified his media appeal. Especially during his early years in Atlanta, similar to his fellow Virginian, Allen Iverson, everywhere Vick went, he exuded black hip-hop culture. He wore popular baggy clothes, shiny jewelry, and often traveled with an entourage of black males, which validated his street credibility. The media salivated at this image because it fed into their stereotypical imaginations of black males in general and more specifically black male athletes. Historically, black male athletes have been viewed as savage, deviant, and hypersexual individuals. Similar to other black entertainers (e.g., hip-hop artists), Vick capitalized on his public persona, which was based on historical stereotypes of black males in the United States.

The relationship between the mass media and black male athletes has been ambivalent at best. On the one end, black male athletes are idolized for their athletic prowess and unique style. Contrarily, they are depicted as dumb jocks, thugs, and mere entertainers. These convoluted messages and images of black male athletes reveal the broader U.S. society's ambiguous perceptions of them. Both LeBron James and Michael Vick are polarizing figures who embody various aspects of the modern day black athlete. They both represent the zenith of athletic ability in their respective sports, the economic potential for black athletes, and a level of incredible resilience, which is reflective of a larger narrative of blacks in the United States. However, in the past they have also been negatively depicted as being selfish, brash, and excessively cocky. Only time will tell if modern day black athletes like LeBron James and Michael Vick will carry on the legacy of the black struggle as it was carried by their predecessors such as Muhammad Ali, Arthur Ashe, Jim Brown, Bill Russell, and Jackie

Robinson. Only then can we determine if they serve as agents of change or simply puppets in the corporate sport machine.

Conclusion

This essay examined how sport media content work to reinforce dominant ideas about race, and more specifically about blacks. We have provided examples of how sport commentary and images have been used to reinforce stereotypical notions about black females and males. Whether it is the angry black women (Serena Williams), the black female from the socioeconomically deprived black-female headed household (Gabby Douglas), the uppity black male who has forgotten his place or the savage brute displayed on the cover of the April 2008 edition of *Vogue* (LeBron James), or the black male villain (Michael Vick), these are reoccurring ideas about blacks that prevail in popular culture.

Race still matters in the United States, despite the progress made in electing President Barack Obama. We are presented with constant reminders in varying social institutions, including sport; an institution that has been praised for being a model for racial progress. Sport has been a burden and a blessing to racial progress, especially as it relates to blacks. Clearly, the blessing has been that it has provided opportunity for social mobility for many black athletes, coaches, and administrators. Another blessing has been that it has provided the black community, specifically, and this nation, with iconic heroes and heroines; many have transcended racial boundaries and have been consumed by mass audiences worldwide. The burden has been how it reinforces historical racist ideologies about black physical superiority and intellectual inferiority. Yet, there are counter narratives to challenge these racist ideologies and the racialized images that are predominant in the sport media content.

In the premiere position of quarterback in American football, blacks athletes are overthrowing age old myths about black intelligence, while out-throwing and out-running their white counterparts (see e.g. at the professional level: Cam Newton with the Carolina Panthers, Russell Wilson with the Seattle Seahawks, Robert Griffin, III, with the Washington Redskins; and at the college level: Eugene "Geno" Smith with West Virginia, and Denard Robinson with the University of Michigan—to name a few).

Their presence in the QB position presents a binary opposition between the pocket QB or drop back passer and the scrambler or option/running QB; the former denoting intellectual superiority, with the latter emphasizing physical superiority. The white QB, obviously, fulfilled the former, where his superior cognitive abilities enabled him to read defenses and make precise judgments in locating an open white receiver. On the other hand, black QBs have historically been labeled as being the latter, where a premium is placed on their physical superiority; their ability to run. Robert Griffin III (RG3) has openly expressed his aversion to being typecast as an option QB when he stated:

> I don't want people to think I'm just an option quarterback. It's not something you can prove, I don't think. Perception is reality so it doesn't matter how many yards you throw for, what you do in practice or what you do in the games. If you can run a little bit you'll always be smacked with that stereotype [Keim, 2012].

This statement speaks volumes of how the public's perception persists in labeling the black QB as an option QB. It also speaks to the role black QBs are contributing to the evolution of the position, specifically, and sport, in general.

Therefore, whether it is black QBs, the success of black female athletes like Gabby Douglas, Carmelita Jeter, Candace Parker, Sanya Richards-Ross, Maya Moore, the Williams sisters, Nzingha Prescod, etc., counter narratives are challenging racial ideologies that have persisted in sport and the broader society. The future of sport looks promising for blacks on all levels. The presentation of sport media content can only increase its sensitivity to archaic racist practices and begin to provide a more accurate representation of racial and cultural diversity that is progressive and inclusive, and not pathological and destructive.

Notes

1. We use the singular version of the word sport to speak collectively about sport as a commercial industry and social institution.
2. The triple tragedy in black society: "the tragedy of thousands upon thousands of black youths in obsessive pursuit of sports goals that the overwhelming majority of them will never attain; the tragedy of the personal and cultural under-development that afflicts so many successful and unsuccessful black sports aspirants; and the tragedy of cultural and institutional underdevelopment throughout black society at least in some part as a consequence of the drain in talent potential toward sports and away from other vital areas of occupational and career emphasis, such as medicine, law, economics, politics, education, and technical fields" (Edwards, 2000, p. 9).

References

Bell, D. A. (1989). *And we are not saved: The elusive quest for racial justice.* New York: Basic.

Bell, D. A. (1992). *Faces at the bottom of the well: The permanence of racism.* New York: Basic.

Carter, A. (2008). Negotiation identities: Examining African American female collegiate athlete experiences in predominantly white institutions. Unpublished dissertation, University of Georgia.

Carter-Francique, A. (2011). A reflection of revolution and its significance for black women in sport." In F. G. Polite and B. Hawkins (Eds.), *Sport, race, activism, and social change: The impact of Dr. Harry Edwards' scholarship and service*, pp. 125–141. San Diego, CA: University Reader/Cognella.

Coakley, J. (2009). *Sports in society: Issues and controversies*, 10th ed. New York: McGraw-Hill.

Douglas, D. D. (2012). Venus, Serena, and the inconspicuous consumption of blackness: A commentary on surveillance, race talk, and new racism(s). *Journal of Black Studies, 43*(2), 127–145.

Du Bois, W. E. B. (1961). *The soul of black folks*. New York: Fawcett.

Edwards, H. (2000). Crisis of black athletes on the eve of the 21st century. *Society, 37*(3), 9–13.

Evert, C. (2006, May). Chrissie's page: Dear Serena. *Tennis, 42*(4), 1 and 12.

Giddings, P. (1984). *When and where I enter: The impact of black women on race and sex in America.* New York: William Morrow.

Gilbert, D. (2010). Dear Cleveland, All of Northeast Ohio and Cleveland Cavaliers Supporters. http://www.nba.com/cavaliers/news/gilbert_letter_100708.html.

Hawkins, B. (1998). The white supremacy continum of images of black men. *Journal of African American Men, 3*(3), 1–19.

Holcomb, D. (2007). Diversity Study. *USA Gymnastics.* http://usagym.org/pages/memclub/winter07/diversity.pdf.

Jackson, J. L., Sr. (2010). The Rev. Jesse L. Jackson, Sr., reacts to Dan Gilbert's open letter." Rainbow Push Coalition. http://www.rainbowpush.org/news/single/rev._jesse_l._jackson_sr._reacts_to_dan_gilberts_open_letter

Johnson, P. (2005). Thirty-five of our most beautiful women. *Essence, 36*(1), 198–231.

Keim, J. (2012, July 7). Redskins Confidential: RG3 Report. *The Washington Examiner.* http://washingtonexaminer.com/article/703711#.UIGBOkJZ4as

Ladson-Billings, Tate, W. (1995). Toward a critical race theory of education. *Teachers College Record, 97*(1), 47–68.

Manning Marable, M. (1998). *Speaking truth to power: Essays on race, resistance, and radicalism.* Boulder, CO: Westview.

Myers, G. (2007). Dogs Bury $100M. http://www.nydailynews.com/sports/football/dogs-bury-100m-article-1.237550.

Powell, S. (2008). *Souled out? How blacks are winning and losing in sports.* Champaign, IL: Human Kinetics.

St. Jean, Y., and J. Feagin. (1998). *Double burden: Black women and everyday racism.* Armonk, NY: M.E. Sharpe.

Sieczkowski, C. (2012, August 6). Serena Williams' crip walk dance criticized as inappropriate. The Huffington Post. http://www.huffingtonpost.com/2012/08/06/crip-walk-dance-serena-williams_n_1747593.html.

Stuarowsky, E. (2011). Is multiple jeopardy the name of the game for black women in sport? In F. G. Polite and B. Hawkins (Eds.), *Sport, Race, Activism, and Social Change: The Impact of Dr. Harry Edwards' Scholarship and Service*, pp. 113–124. San Diego, CA: University Reader/Cognella.

An Ethic of Care: Black Female College Athletes and Development

Akilah R. Carter-Francique

Little is known about the experiences of today's black female college athletes and how they contribute to their development (Bruening, 2005; Person,
Benson-Quaziena, & Rogers, 2001; Smith, 2000). What is known is that black
female college athletes' experiences, historically and contemporarily, have been
demarked by racial and gender stereotypes, social isolation and alienation,
silencing, a thirst for mentorship, and the on-going development of coping
mechanisms within their daily environment (Bruening, Armstrong, & Pastore,
2005; Carter, 2008; Carter & Hart, 2010; Carter & Hawkins, 2011). Many of
these experiences occurred within the context of the Predominantly White
Institutions of Higher Education (PWIHE), and while black female participation extends beyond the realm of the PWIHE, to Historically Black Colleges
and Universties (HBCU), the impetus of their experiences is rooted in the
historical oppression based on their race, class, and gender (Bruening, 2005;
Smith, 2000).

These overlapping and oppressive categorizations, "double burdens"
(Smith, 2000), "multiple jeopardies" (King, 1988), or "intersectionality"
(Crenshaw, 1991) often render black women and black female athletes as "de
mules of the world" (Hurston, 1990, p. 14). Oglesby (1981) supports this sentiment and contextualizes the perseverance of black female athletic achievements:

> the black sportswoman is unknown and, of course, unheralded. This is a tragic
> loss for the American community, black and white, male and female, for many
> reasons. Not the least among these reasons is the fact that the black American

sportswoman has performed a prodigious psychological achievement, the understanding of which could be beneficial to all. To become a fine athlete she has to develop an assessment of herself in the face of a society which devalued her, as both a female and a black [p. 1].

Recognizing these feats, the purpose of this chapter is to explicate the need, benefit, and propose an epistemological framework to address black female college athletes social development.

This essay will explore the issues surrounding the development of black female college athletes whom attend PWIHEs and programmatic benefits of fostering social development. The first section will discuss black female college athletes. This section will present the historical and contemporary journey of black female athletes. The second section will discuss aspects of development to illuminate the need for social development. This section will outline the cultural premises, identity formation, theoretical frameworks, and programs which have been used to develop black students in higher education. The third section will identify an epistemological framework for program implementation for black female college athletes. This section will propose a paradigmatic framework reflective of black women, and provide components of the framework to address their social development.

Black Female College Athletes

In the realm of sport, black girls and women have a rich history of athletic engagement and performance. Malveaux (1993) contends, "the teamwork needed to participate in sport teaches students life lessons about cooperation, human relations, dignity and poise" (p. 54). However, for black females these historical and contemporary experiential endeavors have been accomplished and endured through the guise of the objectified Other,[1] as the structural barriers of racism, sexism, and classism are maintained in the realm of sport (Bruening, 2005; Smith, 2000). Based on this notion and acknowledging the purpose of this chapter, a black feminist standpoint epistemology is used to articulate the experiences of black female college athletes. A black feminist standpoint epistemology centers the experiences of black women while considering how the nature of their intersectionality (e.g., race, class, gender, sexual orientation) impacts their experiences (Collins, 2000) and provides an alternate framework for college athlete development.

Historical Experiences

The black female college athlete experience began within the walls of HBCUs in the early 1900s (Cahn, 1998; Davis, 1992). Amelia Roberts advocated for black females and proposed the conceptualization of physical education and athletic programs at Tuskegee Institute (known today as Tuskegee University) in 1927. In 1929, Tuskegee Institute created its first women's track and field team lead by head coach Cleveland Abbott, which produced Olympic greats such as Alice Coachman (1948) and Nell Jackson (1948). The efforts at Tuskegee Institute were not in isolation, as other HBCUs followed suit creating athletic programs at Prairie View A&M (Texas), Alabama State College, Florida A&M, Alcorn College (Mississippi), Fort Valley State College (Georgia), and Tennessee A&I (known today as Tennessee State University) (Cahn, 1998). Thus, the women of Tuskegee Institute forged a way, and the women of Tennessee State University (TSU) would continue to elevate black women in the sport of track and field. Under the direction of head coach Edward Temple, TSU would produce more Olympic greats such as Emma Reed (1948), Mae Faggs (1948, 1952, 1956), Barbara Jones (1952, 1960), Willye White (1956, 1960, 1964), Wilma Rudolph (1956, 1960), and Wyomia Tyus (1964, 1968) (Davis, 1992; Wiggins, 2007). Their accomplishments established black females athletes as an international force; however, as a consequence to their national and international notoriety, black female athletes' physicality reaffirmed dominant (e.g., white, male, upper-class) gender conceptions of womanhood. Thus, the negative and mythical imagery of black women as masculine and animalistic was globally juxtaposed to the feminine beauty and elegance of white women.

These negative conceptions and myths, stemming from the dominant culture were evident within and throughout the United States, but for black female college athletes HBCUs and their athletic programs created a protective barrier against the negativity (Cahn, 1998). For example, black female college athletes during this time period conveyed, "Traveling across the South and into the northern cities brought young athletes out of the protective fold of black institutions and communities. They encountered the harsh realities of southern segregation and the more confusing, unwritten rules of northern racism" (Cahn, 1998, p. 123). Thus, the overt discrimination incurred during the segregated '30s, '40s, '50s and '60s challenged notions of black cultural affirmations, empowerment, and racial uplift. But, black female college athletes were "insulated from wider cultural criticism by their immediate surroundings, athletes rejected interpretations that conflicted with their own" (p. 122); and as such they were able to render these realities within the supportive HBCU institutional environment.

Despite the racial and gender challenges and akin to Malveaux's (1993) assertion, black female college athletes were cognizant of how their athletic participation served as a "site for personal and social transformation" (Cahn, 1998, p. 121). Thus, while traveling to and from athletic competitions illuminated the harsh realities of racism, their travels and athletic performances revealed their significance as black women in the United States. The opportunities to travel, receive an education, and have the support of students and the black community enabled black women to persevere and reach their potential as athletes.

Yet, for black female college athletes and administrators, the 1960s and 1970s would experience a shift in racial and gender practices due to key social movements (e.g., Civil Rights Movement, Women's Movement). These movements would produce legislative acts (e.g., Title VII of the Civil Rights Act of 1964, Title IX of the Education Amendment of 1972) which would impact the nature of college sport by: (a) integrating predominantly white institutions of higher education to include their athletic programs, (b) impacting participation and administrative/coaching rates, and (c) affecting the quality and quantity of support services black college athletes received.

Historical Legislation Impact on Contemporary Representation

As stated, the Civil Rights Movement and the Women's Movement would produce legislation creating access and opportunities in the name of social justice. Through the Civil Rights Movement, the Civil Rights Act of 1964 was enacted forbidding discriminatory practices (e.g., access, treatment) based on a person's race and/or gender. Similarly, the Women's Movement produced the enactment of Title IX of the Education Amendment of 1972[2] (Title IX), which forbid discriminatory practices specifically in educational program and their athletic programs. While the goal of this legislation was to address issues of racial and gender discrimination, a number of unintended consequences resulted.

For instance, according to scholars black females in college sport (i.e., athletes, administrators, coaches) have fallen victim to the unintended consequences of Title IX (see Gill, 2011; Singer & Carter-Francique, 2012; Smith, 2000). In 2012, Title IX celebrated its fortieth anniversary. At that time, researchers and scholars noted participation rates of girls and women were at an all-time high; however, black girls and women's athletic participation rates remained behind that of white girls and women (Acosta & Carpenter, 2012). For example, at institutions of higher education in 2012, black females represent 16 percent of all participants; compared to 62.5 percent, 24.9 percent, and 70.6 percent of white males, black males, and white females respectively at the National Collegiate Athletic Association (NCAA) Division I level (Lapchick, Hoff, & Kaiser, 2011). However, within that 16 percent, black women represent 51.0 percent percent of basketball participants, 29.1 percent percent of outdoor track and field, and 7.7 percent of softball participants

(Lapchick, et al., 2011). Thus, black female athletes participation rates are lower than black males and white females; however, they remain overrepresented in the middle and lower class sports of basketball and track and field. The efforts of Title IX increased access and opportunities (e.g., grant-in-aid) for black females in intercollegiate sport, but limitations remain in the variety of sports participated in as the Other.

In addition to black females' underrepresentation as participants at the college level, black female representation as athletic administrators and coaches reflect similar imagery. Acknowledging the aforementioned class constructs, black female administrators and coaches have limited access and opportunities to rise from participant to professional. For example, black females represent 3.3 percent, 1.4 percent, 1.2 percent of head coaches in women's sports at the Division I, II, and III levels respectively, 6.9 percent, 4.2 percent, 1.9 percent of assistant coaches in women's sports at the Division I, II, and III levels respectively, 0.7 percent, 0.8 percent, 0.4 percent athletic director at the Division I, II, and III levels respectively, 2.9 percent, 6.3 percent, 2.1 percent associate and assistant athletic directors at the Division I, II, and III levels respectively (Lapchick et al., 2011). Interestingly, black females represent a higher percentage in the position of senior women administrators with 10.1 percent, 15.4 percent, and 4.2 percent at the Division I, II, and III levels. Therefore, while Title IX was enacted to address issues of discrimination, black females in sport face continue to face numerous challenges based on the intersections of their race, gender, and class status.

Again, realities of intersectionality situate black females on the margins as participants, coaches, and administrators. Abney (1998, 2007) states negotiating issues of marginalization can be deemed substantial; specifically, in addition to the sociocultural and structural barriers black females must contend with in their pursuit towards advancement in sport coaching and administration: (a) society's attitude towards women and racial minorities, (b) stereotypes, (c) poor media images, (d) structural barriers (e.g., office politics, formal and informal rules), (e) dead-end positions and the glass ceiling effect, (f) politics, (g) career resources and networks, (h) absence of role models and mentors, (i) stacking, and (j) position clustering (e.g., assistant coach). Thus, while sociocultural (e.g., white supremacy, patriarchy) and sociohistorical (e.g., Title IX) barriers permeate society, they ultimately limit black females' growth, development, and career opportunities/advancement.

Contemporary Experiences

Since the passage of the respective racial and gender legislation, black female college athletes' rates of participation have increased. For example, black female college athletes visibility at the division I level has increased from 13.8 percent during the 1999–2000 academic year to 16.0 percent during the 2009–2010 academic year (see Lapchick et al., 2011). The 2.2 percent increase in participants within the ten year span encompass 50.6 percent of the female athletes in basketball, 2.2 percent in lacrosse, 5.3 percent in soccer, 8.2 percent in softball, 28.2 percent and 27.5 percent in indoor and outdoor track and field respectively, and 11.6 percent of the female athletes in volleyball (Brown, 2011). However, as previously stated, black female administrators and coaches are underrepresented in college sport leaving black female athletes with limited mentors and role models in PWIHE environment. Abney (2007) affirms this reality stating, "In most traditionally white institutions, the African American woman athlete lacks African American women administrators and coaches with whom she can identify" (p. 60). Accordingly, this reality causes black female college athletes to rely on peer relationships and family members to negotiate and cope with their developmental challenges (see Carter & Hart, 2010; Carter & Hawkins, 2011).

Research examining the experiences of black female college athletes is not overwhelming, but it is emerging as an area of interest. Hence, black female college athletes' lived experiences present issues of (a) perceived treatment in the athletic environment (Bruening et al., 2005; Foster, 2003; Withycombe, 2011), (b) academic success (Sellers, Kuperminc, & Damas, 1997), (c) identity development and negotiation (Carter, 2008), (d) perceptions of mentoring and mentoring preferences (Carter & Hart, 2010), and (e) adoptive coping styles and strategies (Carter & Hawkins, 2011). Much of the aforementioned research provide a critical examination of the respective experiential issues employing the tenets of critical race theory and/or the themes of black feminist thought. The critical frameworks elucidated discriminatory and marginalizing practices within the PWIHE athletic environment; while simultaneously linking black female college athlete experiences to the greater black female collective within the United States. Therefore, the experiential research on black female college athletes reaffirmed how they too are silenced, stereotyped, alienated and isolated, and rendered invisible (Bruening, 2005; Smith, 2000; Withycombe, 2011).

For example, in 2005, Bruening, Armstrong, and Pastore explored the experiences of black female college athletes at PWIHEs. Employing black feminist thought, this qualitative study revealed black female college athletes were silenced by the media, their coaches, and on campus administration. For instance, when they brought forth personal and/or gender issues (e.g., need for greater media exposure) to coaches and administration, their request were denied. The black females felt this was attributed to their intersectionality, and that black male athletes and white female athletes took priority. Thus, sociocultural norms and structural personnel limited black female college athletes through silencing their voices and attempts to be agents of change.

Silenced experiences and structural challenges are running themes throughout the available scholarship on black female college athletes (Carter, 2008; Foster, 2003; Withycombe, 2011). The resultant impact of silencing, structural challenges, as well as negative stereotypes and limited support (e.g., on-campus mentors), created an atmosphere in which black female college athletes had to develop styles and strategies to cope with their realities. In 2011, Carter and Hawkins examined black female college athlete experiences within a PWIHE, and the factors that contributed to their need and adoption of coping styles and strategies. Similar to the experiences of black male college athletes (see Donnor, 2005; Hawkins, 2001, 2010; Sailes, 1998; Singer, 2008), black female college athletes also experience alienation and isolation based on their status as black athletes on PWIHE. Through their investigation, the researchers determined that on-campus racism and the negotiation and development of their identity as black females whom participated in sport contributed to their need to cope. Hence, the coping styles (e.g., avoidance) and coping strategies (e.g., journaling, talking with friends and family, praying) elicited patterns akin to those utilized in the black community and black female culture.

These research studies reaffirm the sociohistorical effects of racism within the realm of sport and the need for supports to foster black female college athletes' social development. However, the contemporary experiences illuminate the structural dynamics within the PWIHE situate black female athletes as the Other and limit their receipt of supports (i.e., counseling, programs) that can address their social development.

Black Female College Athlete Development

As presented, black female college athletes are silenced, stereotyped, and invisible (Bruening, 2005; Smith, 2000; Withycombe, 2011); however, "high visibility" (based on enrollment and media coverage) (Person, Benson-Quaziena, & Rogers, 2001) as college athletes can generate stress and anxiety. Due to these challenges and black female college athletes' intersectionality, scholars assert the need to identify sources of support to mitigate social and emotional challenges (Howard-Hamilton, 1993; Person et al., 2001). Thus, there is a need to identify sources of support that can help black female college athletes cope with their realities, while simultaneously developing a strong identity, positive self-concept, and realistic plan for life after college. But the intersectionality experienced by black female college athletes warrants an understanding of her specific developmental intersections—black female, college athlete, and black student.

Social Development of Black Female Athletes

Black female participation in athletics has traditionally been encouraged and supported within the black community (Edwards, 1973; Hanks, 1979). Juxtaposed to white females' historical sport journey, in the black community black females "can be strong and competent in sport and still not deny her 'womanliness.' She can even win respect and high status" (Edwards, 1973, p. 233); as exhibited by the accolades of Wilma Rudolph and the black female college athletes of the past. Thus, black female college athletes' socialization and values, or social development, stem initially from the family and community environment.

According to Johnson (1981) socialization includes the "preparation of newcomers for life in their social, economic, physical, cultural and extraphysical surroundings" (p. 25) based on their societal group. And as such, Collins (2000) conveys that black female children and adolescents learn from their mothers the socialization skills necessary for their survival. Subsequently, black female youth:

> learn to expect to work, to strive for an education so they can support themselves, and to anticipate carrying heavy responsibilities in their families and communities because these skills are essential to their own survival and those for whom they will eventually be responsible [Collins, 2000, p. 183].

Hence, black mothers strive to socialize their daughters and educate them on the skills necessary to navigate any environment and institution.

College Athlete Development: Theories and Models

In the college athletic environment, black female college athletes do not have the presence of their mothers, but instead must rely upon the skills their mothers (and families) instilled during their youth. Isolated and often alienated from the general student body, black female college athletes main source of support come in the form of her athletic coaches and athletic-academic advisors (Carter & Hart, 2011; Howard-Hamilton & Sina, 2001). These coaches and administrators are often charged with the duties of assisting college athletes primarily with their academic and athletic development.

Fostering college student development involves a number of factors to include acknowledging the role of students' values, attitudes, self-concepts, aspirations, academic achievements, career development, and overall satisfaction within the greater context of the institution of higher education (Astin,

1977). Hence, college athlete development theories have often incorporated cognitive and psychosocial developmental theories to address their development (Howard-Hamilton & Sina, 2001). Cognitive development theories focus on how a person learns, reasons, and make sense of their life experiences. These theories include Kohlberg's (1984) moral development and Perry's (1999) intellectual and moral development, as each of these stage models aims to resolve a moral problem. The psychosocial development theories focus on determining self-concept, the parameters of personal relationships, and life-long goals. These theories include Erickson (1980) and Chickering and Reisser's (1993) stage models, which address key aspects of adolescent development to include industry and identity (Erickson, 1980) and interdependence (Chickering & Reisser, 1993). Howard-Hamilton and Sina (2001) explicate the majority of college athletes achieve their sense of industry prior to or upon their arrival to the college campus due to their recognition as athletes; conversely, identity development is often not achieved upon or during their college athlete tenure; and thus, college athletes are "likely to face great challenges in addressing identity" (p. 37). But it must be noted, these psychosocial development models are based on research with privilege white males; and, as such the theories are not applicable to all populations (i.e., racial/ethnic minorities, gendered minorities) (Reisser, 1995). Therefore, understanding identity development for racial and gendered minorities is often limited through utilizing the aforementioned theories.

While cognitive and psychosocial development are important issues to address academic and athletic development, social development and identity remain. But these issues must be addressed with the full consideration of black female college athletes' intersectionality. Black female college athletes' social development *and* identity development warrant theoretical frameworks and models that acknowledge their historic subjugation and address their specific standpoint as black women.

Identity Development and College Students of Color

In the university environment, understanding racial and ethnic identity development can arm higher education practitioners (i.e., faculty, academic advisors, tutors) with the knowledge to facilitate academic successes for all students of color, to include black female college athletes. Acknowledging students' racial and ethnic identity development can provide insight on students' social and cognitive development within the historically oppressive environment of the PWIHE (Torres, Howard-Hamilton, & Cooper, 2003). Nevertheless, persons of an "oppressed and exploited minority" (Erickson, 1968, p. 303) may internalize the negative sociocultural and sociohistorical stereotypes perpetuated by the dominant culture (Steele & Aronson, 1995). Therefore, obtaining "information about a person's racial identity does not reveal anything about her or his cultural socialization, except perhaps how much the person values her or his socioracial group's traditional culture" (Helms & Cook, 1999, p. 98). Thus, internalization of the master narrative could potentially thwart minority students' achievement of a healthy development.

In 1990, Phinney and Alipuria explored the role of ethnic identity on minority (e.g., Asian, black, Latino/a) college students' self-esteem whom attended predominantly minority universities. Acknowledging Erickson's (1968) framework, and extending the work of minority scholars' investigations of ethnic identity on overall identity development (Cross, 1978; Helms, 1990; Tajfel, 1978), Phinney and Alipuria (1990) found that the ethnically and racially diverse minority students had a need to understand how their ethnic identity contributed to their overall identity and self-esteem. While there were differences in each of the respective minority groups, the results revealed minority students felt searching for and understanding their ethnic identity was important to their sense of self, or self-esteem. Furthermore, determining their ethnic identity was found to play a significant role in how they responded when making major life decisions (Waterman, 1985). Thus, for minority college students rendering their ethnic identity played a significant role in their overall identity formation and addressing the final stage of adolescent development.

While Phinney and Alipuria's (1990) findings are significant, the students within their study attended racially diverse universities, which may embrace and celebrate the notion of racial and ethnic diversity. Conversely, racial and ethnic minorities that attend PWIHEs have been noted to experience difficulties adjusting and developing as whole persons due to the historic realities of white supremacy and patriarchy (Allen, 1985; Fleming, 1984; Nettles, 1988; Nettles, Thoeny, & Gosman, 1986; Suen, 1983; Torres et al., 2003). Again, white supremacy and patriarchy in society and PWIHEs are rooted in the notion of power, oppression, and exploitation thus subordinate the Other. Racial identity development, then, becomes a significant developmental issue for adolescent minorities as it: (a) impacts the "degree and quality of involvement that is maintained with one's own culture and heritage," (b) address "ways of responding to and dealing with the dominant group's often disparaging views of their group," and (c) affects the overall "impact of these factors on the psychological well-being" (Phinney, 1990, p. 499). Subsequently, scholars have suggested ways to address racial identity, socialization, and development for blacks and black college students that encourage linking to their cultural roots (see Robinson & Howard-Hamilton, 1994; Torres et al., 2003).

Black College Students and the Afrocentric Paradigm

Similar to the development theories and models, identity development models are also designed to address white, male, privileged persons. However, with the increased diversification (i.e., race, sexual orientation) of college campuses (Howard-Hamilton & Sina, 2001; Rendon, 1994); the implementation of theories, models, programs, and services should reflect the diversity.

Black college students whom attend PWIHEs are not monolithic, therefore, each come to the campus with various challenges and various ways in which they feel are appropriate to address those challenges. Torres, Howard-Hamilton, and Cooper (2003) state "for members of racial and ethnic groups, it is not the concept of adapting to the context that causes problems but the experience of oppression that leads" (p. 17), to experiences of subordination which create challenges in the development of identity, self-esteem, and psychological well-being. Determining the appropriate theories, models, programs, and services scholars suggest conducting a needs assessment to discern the developmental needs of racially and ethnically diverse students.

In particular, McEwen, Roper, Bryant, and Langa (1990) center black college students' developmental needs. They suggest addressing nine dimensions before implementing programs, which include: (a) developing ethnic and racial identity, (b) interacting with the dominant culture, (c) developing cultural aesthetics and awareness, (d) developing identity, (e) developing interdependence, (f) fulfilling affiliation needs, (g) surviving intellectually, (h) developing spirituality, and (i) developing social responsibility. See Table 1 for more detail. The goal of addressing the nine dimensions prior to program implementation is to ensure black college students inclusiveness and promote a sense of multiculturalism among majority students (Howard-Hamilton, 1997; McEwen et al., 1990). Furthermore, the culmination of the nine factors reveals how black college student developmental programs can promote cognitive and social-emotional changes and infuse principles and values which reflect their African heritage, or the Afrocentric paradigm.

Table 1. Nine developmental tasks factors of African American students

Developmental tasks	Explanation
Developing ethnic and racial identity	Addressing thoughts and concerns regarding ethnic and racial identity in an effort to develop skills to protect one's identity.
Interacting with the dominant culture	Understanding the nature of assimilation, acculturation, and determining ways to interact with white students.
Developing cultural aesthetics and awareness	Acquiring knowledge and appreciation for one's culture and the culture of others.

Developing identity	Acquiring knowledge to aid in the development of one's identity to include referencing personal and social environments to maintain self-concept.
Developing interdependence	Encouraging independent and autonomous skills within nurturing relationships.
Fulfilling affiliation needs	Encouraging the development of meaningful networks within and outside of the campus environment.
Surviving intellectually	Understanding one's intellectual deficiencies and obtaining support can aid with other developmental areas.
Developing spirituality	Promoting and providing access to religious affiliations and engagement.
Developing social responsibility	Encouraging service-learning opportunities.

The Afrocentric paradigm is rooted in the social sciences and based on the historical and traditional concepts of African peoples and contemporary practices of African Americans. Moreover, the Afrocentric paradigm is rooted in the Nguzo Saba value systems that include seven basic values: (a) unity, (b) self-determination, (c) collective work responsibility, (d) cooperative economics, (e) purpose, (f) creativity, and (g) faith (see Karenga, 1980). These seven basic values promote a cultural and ethnic standpoint which foster social unity and development (e.g., spiritual, moral) (Karenga, 1980, 1993).

Accordingly, Schiele (1996) suggests the goal of the Afrocentric paradigm is to: (a) "promote an alternative social science paradigm more reflective of the cultural and political reality of African Americans; (b) dispel the negative distortions about people of African ancestry by legitimizing and disseminating a worldview that goes back thousands of years; and (c) promote a worldview that will facilitate human and societal transformation toward a spiritual, moral, and humanistic ends and that will persuade people of different cultural and ethnic groups that they share a mutual interest" (p. 286).

Therefore, the Afrocentric paradigm reflects a unique cultural perspective and an alternative perspective to the traditional Eurocentric framework that is often used as a universal lens to understand social phenomena (Asante, 1991; Robinson & Howard-Hamilton, 1994; Schiele, 1996). Based on the basic values and goals of the Afrocentric paradigm, scholars purport its usage to address black college student development.

Scholars express the Afrocentric paradigm to foster black students and black college student development often manifest in rites of passage programs (Brookins, 1996; Brooks, West-Olatunji, & Baker, 2005; Pinkney, Outley, Blake, & Kelly, 2011; Warfield-Coppock, 1992a, 1992b) and/or historically black Greek letter organizations (Giddings, 2007; Kimbrough, 1995, 2009; Kimbrough & Hutcheson, 1998). Rites of passage framework and programs for black students are rooted in the Afrocentric paradigm; and consist of a series of ceremonial processes to educate, develop, socialize, and mature young people into responsible, character driven leaders and adults (Brooks, et al., 2005; Warfield-Coppock, 1992b). These programs provide a safe space to develop and support black college students' academic, social, and leadership acumen; but the structural design of intercollegiate athletics (e.g., practice, competition, travel) often limit the opportunity to reap the benefits and participate in these programs and organizations.

Black Female College Athlete Development Framework

As expressed, the sociohistorical and sociocultural constructs play a significant role in shaping black female college athletes' experiences. And Howard-Hamilton (2003) reminds us that "the development and socialization of African American women have been moulded and understood within the framework of perceptions and agendas of members of the dominant society" (p. 20). The oppressive forces and perceptions reaffirm the power of a white supremacy, patriarchy, and capitalistic ideology within the college sport. Thus, for black female college athletes a black feminist standpoint epistemology becomes readily apparent to contextualize, understand, and provide strategies for survival. The black feminist standpoint epistemology centers the black females within its dissemination and cultivation of knowledge, and in-turn recognizes how power relations affect that knowledge. Once the power dynamics are determined in the construction of knowledge, the paradigmatic frameworks can be utilized to understand black female college athletes' positionality within their social institutions and networks. Therefore, to properly develop and incorporate an instructional framework it is important to perform an assessment, like McEwen, Roper, Bryant, and Langa's (1990) nine dimensions, to understand the strengths and limitations of the organization's ability to deliver a culturally appropriate program.

The Structure of College Athletics and College Athlete Development

The organizational structure of college athletics has been described in a multitude of ways. Some acknowledge college athletics for its opportunity to provide athletic and academic opportunities (insert citation); while other chastise college athletics for its seemingly commercialized focal point (Duderstadt, 2000; Hawkins, 2001; 2010; Sperber, 2000; Zimbalist, 2001). Davis (1994) highlights these competing models as the amateur/education model and the commercial/education model. The amateur/education model present college athletics as student driven; and thus, reflects college athletes' can receive all the educational, physical, psychological, and social benefits that athletic participation offers. While, the commercial/education model present college athletics as a business, in which college athletes are the labor force and receive little to no educational, psychological, or social benefits. Therefore, these competing models and perceptions are noteworthy, as it questions the nature of college athletics and thus the experiences of college athletes, to include their development.

CHAMPS/Life Skills

The National Collegiate Athletic Association took notice of these ongoing debates, as well as college athletes' on-going developmental challenges. In 1994 the NCAA introduced Challenging Athletes' Minds for Personal Success (CHAMPS). CHAMPS is a life skills program designed to "maintain intercollegiate athletics as an integral part of the campus educational program and the student-athlete as integral part of the student body" (National Collegiate Athletic Association [NCAA], 2008). Moreover, this program was designed to support the developmental needs of college athletes through five commitments: academic excellence, athletic excellence, personal development, career development, and engage in community service.

The NCAA and its educational staff provide program materials, resources (e.g., needs assessment instrument, program administration guide, access to online materials) to enable administrators to implement programming. Yet again, it must be noted that each NCAA member institution has autonomy in program delivery, thus programming and commitment implementation is based on institutional needs (NCAA, 2008).

Afrocentric Feminist Epistemology and Framework

Acknowledging the dynamics of college athletics and the purpose of CHAMPS/Life Skills is important. However, considering McEwen and colleagues' (1990) nine developmental factors it becomes apparent the need for CHAMPS/Life Skills administrators, and athletic administrators in general, to acquire an understanding of cultural responsiveness. More specifically, there is a need to understand the value of infusing culturally relevant pedagogy within college athlete developmental programming (see Ladson-Billings, 1995a, 1995b). Therefore, acknowledging the aforementioned culturally relevant paradigmatic framework for black college student social development, it is reasonable to suggest its utilization for the social development of black female college athletes.

The Afrocentric paradigm enables black college students an opportunity to have voice, be self-reflective, acknowledge their cultural heritage, and provide knowledge and wisdom to combat the negative stereotypes and rhetoric that pervade society and other social spaces such as the PWIHE and college athletics. Yet, due to the black female college athletes' gendered categorization, Collins (2000) purports the use of the Afrocentric paradigm in conjunction with the feminist paradigm. The feminist paradigm, like the Afrocentric paradigm, address issues and experiences of oppression from the power binaries of sex and gender to allow women to have a voice, create a space for empowerment, and provide strategies and wisdom to overcome "white capitalistic patriarchy." Accordingly, feminist issues and experiences transcend the established categories of race, ethnicity, class, sexual orientation, and religion. Thus, black females have access to another epistemological standpoint that can meet the developmental needs of black females known as Afrocentric feminist epistemology (Collins, 2000).

Afrocentric feminist epistemology was borne out of a combination of the Afrocentric standpoint and the feminist standpoint. It acknowledges how the power dynamics and binary thinking can subordinate black females; and thus, provides an understanding of the black female experience and presents strategies to foster resistance within society's power dynamics, or "matrix of domination" (Collins, 2000). The Afrocentric feminist epistemology is situated in the daily experiences of black females and is comprised of four dimensions: (a) the lived experience as a criterion of meaning, (b) the use of dialogue in the assessing knowledge claims, (c) the ethics of caring, and (d) the ethic of personal accountability (see Collins, 2000). Each of these dimensions addresses aspects of the black female experience, which allow them to endure, thrive, and overcome in their multi-oppressive reality. Thus, using personal stories and narratives to validate knowledge; applying religious based principles for guidance and transfer of wisdom; and, establishing accountability for the dissemination of information each aid in socialization. Hence, Afrocentric feminist epistemology encourages ethical behavior and values, while simultaneously challenging dominant ideologies.

Implementing the Afrocentric Feminist Epistemology and Framework

Afrocentric feminist epistemology creation spoke to the need to understand and provide a method of resistance such that black females are able negotiate their oppressive realities and contextualize how their race, gender, and class intersections render them invisible and Othered. Akin to the black female collective, the aforementioned historical and contemporary oppressive realities also render black female college athletes invisible, the objectified Other, and silenced within the PWIHE environment (Bruening, 2005; Bruening et al., 2005; Carter, 2008). Therefore, utilizing this epistemological lens as a model and framework to address black female college athletes' social development should prove beneficial.

In particular, the Afrocentric feminist epistemology presents two dimensions that could translate into a model and/or framework to assist black female college athletes' social development (a) the lived experience as a criterion of meaning and (b) the ethics of care. The first, lived experience as a criterion of meaning emphasizes the notion of knowing to include knowledge and wisdom. According to Collins (2000), "Living life as black women requires wisdom because knowledge about the dynamics of intersecting oppressions has been essential to U.S. black women's survival. African American women give such wisdom high credence in assessing knowledge" (p. 257). Consequently, black females whom have had experiences as the Other are called upon as experts to provide information and understanding; and subsequently, serve as mentors to other black females.

Black females serving as mentors are in alignment with the Afrocentric paradigm. The aforementioned rites of passage programs outline components that promote positive social development for black youth such as mentoring (Brooks, West, Olantunji, & Baker, 2005; Pinckney et al., 2011; Warfield-Coppock, 1992b). Mentoring, in a rites of passage program, assist the protégé through their individual development by attaining knowledge and wisdom and fostering resilience to become a productive member of society (Pinckney et al., 2011; Warfield-Coppock, 1992b). Additionally, mentoring with respect to college student development aids in the retention of black college students (Cheatham & Berg-Cross, 1993). Nevertheless, the notion of mentoring is a practical example of Afrocentric feminist epistemology, but the notion of mentoring from the Afrocentric feminist epistemological is framed as "mothering" or "othermothering" (Collins, 2000; James, 1993).

"Mothering" or "othermothering" is described as persons who assist biological mothers in rearing children either formally or informally (Collins, 2000; James, 1993). These persons, often female, consist of grandmothers, aunt, sisters, cousins, and/or other fictive kin. Thus, within institutions of higher education black female faculty and staff can serve as othermothers, mentors, and role models for black female college athletes. For example, Guiffrida (2005) examined black college student-faculty relationships at a PWIHE and found black students sought out black faculty to serve as mentors. According to the black college students, the black faculty exhibited characteristics of trust, familiarity, and experiential validation, which served as rationale for the forged relationships. Similarly, Carter and Hart (2011) examined black female college athletes perspective of mentors and mentoring, and similar to Guiffrida (2005), found that black female college athletes desired mentors whom were familial (e.g., mother, sister); however, in absence of familial support black female college athletes welcomed non-familial mentors as long as a level of trust was exhibited.

Each of these research studies present the benefit of black faculty and staff serving as mentors. But as presented, there is an underrepresentation of racial minorities in PWIHEs (e.g., faculty, staff, athletic coaches and administrators) that can fulfill these roles. Therefore, while this dimension does present one practical example for developing black female college athletes socially, implementing a more comparable framework is necessary to meet the needs of the black female college athletes and acknowledge the limitation of the institution and organizational structure.

The second dimension, the ethics of caring emphasizes the importance of "personal expressiveness, emotions, and empathy" (Collins, 2000, p. 263). More specifically, Afrocentric feminist epistemology maintains three interconnected components, which centralize black female experiences and knowledge claims. The components consist of (a) personal uniqueness, (b) emotional dialogues, and (c) empathy. The ethics of caring also has roots in feminist epistemology (Gilligan, 1993).

The first component, personal uniqueness, recognizes the black collective as African descendants, and all spiritually connected; and therefore, they express their spirituality, their power, and their energy in unique and individualistic ways. Thus, per Solórzano, Ceja, and Yosso (2000) and Solórzano and Villalpando (1998) creating "safe social spaces" and "counter social spaces" within PWIHEs can allow black female college athletes to "come as they are" and express themselves without surveillance. Each of their studies revealed the conception of "safe social spaces" and "counter social spaces" are essential to the development (e.g., academically, athletically, socially) and survival of marginalized groups; and as such, colleges and universities support of black student organizations, black sororities and fraternities, and black student-organized study halls serve to support their personal uniqueness (Solórzano et al., 2000; Solórzano & Villalpando, 1998). Furthermore, the praxis of culturally relevant pedagogy encourages a student-centered philosophy (Ladson-Billings, 1995a, 1995b) and similarly to the notion of safe social spaces and counter social spaces, culturally relevant pedagogy also supports the personal uniqueness of marginalized students.

The second component, the appropriateness of emotions in dialogues recognizes the value of emotion in verbal exchange. Collins (2000) exclaims,

"Emotion indicates that a speaker believes in the validity of an argument" (p. 263). Black females' emotional expression is often unwanted, as the combination of their racial and gendered intersections leaves the black female voice marginalized and emotional expressions suppressed. In 1993, Signithia Fordham explored black female academic experiences, gender "passing," and methods of resistance in an educational environment. Fordham's (1993) study revealed how black female students' gendered selves and use of voice were often challenged by and juxtaposed to the dominant culture's conception of womanhood. Depending on the dominant conceptions of womanhood and the cultural environment (i.e., predominantly white v. predominantly black), black female students achieved academically whether they were silent or loud. Fordham's (1993) research revealed the majority of black females adopted the dominant cultures' value of womanhood, and remained silent in an effort to achieve academically and survive in dominant society. Thus, the students negotiated the educational environment and adopted methods that abandoned their culture.

Conversely, Henry's (1998) examination of black girls' academic experiences in an African-centered school revealed the young black females also had to negotiate (a) gender and the dominant culture's definition of womanhood, (b) their multiple identities as black girls, (c) single gendered and co-gendered spaces and self-expression, and (d) appropriate theoretical frameworks (e.g., black feminist v. black nationalist) to thrive academically and socially. Thus, with regard to voice and emotion, black females need to articulate (e.g., speak, write) their experiences in a safe space and within a safe space that will validate and embrace their articulations (Henry, 1998; Omolade, 1994).

The third component is empathy, which encourages the development of empathy, engaging black females in situations which they can learn how to understand, have sympathy, and be responsive when her "sister" is in need. The creation of safe spaces is important to support the developmental process of empathy, but having the skills and experiences is also necessary. In 2011, Carter and Hawkins examined black female college athlete experiences and their coping methods within the PWIHE environment. They found that the black female athletes were often alienated due to their intersectionality; and subsequently, isolated themselves from issues and/or persons of conflict. They chose an avoidance coping style to manage their experiential realities and selected coping strategies (e.g., talking, journaling, listening to music, reading their Bible) reflective of the black community and the black female collective. Carter and Hawkins (2011) determined, again, black female college athletes needed "safe spaces" to help them contextualize their experiences as the Other and utilize the safe space as a site for social support.

Black females' ability to establish coping styles and strategies to negotiate their experiential realities is essential. According to Watt (2003), black female college students' use of religion and spirituality to cope with their othered experiences proved beneficial in the PWIHE. Their use of religion and spirituality also served as a strategy of resistance and ultimately aided in the black female college students ability to develop a healthy identity. Thus, through their ability to cope with their oppressive realities, they were better able to understand and empathize with other black females trials through their spirituality.

Implications for Practitioners

In 2003, Howard-Hamilton suggested black feminist thought as a theoretical framework to explicate the experiences of black females in the PWIHE, and some scholars who have examined black female college athletes have followed suit. Whether a person interprets black feminist thought as black feminist standpoint epistemology or Afrocentric feminist epistemology, this lens centers the experiences of black females. Therefore, Afrocentric feminist epistemology has proved fruitful in deconstructing the experiences of black females while simultaneously addressing the sociocultural and sociohistorical traditions that advocate for social justice, emancipation, and the empowerment of black females. Hence, if Afrocentric feminist epistemology can articulate black females' past and current experiences, it would be prudent to implement its traditions and philosophies to cultivate black females and black female college athletes of today and tomorrow.

Black female division I college athlete experiences' at PWIHE are not comparable to their foremothers' experiences at HBCUs. However, culturally responsive practitioners should identify how their foremothers' survival strategies and black student development theories can be utilized and integrated into the current PWIHE and intercollegiate athlete model. Thus, practitioners should recognize black female college athletes' predisposed developmental challenges and the availability of resources (i.e., mentors, on- and off-campus programs and organizations, churches) to attend to their developmental needs. So, whether those needs are met within the collegiate athletic environment or through collaborative efforts within the university (i.e., black student organizations, department of multicultural services) or through the community (i.e., black churches, black female community leaders) it is important that black female college athletes feel supported, empowered, and valued.

Through this essay, information was presented that explicated the need for, benefits of, and epistemological propositions for the addressing the social development of black female college athletes. Employing the Afrocentric feminist epistemological framework presents a viable option for structuring black female college athletes' social development programs and services. Fostering their social development through the practice of "othermothering" is a historical tradition that has proven benefits, and should be a continued practice to support the development of these women socially, academically, and athletically. Likewise, the ethic of care provides key components that can be adapted to programs and services. Hence, embracing their individuality, self-expression, and promoting compassion are on par with diversity initiatives, college student development, and aspects of the collegiate athletic mission. Additionally, there is added value in employing Afrocentric feminist epistemological dimension of the ethic of care, as it can be considered an inclusionary framework for its ability to address any students whom may be experiencing marginalization in a college environment.

Black female college athletes are a growing population with increasing visibility and while their societal positions and historic journey have created a multitude of challenges limiting their development, it is imperative that practitioners take heed and support these phenomenal females. As presented, up until today the "black American sportswoman has performed a prodigious psychological achievement" (Oglesby, 1981, p. 1) often in isolation and with limited support, but the time has come to *support* her, *care* for her, and *understand* her, as it will be beneficial to her and "beneficial to all."

Notes

1. The Other is defined as "the enslaved African women" (Christian, 1985, p. 160) whose mere existence justifies oppressive practices. Thus, black female representation is in diametrical opposition to dominant culture (Collins, 2000).

2. Title IX of the Education Amendment of 1972 states that "No person in the United States shall, on the basis of sex, be excluded from participation in, be denied the benefits of, or be subjected to discrimination under any education program or activity receiving Federal financial assistance" (United States Department of Labor, http://www.dol.gov/oasam/regs/Statutes/titleix.htm).

References

Abney, R. (1998). The effect of role models and mentors on the careers of black women athletic administrators and coaches in higher education. Unpublished dissertation, University of Iowa, Iowa City.

Abney, R. (2007). African American women in intercollegiate coaching and athletic administration: Unequal access. In D. Brooks and R. Althouse (Eds.), *Diversity and Social Justice in College Sport: Sport Management and the Student Athlete*, pp. 51–75. Morgantown, WV: Fitness Information Technology.

Acosta, V., and L. Carpenter (2012). Women in intercollegiate sport: A longitudinal, national study thirty-five year update, 1977–2012. Retrieved October 1, 2012 from http://acosta carpenter.org/AcostaCarpenter2012.pdf.

Allen, W. R. (1985). Black student, white campus: Structurally interpersonal, and psychological correlations of success. *Journal of Negro Education, 54,* 134–147.

Asante, M. K. (1991). The Afrocentric idea in education. *The Journal of Negro Education 60*(2), 170–180.

Astin, A. (1977). *Four critical years: Effects of college on beliefs, attitudes, and knowledge*. San Francisco, CA: Jossey-Bass.

Brookins, C. C. (1996). Promoting Ethnic Identity Development in African American Youth: The Role of Rites of Passage. *Journal of Black Psychology 22*, 338–417.

Brooks, M., C. West-Olantunji and J. Baker (2005). Use of rites of passage programs to foster resilience in African American students. *Missouri School Counselor Association's The Counseling Interviewer 37* (4), 54–59.

Brown, G. (2011 December 4). Demographics data show more inclusive trends: Searchable online database replace previous reports. National Collegiate Athletic Association: Latest News. Retrieved on September 14, 2012 from http://www.ncaa.org/wps/wcm/connect/public/ncaa/resources/latest+news/2011/december/demographics+data+show+more+inclusive+trends.

Bruening, J. (2005). Gender and racial analysis in sport: Are all the women white and all the blacks men? *Quest 57*, 340–359.

Bruening, J., K. Armstrong and D. Pastore (2005). Listening to the voices: The experiences of African American female student athletes. *Research Quarterly for Exercise and Sport 76*(1), 82–100.

Cahn, S. K. (1998). *Coming on strong: Gender and sexuality in the twentieth-century women's sports*. Cambridge, MA: Harvard University Press.

Carter, A. (2008). Negotiation identities: Examining African American female collegiate athlete experiences in predominantly white institutions. Unpublished dissertation, University of Georgia.

Carter, A. R., and A. Hart (2010). Perspectives of mentoring: The black female student-athlete. *Sport Management Review 13*, 382–394.

Carter, A. R., and B. J. Hawkins (2011). Coping strategies Among African American female collegiate athletes in the predominantly white institution. In K. Hylton, A. Pilkington, P. Warmington, and S. Housee (Eds.), *Atlantic crossings: International dialogues in critical race theory*, pp. 61–92. Birmingham, UK: Sociology, Anthropology, Politics (C-SAP), Higher Education Academy Network.

Cheatham, H. E., and L. Berg-Cross (1993). College student development: African Americans reconsidered. In L. C. Whitaker and R. E. Slimak (Eds.), *College Student Development*, p. 167–192. New York: Haworth.

Chickering, A. W., and L. Reisser, L. (1993). *Education and identity*, 2d ed. San Francisco, CA: Jossey-Bass.

Collins, P. (2000). *Black feminist thought: Knowledge, consciousness, and the politics of empowerment*, 2d ed. New York: Routledge.

Crenshaw, K. (1991). Mapping the margins: Intersectionality, identity politics, and violence against women of color. *Stanford Law Review 43* (6), 1241–1299.

Cross, W. E. (1978). The Thomas and Cross models of psychological nigreascence: A review. *Journal of Black Psychology 5* (1), 13–31.

Davis, M. D. (1992). *Black American women in Olympic track and field: A complete illustrated reference*. Jefferson, NC: McFarland.

Davis, T. (1994). Intercollegiate athletics: Competing models and conflicting realities. *Rutgers Law Journal 25* (2), 269–327.

Department of Labor (2012). Title IX of the Education Amendments of 1972: 20 U.S.C. Sect. 1681. Retrieved on September 16, 2012, from http://www.dol.gov/oasam/regs/Statutes/titleix.htm.

Donnor, J. K. (2005). Towards an interest-convergence in education of African American football student athletes in major college sports. *Race Ethnicity and Education 8* (1), 45–67.

Duderstadt, J. (2000). *Intercollegiate athletics and the American university: A university president's perspective*. Ann Arbor: University of Michigan Press.

Edwards, H. (1973). *Sociology of sport*. Homewood, IL: Dorsey.

Erickson, E. (1968). *Identity: Youth and crisis*. New York: Norton.

Erickson, E. (1980). *Identity and the life cycle*. New York: W. W. Norton.

Fleming, J. (1984). *Blacks in college*. San Francisco, CA: Jossey-Bass.

Fordham, S. (1993). "Those loud black girls": (Black) women, silence, and gender "passing" in the academy. *Anthropology and Education Quarterly, 24* (1), 3–32.

Foster, K. M. (2003). Panopticonics: The control and surveillance of black female athletes in collegiate athletic programs. *Anthropology & Education Quarterly, 34* (3), pp. 300–323.

Giddings, P. (2007). *In search of sisterhood: Delta Sigma Theta and the challenges of the black sorority movement*. New York: HarperCollins.

Gill, E. L. (2011). The Rutgers women's basketball and Don Imus controversy (RUIMUS): White privilege, new racism, and the implication for college sport management. *Journal of Sport Management 25*, 118–130.

Gilligan, C. (1993). *In a different voice: Psychological theory and women's development*. Cambridge, MA: Harvard University Press.

Guiffrida, D. A. (2005). Othermothering as a framework for understanding African American students' definition of student-centered faculty. *The Journal of Higher Education, 76* (6), 701–723.

Hanks, M. (1979). Race, sexual status, and athletics in the process of educational achievement. *Social Science Quarterly, 60*, 482–496.

Hawkins, B. (2001). *New plantation: The internal colonization of black student-athletes*. Winterville, GA: Sadiki.

Hawkins, B. (2010). *The new plantation: Black athletes, college sports, and predominantly white NCAA institutions*. New York: Palgrave Macmillian.

Helms, J. (1990). *Black and white racial identity: Theory, research, and practice*. Contributions in African American and African Studies. New York: Greenwood.

Helms, J. E., and D. A. Cook (1999). *Using race and culture in counseling and psychotherapy: Theory and process*. Needham Heights, MA: Allyn and Bacon.

Henry, A. (1998). Invisible and womanish: Black girls negotiating their lives in an African_centered school in the USA. *Race, Ethnicity, and Education, 1* (2), 151–170.

Howard-Hamilton, M. F. (1993). African-American female athletes: Issues, implications, and imperatives for educators. *NASPA Journal, 30* (2), 153–159.

Howard-Hamilton, M. F. (1997). Theory to practice: Applying developmental theories relevant to African American men. *New Directions for Student Services, 80*, 17–30.

Howard-Hamilton, M. (2003). Theoretical frameworks for African American women. *New Directions for Student Services, 104*, 19–27.

Howard-Hamilton, M. F., and J.A. Sina (2001). How college affects student athletes. *New Directions for Student Services, 93*, 35–45.

Hurston, Z. N. (1990). *Their eyes were watching God*. New York: Harper Perennial.

James, S. M. (1993). Mothering: A possible black feminist link to social transformation? In S. M James and A. P. A. Busia, *Theorizing black feminisms: The visionary pragmatism of black women*, pp. 44–54. London: Routledge

Johnson, R. C. (1981). The black family and black community development. *Journal of Black Psychology, 8*, 35–52.

Johnson, V. D. (2001). The Ngzubo Saba as a foundation for African American student college student development theory. *Journal of Black Studies, 31* (4), 406–422.

Karenga, M. (1980). *Kawaida theory*. Los Angeles, CA: Kawaida.

Karenga, M. (1993). *Introduction to black studies*, 2d ed. Los Angeles, CA: University of Sankore Press.

Kimbrough, W. M. (1995). Self-assessment, participation, and value of leadership skills, activities, and experiences for black students relative to their membership in historically black fraternities and sororities. *The Journal of Negro Education, 64* (1), 63–74.

Kimbrough, W. M. (2009). The membership intake movement of historically black Greek-letter organizations. *NASPA Journal, 46* (4), 603–613.

Kimbrough, W. M., and P. A. Hutcheson (1998). The impact of membership in black Greek-letter organizations on black students' involvement in collegiate activities and their development of leadership skills. *The Journal of Negro Education, 67* (2), 96–105.

King, D. (1988). Multiple jeopardy, multiple consciousness: The context of a black feminist ideology. *Journal of Women Culture and Society, 14* (1), 42–72.

Kohlberg, L. (1984). *Philosophy of moral development.* New York: Harper and Row.

Ladson-Billings, G. (1995a). But that's just good teaching! The case for culturally relevant pedagogy. *Theory Into Practice, 34* (3), 159–165.

Ladson-Billings, G. (1995b). Toward a theory of culturally relevant pedagogy. *American Educational Research Journal, 32*(3), 465–491.

Lapchick, R., B. Hoff and C. Kaiser (2011, September 3). The 2010 racial and gender report card: College sport. Orlando: Institute for Diversity and Ethics in Sport, University of Central Florida.

Malveaux, J. (1993). Sport scholars aren't the only outstanding students. *Black Issues in Higher Education, 12,* 54.

McEwen, M. K., L. D. Roper, D. R. Bryant and M. J. Langa (1990). Incorporating the development of African-American students into psychosocial theories of student development." *Journal of College Student Development, 31* (5), 429–436.

National Center for Education Statistics (2011). The condition of education. Retrieved on September 12, 2011 from http://nces.ed.gov/pubs2011/2011033.pdf.

National Collegiate Athletic Association [NCAA] (2008). NCAA CHAMPS/Life skills program: 2008–2009. Retrieved on October 3, 2012 from http://www.ncaapublications.com/productdownloads/LS08.pdf.

National Collegiate Athletic Association (2012, 17 August). Office of the president. http://www.ncaa.org/wps/wcm/connect/public/NCAA/NCAA+President/On+the+Mark.

Nettles, M. T. (1988). Toward black undergraduate student equality in american higher education. New York: Greenwood.

Nettles, M. T., A. Thoeny and E. Gosman (1986). Comparative and predictive analyses of black and white students' college achievement and experience. *Journal of Higher Education, 57,* 289–318.

Oglesby, C. A. (1981). Myths and realities of black women in sport. In T. S. Green, C. A. Oglesby, A. Alexander, and N. Franke (Eds.), *Black women in sport.* Reston, VA: AAHPERD.

Omolade, B. (1994). *The rising song of African American women.* New York: Routledge.

Perry, W. G. (1999). *Forms of intellectual and ethical development in the college years: A scheme.* San Francisco, CA: Jossey-Bass Higher and Adult Education Series.

Person, D. R., M. Benson-Quaziena and A. Rogers (2001). Female student athletes and students of color. *New Direction for Student Services, 93,* 55–64.

Phinney, J. S. (1990). Ethnic identity in adolescents and adults: review of research. *Psychological Bulletin, 108*(3), 499–514.

Phinney, J. S., and L. L. Alipuria (1990). Ethnic identity in college students from four ethnic groups. *Journal of Adolescence, 13,* 171–183.

Pinckney, H. P., C. Outley, J. J. Blake and B. Kelly (2011). Promoting positive youth development of black youth: A rites of passage framework. *Journal of Park and Recreation Administration, 29* (1), 98–112.

Reisser, L. (1995). Revisiting the seven vectors. *Journal of College Student Development, 36*(6). 505–511.

Rendon, L. I. (1994). Validating culturally diverse students: Toward a new model of learning and student development. *Innovative Higher Education, 19* (1), 33–51.

Robinson, T. L., and M. F. Howard-Hamilton (1994). An Afrocentric paradigm: Foundation for healthy self-image and health interpersonal relationships. *Journal of Mental Health Counseling, 16*(3), 327–339.

Sailes, G.A. (1998). The African American athlete: Social myths and stereotypes. In G.A. Sailes (Ed.), *Contemporary themes: African Americans in sport,* pp. 183–198. New Brusnwick, NJ: Transaction.

Sailes, G. A. (1998). "A comparison of professional sports career aspirations among athletes." In Sailes, G. (Ed.), *African Americans in sport,* pp. 261–269. Somerset, NJ: Transaction.

Schiele, J. H. (1996). Afrocentricity: An emerging paradigm in social work practice. *Social Work,* *41* (3), 284–294.

Sellers, R. M., G. P. Kuperminc, and A. Damas (1997). The college life experiences of African American women athletes. *American Journal of Community Psychology,* 25 (5), 699–720.

Singer, J.N. (2008). Benefits and detriments of African American male athletes' participation in a big-time college football program. *International Review for the Sociology of Sport, 43* (4), 399–408.

Singer, J. N., and A. R. Carter-Francique (2012). Representation, participation, and the experiences of racial minorities in college Sport. In G. Sailes (Ed.), *Sports in higher education: Issues and controversies in college athletics,* pp. 113–138. San Diego, CA: Cognella.

Smith, Y. (2000). Sociohistorical influences on African American elite sportswomen. In D. Brooks and R. Althouse (Eds.), *Racism in college athletics: The African American athletes' experience,* 2d ed., pp. 173–198. Morgantown, WV: Fitness Information Technology.

Solórzano, D., M. Ceja, and T. Yosso (2000). Critical race theory, racial microaggressions, and campus racial climate: The experiences of African American college students. *The Journal of Negro Education, 69* (1/2), 60–73.

Solórzano, D., and O. Villalpando (1998). Critical race theory, marginality, and the experience of minority students in higher education. In Torres and T. Mitchell (Eds.), *Emerging issues in the sociology of education: Comparative perspectives,* pp. 211–224. Albany: State University of New York Press.

Sperber, M. (2000). *Beer and circus: How big-time college sports has crippled undergraduate education.* New York: Henry Holt.

Steele, C. M., and J. Aronson (1995). Stereotype threat and the intellectual test performance of African Americans. *Journal of Personality and Social Psychology, 69* (5), 797–811.

Suen, H. (1983). Alienation and attrition of black college students on predominantly white campuses. *Journal of College Student Personnel, 24,* 117–121.

Tajfel, H. (1978). *Differentiation between social groups: Studies in the social psychology of intergroup relations.* Oxford, England: Academic.

Toldson, I. A., and C. W. Lewis (2012).*Challenge the status quo: Academic success among school-age African American males.* Washington, D.C.: Congressional Black Caucus Foundation.

Torres, V., M. F., Howard-Hamilton, and D. Cooper (2003). Identity development of diverse populations: Implications for teaching and administration in higher education. *ASHE-ERIC Higher Education Report, 29* (6). Hoboken, NJ: Wiley Periodicals.

Warfield-Coppock, N. (1992a). The rites of passage: Extending education into the African American community." In M. Shujja (Ed.), *Too much schooling, too little education: A paradox in African American life,* pp. 377–394. Trenton, NJ: African World.

Warfield-Coppock, N. (1992b). The rites of passage movement: A resurgence of African-centered practices for socializing African American youth." *The Journal of Negro Education, 61* (4), 471–482.

Waterman, A. (1985). Identity in the context of adolescent psychology. In A. Waterman (Ed.), *Identity in adolescence: Process and contents,* pp. 5–24. San Francisco, CA: Jossey-Bass.

Watt, S. K. (2003). Come to the river: Using spirituality to cope, resist, and develop identity. *New Directions for Student Services, 104,* 29–40.

Wiggins, D. K. (2007). Climbing the racial mountain: A history of the African American experience in sport." In D. Brooks and R. Althouse (Eds.), *Diversity and social justice in college sport: Sport management and the student athlete,* pp. 21–47. Morgantown, WV: Fitness Information Technology.

Withycombe, J. L. (2011). Intersecting selves: African American female athletes' experiences of sport. *Sociology of Sport Journal, 28,* 478–493.

Zimbalist, Andrew (2001). *Unpaid professionals: Commercialism and conflict in big time college sports.* Princeton, NJ: Princeton University Press.

Right Place, Right Time: The Galvanization of Brooklyn During the Robinson Years

Demetrius W. Pearson

Introduction

This socio-cultural and historical essay discusses the salient impact that the signing of Jackie Robinson had on the borough of Brooklyn, American sport, and post-war society. It also highlights the iconic legacy forged over time by this seminal occurrence during an era where federally sanctioned segregation was the norm in basically all aspects of American society. Ironically, during this period, baseball was America's national pastime and symbolic of the country's value system. What took place in Brooklyn was perceived by many as unthinkable, inconceivable, unconscionable, and un–American (Peterson, 1999). However, the contractual agreement consummated on October 23, 1945, and executed several years later provided the impetus for the questioning of civil liberties, and ultimately social change in America.

In 1947 Brooklyn and its beloved baseball franchise, the Dodgers, became the most controversial sport team in American history when Jackie Robinson took the field. This landmark event, known as "Baseball's Great Experiment" (Gems, Borish, & Pfister, 2008; Tygiel, 1983), was arguably the most salient moment in American sport and post–World War II society. It was the first time during the twentieth century that an African American baseball player suited up and played for a major league team. According to the late Arthur Ashe (1993), the integration of Major League Baseball could not have occurred

20 years earlier for a variety of reasons. Yet, a business savvy, innovative lawyer in concert with a supremely confident West Coast transplant galvanized a culturally eclectic community, and changed the landscape of sport forever. The relationship (business and personal) between Branch Rickey and Jackie Robinson, along with the goading national black press (Austin, 1997), superseded sport and was instrumental in impacting American social policy. Kahn (1972) metaphorically compared Robinson's integration of Major League Baseball to Brown vs. Board of Education of Topeka.

Historical Overview

The Brooklyn Dodgers, presently known as the Los Angeles Dodgers, are arguably one of the most storied professional sport franchises in American history. Noted for their mid-twentieth century exploits both on and off the baseball diamond, the Brooklyn Dodgers were the quintessential sport franchise to epitomize social integration. No other sport team has been so lauded for its front office decisions, talent scouting, player selection, frugality, and community support during the post-war years than the Brooklyn Dodgers. They were symbolic of the changing face of American sport and society through their social integration and westward migration.

The early Brooklyn Dodgers franchise was known by several different names during the late 1800s and early 1900s including Ward's Wonders, Foutz's Fillies, Hanlon's Suberbas, Bridegrooms, Robins, and Trolley Dodgers. The latter name, which was used and dropped several times during the franchise's history, came about as a result of the maze of trolleys that crisscrossed the New York borough around the turn of the century (Baseball Reference, 2012). The team joined the American Association, an early rival to the National League in 1884, and won the league pennant in 1889 under the name Brooklyn Bridegrooms (because many players had recently married). Following the 1889 season the Bridegrooms, along with the Cincinnati Reds, withdrew from the American Association to join the National League. In their inaugural season they won the pennant and played the American Association's Louisville Colonels in the 1890 World Series, which ended in a 3 to 3 draw with one tie game.

The early success of the Brooklyn franchise was short lived as the team maintained a mediocre record throughout the first decade of the twentieth century. However, brief success was experienced in 1914 when the team (Brooklyn Robins) won the pennant and appeared in the World Series against left-handed pitcher Babe Ruth. Frequent name changes, new ownership, and intermitting success characterized the Brooklyn ball club during the 1920s and

1930s. Under the ownership of Charlie Ebbets a new stadium (Ebbets Field), was built, which would be a staple for the team from 1913 until their move to Los Angeles in 1957.

The Borough of Brooklyn

Over the years Brooklyn has been referred to as the "side door" to the Statue of Liberty because of its long history of ethnic diversity (Simon, 2002). During the post–World War II era Brooklyn was a heterogeneous amalgamation of clans, villages, and enclaves comprised of Italians, Irish, Poles, Swedes, and Germans in Bensonhurst; transplanted blacks from the south inhabited Stuyvesant Heights; Russians, Syrians, and West Indians settled in Greenspoint; while Newfoundlanders took residence in Prospect Park West. Census data indicate that more than a third of the borough's population was Jewish in the mid–1940s (Simon, 2002). They resided in Williamsburg, Bensonhurst, and Crown Heights. Kahn (1972) fondly and reminiscently depicted Brooklyn as an ethnically diverse environ with remarkable schools, fine libraries, second run movie houses, eclectic neighborhoods, and lovely stretches of acreage.

Unique in many respects, the ethnic diversity of Brooklyn was instrumental in the "Great Experiment" of Branch Rickey, the part owner and general manager of the Brooklyn Dodgers in 1947. He believed that the multiple aspects of Brooklyn's diversity (i.e., ethnicity, geographic locale, SES, social environment, architectural design, etc.) would facilitate his integration plan for the Dodgers. Unlike their crosstown rivals, the Dodgers' organization was uniquely "un-Yankee like" in that they cultivated a working class fan base. As a result, affordable ticket prices designed to increase beer sales, Sunday doubleheaders, "ladies day" ticket discounts, and night games were scheduled to accommodate work schedules and induce the working class fan. The communal relationship between "Brooklynites" and the Dodgers was shaped during the 1950s due to the many players that lived among the fans, and often used the same public transportation. As a result, the Dodgers perceptually represented neighborhood and community related baseball. Ebbets Field was also thought to be a neighborhood venue because of its intimate confines.

Post-war America and Mid-century Changes

The legendary success and iconic moments of the Brooklyn Dodgers franchise occurred after World War II. They were symbolic of the changing face of American sport and society at a time when a social renaissance and mid-century revolution of sorts were underway. Austin (1997) noted that when Jackie Robinson took the field in 1947 it signaled the start of a change process that eventually transformed the social conscience of the Brooklyn Dodgers and all of baseball. At the height of their National League supremacy (1945–1957) the nation witnessed and experienced numerous noteworthy social and political events. Some of the more notable historical events were: (1) the signing of Jackie Robinson and the integration of Major League Baseball; (2) President Truman's signing of Executive Order 9981 desegregating the armed forces; (3) the landmark school desegregation case Brown v. Board of Education; (4) the Civil Rights Movement and the Montgomery Bus Boycott; (5) the Soviet Union's emergence as a superpower and the Cold War era; (6) the "Red Scare" and McCarthyism; (7) Sputnik I and the space race; and (8) the westward expansion of Major League Baseball with the exodus of the Brooklyn Dodgers and New York Giants.

Televised sport coverage aided baseball in maintaining its national pastime status, as well as the relocation of the Dodgers and Giants. Their National League inter-city rivalry continued with far greater profits (via increased market shares) because the league was comprised of only 16 teams. There were no franchises south of Washington, D.C., and west of St. Louis. Therefore the market shares of these transplant franchises grew exponentially due to their novelty and limited competition.

Social Integration and Organizational Culture

Although the Dodgers were somewhat successful prior to team president and part owner Branch Rickey's arrival, they became a national phenomenon under his leadership. Much of the Dodgers post-war success can be attributed to his administration and shrewd business acumen. His prescient vision and "stealth-like" negotiations enabled him to build the organization into a perennial contender, facilitate social change, and create an iconic national brand that has endured for over a half century after the team relocated. During his tenure he was aided by the controversial Leo "the Lip" Durocher, who was the manager of the Dodgers when Robinson was called up to the major league team.

Rickey's successful integration of Major League Baseball, with the signing of Jackie Robinson, is viewed as his most salient career accomplishment. Often confused and misconstrued as a humanitarian social statement, Rickey's signing of Robinson and other elite Negro League ball players was financially motivated. He saw a reservoir of untapped Negro League talent, and was willing to negotiate and often exploit the vast resources. According to Ward and Burns

(1994), Rickey was quoted as stating: "The greatest untapped reservoir of raw material in the history of the game is the black race. The Negroes will make us winners for years to come, and for that I will happily bear being called a bleeding heart and a do-gooder and all that humanitarian rot" (p. 254). His talent scouting and signing of Negro League players enabled him to have four in uniform in 1950, when baseball had only nine. The Dodgers eventually signed 16 Negro League players, and became the team of choice for black Americans.

However, the organizational climate and culture within the Brooklyn Dodgers' franchise was not initially supportive of Rickey's social integration plans. Clay Hooper, manager of the Montreal Royals, the Dodgers' AAA minor league farm club, was not thrilled when he was informed that he had inherited Jackie Robinson in 1945. A native Mississippian, Hooper questioned the rationale of this directive: "Do you really think a nigger's a human being?" (Ward & Burns, 1994, p. 287). He allegedly begged Branch Rickey not to put him in charge of this integrated ball club. In time Hooper's fears and apprehensions subsided due to Robinson's work ethic, athletic prowess, intellect, and temperament. After the Montreal Royals won the league championship and the Little World Series, Hooper grabbed Robinson by the hand and stated: "You're a great ballplayer and a fine gentleman.... It's been wonderful having you on the team" (Ward & Burns, 1994, p. 289).

An anti-integration sentiment was pervasive at the major league level and on the Brooklyn Dodgers as well. Knowing that discrimination and bigotry were rampant within his own organization, and Jim Crow laws throughout the south would exacerbate the quest to desegregate the team, Rickey transferred the Dodgers training camp from Florida to Cuba in 1947. He also scheduled additional games in Panama during spring training with the Royals (Austin, 1997). This was a ploy designed to "soft sell" and show Robinson's baseball skills to the Dodgers' major league players and baseball writers. In a staged seven-game series against the Dodgers Robinson (playing for the Royals) batted .625 and stole seven bases. Ironically, as oppose to gravitating toward the "novel phenom," the ploy appeared to alienate several players. For some it raised questions about job security, whereas for others it was the audacity of having to play against and/or with a black player.

Three players (Dixie Walker, Eddie Stanky, and Bobby Bregan), in particular, were outraged by Rickey's "clandestine" ploy and attempted to thwart his overall plan by drawing up a petition. It suggested that they would prefer to be traded than to play with a black teammate. They solicited other Dodger players to sign the petition. With the aid of his oft outspoken manager, Leo Durocher, Rickey quelled the rebellion by threatening to trade any player who persisted with the protest and chose not to play with Robinson. Durocher told the players that Robinson was going to make them rich, after which he emphatically informed them what they could do with their petition (Ward & Burns, 1994). One player, Kirby Higbe, who maintained his anti–Robinson position and refused to comply with Rickey's mandate was summarily traded to the Pittsburgh Pirates.

The Robinson Effect and Major League Baseball

Branch Rickey and Jackie Robinson's successful partnership helped galvanize the Dodgers' fandom, placed social integration in the forefront of American society, and paid substantial dividends at the gate. Their unconventional alliance, which was chronicled throughout Robinson's playing career, was the genesis for integration in most American sport forms. National tabloids condemned and vilified them for threatening baseball's purity and status quo, while others extolled the courage of the organization and sacrifices made by its players. However, Rickey and Robinson found themselves in the right place at the right time. The Great Baseball Experiment was a tremendous gamble at the time, but Rickey's cunning business acumen helped skew the bet in his favor, which benefitted him in many ways.

Although there was much discussion and role-playing between Rickey and Robinson prior to his professional baseball debut, the overt hostility, taunts, racial epitaphs, death threats, and social injustices nearly brought on a nervous breakdown while in the minor league. In spite of the malevolent behavior toward Robinson during his rookie year on the Dodgers' AAA farm team he led the International League in batting (.349), stolen bases (49), and fielding average (.985). He also scored 113 runs, hit 25 doubles, and drove in 66 runs while leading his team to the league championship and victory in the Little World Series. What fans witnessed in the minor league is what Brooklyn and Major League Baseball fans would routinely see when the Dodgers played.

Few disagree that Jackie Robinson was the right person to integrate Major League Baseball. Even though he was not the most skilled ballplayer in the Negro League, he was the best candidate to fulfill Rickey's master plan for baseball. "Negro League players, as a group, agreed that Robinson wasn't the best player in the league when he was chosen in 1945. There were other players who were considered "can't misses" talent-wise" (McNary, 2003, p. 156). Many who watched him over the years were of the opinion that baseball may not have even been his fourth best sport. He may have been a better golfer than baseball player (McNary, 2003). However, Rickey saw many attributes beyond Robinson's athletic prowess. He was obviously aware of Robinson's athletic pedigree, due, in part, to his brother Mack's second place finish in the 200 meters to Jesse Owens at the 1936 Olympic Games. Of particular interest to Rickey were character traits unfound in other Negro League players: innate intelligence, unflappable temperament, indomitable courage, and experience as an army officer. Unlike his counterparts, Robinson had also been exposed to integrated sports from his college days in Los Angeles.

As a collegian Robinson excelled in four sports (i.e., baseball, track, football, and basketball), and was so skilled in football and basketball that he could have played both professionally. He was a two-time Pacific Coast Conference scoring champ, and arguably the best all-around player of his time at UCLA, prior to joining the military in 1941. Unbeknownst to most he did play professional basketball briefly with the Los Angeles Red Devils, an integrated team in 1946, after playing summer baseball on the Dodgers minor league club in Montreal. During his collegiate football career he played alongside film legend Woody Strode and All-American Kenny Washington. Both would eventually be among the first black players to re-integrate professional football in 1946.

Robinson's impact on the borough of Brooklyn and Major League Baseball were immediate. Although his debut performance was unheralded, the mere presence of the 26-year-old black rookie on Opening Day drew a capacity crowd of 26,623 at Ebbets Field, more than half of which were black (Ward, Burns, & O'Connor, 1994). In time his exceptional baseball skills would match the many attributes that Branch Rickey saw in Robinson. Even the many fans that wished him to fail had to admit that they were intrigued by his aggressive style of play. "Robinson used bunting, speed, aggressive base-running, and the element of fear in order to dominate the game" (McNary, 2003, p. 159). His daring style of play had been absent from Major League Baseball for many years, but a staple in the Negro League. Some contend that Robinson nearly single-handedly revived the stolen base and bunt as offensive weapons in baseball. Ironically, his style of play would be a fixture in baseball until the "steroid era" of the late twentieth century where the home run became the most coveted offensive weapon. A resurgence of the Robinson style of play (i.e., bunting and stealing bases), to some extent, has reemerged in Major League Baseball as "small ball."

Unparalleled Prosperity and Fan Galvanization

Throughout Robinson's sterling ten-year career with the Dodgers the borough of Brooklyn, as well as the other National League cities where he played, set attendance records (Gems, Borish, & Pfister, 2008). The Dodgers success sparked national interest in the tabloids and on the radio broadcasts.

Wendell Smith, sports editor for the *Pittsburgh Courier*, chronicled the attendance trends during Robinson's initial year in Major League Baseball. He indicated that new attendance records were set in Philadelphia, Pittsburgh,
Cincinnati, and Chicago. National League attendance was so good that Smith
wrote: Jackie's nimble / Jackie's quick, ... Jackie's making the turnstiles click"
(Ward & Burns, 1994, p. 292). Robinson's popularity was so nationally pervasive that when the Dodgers played the Cardinals black fans in Kansas City
chartered buses to see him play in St. Louis. This was also true in other southern cities where enthusiastic black fans boarded a train in Norfolk, Virginia,
nicknamed the "Jackie Robinson Special" to attend his games in Cincinnati
(Ward, Burns, & O'Connor, 1994). Robinson and Rickey's partnership converted a generation of blacks into loyal Dodger fans, as well as others supportive of racial integration in baseball.

Fan excitement and attendance were highly correlated during the Robinson years, and certainly in Brooklyn. A decade before the Dodgers' east coast
exodus they had made more money than any other National League franchise.
Their home game attendance reached a record high 1.8 million fans in 1947,
far exceeding the league average of 1.2 million, which also spiked in Robinson's
inaugural season (Davies, 1994). They even made more money than their cross-
town American League rival Yankees from 1952 to 1956 (Rossi, 1999).

Black fans reacted to everything Robinson did on the field, as well as
other Brooklynites. "Everyone was yelling, 'Jackie, Jackie, Jackie,'" a Jewish fan
recalled, "and I was yelling with them. And suddenly I realized that behind
me someone was yelling 'Yonkel, Yonkel, Yonkel,' which is Yiddish for 'Jackie'"
(Ward & Burns, 1994, p. 291). The social integration plan of Rickey worked
twofold in Brooklyn, as stellar Negro League players were signed by the
Dodgers and newly urbanized black city dwellers became devoted fans. Their
allegiance switched from the Negro Leagues to the Brooklyn Dodgers.

"Dem Bums" and Altruism

The Brooklyn Dodgers of the mid–1940s and 1950s were affectionately
dubbed "Dem Bums" and "Lovable Losers" by their devoted fans. The
monikers were employed as terms of endearment for one of baseball's unluckiest teams. While the Dodgers had difficulty winning the World Series against
their cross-town rival Yankees, they had established an extremely loyal fan
base. Even fans that went afoul of the law, literally during their dying days,
inquired about Dem Bums. Koch (1999, para. 5) documented one such situation: "Brooklynites were not surprised when, on April 21, 1941, a former
native sat in the electric chair at the Massachusetts State Prison and said to

the guards: 'One last thing. Did the Bums win against the Giants today?'"
This unwavering support for the Dodgers was somewhat symbolic of the hardships endured by its largely immigrant and migratory fan base that perceived
themselves as "underdogs," with respect to their wealthier American League
rival Yankees. During the integration of the Dodgers fans and players alike
were ambivalent about this social experiment. However, their fears and apprehensions were assuaged by the brilliant play and sportsmanship of Robinson
and other newly recruited black players.

From the players' perspective their team loyalty was put to the test both
on and off the field as they were bombarded with uncomplimentary comments
and racial slurs by opposing teams and their hostile fans on a daily basis.

> When the Phillies arrived for a three-game series, they began shouting racial
> epithets during batting practice and kept it up until the last out—"Nigger, go
> back to the cotton fields"; "We don't want you here, nigger"; "Hey, snowflake,
> which one of you white boys' wives are you dating tonight?" The Phillies'
> Southern-born manager, Ben Chapman, led the jeering, and Robinson came
> close to cracking [Ward & Burns, 1994, p. 291].

Opposing pitchers intentionally threw at Dodger players, and often referred
to those who played with him as "whores" (Kahn, 1972, p. xvi). Kahn (1972)
also noted that Robinson was at the core of every racial epithet, and the
Dodgers who played with and ultimately befriended him became "nigger
lovers" and "monkey fuckers" by bench jockeys.

Ironically the constant haranguing, social injustices, unsportsmanlike
play, and overt racial hatred toward the Dodgers facilitated their bonding as
a team. They stood together as a team, in spite of the rude receptions and
adverse conditions they encountered.

> One critical series in April was when the Philadelphia Phillies played the
> Dodgers in Brooklyn. The Phillies manager, Ben Chapman, ordered his play-
> ers to use verbal taunts to see if Robinson "can take it." All accounts described
> the taunting as unrelenting and unusually cruel. In the second game of the
> Phillies series, Dodgers players began responding to the taunts. Dodgers
> infielder Eddie Stanky called Chapman a coward. Dodgers pitcher Dixie
> Walker also reprimanded Chapman [Austin, 1997, p. 105].

The display of civility and support by these two particular Dodgers, who inci-
dentally were among the anti–Robinson group that drew up a petition request-
ing a trade if he joined the team, was noteworthy and symbolic of the team's
resolve. The incident with the Philadelphia Phillies, and racist manager, was
so blatant and caustic that fans sitting in the dugout area wrote letters of
protest to the baseball commissioner. The press also found the behavior of
the Phillies' manager despicable and chronicled the account. The outrage
eventually moved Commissioner Chandler to notify the Philadelphia Phillies

owner that punitive action would be taken by the league if the harassment of Robinson did not cease (Austin, 1997; Peterson, 1999). In retrospect, the Dodgers' struggles against racism became a spectator rallying point for respect. Kahn (1972) lionized the stance taken by the Dodgers in his epic novel entitled *The Boys of Summer* when he wrote "without pretense or visible fear these men marched unevenly against the sin of bigotry" (p. xvi).

Despair and Disappointment

In spite of the Dodgers' financial windfall and National League success, during the "Robinson years" (1947–1956), they won but one World Series (1955) out of six attempts. Thus, the rallying cry became "wait till next year!" Unfortunately, there was no next year in 1957 as Jackie Robinson opted to retire instead of accepting a trade to National League rival New York Giants. Also, the on-going feud between city officials and Dodgers president Walter O'Malley led to municipal strife and political posturing primarily around the location of a new stadium. Hence, key administrative decisions both galvanized the community and later alienated fans.

The irreconcilable differences eventually sent the franchise to the West Coast and its virgin baseball environs (Light, 1997). The team relocated to Los Angeles to the disappointment of its devoted fans. The shock and bewilderment of the relocation news was devastating to the borough's fandom that had suffered through the many ups and downs of the franchise over the years. A sense of betrayal engulfed the devotees, who immediately blamed the club's perceived Machiavellian-style president and majority owner Walter O'Malley for the move (Ellsworth, 2005). As a result, Dodger fans viewed him as one of the most villainous individuals in history behind Hitler and Stalin (Prince, 1996). Although many adult fans during the "heyday" of Dem Bums are sparse, contempt and resentment toward O'Malley have surfaced well after the team's East Coast exodus. "Following his death in 1979, effigies of the Dodger owner O'Malley were burned in the streets of Brooklyn" (Ellsworth, 2005, p. 20).

Legacy and Nostalgic Lore

After more than a half-century since their unceremonious departure from Brooklyn, and relocation to Los Angeles, the Dodgers are still among the best-known sport franchises of all time. Unlike their crosstown National League rival Giants the Dodgers have always been steeped in nostalgic lore. Simon (2002) noted that the Dodgers still maintain the most iconic logo of any transplant team in American sport history. The name has been so enduring that it rivals teams that have come into baseball by expansion over the years.

Interestingly, unparalleled empathy between the fans and team emerged during Robinson's ten-year career, and games played at Ebbets field. Regardless of their strivings and successes fans often felt they were overlooked and unrewarded, which elicited an unwavering kinship. Unlike other baseball teams that relocated, the Dodgers were a prosperous franchise. Their move west was such a success that the club became the richest in the majors (Rossi, 1999). Sport historians and social theorists alike contend that the Dodgers' westward migration, along with the Giants, was one of the most influential forces that shaped organized sports in the post–1950 era (Rader, 2004). This was partly due to the fact that both the Dodgers and Giants were the most successful National Leagues teams in history in 1957.

Conclusion

In retrospect, an examination of the socio-cultural and historical impact of Jackie Robinson on Brooklyn, baseball, and American society during his playing career demonstrates the power and pervasiveness of sport. A limited integration state of mind emerged from the baseball diamond via the Robinson-Rickey pact. Some contend that post-war timing, the utilization of previously untapped resources, and potential economic prosperity were factors in this mid-century renaissance. Yet, due to the controversial social change that took place within the Dodgers franchise, national tabloids chronicled the team more than any other franchise previously. The black press was obviously interested in, and supportive of, the Dodgers' organization for its courageous stance. They not only became a national team, among those who sought a more liberal America, but a national issue. Needless to say, the Dodgers, and grudgingly Major League Baseball, were ahead of the country with regard to social integration. Davis (1994) seemed to put the Great Experiment in perspective with the following statement: "The symbolism provided by the integration of the national pastime was clear: race relations in the United States would never return to their prewar status" (pp. 10–11).

Robinson's triumph over the immense pressures and incredible obstacles placed in his path were laudable in many respects. His courage, perseverance, and altruism on the field of play were the epitome of "baseball martyrdom," exemplified by his post-career health conditions and untimely death at the age of 53. Peterson (1999) stated that Rickey's judgment was prophetic and vindicated through Robinson's success and the social changes that occurred in baseball and other American sports.

The integration of baseball during the "modern era" by Robinson and Rickey has been often compared with the landmark school desegregation case Brown vs. Board of Education of Topeka. The ramifications of these two socio-cultural, historical, and political events helped shape public policy and a nation. In a sense, and in so many ways, the Dodgers' games that were played at Ebbets Field metaphorically served as a "sociological incubator" of what American society was and what it could be in the future.

References

Ashe, A. R. (1993). *A hard road to glory: A history of the African American athlete since 1946*, Vol. 3. New York: Amistad.

Austin, J. R. (1997). A model for facilitating controversial social change in organizations: Branch Rickey and the Brooklyn Dodgers. *Journal of Applied Behavioral Science, 33* (1), 101–118

Baseball Reference (2012). *Brooklyn Dodgers*. Retrieved from http://www.baseballreference.com/bullpen/Brooklyn_Dodgers#Home_Ballparks.

Davies, R. O. (1994). *America's obsession: Sports and society since 1945*. Fort Worth, TX: Harcourt Brace.

Ellsworth, P. (2005). The Brooklyn Dodgers' move to Los Angeles: Was Walter O'Malley solely responsible? *Nine: A Journal of Baseball History and Culture, 14* (1), 19–40.

Gems, G. R., L. J. Boris and G. Pfister (2008). *Sports in American history: From colonization to globalization*. Champaign, IL: Human Kinetics.

Kahn, R. (1972). *The boys of summer*. New York: Harper and Row.

Koch, A. (1999, December 3). The ultimate fan remembers "Dem Bums." *The Melrose Mirror*. Retrieved from http://melrosemirror.media.mit.edu/servlet/pluto?state=30303470616765 30303375765625061676530303269643030334333343030.

Light, J. F. (1997). *The cultural encyclopedia of baseball*. Jefferson, NC: McFarland.

McNary, K. (2003). *Black baseball: A history of African-Americans and the national game*. Bramley Road, England: PRC.

Peterson, R. (1999). *Only the ball was white: A history of legendary black players and all-black professional teams*. New York: Gramercy.

Prince, C. E. (1996). *Brooklyn's Dodgers: The Bums, the borough, and the best of baseball, 1947–1957*. New York: Oxford University Press.

Rader, B. G. (2004). *American sports: From the age of folk games to the age of televised Sports*, 5th ed. Upper Saddle River, NJ: Prentice Hall.

Rossi, J. P. (1999). *A whole new game: Off the field changes in baseball, 1946–1960*. Jefferson, NC: McFarland.

Simon, S. (2002). *Jackie Robinson and the integration of baseball*. Hoboken, NJ: Wiley and Sons.

Tygiel, J. (1983). *Baseball's great experiment: Jackie Robinson and his legacy*. New York: Oxford University Press.

Ward, G. C., and K. Burns (1994). *Baseball: An illustrated history*. New York: Knopf

Ward, G. C., K. Burns, and J. O'Connor (1994). *Baseball, the American epic*. New York: Knopf.

The Athletic Industrial Complex: Conference Realignment, Race and Title IX

Earl Smith

I'm going to let those people play their games. I think they'll be doing that for the next 20 years. If they could figure it out and get it done in the next year, we wouldn't have to think about it. Maybe they should just have a draft, each conference should just draft teams ... except then they'd have to make a decision and they wouldn't be able to figure it out. Eventually, they'll get this thing figured out. They'll get all the teams moved and then in a year or two someone will say We need to take somebody, ... But I'll be long gone by then. Rivalries don't matter to anyone anymore.... If you ask someone at West Virginia if they like going to Texas Tech or Texas A&M and all those places, ask their fans whether they really like that. Maybe they do. I don't know. I don't get it. It's just the way it's going. There's nothing you can do about it. Like I said, if these guys (the conference commissioners) were running the United States in colonial times, Brazil and Argentina would be states because they have something we need. It's a great country.
—Jim Boeheim, Syracuse University Men's Basketball Coach
USA Today, November 22, 2012

Introduction

Let me begin with a few definitions to clarify the main concepts addressed in this essay.

For the purposes of this discussion I am using the term "race" as scholars, and sociologists in particular, use it. According to the American Anthropological Association's statement on race (1998)[1]: "Race is a classification system

71

used to categorize humans into large and distinct populations or groups by physical appearance, geographic ancestry, culture, history, language, ethnicity, and social status."

Sociologists, however, have modified this definition to focus on the social nature of race. Specifically, we argue that race is a social construct; that though individual characteristics of human beings pass down or are inherited, that the categories of race are mutable and highly influenced by ideology, politics and power.

The concept "conference realignment" refers to the movement of colleges and universities among NCAA designated conferences. Between 2010 and 2012 the term took on new meaning as literally dozens of schools began hopping from conference to conference and true power conferences began to emerge.

Claiming the coining of the term "Athletic Industrial Complex," it remains clear to me that the idea comes from President Dwight D. Eisenhower. I use the term Athletic Industrial Complex (AIC) in the same manner that sociologist C. Wright Mills and former President Dwight Eisenhower used the term "military industrial complex." AIC refers to the fact that athletics - sports—are now firmly embedded into American society and most other institutions, from the hotel and entertainment industry to construction to clothing and transportation. Advertising is the main institution where sports are used to sell goods.

Having provided working definitions of each concept, I turn now to deeper discussions of each concept and an examination of the intersections of each.

The Athletic Industrial Complex

At the college and university level I argue here that the primary mechanism that drives the exploitation of student athletes, the mechanism that plants them firmly in the "periphery" of the economics of intercollegiate sport, is the AIC. The AIC is about more than just the exploitation of student athletes, however. It is an institution embedded in both higher education and the global sports economy and as such it has the power to shape hegemonic ideology and collude with other institutions in the enterprise of sports. For example, every Memorial Day weekend in the United States NASCAR partners with the military to recognize the contributions of military personnel. Similarly, on Thanksgiving and Christmas the sports programs often "advertise" that the NFL or NBA games we are watching while we eat our turkey or unwrap our gifts are being broadcast through the generosity of sports networks like ESPN to our troops in Iraq and Afghanistan. This collusion furthers both the dominance of the ideology of the AIC as well as the expansion of global sports markets.

This conflation of hegemonic ideologies of heroes—both military and sports—is perhaps illustrated most compellingly by the case Pat Tillman who left his "job" as a professional football player and enlisted in the military after the 9/11 tradegedy to serve his country. Tillman was killed in Afghanistan in what would become a highly controversial event, primarily because the U.S. military lied about the details of his death only revealing after significant pressure from his family the fact that Tillman was killed by friendly fire by a unit in which his brother was serving. The Tillman family claims that the government has still not been totally honest about the circumstances surrounding his death. Perhaps what makes the sting even greater is the fact that the U.S. government, including then President George Bush, hailed Tillman's courageous decision to leave sports and enter the military. His picture and story were plastered everywhere and his family now feels that he was taken advantage of in life and ignored in death (Krakauer 2009).

Another key feature of the AIC is the global expansion of both professional and intercollegiate sports. And, it is in the professional ranks where the vastness of the AIC is witnessed. For example, there was a debate in the United States over the fact that the 2014 Super Bowl would be played in New York—actually in New Jersey. Because the Super Bowl is played in February, opponents of this decision argue that fans won't want to come and spend money because Super Bowl fans—especially those from the populous northern cities like New York and Chicago—look forward to attending the Super Bowl somewhere in the Sunbelt where they will be assured warm, sunny weather. The proponents of the decision argue that the decision is not about anything other than money and that (1) the majority of viewers of the Super Bowl whom the advertisers pay to reach will not attend the game anyway, they'll be watching it on TV in the comfort of their own homes, and (2) corporations will continue to pay for luxury boxes for their executives regardless of the weather and location of the Super Bowl. And, proponents suggest that the rental of luxury boxes will be enhanced by the fact that the game will be played in a new, billion dollar stadium, with luxury boxes outfitted with all of the latest amenities.

Furthermore, we can speculate that the NFL's interest in promoting interest in American football abroad—particularly in Western Europe where they stage exhibition games every year—may be tied to the decision to hold the Super Bowl in New York. Europeans who have been courted and cultivated by the NFL would likely see the chance to combine a vacation to New York City with the opportunity to attend the Super Bowl as a "win-win" and thus the NFL may boost the attendance of wealthy Europeans and thus open additional doors of opportunity to expand interest and viewership in Europe.

Not to lose sight of the argument, the AIC is also alive and well in college athletics and conference realignment, which I will examine shortly, is one of the last iterations of this phenomenon.

Intercollegiate athletics offers a rich site for the interrogation of the AIC in part because it is so widely varied by both division and by sport. The discussion will focus almost exclusively on college football at the Football Bowl Subdivision (FBS) level because this is the primary site where the AIC is evident. In contrast, for example, to the resources available at most of the 120 FBS football programs, the vast majority of sports, including track and field, volleyball, and even the country club sports of tennis and golf, could never be considered beneficiaries or exemplars of the AIC.

Beginning at the near the end of the twentieth century, the AIC exploded in college football; head coaches commanded salaries of more than $2 million per year, regardless of the success of their teams, athletic departments remodeled or built new football stadiums and locker rooms that often cost in the tens of millions of dollars (*renovations* in the mid–2000s routinely ran close to $50 million) and 70 teams play in bowl games each season. As I will demonstrate subsequently, this explosion of the AIC in college football is the driving force behind conference realignment and carries with it negative implications that are racialized and gendered.

Race, Ethnicity and the Decennial Census

Many scholars who talk about race and sport argue that certain racial groups are imbued with physical qualities that pre-dispose them to athleticism, and in particular, qualities that make them successful as sports such as basketball, football and track and field. Yet, when one applies a racial analysis to athletic prowess utilizing the concept of race as a social concept it is quickly revealed that it is not race itself that is correlated with athletic prowess but instead a set of qualities that often, but not always, co-exist with racial identification and are inheritable.

One easy way to understand this misapplication of the term race is to look at the U.S. Census, wherein Americans are enumerated every 10 years. Some of the best illustrations of the social construction of race come from analyzing the census categories over time. For example, in the 1860 census, there were three racial categories: "white," "negro" or "mulatto."

Immediately following the Civil War, a special census was taken in 1865. In this census, those who identified as "negro" or "mulatto" were asked again to confirm their racial identity. Part of the purpose of this special census was to offer "negroes" a chance to be returned to Africa. Never mind the fact that only a small percentage of "negroes" had ever been to Africa. Most were born here in the United States.

The category "mulatto" disappeared in both terminology and sentiment until 2000. In the 2000 census, for the first time since the mid–1800s, individuals could choose more than one race. To be clear, there is no racial category "mixed," or "bi" but people can choose "white" and "black" or "white" and "Asian." As a result, about 13 percent of the U.S. population now identifies as multi-racial, with more than one race.

The 2000 census was also important because the census moved the designation "Hispanic" out of the set of racial categories and into a special designation of "ethnicity." Interestingly "Hispanic" is the only ethnic category currently in the U.S. census.

So, bringing it closer to sport, imagine someone like Sammy Sosa or Albert Pujoles. According to the 1990 census, both men's race was "Hispanic." In 2000 and again in 2010, they now had to decide if they were "black," "white," "Asian/pacific islander" or "native American/Alaskan native." They were no longer Hispanic; at least in terms of the racial categories designated by the U.S. government.

Both men are the same people in 1990 and 2000, the traits we identify as "racial"—skin tone, hair texture, etc. did not change, but their racial identity, according to the U.S. government, did.

Not surprising, in 2000 the majority of "Hispanics" left the racial category blank. It didn't make sense to them that they were anything other than "Hispanic." These are examples of what sociologists mean when they say that race is a social construct.

Race (Still) Matters

With that out of the way it can be clearly stated that race still matters in the United States. And, though this essay is about race and sport, as I have argued elsewhere (Smith 2007/2009), the sports world is a microcosm of the larger society, and thus, to provide a context, I present evidence on the impact of race in several other areas of social life.

Interpersonal Relationships: Though there is evidence that we have achieved some measure of integration and interracial interactions among young children, by the time they reach high school, the vast majority of white and black children occupy spaces that are nearly entirely segregated, save for the playing fields and courts of sports. Schools are segregated, dating is segregated, churches are segregated and many workplaces are segregated, at least when we consider the types of work that men and women perform inside of large companies.

Corporal Punishment: It has been shown that African American children are on the receiving end of corporal punishment more so than children of other race and ethnic group. In a 2012 report the Department of Education notes that: "Although black students made up only 18 percent of those enrolled in the schools sampled, they accounted for 35 percent of those suspended once, 46 percent of those suspended more than once and 39 percent of all expulsions, according to the Civil Rights Data Collection's 2009–10 statistics from 72,000 schools in 7,000 districts, serving about 85 percent of the nation's students. The data covered students from kindergarten age through high school. One in five black boys and more than one in 10 black girls received an out-of-school suspension. Overall, black students were three and a half times as likely to be suspended or expelled than their white peers."

Secretary of Education Arne Duncan, in a speech at Howard University on March 6, 2012, noted that African American students are five times as likely to be suspended as their white peers. He put it thus: "The power of the data is not only in the numbers themselves, but in the impact it can have when married with the courage and the will to change. The undeniable truth is that the everyday educational experience for many students of color violates the principle of equity at the heart of the American promise. It is our collective duty to change that."

*Incarceration:*Despite the fact that African American men make up only 6 percent of the total U.S. population, they constitute nearly half of all prisoners in state and federal institutions as well as under supervision in parole and/or probation status. And, as I have noted (Smith & Hattery 2010), this over-incarceration of African American men is associated with poverty, unemployment, high school drop-out rate, single parent families, HIV/AIDs and even intimate partner violence.

Employment: In a paper by Marianne Bertrand and Sendhil Mullainathan entitled "Are Emily and Greg More Employable than Lakisha and Jamal?: A Field Experiment on Labor Market Discrimination." (NBER Working Paper No. 9873) the authors found that job applicants with names like Lakisha, Jamal and others were hindered in obtaining employment. More specifically, the researchers sent out over 5,000 resumes, some with stereotypically black-sounding names, and some with stereotypically white-sounding ones. They found that job applicants with white sounding names needed to send about 10 resumes to get one callback; those with African-American names needed to send around 15 resumes to get one callback.

Good credentials had more of an effect on the fate of white-sounding applicants than of black-sounding ones—while people named Greg could look forward to more callbacks if they had more experience, the same wasn't necessarily the case for people named Jamal.

Housing: A paper published by the organization United for a Fair Economy addressed head on the issue of the housing crisis for African Americans. The work shows that home ownership in the United States is still a central part of the quintessential American Dream. Yet, by 2009, in the hands of the mortgage lending industry, subprime loans became predatory loans—a faulty product that was ruthlessly hawked even though financial institutions were aware of its defects. Even a surface check of the demographics shows that, in city after city, a solid majority of subprime loan recipients were African Americans and other low-income people of color (http://www.faireconomy.org/dream).

Additionally, a study by the Woodstock Report entitled "Struggling to Stay Afloat: Negative Equity in Communities of Color in the Chicago Six County Region" reported that in predominantly African American communities in Chicago, 40.5 percent of borrowers are underwater on their mortgages—that is, they owe more than the home is worth—and that these rates are two and a half times higher than foreclosures in predominantly white communities (Clark 2011, http://brr.berkeley.edu/2012/03/in-predominantly-black-or-latino-neighborhoods-in-chicago-40-of-mortgages-are-under water/).

Other studies reveal the same thing. African American homeownership rates have plummeted nearly 6 percent to 46.2 percent after peaking in 2004. This is more than twice the decline of any other racial or ethnic group. Overall, 11.3 percent of owner-occupied mortgage housing units had "underwater" mortgages, a mortgage arrangement in which homeowners essentially owe more debt on their property than its current market value. African American "underwater" mortgages stand at 35 percent (and 18 percent for whites). Note that the loss of homeownership is more than the difference between a mortgage payment and a rent check; purchasing property is the key to building wealth and accessing the American Dream (Smith & Hattery 2012).

College Attainment: Contrary to popular belief about the unfairness of any variety of Affirmative Action Programs, and their placing African Americans in high numbers into select colleges and universities around the country, African Americans lag far behind in both getting into college and exiting college with a degree in hand (Smith & Hattery 2012). In a paper by Grace Kao and Jennifer Thompson entitled "Racial and Ethnic Stratification in Educational Achievement and Attainment" (Annual

Review of Sociology Vol. 29, 2003, pp. 417–442, http://www.jstor.org/ stable/30036974) they convincingly show that despite high aspirations among African American youth wanting to attend college in the end there is lower subsequent attainment. This research is followed in a study by the Lumina Foundation showing that one of the major impediments to college attainment for blacks is the large number of black men, ages 16-24 in the prison pipeline instead of on the path to college (http://www. luminafoundation.org/newsroom/newsletter/archives/2009-11.html). And, finally (but unknown to some), race matters in the sports world:

It matters what sports you play.
It matters which positions you play in some team sports.
It matters whether you can coach and/or own a team.
Gender also matters.

This essay demonstrates that at the intercollegiate level race and gender matter in sports and that conference realignment matters so much so that no one has stepped back from the euphoria that money does to university presidents, NCAA officials, athletic directors, coaches, to seriously consider the unintended or unanticipated consequences (Merton 1936) of the race and gender implications of conference realignment.

Conference Realignment and Title IX

Conference realignment will have significant and negative consequences that are both gendered (Title IX) and racialized. Specifically, conference realignment will create different experiences for athletes playing different sports, and because of the ways in which sports are completely segregated by gender and highly segregated by race this will produce differential experiences based on both gender and race.

The illustration used is from the University of Houston which has recently joined the Big East Conference. As a result of leaving Conference USA and joining the Big East, the Houston football team will routinely be making cross-country flights to play conference games. Anyone who flies across the country regularly knows the toll these flight, especially taken frequently, take on the body. They are exhausting. Furthermore, even if the team charters commercial planes, these trips will keep the players away from campus far longer than they were while participating in a conference in which they were the geographic center.

And because the football team is primarily African American (and the same will hold for men's basketball as well, the sport that will also likely travel throughout the conference), the impact of extended travel and time away from campus will be disproportionately be borne by African American men. And, we need not review in any detail the graduation rate data to be certain that the group required to spend the most time away from campus is the same group that can least afford to do so.

This is definitely the case for the University of Houston. Houston is already struggling to graduate African American men who play football and this additional travel and time away from campus will exacerbate this struggle.

As noted previously, one of the outcomes of the AIC explosion in football and to a lesser degree men's basketball—which is diminished only because of the size of the roster and coaching staff as well as the size of the arena—conference realignment has significantly furthered the chasm between the revenue generating sports and all other sports, often referred to as "non-revenue generating" or Olympic sports. In a previous study (Hattery, Staurowsky & Smith, 2008), my research demonstrated that regardless of the success of the football team or the women's soccer team, most of the athletic budget dollars are appropriated for football and men's basketball. And, as the pot shrinks, I anticipate that there will be very little if any negative impact on football, a team which will now incur even greater travel costs, the chasm will only grow.

As a result, women student athletes—regardless of race—and white male student athletes will have a *much different experience, and I would argue inferior experience,* than their peers on the football team. It is highly likely that women's sports and the Olympic sports will see their budgets trimmed as a result of the increased cost of their own travel as well as the travel of the football team that results directly from conference realignment. This could impact coaches' salaries, the number of assistant coaches, equipment, food, and so on. Or, they might see some of their travel cut entirely.

For example, the soccer team might be able to schedule fewer non-conference games—which is critically important for rankings—or they might see the conference split into north and south or east and west with teams only playing those on their "side." This is particularly troubling because as my other research has shown, women's basketball has provided incredible opportunities for African American women (Hattery, Staurowsky & Smith 2008). If women's basketball is forced to cut their budget in order to accommodate additional travel for football this will adversely impact hundreds of African American women and turn back the clock on the gains made under Title IX.

Conclusion

I fully understand the reasons why Houston wants to join the Big East Conference:

- The Big East is a Football Bowl Subdivision (FBS) or Automatic Qualifier (AQ) conference which is the only pathway to the Bowl Championship Series (BCS) bowls
- Houston feels that despite their 12–1 season in 2011, because they were not in an AQ conference they were denied the opportunity to play in a BCS bowl which would have offered a bigger stage to play on and a significantly higher payout

Yet, this argument is that the move is very risky.

- Playing in an AQ conference is no guarantee of playing in a BCS bowl. Houston would still have to win the conference and the Big East is competitive, at least for the moment, until more and more shifting occurs as a part of the conference realignment tsunami
- In other research conducted, the data demonstrate that despite the huge "payout"—$17 million for playing in the Orange Bowl—once the funds are dispersed to all of the conference members and expenses have been paid to host travel parties, travel for auxiliary staff like cheerleaders, the band and the travel for 100 plus players, 15 to 20 coaches, their families etc., including the requirement to buy blocks of tickets, few schools actually make a profit (Clotfelter 2011)
- The costs associated with joining the Big East, the additional travel, and the costs associated with the coveted bowl games all come at a time when the economy is still in recession and most universities are cutting back in their general expenses simply to keep their doors open.

With regards to athletics in particular, conference re-alignment will have the following consequences:

1. It will negatively impact the academic performance and graduation rates for African American male athletes.
2. It will negatively impact the experience of women athletes playing all sports, making it very difficult if not impossible to honor the spirit of Title IX.
3. It will negatively impact all of the Olympic sports men play. And because these sports are mostly played by white men it will racialize the experiences of male athletes.
4. It will highlight the fact that the Olympic sports exist to serve a few distinct purposes:
   a. To meet the legal requirements of Title IX.
   b. To ensure that the student-athlete body overall is integrated and diverse.
   c. To ensure that institutions can meet their APR, as all of the grad-

uation rate data confirm that graduation rates are generally significantly at or above the college average for Olympic Sport athletes while the rates for football and men's basketball are at or below the college-wide average.

d. To allow the NCAA to advertise that many thousands of student athletes will "go pro" in something other than sports.

Despite what anyone in the National Collegiate Athletic Association or any Athletic Director says, the purpose of the Olympic sports is *not* to provide a high level athletic experience for student athletes. The Olympic sports exist *only* to make the NCAA and member institutions look like they care about the non-athletic experience of student athletes. If college football were disconnected from the university and run like the minor league programs in baseball and hockey, the Olympic Sports would cease to have a purpose and they would likely disappear—at least at the intercollegiate level, fully funded by the University. They might exist only as club and inter-mural sports only.

So what does this entire scenario mean? Taken together, it means that Conference Realignment, the push to create mega-conferences, thus shutting out many, many institutions that live under the moniker such as "mid-majors" etc., the Pacific 12, Atlantic Coast Conference, Big 12, Big 10, Southeastern Conference and the Big East will have the intercollegiate sport landscape covered for themselves.

With relationships with the Bowl Conference Series (BCS) these conferences can pick and choose (or not) who plays in what post-season bowl games. The ability to control scheduling and football revenues also sends the message that the controlling body of intercollegiate sports is in trouble.

In late 2012 NCAA President Mark Emmert said as much when he made the declaration that institutions interested in leaving the member association, the NCAA, should do so. He put it thus (Whiteside 2012): "If BCS schools or any other schools decide they'd be better served by having their own association, then they can and should go do that." This type of assessment would never have been possible just five years ago. But with the growing independence taking place in college sports (e.g., Notre Dame and the University of Texas, Austin, brokering their own television contracts (Rosenberg 2011) for football games, both home and away), conference commissioners, university presidents, and athletic directors may come to see their best interests are not aligned with the NCAA and may no longer be served best by continued membership in the NCAA. One "canary in the mine" illustration may be seen in the University of Notre Dame football being able to operate completely outside of the conference structure and yet compete, at least in 2013, in the highest level BCS bowls, including an opportunity to play for the National Championship.

How all of this jockeying will play out is unpredictable. What is not unpredictable is that nothing that has taken place in the past two to three years in terms of conference realignment has come with the best interests of the student-athletes in mind or with concern over preserving the gains of Title IX. And, to a lesser extent none of the conference movement really took into consideration the interests of men's basketball. It was and is all about football & money.

New York Times columnist Joe Nocera, in "Show Me the Money" (December 10, 2012), pointing to the International Management Group (IMG) sponsored conference and noting that student athletes interests were absent, said:

> The annual IMG Intercollegiate Athletics Forum ...is the kind of meeting where football games are routinely described as "product," television networks are "distribution channels," and rooting for State U. is an example of "brand loyalty." The university presidents, conference commissioners, athletic directors and corporate marketers who attend spend very little time mouthing the usual pieties about how the "student-athlete" comes first. Rather, they gather each year to talk bluntly about making money.

Finally, as sociologist Merton (1936) put it sometimes our purposeful actions have unintended consequences. This fact, to be sure, is one way of seeing the Athletic Industrial Complex, conference realignment and the changing landscape of intercollegiate sports. But, it is not all centered at the college level. As stated above, professional sports, on an even grandeur scale, is caught up in the whole aurora of hyper-commercialism to the extent that NASCAR is struggling to fill the expanded stadiums/tracks built in places far from the south (e.g., Michigan, Maine, California) and all of the professional leagues (NBA, MLB, NHL) have been struck by players strikes, "lockouts" and contract negotiations never before seen in the sports world. What are the overall concerns: money.

Where does it all ends? We don't know yet. What we do know is that the analysis provided here hints at a sports world way out of control.

Notes

1. "American Anthropological Association Statement on Race," AAA (1998–05–17), aaanet.org. Retrieved January 4, 2011.

References

Bertrand, Marianne, and Sendhil Mullainathan. 2003. Are Emily and Greg more employable than Lakisha and Jamal? A field experiment on labor market discrimination. NBER Working Paper No. 9873.

Bonilla-Silva, Eduardo. 2009. *Racism without racists: Color-blind racism and the persistence of racial inequality in the United States*. Lanham, MD: Rowman and Littlefield.

Branch, Taylor. "The shame of college sports." *The Atlantic*. http://www.theatlantic.com/magazine/archive/2011/10/the-shame-of-college- sports/8643/?single_page=true.

Clark, Sherri Lawson. 2012. In search of housing: Urban families in rural contexts. *Rural Sociology* 77(1): 110–134.

Clotfelter, Charles. 2011. *Big-time sports in American universities*. New York: Cambridge University Press.

Hattery, Angela J., Earl Smith and Ellen Staurowsky. 2008. They play like girls: Gender equity in NCAA sports." *The Journal for the Study of Sports and Athletes in Education*. 1(3): 249–272.

Krakauer, J. 2009. *Where men win glory : The odyssey of Pat Tillman*. New York: Doubleday.

Merton, Robert. 1936. The unanticipated consequences of purposive social action. *American Sociological Review* 1:894–904.

Nocera, Joe. 2012, December 10. "Show me the money." *New York Times*, http://www.nytimes.com/2012/12/11/opinion/nocera-show-me-the-money.html?hp.

Rosenberg, Michael. 2011, January 20. University of Texas' TV network is a lucrative web of conflicts. *Sports Illustrated*. http://sportsillustrated.cnn.com/2011/writers/michael_rosenberg/01/20/texas.tv/index.html#ixzz2F1P2N8dj.

Schwartz, Robert. 2001, May 3. Racial profiling in medical research. *New England Journal of Medicine 344* (18): 1392–1393.

Smith, Earl. 2009. *Race, sport and the American dream*. Durham, NC: Carolina Academic.

Smith, Earl, and Angela Hattery. 2010. *Prisoner reentry and social capital: The long road to reentry*. Lanham, MD: Lexington.

Smith, Earl, and Angela Hattery. 2012. *African American families: Myths and realities*. Lanham, MD: Rowman and Littlefield.

USA Today. 2012, November 22. Jim Boeheim sounds off on conference realignment. http://www.usatoday.com/story/sports/ncaab/2012/11/22/jim-boeheim-ncaa-conference-realignment/1721455/.

Whiteside, Kelly. 2012. College sports administrators recognize growing gulf. *USA TODAY*, http://www.usatoday.com/story/sports/ncaaf/2012/12/05/ncaa-membership-power-conferences-img-iaf/1749365/.

Encountering the Undead: An Open Letter on the Persistent Problem of Native American Mascots

C. Richard King

To Whom It May Concern:

I apologize for the impersonal salutation. Two decades of study have taught me that the controversy over Native American mascots largely derives from impersonal forces, particularly white privilege, anti–Indianism, and the political economy of the sport-media complex, and that any possibility of change hinges on a shift among the nameless masses. Too few fans, educators, alumni, policy makers, and pundits have had to come to terms with the conditions that continue to make such imagery and rituals pleasurable, powerful, and profitable.

The persistence of such celebrations of white supremacy and the genocidal impulses animating U.S. settler society is especially striking in era that has proclaimed the end of racism and the ascendency of colorblindness. Ten, fifteen, years ago, one might have reasonable thought that such icons and practices were dead (or dying), but in retrospect, they were perhaps better understood to be undead. Indeed, in keeping with the reigning preoccupations of the day—vampires and zombies—perhaps on the language of the monstrous and the grotesque can make the entanglements of race, power, and sport spectacle legible. While the return or call for return of Native American mascots at the University of Illinois, Dartmouth College, Stanford University, and Eastern Michigan University conjure images of raising the dead, the long history of playing Indian at halftime are equally reminiscent of people thriving off the life-forces of sacrificed alters or the trophies a serial killer takes from his victims. I know these metaphorical framings might be read as hyperbolic, but I find myself at a loss for a vocabulary and lens with which to make sense of the appropriation, exploitation, and violence—symbolic and material—animating with American Indian mascots. That said, perhaps I move to the irrational register too quickly, when a summary of scholarly findings and a logical discussion would better serve as a foundation for understanding and engagement.

To begin down this path, let me introduce myself. My name is C. Richard King. I am currently a professor of comparative ethnic studies at Washington State University. I have advanced degrees in cultural anthropology: a MA in anthropology for the University of Kansas (1992) and a PhD from the University of Illinois (1996). My research and teaching centers on the meaning of race and ethnicity, the history of racism, and the popular understandings of American Indians. I have dedicated nearly two decades to the study of Native American mascots. I have written extensively on the history and significance of Indian iconography (naming, imagery, and rituals) in sports. In addition to three monographs on contemporary Native American life generally, I have written or co-written over two dozen articles and/or book chapters on the Native American mascot controversy, while also co-editing an award winning anthology of essays on the subject, co-authoring a study of race and racism in college athletics that examines mascots along with other forms of racialism, and more recently editing a sourcebook on the controversy.

Native American mascots hurt American Indians. When referring to Native American mascots, I not only mean the individual who dons a costume and plays at being Indian to entertain and excite the crowd, but I also refer to a whole of associated beliefs and behaviors, including the use of Indianness to name and represent sports teams, the creation of visual representations in school logos, student performances at half-time, the antics of fans, the cheers, placards, and demeanor of opposing players and fans, and the proliferation of spirit boosting events and iconography throughout the local community.

My research has led me to the conclusion that Native American mascots injure students and communities, most especially American Indians and their futures. In fact, I am so convinced by my findings that I worked with Iowa Civil Rights Commission in 2002 to draft a resolution outlining the deleterious effects of Indian iconography in interscholastic athletics and served as lead author of the resolution opposing American Indian mascots endorsed by the North American Society for the Sociology of Sport that found the images, names, and practices associated with them denigrate indigenous people, their civil rights, their cultures and spiritualities, and their sovereignty.

The harms associated with Native American mascots can be enumerated as follows:

a. They perpetuate false, stereotypical images of indigenous cultures and histories. Native American mascots, importantly, relying on well-worn clichés, have incorporated the sub-human buffoon, the burlesque carica-ture, most familiar perhaps in the Cleveland Indians' Chief Wahoo, the bulbous nosed, laughing Native, and super-human warrior, proud and bel-licose like Florida State University's Chief Osceola. In either case, as Native American mascot stereotype, they deny American Indian people (students, fans, citizens) complete personhood. Native American mascots hurt first and foremost by dehumanizing Native Americans.

b. Because Native American mascots distort Indianness, encouraging peers and the general public to misrecognize and mistreat living and breathing Indian peoples, they injure the self-esteem of individual Native Americans, precisely because stereotyping demeans, belittles, devalues, calls into ques-tions, makes invisible, and humiliates.

c. Even when well intentioned, Native American mascots contribute to anti–Indian racism in the U.S. as ubiquitous, pervasive and persistent symbols and spectacles. More insidious still, as they make anti–Indian racism acceptable and even fun, they trivialize not simply the people they harm but also the acts of causing harm to them.

d. Native American mascots terrorize American Indian peoples. They do not simply offend many of them, but make them scared to speak up, uncomfortable at school, unwelcome at sporting events. They become targets of ridicule, name calling, and even physical assaults. For instance, at the University of Illinois, Native American students have reported that attendance at games evoked shame and marginalization, while those who protested Chief Illiniwek were subject to racial slurs and physical threats. Meanwhile, at the University of North Dakota, American Indian students were called names, including "Prairie Nigger," told to go back to the reser-vation, and threatened with harm if the school mascot were to be retired. Given their pervasiveness and persistence as anti–Indian emblems, it is likely that Native American mascot play no small role in making Native Americans the most common victims of violent assaults in the U.S.

e. Native American mascots prevent American Indians from full and equal enjoyment of public accommodations.

f. Native American mascots foster racial harassment.

g. Native American mascots undermine the expectation of equal treatment for indigenous peoples in public life, curtailing the expression and enjoy-ment of full citizenship.

h. Native American mascots constitute one prominent form of racial microaggression, small, invisible acts that at a local level together cause individual and collective trauma. As such, they transform learning environments into hostile environments. In turn, they contribute in part to a widening achievement gap and to a high dropout rates for indigenous students.

i. Native American mascots allow the dominant society to define Indianness, undermining indigenous identity, tradition, and sovereignty.

j. Native American mascots abuse indigenous spirituality, misusing sacred objects (eagle feathers for instance) and rituals for the sake of school spirit and local traditions.

k. Native American mascots promote divisiveness and factionalism in Native nations, because institutions often reward Native individuals who endorse their symbols and spectacles as acceptable, often in spite of the vocal opposition of duly elected tribal bodies. In this respect they are very similar to the divide and conquer mentality associated with treaty-making.

Evidence of these harms is far too numerous to note here, but includes the following:

a. Careful study of the origins of mascotting reveals its deep connections with American imperial expansion, racism, and anti–Indianism.

b. The team symbols, school songs, yearbooks, fan behavior, tee-shirts, media coverage and related texts all give voice to the dehumanizing, terrifying, and otherwise damaging content and effects of Native American mascots.

c. The arguments offered up by defenders of mascotting further underscore the harms associated with Native American mascots. They purport to honor Native Americans, but do not listen to them or take their concerns seriously. They parade one or two individuals in front of the public, disregarding the proclamations and condemnations of countless political and tribal organizations. They claim not to intend harm, suggesting they know that "their" Indians hurt actual Indians. Worse, as noted above, their literature often includes hate speech and their actions at places like the University of Illinois and the University of North Dakota seem intended to intimidate through violence.

d. The actions and comments of Indians also speak to the extent of harm. Native Americans in newspaper columns and letters to the editors, in public demonstrations and legal cases, in political petitions and everyday conversation talk personally and painfully about the harms associated with mascotting.

e. Many polls of Native Americans also attest to the deleterious effects of mascotting.

f. Schools have recognized the uncomfortable origins and hurtful implications of their "Indians." Stanford nearly 30 years ago dropped their offensive mascot and more recently Marquette, Syracuse, Miami of Ohio, and

St. John have followed suit. Other colleges, such as Iowa and Wisconsin have policies prohibiting the scheduling of opponents with Native American mascots. State boards of education and civil rights commissions in Nebraska, Minnesota, New York, and Michigan have recommended that schools discontinue the use of Indian symbols. And local school boards in Los Angeles, Dallas, and beyond have changed mascots. Most recently, the Oregon State Board of Education banned the use of American Indian imagery, names, and mascots on penalty of losing state education funds.

g. In the same spirit, a number of newspapers have refused to print offensive team names in their coverage of sports. Most recently, the fall of 2012, the *Kansas City Star* indicated it would no longer refer to the Washington, D.C. football team as the R*dskins and *The City Paper*, an independent weekly in the nation's capital, asked its readers to help it select an alternate name for the franchise.

h. An array of local, regional, and national organizations have condemned Native American mascots. All American Indian organizations, from the Great Lakes Inter-Tribal Council to the National Congress of American Indians, have spoken out against mascots. Other organizations devoted to racial justice, such as the National Association for the Advancement of Colored People, have encouraged the discontinuation of athletic icons. Moreover, professional and scholarly organizations, including the American Anthropological Association, and the National Education Association have taken positions against mascots.

i. In 2005, the National Collegiate Athletic Association banned the use of Native American mascots, imagery, and names, denying schools that used such iconography the opportunity to participate in post-season competitions. They took this action because it believed a preponderance of the evidence demonstrated such symbols and practices produced hostile environments.

j. Dr. Stephanie A. Fryberg and her colleagues have conducted empirical research verifying the harms associated with Native American mascots. In her dissertation, completed at Stanford University, as well as forthcoming publications, Dr. Fryberg has demonstrated that stereotypical images of American Indians, particularly those used in connection with sports, (i) reduces American Indian students' self-esteem, (ii) lowers students' belief that their communities can address problems facing them, (iii) limits the kind, quantity, and quality of future roles and achievements they envision for themselves, and (iv) impacts those who claim to find nothing wrong with sport mascots most adversely.

k. Dr. Chu Kim-Prieto and her colleagues found that Native American mascots not only reinforce deleterious stereotypes about American Indians, but also prime those who see them to have negative ideas about other ethnic groups.

l. In its 2005 resolution calling for an "immediate retirement" of American Indian mascots and nicknames, the American Psychological Association concurred that they perpetuate stereotypes, foster hostile environments, and endanger indigenous students, noting in part that they impair "the educational experiences of members of all communities—especially those who have had little or no contact with Indigenous peoples...[and] can lead to negative relations between groups."

Importantly, the ways in which defenders of Native Americans mascots advance their arguments often intensify the harms associated with them.

a. Defenders repeatedly point to their intentions. They intend honor and respect, but when the creation of learning environments and inclusive communities hinges on effects, and not just intentions, outcomes and impacts matter and merit greater attention. Whatever their intentions, their naming, chants, images, and dances do not honor, nor do they respect. They distort and dehumanize. They reflect a bygone era in which the domination of Native Americans celebrated.

b. They cast themselves as misunderstood, under assault, and injured. Reframing their traditions and identities as under attack and imperiled allows them to present themselves as victims.

c. They cast critics as overly sensitive and politically correct, denying that issues raised have any relevance or importance. Dismissal and denial reinforce the normalcy and force of everyday racism, while also working to render its existence invisible.

d. They draw false equivalences between American Indian mascots and those representing other ethnic groups. In the process, they neglect important differences: whereas some number of ethnic mascots, like the Fighting Irish were created by the group they represent, and others represent peoples who no longer exists, such as Viking or Saxons; American Indian mascots were created largely by European Americans and remain living people embodying vibrant cultures.

The evidence is clear. Native American mascots reflect and reproduce white supremacy and anti–Indianism. They emerge from and express ugly, false, and dehumanizing understandings of indigenous peoples, dressed up and denied as honor, tradition, and respect. They reinforce the entitlements of settler society to Indianness, endorsing appropriation and abuse. Not surprisingly, they have a number of deleterious effects, distorting and damaging indigenous peoples, cultures, and histories. They negatively impact how American Indians and others value difference, amplifying racism, directed at indigenous peoples and others, directed internally and externally. They marginalize Native Americans, making them a joke, a trophy, a totem, while denying them rights and opportunities extend to other Americans. In short, Native American mascots keep racism alive, making it fun, normal, and acceptable.

I am not certain if this marshaling of logic, fact, and truth will make a difference. I fear it will not. Positions hardened in the defense of white privilege tend to dismiss evidence and the entitlements and comforts of settler society tend to accept the legitimacy of claims on Indianness as settled questions. Unfortunately, even if I were to appeal to the irrational, employing monstrous metaphors as I did at the start of this letter I worry the real issues might get lost. All of this, dear reader, leaves me at a loss: how do we make concrete the persistence of racism after its reported demise? How do we make material the harmful effects of ideas and practices so many not only accept but embrace? How do we bring the practice of playing Indian at half-time to an end? I would welcome your thoughts.

Thank you for taking the time to read this. I look forward to your response.

References

American Indian Opinion Leaders (2001). American Indian mascots; Respectful gesture or negative stereotype? *Indian Country Today, 21* (8), A5.

Baca, L. (2004). Native images in schools and the racially hostile environment. *Journal of Sport and Social Issues, 28,* 71–78.

Berkhofer, R. F. (1978). *The White man's Indian: Images of the American Indian from Columbus to present*. New York: Vintage/Random House.

Bird, S. E. (Ed.) (1996). *Dressing in feathers: The construction of the Indian in American popular culture*. Boulder: Westview.

Churchill, W. (1994). Let's spread the fun around. In *Indians are us? Culture and genocide in native North America* (pp. 65–72). Monroe, ME: Common Courage.

Clark, A. T. (2005). Wa a o, wa ba ski na me ska ta! "Indian" mascots and the pathology of anti-indigenous racism, in Amy Bass, editor, *In the game: Race, identity, and sports in the twentieth century*, 137–166. New York: Palgrave Macmillan.

Clarkson, G. (2003). Racial imagery and Native Americans: A first look at empirical evidence behind the Indian mascot controversy. *Cardozo Journal of International and Comparative Law, 11,* 393–407.

Claussen, C. L. (1996). Ethnic team names and logos: Is there a legal solution? *Marquette Sports Law Journal, 6,* 409–421.

Clegg, R. (2002). American Indian nicknames and mascots for team sports: Law, policy, and attiuide. *Virginia Sports and Entertainment Law Journal, 1,* 274–282

Condit, C. M. (1989). The rhetorical limits of polysemy. *Critical Studies in Mass Communication, 6,* 103–122.

Connolly, M. R. (2000). What's in a name? A historical look at Native American related nicknames and symbols at three U.S. universities. *Journal of Higher Education 71,* 515–547.

Coombe, R. J. (1999). Sports trademarks and somatic politics: Locating the law in critical cultural studies. In R. Martin and T. Miller (Eds.), *SportCult*, pp. 262–288. Minneapolis: University of Minnesota Press.

Davis, L. R. (1993). Protest against the use of Native American mascots: A challenge to traditional, American identity. *Journal of Sport and Social Issues, 17*, 9–22.

Davis, L. R. (2002). The problems with Native American mascots. *Multicultural Education, 9*, 11–14.

Davis, L.R. (2007). "Eliminating Native American Mascots Ingredients for Success." *Journal of Sport & Social Issues, 31* (4), 340–373.

Davis, L. R., and M. Rau (2001). Escaping the tyranny of the majority. In C. R. King and C. F. Springwood (Eds.), *Team spirits: Essays on the history and significance of Native American mascots* (pp. 304–327). Lincoln: University of Nebraska Press.

Deloria, P. (1998). *Playing Indian*. New Haven: Yale University Press.

Eckert, R. C. (2001). Wennebojo meets the Mascot: A trickster's view of the Central Michigan University mascot/logo. In C. R. King and C. F. Springwood (Eds.), *Team spirits: Essays on the history and significance of Native American mascots* (pp. 64–81). Lincoln: University of Nebraska Press.

Eitzen, D. S., and M. B. Zinn (1989). The de-athleticization of women: The naming and gender marking of college sport teams. *Sociology of Sport Journal, 7*, 362–369.

Eitzen, D. S., and M. B. Zinn (1993). The sexist naming of collegiate athletic teams and resistance to change. *Journal of Sport and Social Issues, 17*, 34–41.

Fisher, D. M. (2001). Chief Bill Orange and the Saltine Warrior: A cultural history of Indian symbols and imagery at Syracuse University. In C. R. King and C. F. Springwood (Eds.), *Team spirits: Essays on the history and significance of Native American mascots* (pp. 25–45). Lincoln: University of Nebraska Press.

Fryberg, S. (2002). *Representations of American Indians in the media: Do they influence how American Indian students negotiate their identities in mainstream contexts?* Unpublished Dissertation, Department of Psychology, Stanford University.

Fryberg, S. (2004). "We're honoring you, dude": The impact of using American Indian mascots. Paper presented at the Annual Meeting of the North American Society for the Sociology of Sport, Tucson, AZ, 4 November.

Gawiser, S. R., and G. E.Witt (1994). *A journalist's guide to public opinion polls*. Westport, CT: Praeger.

Green, R. (1988). The tribe called wannabee: Playing Indian in America and Europe. *American Journal of Folklore, 99*, 30–55.

Hall, S. (1984). Encoding/decoding. In S. Hall, D. Hobson, A. Lowe and P. Willis (Eds.), *Culture, media, language: Working papers in cultural studies, 1972–79* (pp. 128–138). London: Hutchinson and the Centre for Contemporary Cultural Studies, University of Birmingham.

Harjo, S. S. (2001). Fighting name calling: Challenging "Redskins" in court. In C. R. King and C. F. Springwood (Eds.), *Team spirits: Essays on the history and significance of Native American mascots* (pp. 189–207). Lincoln: University of Nebraska Press.

Heck, M. C. (1984). The ideological dimension of media messages. In S. Hall, D. Hobson, A. Lowe and P. Willis, eds., *Culture, media, language: Working papers in cultural studies, 1972–79*, pp. 122–127. London, England: Hutchinson and the Centre for Contemporary Cultural Studies, University of Birmingham.

Kelber, B. C. (1994). "Scalping the Redskins": Can trademark law start athletic teams bearing Native American nicknames and images on the road to reform? *Hamline Law Review, 17*, 533–588.

King, C. R. (1998). Spectacles, sports, and stereotypes: Dis/playing Chief Illiniwek. In *Colonial discourse, collective memories, and the exhibition of Native American cultures and histories in the contemporary United States* (pp. 41–58). New York: Garland.

King, C. R. (2001). Uneasy Indians: Creating and Contesting Native American Mascots at Marquette University. In C. R. King and C. F. Springwood (Eds.), *Team spirits: Essays on the history and significance of Native American mascots* (pp. 281–303). Lincoln: University of Nebraska Press.

King, C. R. (2002). Defensive dialogues: Native American mascots, anti–Indianism, and educational institutions. *Studies in Media & Information Literacy Education, 2 (1)*. http://www.utpress.utoronto.ca/journal/ejournals/simile.

King, C. R. (2003). Arguing over images: Native American mascots and race. In R. A. Lind (Ed)., *Race/gender/media: Considering diversity across audiences, content, and producers.* Boston: AB-Longman.

King, C. R. (2004). Borrowing power: Racial metaphors and pseudo–Indian mascots. *CR: The New Centennial Review, 4,* 189–209.

King, C. R. (2006). Being a warrior: Race, gender, and Native American mascots. *International Journal of the History of Sport 23*(2), 315–330.

King, C. R., and C. F. Springwood (2000). Choreographing colonialism: Athletic mascots, (dis)embodied Indians, and EuroAmerican subjectivities. *Cultural Studies: A Research Annual, 5,* 191–221.

King, C. R., and C. F. Springwood (2001a). *Beyond the cheers: Race as spectacle in college sports.* Albany: State University of New York Press.

King, C. R., and C. F. Springwood (Eds.) (2001b). *Team spirits: Essays on the history and significance of Native American mascots.* Lincoln: University of Nebraska.

King, C. R., E. J. Staurowsky, L. Baca, L. R. Davis and C. Pewewardy (2002). Of polls and race prejudice: *Sports Illustrated*'s errant "Indian wars." *Journal of Sport and Social Issues, 26,* 382–403.

Landreth, M. (2001). Becoming the Indians: Fashioning Arkansas State University Indians. In C. R. King and C.F. Springwood (Eds.), *Team spirits: Essays on the history and significance of Native American mascots* (pp. 46–63). Lincoln: University of Nebraska Press.

LeBeau, P. R. (2001). The fighting braves of Michigamua: Adapting vestiges of American Indian warriors in the halls of Academia. In C. R. King and C. F. Springwood (Eds.), *Team spirits: Essays on the history and significance of Native American mascots.* Lincoln: University of Nebraska Press.

Likourezos, G. (1996). A Case of first impression: American Indians seek cancellation of the trademarked term "Redskins." *Journal of the Patent and Trademark Office Society, 78,* 275–290.

McEwan, P. J., and C. Belfield (2004). What happens when schools stop playing Indian? http://www.wellesley.edu/Economics/mcewan/Papers/playing.pdf. Accessed May 5, 2004.

National Spectator Association. (1999). Fan Poll. Available online at http://www.nsa.com/Poll1.cfm?Poll_ID=260.

Native American Journalists Association. (2003). Reading red report 2003: A call for the news media to recognize racism in sport team nicknames and mascots. http://www.naja.com/docs/2003ReadingRed.pdf.

Nuessel, F. (1994). Objectionable sports team designations. *Names: A Journal of Onomastics, 42,* 101–119.

Pace, K.A. (1994). The Washington Redskins and the doctrine of disparagement. *Pepperdine Law Review, 22,* 7–57.

Peter Harris Research Group (2002). Methodology for *Sports Illustrated* survey on the use of Indian nicknames, mascots, etc. Document shared with Ellen Staurowsky in January 2003.

Pewewardy, C. D. (1991). Native American mascots and imagery: The struggle of unlearning Indian stereotypes. *Journal of Navaho Education, 9,* 19–23.

Pewewardy, C. D. (1998). Fluff and Feathers: Treatment of American Indians in the literature and the classroom. *Equity and Excellence in Education, 31,* 69–76.

Pewewardy, C. D. (2001). Educators and mascots: Challenging contradictions. In C. R. King and C. F. Springwood (Eds.), *Team spirits: Essays on the history and significance of Native American mascots* (pp. 257–279). Lincoln: University of Nebraska Press.

Pickle, D. (2002). Members to be queried on Indian mascot issue. *The NCAA News,* n.p. Retrieved from http://www.ncaa.org/news/2002/20020401/active/3907n02.html on November 4, 2002.

Price, S. L. (2002, March 4). The Indian wars. *Sports Illustrated, 96* (10), 66–72.

Prochaska, David 2001. At home in Illinois: Presence of Chief Illinwek, absence of Native Americans. In C. R. King and C. F. Springwood (Eds.), *Team spirits: Essays on the history and significance of Native American mascots* (pp. 157–188). Lincoln: University of Nebraska Press.

Rodriquez, R. (1998). Plotting the assassination of Little Red Sambo: Psychologists join war against racist campus mascots. *Black Issues in Higher Education, 15* (8), 20–24.

Rosenstein, J. (2001). "In whose honor?" Mascots, and the media. In C. R. King and C. F. Spring-wood (Eds.), *Team spirits: Essays on the history and significance of Native American mascots* (pp. 241–256). Lincoln: University of Nebraska Press.

Sigelman, L. (1998). Hail to the Redskins? Public reactions to a racially insensitive team name. *Sociology of Sport Journal, 15*, 317–325.

Simms, R. (2002, June 13). Do you favor or oppose keeping Native American mascots for high school, college, or professional sport teams? *King County Weekly Poll*. Retrieved from http://www.metrokc.gov/exec/survey/feedback mascots.html on November 4, 2002.

Spindel, C. (2000). *Dancing at halftime: Sports and the controversy over American Indian mascots.* New York: New York University Press.

Splichal, S. (1999). *Public opinion: Developments and controversies in the twentieth century.* Lanham, MD: Rowman and Littlefield.

Springwood, C. F. (2001). Playing Indian and fighting (for) mascots: Reading the complications of Native American and EuroAmerican alliances. In C. R. King and C. F. Springwood (Eds.), *Team spirits: Essays on the history and significance of Native American mascots*. Lincoln: University of Nebraska Press.

Springwood, C. F., and C. R. King (2000). Race, power, and representation in contemporary american sport. In P. Kivisto and G. Rundblad, (Eds.), *The color line at the dawn of the twenty-first century* (pp. 161–174). Thousand Oaks, CA: Pine Valley.

Stapleton, B. (2001). *Redskins: Racial slur or symbol of success?* San Jose, CA: Writers Club.

Staurowsky, E. J. (1998). An act of honor or exploitation? The Cleveland Indians' use of the Louis Francis Sockalexis story. *Sociology of Sport Journal, 15*, 299–316.

Staurowsky, E. J. (1999). American Indian imagery and the miseducation of America. *Quest, 51*, 382–392.

Staurowsky, E. J. (2000). The Cleveland Indians: A case study in cultural dispossession. *Sociology of Sport Journal, 17*, 307–330

Staurowsky, E. J. (2001). Sockalexis and the making of the myth at the core of the Cleveland "Indians" imagery. In C. R. King and C. F. Springwood (Eds.), *Team spirits: Essays on the history and significance of Native American mascots* (pp. 82–107). Lincoln: University of Nebraska Press.

Trainor, D. J. (1995). Native American mascots, schools and the Title VI hostile environment analysis. *University of Illinois Law Review, 5*, 971–997.

University of North Dakota. (2000). Name commission poll. http://www.und.edu/name commission/index.html.

USA Weekend (1997). Chief Wahoo poll. http://www.usaweekend.com/quick/results/chief_wahoo_qp_results.html.

Vanderford, H. (1996). What's in a name? Heritage or hatred: The school mascot controversy. *Journal of Law and Education, 25*, 381–388.

Williams, D. M. (2006). Patriarchy and "The Fighting Sioux": A gendered look at racial college sports nicknames. *Race, Ethnicity and Education. 9*(4), 325–340.

Williams, D. M. (2007). No past, no respect, and no power: An anarchist evaluation of Native Americans as sports nicknames, logos, and mascots. *Anarchist Studies. 15* (1), 31–54.

Williams, D. M. (2007). Where's the honor? Attitudes on the "Fighting Sioux" nickname and logo. *Sociology of Sport Journal, 24*(4), December.

The Case for Tennessee State as an Expansion Member of the SWAC: Economic Impact

J. Kenyatta Cavil

In today's hyper-connected world, it is often easy to get so immersed in doing day-to-day business that strategic planning initiatives are lost on online message boards and sports talk-radio shows. This writer thinks the case can be made for Tennessee State University's athletics program to move to the Southwestern Athletic Conference (SWAC). Indeed, the time is now for the conference to get to 16 members from its current state and attempt to strategically solidify its future in a crowded marketplace.

The question as to whether Tennessee State is maximizing its potential as a current and long-time member of the Ohio Valley Conference (OVC) as it pertains to its athletic programs must constantly be asked and reevaluated in terms of the best business practices. This essay reviews Historically Black Colleges and Universities (HBCUs) and also reviews the alignment of Tennessee State as an expansion member of the SWAC and the projected economic impact of such a move. According to Cavil (2006), the Mid-Eastern Athletic Conference (MEAC) league administrators, athletic directors and presidents/chancellors, were split among many different aspects of conference expansion. This essay seeks to provide benchmark information to allow fans, alumni as well as university and conference leaders to better answer this question on the expansion of the SWAC with Tennessee State University as the newest member.

As HBCUs' athletic programs continue to grow, expand and operate in the National College Athletic Association (NCAA), National Athletic Intercollegiate Association (NAIA), National Junior College Athletic Association

(NJCAA) or United States Collegiate Athletic Association (USCAA), and with the increased commitment to athletics from regional and national branded Historically White Colleges and Universities' (HWCUs) athletic programs operating at the highest level, in the NCAA as member of the Division I Football Bowl Subdivision (FBS), Bowl Championship Series (BCS), it is important to examine the current status of HBCUs' athletics programs and their conference associations.

History of Black Colleges and Universities

Historically black colleges and universities are institutions of higher education in the United States that were established since the early 1800s with the primary goal of educating African Americans and serving the African American community. Although there are 24 HBCUs classified with the NCAA Division I affiliation, there are 105 HBCUs in the United States, the District of Columbia, and the U.S. Virgin Islands, including public and private, two-year and four-year institutions, medical school, university law schools, business colleges, technical institutes and community colleges. All are in the former states and territories of the United States that held Africans as slaves except for five, Central State University (Ohio), Cheyney University (Pennsylvania), Lewis College of Business (Michigan), Lincoln University (Pennsylvania) and Wilberforce University (Ohio) as well as the now-defunct Western University (Kansas).

The first HBCU to be established was Cheyney, located in Cheyney, Pennsylvania. It was founded in 1837. The First Morrill Act enacted on July 2, 1862, made higher education available Americans with federal support for state education. Ten years later, the Freedmen's Bureau helped to provide support to a small number of HBCUs (Brazzell, 1992). Following, the Civil War in 1865, the Thirteenth Amendment abolished slavery and reconstruction in the South began. While the Fourteenth, and Fifteenth Amendments compelled states to provide public education for former slaves and other black Americans (Brown, 1999). Historically, black colleges and universities struggled significantly with legislations and court decisions such as the Jim Crow laws in the South. These struggles led to the rise and fall of a number of HBCUs. The Second Morrill Act of 1890 mandated that those funds be extended to institutions that enrolled black Americans and led to the establishment of an additional nineteen HBCUs across the United States (Mance, 2003). The Second Morrill Act of 1890 ultimately strengthened the prevailing doctrine of segregation.

In 1954 the U.S. Supreme Court decision *Brown vs. Board of Education*

broke the barrier of separate but equal policy in schools. Even after that decision, HBCUs were the best opportunity for most blacks interested in attending
college. This was during the Civil Rights Movement era, and black colleges
continued to produce successful African Americans, despite their fight for
existence (Allen, 1986).

According to the Higher Education Act of 1966, a Historically Black
College and University is defined as: "any historically black college or university that was established prior to 1964, whose principal mission was, and is,
the education of black Americans, and that is accredited by a nationally recognized accrediting agency or association determined by the Secretary [of
Education] to be a reliable authority as to the quality of training offered or is,
according to such an agency or association, making reasonable progress toward
accreditation" (U.S. Department of Education, 2010). HBCUs have a strong
and storied tradition with over 130 years of educational service to African
American students.

HBCU Sports

College athletics in the United States has prospered significantly since
its inception. American intercollegiate athletics have seen millions of spectators go through the turnstyles each year. College football is an integrated part
of campus activities positioning itself above other sports both in terms of revenues and expenses (Suggs, 1998). According to Deschriver and Jensen (2002),
National Collegiate Athletic Association (NCAA) universities such as the
University of Tennessee attract over 100,000 attendees for each home football
games, and ticket revenues alone can eclipse $3 million for a single game. In
2007, 619 schools combined for over 48 million people attending NCAA football games which included all division levels (I—Football Bowl Subdivision
(FBS), I—Football Championship Subdivision (FCS), II, and III) (Johnson,
2008). NCAA Division I teams, with the exception of a few independent
operating programs, are organized into conferences.

Attendance is a major component of sport consumption. Sport economic
literature dealing with attendance has garnered a great deal of interest
(DeSchriver, 2007). According to Johnson (2007), although all-time records
were not set in the Division I Football Championship Subdivision, classification's numbers were up for the second straight season. Over five and half million fans saw FCS games in 2007, this was the fourth-highest total in that
subdivision and was up 238 fans per game from the previous year. Historically
black colleges and universities (HBCU) Classic games have occurred for more
than 80 years across America with large attended contests, as well. In fact, the

Magic City Classic, the match-up of Alabama's two HBCU state schools, surpassed the Florida Classic (65,367) in attendance this year for the first time and it set an all-time record for game of 68,593 (Williams, 2008). The top six attended HBCU Classic games each had attendance over 50,000 fans. While the Southwestern Athletic Conference (SWAC) a conference made up of black universities and a FCS member held on to its top spot once again with 15,614 fans per game (Johnson, 2007). Armstrong's (2002) research suggests that cultural factors significantly influence African Americans' motives for attending black college football games. McClelland (2011) suggests that the unequal distribution of resources has impacted the dynamics of HBCU academics and athletics.

Tennessee State University

According to the Tennessee State University website, Tennessee State University is a comprehensive urban coeducational land-grant university founded in 1912 in Nashville (Tennessee State University History, n.d.). The present-day Tennessee State University exists as a result of the merger on July 1, 1979, of Tennessee State University and the former University of Tennessee at Nashville.

Through successive stages, Tennessee State has developed from a "normal" school for Negroes (an institution to educate teachers) to its current status as a national university with students from 44 states and 38 countries. The 500-acre main campus, with more than 65 buildings, is located in a residential setting. The Avon Williams Campus is located downtown, near the center of the Nashville business and government district.

In 1957, the school became the first historically black college to win a national basketball title, winning the National Association of Intercollegiate Athletics (NAIA) championship. In fact, the legendary coach John B. McLendon led Tennessee State to three consecutive national championships (NAIA: 1957-58-59 when it was called Tennessee A&I State University). In 1986, Tennessee State joined the OVC. The football team, like all other OVC members, competes in the Football Championship Subdivision (the former I-AA). According to the Tennessee State University website, by 2009, approximately 100 of its football players had been drafted by the National Football League, many of whom did so under the guidance of another legendary Tennessee State coach, John A. Merritt (Tennessee State University History, n.d.). Among them were Ed "Too Tall" Jones, Joe Gilliam, Claude Humphrey, Mike Hegman, and Richard Dent. At Tennessee State, Merritt had four undefeated seasons, claimed four Midwestern Conference titles, seven black College Football

Championships (1965, 1966, 1970, 1971, 1973, 1979, and 1982) and earned the school's first-ever National Collegiate Athletic Association (NCAA) Division I-AA playoff victory in 1982. His coaching record at Tennessee State was 174–35–7, resulting in an 82 percent winning percentage.

City of Nashville

According to the Vanderbilt Center for Nashville Studies, the City of Nashville has five major sporting venues with a seating capacity of 10,000 or greater (Burgener, 2010). LP Field (capacity 69,798), Bridgestone Arena (capacity 17,113 for hockey, approximately 18,000 for basketball), Vanderbilt Stadium (capacity 39,720), Vanderbilt's Memorial Gym (capacity 14,158), Greer Stadium (capacity 10,052), Tennessee State's on-campus Hale Stadium (capacity 15,000), and Howard Gentry Complex (capacity 10,500), also at Tennessee State.

LP Field is a shared facility, home of the Titans, the Tennessee State University Tigers, and the Music City Bowl. The Howard Gentry Complex at Tennessee State University is a dynamic facility. The complex also includes a 220-yard indoor track, and a thirty-five meter, eight-lane swimming pool. (This indoor track facility would become in the only indoor track facility in the SWAC.) Tennessee State has also recently completed an indoor football practice facility.

The expansion of the SWAC with Tennessee State University provides the potential for match-ups should increase home attendance, as well as Classic game match-ups that lead to large attendance numbers seen through the conference attendance prowess. According to the NCAA website, the SWAC has been the top attended football conference in the NCAA Division I FCS, 33 times in the last 34 years (NCAA Statistics, 2012). As a league in 2012, the SWAC averaged 12,944 fans at each of its 53 home contests. In addition economic indicators suggests that with increased attendance for football contest associated with SWAC fans traveling from out-of-town to follow their team, they are likely to stay for a night, eat in local restaurants and make other purchases in local establishments (and when that includes major metropolitan cities for neutral site Classic games; the stay becomes two or three days).

These types of economic indicators create a unique marketability based on brand awareness for the SWAC and its member institutions as measured in one's economic impact. Many corporations seek to align their products with strong and well branded organizations that allow that business to align their products and services with potential customers. Economic impact is defined as out-of-town dollars spent on food, lodging (total nights housed and average room cost per night), and operational spending based on a formula used to calculate visitors spending.

A move to the SWAC for Tennessee State could mean even more than the "bump" one naturally gets from moving to a conference where one will host teams like Alabama A&M, Alabama State, Southern, and Grambling State. As mentioned, Tennessee State plays in a state-of-the-art professional football stadium. The Tigers have recently renovated their on-campus basketball arena and football stadium, the latter being the famous "Hole," to play several selected home games.

Although Tennessee State currently operates their athletic programs as a member of the NCAA FCS Division I classification, it stands to reason that there is greater potential to raise revenue with conference realignment as a member of the SWAC (which also operates as a NCAA Division I FCS program). If Tennessee State were to join the SWAC, the profile of both Tennessee State University and the SWAC would likely be grander in scale.

The conference expansion of Tennessee State would align the Tigers with historic rivals such as Southern, Grambling State, and Texas Southern. More importantly, it would open the expansion of the SWAC in a state with a strong radio and media markets. Tennessee State holds a solid relationship with Nashville via the association of the John A. Merritt Classic played in the LP Field. First played in 1999, the Classic honors John A. Merritt, the legendary Tennessee State University football coach who led the Tigers from 1963 to 1983. The John A. Merritt Classic with a conference opponent would gain additional importance as well as the addition of the Southern Heritage Classic to the SWAC games product inventory. More products added to a conference's inventory will provide great leverage for negotiating these products in the sport industry (i.e. media, merchandise, and sponsorship).

The revenue sharing distribution formula for the SWAC is based on shares (total = 15.5 shares). As a member of the conference, each institution is automatically awarded one share (subtotal = 10 shares). Each institution's athletic program has an opportunity to win one share for the following: football championship, men's basketball regular season championship, men's tournament championship, women's basketball regular season championship and or women's tournament championship as well as a half of a share for a football championship runner-up appearance (subtotal = 5.5 shares). In case of a tie for a regular season championship, the share is split between those teams that were tied.

The Arkansas at Pine Bluff Golden Lions 2012 football schedule featured a match-up between the Tennessee State and SWAC member Arkansas-Pine Bluff (UAPB Football Schedule, 2012). This could become a border-state rivalry game. With Tennessee State as a member of the SWAC, such a game could become a conference match-up, and provide greater opportunity to leverage another Classic with a major title sponsor and renegotiated media broadcast rights, such as McDonald's and ABC/ESPN, for increased revenues

for the conference and it members through revenue sharing governance policies. Each Classic featuring Tennessee State and a current SWAC member
institution with attendance that could rival the Magic City Classic game
between Alabama A&M and Alabama State could bring $60,000 to $80,000
between the two teams from television shares. One should note that the
SWAC revenue sharing distribution does not include television shares.

The conference generates revenues from the following: NCAA alloca-
tions, BCS distributions, conference member yearly dues, media rights (ESPN,
etc.), sponsorships, conference events and CD/fund/money market accounts.

What kind of money can a Tennessee State home conference game as a
member of the SWAC played at LP Stadium as a Classic bring in and conference games as a member of the SWAC played on campus? According to the
Vanderbilt Center for Nashville Studies report titled "The State of Sports in
Nashville," the Music City Bowl, is similar in nature in many ways to the John
A. Merritt Classic that the bowl averages more than 34,000 in attendance per
year. The 2009 game between the University of Kentucky and Clemson University produced a $12.6 million impact on the local economy. Although it
should be noted that many fans choosing to attend the John A. Merritt Classic
or any similar HBCU Classic game would likely not stay the night or at least
as many nights like the above listed bowl game attendees, it provides a general
idea of potential economic impact.

The Southern Heritage Classic in Memphis, Tennessee, featuring the
Tennessee State Tigers and the Jackson State Tigers becomes a conference
game with Tennessee State accepting the invitation to join the conference.
According to a report prepared by Dr. Richard Irwin, director of the University
of Memphis Bureau of Sport and Leisure Commerce, the 2008 Southern Heritage Classic game had a $16.2 million economic impact on the city (Classic
History, n.d.).

This economic impact number continues to grow, according to a study
by the University of Memphis' Sparks Bureau of Business and Economic
Research that found that in 2011, the Southern Heritage Classic had an economic benefit of $21 million (Classic History, n.d.). The 2011 figure repre-
sented a 25 percent increase from the analysis done in 2008. This provides
additional leverage for Tennessee State, Jackson State, and the SWAC with
potential sponsors.

The real question is whether Tennessee State University's new president,
Dr. Glenda Baskin Glover, a licensed attorney and certified public accountant,
(bachelor's degree in Mathematics from Tennessee State University, a MBA
from Clark-Atlanta University, a J. D. from Georgetown University Law Center, and a Ph.D. in business economics and policy from George Washington
University), would be open to conference realignment and admittance to the

SWAC. Currently, SWAC Commissioner Duer Sharp and the SWAC presidents and chancellors have offered an open invitation to Tennessee State University to join the conference.

One company listed in the Fortune 500 is headquartered in Nashville and a total of eight Fortune 500 companies are located in the State of Tennessee. Why is this important? Adding Tennessee State gives the SWAC a better ability to market to Nashville-based businesses.

In conclusion, adding Tennessee State to the SWAC gives the conference a tangible location in the nation's thirtieth largest city, forty-fourth largest metropolitan area, and a large media market. It gives the conference access to a new market.

Southwestern Athletic Conference (SWAC) Affiliation History

According to the SWAC website, Prairie View A & M University is an original founding member of the SWAC in 1920 (SWAC History, n.d.). At that time, eight men representing six colleges from the state of Texas met to discuss collegiate athletics and the many challenges that face their respective institutions. By the time the session in Houston had concluded, they had founded an athletic league that has slowly become one of the leading sports associations in the world of collegiate athletics, the Southwestern Athletic Conference.

The founding fathers of the original "Super Six" were C.H. Fuller of Bishop College, Red Randolph and C.H. Patterson of Paul Quinn, E.G. Evans, H.J. Evans and H.J. Starns of Prairie View A & M, D.C. Fuller of Texas College and G. Whitte Jordan of Wiley College.

Although there is considerable disparity in institutional enrollments, the Southwestern Athletic Conference provides challenging competition, and it is geographically manageable because most team travel can be accommodated by bus transportation (see Table 1). Conference realignment with Tennessee State as an expansion member of the SWAC based on a comprehensive study "Southwestern Athletic Conference (SWAC) to 12 ~ 14 ~ 16 HBCUs Expansion Study" by THG Agency (2012), reveals, the SWAC would provide Tennessee State with the following:

1. Alignment of Tennessee State with the SWAC and its member institutions would provide Tennessee State a partnership with more institutions that have similar athletic revenue operating budgets which provides for a stronger opportunity for Tennessee State to create competitive balance in athletics.

Name	Location	Status	Enrollment 2010	Football Stadium	Basketball Stadium	Men SWAC	Women SWAC	Non SWAC
Eastern Division								
Alabama A&M	Huntsville, AL	Public	5,814	21,000	6,000	8	9	1
Alabama State	Montgomery, AL	Public	5,705	30,000	7,400	8	10	
Alcorn State	Lorman, MS	Public	3,682	22,500	7,000	8	10	
Miss. Valley State	Itta Bena, MS	Public	2,500	10,000	5,000	8	9	
Jackson State	Jackson, MS	Public	8,687	62,000	8,000	8	10	
Western Division								
Ark. at Pine Bluff	Pine Bluff, AR	Public	3,232	12,500	4,500	8	8	
Grambling State	Grambling, LA	Public	4,994	19,600	7,500	6	9	
Prairie View A&M	Prairie View, TX	Public	8,456	6,000	5,520	8	10	
Southern	Baton Rouge, LA	Public	7,313	29,000	7,500	6	9	
Texas Southern	Houston, TX	Public	10,026	22,000	8,100	7	9	
———						OVC	OVC	
**Tennessee State	Nashville, TN	Public	8,456	69,798	10,500	7	8	

*There are currently 10 members in the SWAC. ** Tennessee State University is a member of the Ohio Valley Conference.

2. Alignment of the Tennessee with the SWAC and its member institutions would provide Tennessee State a partnership with more institutions with similar enrollment size; this has a direct relationship with athletic revenue operating budgets.

3. Alignment of Tennessee State with the SWAC and its member institutions would provide Tennessee State a larger academic and athletic recruiting footprint (further extends the current Alabama and Mississippi landscape and introduces the Texas and Louisiana landscape).

4. Alignment of Tennessee State with the SWAC and its member institutions would provide Tennessee State an opportunity to likely increase football attendance (i. e. SWAC 2010 = 14,605 average compared to OVC 2010 = 8,308 average according the NCAA.org).

5. Alignment of the Tennessee with the SWAC and its member institutions would provide Tennessee State with an opportunity to move from a regional conference alignment to a multi-regional (national marketing

platform and athletics brand awareness) conference alignment still in a contiguous state footprint.

6. Alignment of Tennessee State with the SWAC and its member institutions would provide Tennessee State a partnership with several academically stronger peer institutions, (DRU) as measured by the Carnegie Classification.

7. Alignment of Tennessee State with the SWAC and its member institutions would provide Tennessee State with the ability to influence other traditionally and culturally rich Carnegie (DRU) classified HBCUs programs, in regionally strong business innovated areas such as: Atlanta, Georgia and the State of Florida.

8. Alignment of Tennessee State with the SWAC and its member institutions would Tennessee State with an opportunity to strategically open doors and it creates an additional platform for Tennessee State's Engineering Program and other strong professional academic units to further directly align itself with a strong corporate engineering job market in Houston and indirectly in Dallas in the strong Texas economic market.

Being in the market is different than simply having access to the market. Houston is the nation's sixth largest radio market and tenth largest television market. (This information is based on a commissioned study for Texas Southern University.) It is also the fourth largest U.S. city. Houston is also the second-most fertile recruiting ground in the SWAC's footprint, with 140 prospects from Houston signing letters of intent for FBS schools in 2011.

Dallas-Fort Worth is home to one HBCU and is the nation's fifth largest radio market (eighth largest black/African American) and fifth largest television market. It is also the eighth largest U.S. city, respectively. It is also the eighth largest U.S. metropolitan area. If that is not enough, ten of the companies listed in the Fortune 500 are headquartered in Dallas, the third largest concentration in the United States tied with Atlanta; three in Forth Worth; and additionally in the region: four in Irving, two in Plano and two Austin-Round Rock.

References

Allen, W. R. (1986). *Gender and campus race differences in black student academic performance, racial attitudes and college satisfaction.* Atlanta: Southern Education Foundation.

Armstrong, K. L. (2002). An examination of the social psychology of blacks' consumption of sport. *Journal of Sport Management, 16,* pp. 267–288.

Brazzell, Johnetta Cross (1992). Bricks Without Straw: Missionary-Sponsored Black Higher Education in the Post-Emancipation Era. *The Journal of Higher Education, 63* (1): 26–49.

Brown, M. C. (1999). *The Quest to Define Collegiate Desegregation.* Westport, CT: Bergin and Garvey.

Burgener, J. L. (2010). The state of sports in Nashville. http://www.vanderbilt.edu/vcns/The_
State_of_Sports_in_Nashville.pdf.

Carnegie Foundation for the Advancement of Teaching (2010). Institution lookup. http://www.
classifications.carnegiefoundation.org/lookup_listings/institutions.php?key=782.

Cavil, J. Kenyatt. (2006). MEAC expansion: To expand or not to expand is the question—a comprehensive review of conference expansion, based on organizational leadership. *I-AA.org Magazine*, 2006 Fall Preview, p. 87.

Classic History (N.d.). The Southern Heritage Classic: A 20-year celebration by Roscoe Nance,
former *USA Today* reporter who has written about black-college football for 34 years. http://
www.southernheritageclassic.com/classic_history.asp.

DeSchriver, T. D. (2007). Much adieu about Freddy: The relationship between MLS Spectator
attendance and the arrival of Freddy Adu. *Journal of Sport Management, 21* (3), 438–451.

DeSchriver, T. D., and P. E. Jensen. (2002). Determinants of spectator attendance at NCAA Division II football contests. *Journal of Sports Management, 16* (4), 311–330.

Johnson, G. K. (2007). Football attendance soars again. NCAA News, retrieved on March 6, 2008,
http://www.ncaa.org/wps/ncaa?ContentID=4232.

Mance, R. (2003). The Morrill Act & 1862 & 1890 & HBCUs, retrieved April 12, 2011, from
http://emergingminds.org/The-MORRILL-ACT-of-1862-and-1890-and-HBCUs.
html?format=pdf.

McClelland, C. F. (2012). Athletic directors' perceptions of the effectiveness of HBCU Division
I-AA Athletic Programs. Ph.D. Dissertation, Texas A&M University.

MEAC History (n.d.). MEAC website, http://www.meacsports.com/ViewArticle.dbml?DB_
OEM_ID=20800&ATCLID=1591845.

NCAA Statistics (2012). NCAA Football Attendance. http://www.ncaa.org/wps/wcm/connect/
public/NCAA/Resources/Stats/Football/Attendance/index.html.

Our History (n.d.). Tennessee State University website, http://www.tnstate.edu/about_tsu/history.
aspx.

Suggs, W. (1998). Only NCAA's state schools turn profits. *Smith & Smith's Sports Business Journal*,
October 18–25, p. 5.

SWAC History (n.d.). SWAC Athletics. http://www.swac.org/ViewArticle.dbml?DB_OEM_
ID=27400&ATCLID=205246152.

THG Agency (2012). Southwestern Athletic Conference (SWAC) to 12 ~ 14 ~ 16 HBCUs expansion study. Unpublished report. Houston, Texas. Michael Washington.

UAPB Football Schedule (2012). Arkansas-Pine Bluff releases 2012 Golden Lion Football schedule.
http://onnidan.com/index.php/component/content/article/1470.

U.S. Census Bureau (2010). Census Bureau map products. http://www.census.gov/geo/www/
maps/CP_MapProducts.htm.

U.S. Department of Education (2010). List of HBCUs—White House initiative on Historically
Black Colleges and Universities. http://www2.ed.gov/about/inits/list/whhbcu/edlite-list.
html.

Williams, L. (2008, January 1–7). Attendance matters: Largest attendance at football games of
2007. *Black College Sports Page*, p 1.

Appendix A

Student Total Enrollment

Southwestern

1	Texas Southern	10,026	4	Tennessee State	8,456
2	Prairie View A & M	8,781	5	Southern	7,313
3	Jackson State	8,687	6	Alabama A & M	5,814

7	Alabama State	5,705
8	Grambling State	4,994
9	Alcorn State	3,682
10	Arkansas at P. B.	3,232
11	Miss. Valley State	2,500
Average		**6,073**

Mid-Eastern

1	Florida A & M	13,089
2	N. Carolina A & T	12,000
3	Howard	10,491
4	N. Carolina Central	8,612
5	Tennessee State	8,456
6	Morgan State	7,427
7	Delaware State	6,235
8	Hampton	5,000
9	S. Carolina State	5,000
10	Savannah State	4,552
11	Maryland at E. S.	4,433

12	Norfolk State	4,179
13	Coppin State	4,000
14	Bethune-Cookman	3,594
Average		**6,816**

Ohio Valley

1	Eastern Kentucky	16,515
2	SIUe	14,055
3	Tennessee Tech	11,768
4	Southeast Missouri	11,510
5	Eastern Illinois	11,167
6	Austin Peay	10,873
7	Murray State	10,800
8	Morehead State	10,215
9	Jacksonville State	9,504
10	Tennessee State	8,456
11	UT Martin	8,400
12	Belmont	6,637
Average		**10,825**

HBCU Football Championship Subdivision Total Enrollment

From Carnegie Classification

	HBCU Division I Institution	2010 Enrollment	2010 Conference Affiliation
1	Florida A & M	13,089	MEAC
2	North Carolina A & T State	12,000	MEAC
3	Howard	10,491	MEAC
4	Texas Southern	10,026	SWAC
5	Prairie View A & M	8,781	SWAC
6	Jackson State	8,687	SWAC
7	North Carolina Central	8,612	MEAC
8	Tennessee State	8,456	OVC
9	Southern	7,313	SWAC
10	Morgan State	7,427	MEAC
11	Delaware State	6,235	MEAC
12	Alabama A & M	5,814	SWAC
13	Alabama State	5,705	SWAC
14	Hampton	5,000	MEAC
15	South Carolina State	5,000	MEAC
16	Grambling State	4,994	SWAC
17	Savannah State	4,552	MEAC
18	Maryland-Eastern Shore	4,433	MEAC
19	Norfolk State	4,179	MEAC
20	Coppin State	4,000	MEAC
21	Alcorn State	3,682	SWAC
22	Bethune-Cookman	3,594	MEAC
23	Arkansas-Pine Bluff	3,232	SWAC
24	Mississippi Valley State	2,500	SWAC

Average 6,575

Appendix B

Carnegie Classification

Southwestern

1	Jackson State	RU/H
2	Tennessee State	DRU
2	Texas Southern	DRU
4	Prairie View A & M	Master's/L
4	Southern	Master's/L
4	Alabama A & M	Master's/L
4	Alabama State	Master's/L
8	Grambling State	Master's/M
8	Alcorn State	Master's/M
8	Miss. Valley State	Master's/M
11	Arkansas at P. B.	Bac/Div.

Average 5.60 = Master's/M

Mid-Eastern

1	Howard	RU/H
2	Florida A & M	DRU
2	N. Carolina A & T	DRU
2	Morgan State	DRU
2	S. Carolina State	DRU
2	Tennessee State	DRU
7	N. Carolina Central	Master's/L
7	Norfolk State	Master's/L

9	Delaware State	Master's/M
9	Hampton	Master's/M
11	Maryland at E. S.	Master's/S
11	Coppin State	Master's/S
13	Savannah State	Bac/A&S
14	Bethune-Cookman	Bac/Div.

Average 5.46 = Master's/M

Ohio Valley

1	Tennessee State	DRU
2	Eastern Kentucky	Master's/L
2	SIUE	Master's/L
2	Tennessee Tech	Master's/L
2	Southeast Missouri	Master's/L
2	Eastern Illinois	Master's/L
2	Austin Peay	Master's/L
2	Murray State	Master's/L
2	Morehead State	Master's/L
2	Jacksonville State	Master's/L
2	Belmont	Master's/L
12	UT Martin	Master's/M

Average 6.00 = Master's/L

HBCU Football Championship Subdivision Carnegie Classification

From Conferences Football Media Guide

	HBCU Division I Institution	Classification	2010 Conference Affiliation
1	Howard	RU/H	MEAC
1	Jackson State	RU/H	SWAC
3	Florida A & M	DRU	MEAC
3	North Carolina A & T State	DRU	MEAC
3	Tennessee State	DRU	OVC
3	Morgan State	DRU	MEAC
3	South Carolina State	DRU	MEAC
3	Texas Southern	DRU	SWAC
9	Prairie View A & M	Master's/L	SWAC
9	North Carolina Central	Master's/L	MEAC
9	Southern	Master's/L	SWAC
9	Alabama A & M	Master's/L	SWAC
9	Alabama State	Master's/L	SWAC
9	Norfolk State	Master's/L	MEAC
15	Delaware State	Master's/M	MEAC
15	Hampton	Master's/M	MEAC
15	Grambling State	Master's/M	SWAC

15	Alcorn State	Master's/M	SWAC
15	Mississippi Valley State	Master's/M	SWAC
20	Maryland-Eastern Shore	Master's/S	MEAC
20	Coppin State	Master's/S	MEAC
22	Savannah State	Bac/A&S	MEAC
23	Bethune-Cookman	Bac/Div.	MEAC
24	Arkansas-Pine Bluff	Bac/Div.	SWAC

Average 5.66 = Master's/M

Appendix C

Athletic Budgets

Southwestern

1	Prairie View A & M	$9.8M
2	Texas Southern	$9.7M
3	Tennessee State	$9.5M
4	Arkansas at P. B.	$9.2M
5	Alabama State	$9.1M
6	Southern	$6.8M
7	Alabama A & M	$6.6M
8	Alcorn State	$5.7M
9	Jackson State	$5.6M
10	Grambling State	$5.4M
11	Miss. Valley State	$4.3M

Average $7.1M

Mid-Eastern

1	Delaware State	$13.7M
2	Norfolk State	$12.4M
3	S. Carolina State	$10.1M
4	Tennessee State	$9.5M
5	Florida A & M	$9.3M
6	N. Carolina A & T	$8.9M
7	Morgan State	$8.7M
8	N. Carolina Central	$7.0M
9	Maryland at E. S.	$4.5M
10	Savannah State	$4.0M
11	Coppin State	$3.0M
12	Bethune-Cookman*	
13	Hampton*	
14	Howard*	

Average $8.2M

Ohio Valley

1	Murray State 77%	$13.3M
2	Eastern Kent 80%	$12.3M
3	Eastern Illinois 71%	$11.9M
4	Tennessee Tech 74%	$9.5M
5	Tennessee St 74%	$9.5M
6	UT Martin 82%	$8.8M
7	Southeast Miss 75%	$8.7M
8	Morehead St 85%	$8.6M
9	Austin Peay 79%	$7.4M
10	SIUE 85%	$6.8M
11	Jacksonville State	
12	Belmont*	

Average $9.7M

*Privately funded institutions are not required to report externally.

HBCU Football Championship Subdivision Budget

From USA Today.com for FY 2010

	HBCU Division I Institution	2010 Budget	2010 Conference Affiliation
1	Delaware State	$13,746,084	MEAC
2	Norfolk State	$12,420,571	MEAC
3	South Carolina State	$10,143,804	MEAC
4	Prairie View A & M	$9,892,725	SWAC
5	Texas Southern	$9,704,666	SWAC

6	Tennessee State	$9,594,782	OVC
7	Florida A & M	$9,352,322	MEAC
8	Arkansas-Pine Bluff	$9,270,585	SWAC
9	Alabama State	$9,104,938	SWAC
10	North Carolina A & T State	$8,908,949	MEAC
11	Morgan State	$8,756,578	MEAC
12	North Carolina Central	$7,027,083	MEAC
13	Southern	$6,859,770	SWAC
14	Alabama A & M	$6,619,752	SWAC
15	Alcorn State	$5,722,855	SWAC
16	Jackson State	$5,680,543	SWAC
17	Grambling State	$5,444,909	SWAC
18	Maryland-Eastern Shore	$4,524,873	MEAC
19	Mississippi Valley State	$4,339,095	SWAC
20	Savannah State	$4,070,032	MEAC
21	Coppin State	$3,072,340	MEAC
22	Bethune-Cookman*		MEAC
23	Hampton*		MEAC
24	Howard*		MEAC

Average $7.8M

*Privately funded institutions are not required to report externally.

Appendix D

Total Revenue Longitudinal Analysis 2006–2011

Southwestern

1	Tennessee State	$10.9M
1	Alabama State	$10.6M
2	Texas Southern	$10.1M
3	Prairie View A & M	$9.5M
4	Arkansas at P. B.	$7.3M
5	Jackson State	$6.9M
6	Southern	$6.7M
7	Grambling State	$6.2M
8	Alabama A & M	$6.0M
9	Alcorn State	$5.9M
10	Miss. Valley State	$4.1M

Average $7.3M

Mid-Eastern

1	Delaware State	$12.5M
2	Norfolk State	$12.1M
3	Tennessee State	$10.9M
4	Florida A & M	$10.1M
5	Morgan State	$9.8M
6	S. Carolina State	$9.8M
7	N. Carolina A & T	$9.2M
8	N. Carolina Central	$8.7M
9	Savannah State	$6.6M
10	Maryland at E. S.	$4.8M
11	Coppin State	$3.4M
12	Bethune-Cookman*	
12	Hampton*	
12	Howard*	

Average $8.7M

Ohio Valley

1	Murray State 72%	$13.6M
2	Eastern Kent 82%	$12.4M
3	Jacksonville S 80%	$12.1M
4	Eastern Illinois 75%	$11.7M
5	Tennessee St 72%	$10.9M
6	Tennessee Tech 75%	$10.7M
6	UT Martin 79%	$9.5M
7	Austin Peay 67%	$9.4M
8	Morehead St 85%	$9.3M
9	Southeast Miss 73%	$9.2M
10	SIUE 87%	$7.2M
12	Belmont*	

Average $10.6M

*Privately funded institutions are not required to report externally.

HBCU FCS Total Revenue Longitudinal Analysis 2006–2011

From USA Today.com for FYs 2006–2011

	HBCU Division I Institution	2006–2011 Total R	Conference Affiliation
1	Delaware State	$12,518,866	MEAC
2	Norfolk State	$12,126,046	MEAC
3	Tennessee State	$10,925,644	OVC
4	Alabama State	$10,614,081	SWAC
5	Florida A & M	$10,148,484	MEAC
6	Texas Southern	$10,108,775	SWAC
7	Morgan State	$9,899,823	MEAC
8	South Carolina State	$9,899,545	MEAC
9	Prairie View A & M	$9,509,384	SWAC
10	North Carolina A & T State	$9,240,731	MEAC
11	North Carolina Central	$8,770,880	MEAC
12	Arkansas-Pine Bluff	$7,302,570	SWAC
13	Jackson State	$6,909,322	SWAC
14	Southern	$6,799,370	SWAC
15	Savannah State	$6,673,458	MEAC
16	Grambling State	$6,212,914	SWAC
17	Alabama A & M	$6,003,172	SWAC
18	Alcorn State	$5,995,743	SWAC
19	Maryland-Eastern Shore	$4,889,052	MEAC
20	Mississippi Valley State	$4,182,130	SWAC
21	Coppin State	$3,484,823	MEAC
22	Howard*		MEAC
22	Hampton*		MEAC
22	Bethune-Cookman*		MEAC

Average $8.2M

*Privately funded institutions are not required to report externally.

Appendix E

Football Attendance

Southwestern

1	Jackson State	24,140
2	Tennessee State	14,861
3	Southern	12,896
4	Alcorn State	11,410
5	Alabama State	11,177
6	Arkansas at P. B.	11,030
7	Grambling State	8,719
8	Texas Southern	8,684
9	Prairie View A & M	6,475
10	Alabama A & M	6,456
11	Miss. Valley State	2,602

Average 14,605

Mid-Eastern

1	Florida A & M	15,913
2	S. Carolina State	14,862
3	Tennessee State	14,861
4	N. Carolina A & T	13,388
5	Norfolk State	11,879
6	Hampton	10,551
7	N. Carolina Central	9,749
8	Bethune-Cookman	6,140
9	Morgan State	5,853
10	Howard	4,868
11	Savannah State	4,243
12	Delaware State	2,948

11	Coppin State*	
14	Maryland at E. S.*	
	Average 10,930	
	Ohio Valley	
1	Jacksonville State	17,330
2	Tennessee State	14,861
3	Southeast Missouri	8,342
4	Tennessee Tech	7,121
5	Eastern Kentucky	6,220

6	Murray State	5,989
7	Eastern Illinois	5,669
8	Austin Peay	4,451
9	Morehead State	4,119
10	UT Martin	4,301
11	Belmont*	
12	SIUE*	
	Average 8,308	

*Does not offer a sanctioned NCAA Division I football program.

HBCU Football Championship Subdivision Attendance

From Conferences Football Media Guide

	HBCU Division I Institution	2010 Attendance	2010 Conference Affiliation
1	Jackson State	24,140	SWAC
2	Florida A & M	15,913	MEAC
3	South Carolina State	14,862	MEAC
4	Tennessee State	14,861	OVC
5	North Carolina A & T State	13,388	MEAC
6	Southern	12,896	SWAC
7	Norfolk State	11,879	MEAC
8	Alcorn State	11,410	SWAC
9	Alabama State	11,177	SWAC
10	Arkansas-Pine Bluff	11,030	SWAC
11	Hampton	10,551	MEAC
12	North Carolina Central	9,749	MEAC
13	Grambling State	8,719	SWAC
14	Texas Southern	8,684	SWAC
15	Alabama A & M	6,456	SWAC
16	Prairie View A & M	6,475	SWAC
17	Bethune-Cookman	6,140	MEAC
18	Morgan State	5,853	MEAC
19	Howard	4,868	MEAC
20	Savannah State	4,243	MEAC
21	Delaware State	2,948	MEAC
22	Mississippi Valley State	2,602	SWAC
23	Coppin State*		MEAC
23	Maryland-Eastern Shore*		MEAC

Average 9,947

*Does not offer a sanctioned NCAA Division I football program.

Appendix F

Academic Progress Rate (APR) 2009–2010

Southwestern

1	Alcorn State	928
2	Alabama A & M	927
3	Alabama State	925
4	Miss. Valley State	920
5	Prairie View A & M	916
6	Arkansas at P. B.	915
7	Tennessee State	912
8	Grambling State	911
9	Southern	899
10	Jackson State	879
11	Texas Southern	813

Average 903

Mid-Eastern

1	Norfolk State	947
2	N. Carolina Central	934
3	Florida A & M	925
4	S. Carolina State	918
5	Bethune-Cookman	916
5	Hampton	916
7	Howard	912
7	Tennessee State	912
9	Morgan State	905
10	Savannah State	900
11	Delaware State	898
12	N. Carolina A & T	872
13	Maryland at E. S.*	
13	Coppin State*	

Average 913

OVC

1	Austin Peay	967
2	Murray State	964
3	Eastern Kentucky	960
4	Tennessee Tech	953
5	Eastern Illinois	949
6	Southeast Missouri	937
7	UT Martin	930
8	Jacksonville State	925
9	Morehead State*	920
10	Tennessee State	912
11	Belmont*	
11	SIUE*	

Average 942

*Does not offer a sanctioned NCAA Division I football program.

HBCU FCS Academic Progress Rate (APR) 2009–2010

From NCAA.com for FYs 2009–2010

	HBCU Division I Institution	2009–2010 APR	Conference Affiliation
1	Norfolk State	947	MEAC
2	N. Carolina Central	934	MEAC
3	Alcorn State	928	SWAC
4	Alabama A & M	927	SWAC
5	Alabama State	925	SWAC
5	Florida A & M	925	MEAC
7	Miss. Valley State	920	SWAC
8	S. Carolina State	918	MEAC
9	Prairie View A & M	916	SWAC
9	Bethune-Cookman	916	MEAC
9	Hampton	916	MEAC
12	Arkansas at P. B.	915	SWAC
13	Tennessee State	912	OVC
13	Howard	912	MEAC
15	Grambling State	911	SWAC

16	Morgan State	905	MEAC
17	Savannah State	900	MEAC
18	Southern	899	SWAC
19	Delaware State	898	MEAC
20	Jackson State	879	SWAC
21	N. Carolina A & T	872	MEAC
22	Texas Southern	813	SWAC
23	Coppin State*		MEAC
23	Maryland at E. S.*		MEAC

Average 909

*Does not offer a sanctioned NCAA Division I football program.

Appendix G

Population

Southwestern

1	Texas Southern	2,257M
2	Tennessee State	605.4K
3	Southern	225.3K
4	Alabama State	202.1K
5	Alabama A & M	179.6K
3	Jackson State	175.0K
5	Arkansas at P. B.	50.3K
9	Miss. Valley State	35.3K
9	Grambling State	21.2K
10	Alcorn State	16.0K
11	Prairie View A & M	7.6K

Average 317.0K

Mid-Eastern

2	Coppin State	637.4K
2	Morgan State	637.4K
3	Tennessee State	605.4K
4	Howard	599.6K
5	N. Carolina Central	405.7K
6	N. Carolina A & T	255.0K
7	Florida A & M	172.5K
8	Hampton	144.2K
9	Norfolk State	144.2K
10	Savannah State	134.6K
11	Bethune-Cookman	63.7K
12	Delaware State	36.5K
13	Maryland at E. S.	28.3K
14	S. Carolina State	13.2K

Average 251.7K

Ohio Valley

1	Tennessee State	605.4K
1	Belmont	605.4K
3	Austin Peay	132.9K
4	Southeast Missouri	37.5K
5	Eastern Kentucky	30.0K
6	Tennessee Tech	27.6K
7	SIUE	24.0K
8	Eastern Illinois	21.0K
9	Murray State	17.7K
10	Jacksonville State	12.,5K
11	UT Martin	10.5K
12	Morehead State	5.9K

Average 126.5K

HBCU Football Championship Subdivision Population

From City-Data.com

	HBCU Division I Institution	*2010 Population*	*2010 Conference Affiliation*
1	Texas Southern	2,257M	SWAC
2	Morgan State	637.4K	MEAC
2	Coppin State	637.4K	MEAC
4	Tennessee State	605.4K	OVC
5	Howard	599.6K	MEAC
6	North Carolina Central	405.7K	MEAC
7	North Carolina A & T State	255.0K	MEAC
8	Southern	225.3K	SWAC
9	Alabama State	202.1K	SWAC
10	Alabama A & M	179.6K	SWAC
11	Jackson State	175.0K	SWAC
12	Florida A & M	172.5K	MEAC
13	Hampton	144.2K	MEAC
13	Norfolk State	144.2K	MEAC
15	Savannah State	134.6K	MEAC
16	Bethune-Cookman	63.7K	MEAC
17	Arkansas-Pine Bluff	50.3K	SWAC
18	Delaware State	36.5K	MEAC
19	Mississippi Valley State	35.3K	SWAC
20	Maryland-Eastern Shore	28.3K	MEAC
21	Grambling State	21.2K	SWAC
22	Alcorn State	16.0K	SWAC
23	South Carolina State	13.2K	MEAC
24	Prairie View A & M	7.6K	SWAC

Average 293.6K

The Leland Giants Baseball and Amusement Association: A Symbol of Race Pride Through Self-Help, 1907–1911

Michael E. Lomax

In 1907, a group of African American businessmen led by Frank Leland and Beauregard Moseley formed the Leland Giants Baseball and Amusement Association (LGBBA). The LGBBA represented the continued efforts of African American entrepreneurs advancing their own economic interests by creating a commercialized amusement. The association consisted of the Leland Giants baseball team, skating rink, dance hall, bowling alley, and a movie theater. The LGBBA was based on a profit motive, but also addressed the wants and needs of Chicago's growing black community, who were excluded from white-owned commercialized amusements. This essay analyzes the factors that led to the consolidation of the Leland Giants into a commercial amusement and recreation enterprise. Three questions will serve to guide the narrative: what were the factors that led to the Leland Giants emerging as the premier black semiprofessional club in the Midwest; how did the LGBBA maintain its symbiotic relationship with white semiprofessional teams, and attempt to exploit Chicago's growing black consumer market; and what were the factors that resulted in its collapse.

At the forefront of this commercial enterprise was the LGBBA's effort to maintain its symbiotic business relationship with white semiprofessional teams, and simultaneously tap into Chicago's growing black consumer market. In 1905, Frank Leland assembled one of black baseball's strongest clubs, resulting in him emerging as the leading black baseball entrepreneur in the Midwest.

He developed a good business relationship with the leading white semipro teams in the Windy City. By 1907, Leland sought to strengthen his team by luring some of the best black players from the East—including Andrew "Rube" Foster—and concurrently making civic ties with black Chicago's business leaders to form the LGBBA. The LGBBA exemplified the attempts by African Americans who accommodated to the widening discrimination in Chicago, and confronted discrimination by creating black institutions. The LGBBA was promoted as a symbol of race pride and racial solidarity through self-help, and the black press utilized the race rhetoric of the era commonly attributed to Booker T. Washington to sell the Association to Chicago's black community. The LGBBA sponsored recreational activities to foster group pride, and engaged in philanthropic endeavors by making donations to institutions in the black community. Throughout its brief history, however, the Leland Giants was the cornerstone of the enterprise.

By 1910, the Leland Giants Baseball and Amusement Association had made tremendous progress in sustaining a successful baseball team, and developing the various recreation enterprises that served Chicago's black community. However, this progress produced a conflict of interest among the Association's management team. In a hostile takeover, LGBBA secretary Beauregard Moseley aligned with the Giant's field manager Rube Foster to force Leland out of the organization. In response, Leland, and former Association members Robert Jackson and Alvin Garrett, formed the Chicago Giants to compete against his old club for gate receipts. By 1911, Foster left the LGBBA and formed a new team, the Chicago American Giants, resulting in Moseley forming a coalition of businessmen to compete against his former field manager and Leland's Chicago Giants. Although Moseley exhibited a sharp business wit, he did not have the acumen to run the baseball operations. He failed to recognize integral parts of the early black baseball business—maintaining both a symbiotic business relationship with white semiprofessional teams, and sustaining consistent press coverage. Leland and Foster made the Leland Giants a successful ball club, and losing these men were more than the LGBBA could endure. By the end of the 1911 season, the LGBBA collapsed at its foundation. Yet it was a testament to these African American entrepreneurs' business savvy that the LGBBA functioned effectively in its brief history.

The Rise of the Leland Giants

Since the early 1890s, William Peters and Frank Leland had been black baseball's leading entrepreneurs in the Windy City. Little is known regarding Peters' early background. He began as a first baseman with the Chicago Unions in 1887 before forming a partnership with Leland, and several other members of Chicago's black community, to transform the club into a full time operation. Leland was born in 1868 in Memphis, Tennessee. He attended college at Fisk University from 1879 to 1886, and in 1887 was on the roster of the Washington Capital City Club of the National Colored League. The Colored League in May disbanded and Leland moved to Chicago where he first became an umpire for the Unions. By the mid–1890s, Leland became the Unions' traveling manager, and along with Peters mastered the barnstorming pattern that made the team the premier semipro club in the Midwest.[1]

Black baseball entrepreneurs would schedule games with white semipros, black and Cuban teams during the season at home and throughout the US. Games were scheduled regionally with clubs that were approximately within a hundred mile radius of a team's home base of operation. When a club developed a reputation as a good gate attraction, black teams would expand their scheduling commitments to other regions of the country. Ideally, a black club would seek to expand their barnstorming tours internationally to Cuba. They would play on the Cuban island during the winter months, return to the United States, and barnstorm their way to their home base prior to the beginning of the regular season. Successful black clubs scheduled approximately 120 to 144 games per year.

The Unions toured the Midwestern states of Indiana, Michigan, Ohio, and Wisconsin during the week and returned to Chicago for Sunday games. They would schedule as many as two or three games on Sunday to maximize the Unions' revenues. Peters and Leland developed several promotional schemes like a winner-take-all series and substantial side bets to generate interest and stimulate competition among the leading white semipro clubs. By 1898, the Unions created what could best be described as a barnstorming rivalry with the Cuban X Giants. Both clubs played Sunday games and billed them as colored championship series, and simultaneously barnstorm the Midwestern states during the week. The Colored Championship series served as a way black baseball entrepreneurs marketed and promoted the black game in the late nineteenth century. To compete for the colored championship, a black club from the Midwest, for example, would have to defeat all the black clubs within their respective region of the country. They would then issue a challenge to play against the top black clubs from another region. Once a black club defeated the top black clubs from each region of the country, they could proclaim themselves as the "World's Colored Champion." Although the informal means of determining the colored champion would lead to controversy, it did generate a lot of publicity for the black game. Creating this rivalry with the Cubans served to heighten the Unions' prestige in the latter half of the 1890s.[2]

In 1901, Leland split with Peters and formed the Chicago Union Giants.

The break up was due to a number of factors. First, the Unions lost their lease on their home grounds on 37th Street and Butler Avenue, resulting in the club being relegated to a traveling team. Peters began to alienate many white semi-pro club managers with his questionable and bizarre behavior. For example, Peters canceled a three-game series with the Marquette club because he inadvertently scheduled the Cuban X Giants on the same day. He made unusual statements in the press like Marquette manager J. P. Keary would get the "best players" in the city to defeat his Unions, who had played the previous day and had traveled all night. The rationale was that the Unions would not be in the best condition to play because the players did not "get their proper rest." Breaking his contract with Keary irritated the Marquette manager and injured the Unions' credibility.[3]

In 1902, Peters and Leland were engaged in a competition for players. According to the *Chicago Tribune*, Peters signed several players who would make the Unions a formidable foe. First, he acquired pitcher and future black baseball magnate Andrew "Rube" Foster from Fort Worth, Texas. Foster was at the beginning of what would be a spectacular career. Peters also signed Andrew Campbell to serve as Foster's catcher. According to the *Tribune*, Campbell played for the Cuban Giants the previous year. To round out his acquisitions, Peters signed Dave Wyatt as the Unions' new shortstop, and pitcher Clarence Lytle. Wyatt played briefly for the Unions in 1898; after his baseball career was over he became a sportswriter for several black newspapers, most notably the Indianapolis *Freeman*. In 1901, Lytle pitched for the Chicago Union Giants.[4]

Peters apparently could not hold on to some of these new players. On June 23, the *Chicago Tribune* reported that Rube Foster pitched for the Union Giants against the Jefferson Grays, and Wyatt played centerfield. Foster struck out seven batters and hit a double in a 12–5 victory. He was equally impressive against the Columbia Giants. On July 28, the *Tribune* reported that Foster struck out ten batters and scattered five hits en route to 7–3 win. Inducing players to jump their contracts only added to the bad blood that existed between Leland and Peters. To add insult to injury, the players that made the Unions the top black club in the Midwest was now on the Union Giants' roster. Harry Buckner, William Binga, Robert Footes, and John Patterson made Leland's Union Giants an exceptional club.[5]

Both the Chicago Unions and Union Giants benefited from Chicago's semiprofessional baseball infrastructure that existed since 1882 when the Chicago Amateur Baseball Association (CABA) was formed. The CABA served essentially as a booking agent, securing leases on several playing grounds throughout the Windy City. They scheduled games for various independent clubs and weekend leagues throughout the city. Chicago had several amateur leagues sponsored by business and industry like the Commercial League, Mercantile League, and Board of Trade League. League clubs in these circuits rarely played the independents because of their caliber of play. In 1898, the CABA collapsed, and from that time on several amateur associations attempted to take their place.[6]

One such organization was the Amateur Manager's Baseball League (AMB). It was unclear when the AMB was formed. On April 7, 1903, the *Chicago InterOcean* reported that William Peters was named treasurer of the league, and George S. Cusack, former president of the CABA, its vice president. Much like the CABA, the AMB functioned as a booking agent, and there was no evidence the league was granted the authority to impose penalties or fines. There was no indication of the league sanctioning a pennant race or sponsoring a championship series at the end of the season. Moreover, there was no evidence to suggest that the Chicago Union Giants was an AMB member.[7]

In 1904, the AMB found itself competing for semipro teams and leagues with a rival organization—the Intercity Baseball Association (IBA). On April 3, 1904, the *Chicago InterOcean* reported that 164 clubs joined the organization with the aspiration of increasing its membership to 250 teams. Amateur loops like the Mercantile, Commercial, West End, and South Athletic Leagues affiliated with the IBA. According to the *InterOcean*, several teams outside the Windy City sought to join the organization. The IBA would offer a banner inscribed "Amateur Champions of the Intercity Baseball Association" to the best amateur team at the end of the season. It was unclear how the best team would be chosen, however.[8]

The IBA became involved in a dispute between Peters and Leland over the use of the name Union Giants. According to the *Tribune*, Peters supposedly "retired" from black baseball and handed control of the club over to Leland. However, this assertion appears to be somewhat inaccurate, given the fact that Peters managed the Unions in 1902 and 1903. A more plausible explanation was that Peters did not field a club in 1904 because of his inability to hold on to top level players like Rube Foster and Dave Wyatt. Nevertheless, according to the *Tribune*, Peters traveled to Springfield, Illinois, and incorporated a club under the name, Union Giants. His actions resulted in the IBA prohibiting its member clubs from scheduling games with Peters' Union Giants. In addition, Leland supposedly sought restitutions in the courts and the IBA supported him.[9]

Leland, apparently, did not follow up on his court litigation. In 1905, he renamed his club the Leland Giants, while Peters continued to call his club the Union Giants. From that time on, William Peters never regained the prominence he had in the mid- and late–1890s. He seemed content on operating as a traveling team, passing the hat to meet expenses. Peters would eventually turn the Union Giants over to his son, Frank, who would manage the club in the 1910s.

The 1905 season was the Leland Giants' finest in its young history. They played a reported 122 games and lost only ten. In one stretch they won 48 straight games. Leland constructed the same managerial configuration the Unions used in the 1890s. He served as manager of the club and William Brown was the team's traveling manager. Leland obtained a lease for a playing grounds on 79th Street and Auburn Avenue. On the field, the Giants were led by their captain and second baseman Nate Harris. Harris began his baseball career in 1900 as a third baseman for the Smoky City Giants, a club organized by Bud Fowler. In 1901, he joined the Columbia Giants, and the following year he coached a football team at Preparatory College in Grand Rapids, Michigan. In 1903 and 1904, Harris traveled east and played for the Cuban Giants and the Philadelphia Giants before returning to Chicago to manage the Lelands. Charles "Joe" Green was the Leland's catcher who began his career in 1903 with the Union Giants. Green would later become a club owner of the Chicago Giants, a charter member of the Negro National League in 1920. After playing one season with the Philadelphia Giants, and the 1904 season with the Union Giants, William Binga returned to play third base for the Lelands. Billy Holland bolstered the Giant's pitching staff. In 1896, Holland was a member of the Page Fence Giants who defeated the Cuban X Giants for the colored championship.[10]

Amid this chaotic situation, Frank Leland emerged as the leading black baseball entrepreneur in the Midwest. The lack of evidence makes it difficult to determine the Leland Giants' ability to generate revenue. The fact that they played over 120 games in 1905 indicates the potential to generate revenue was promising. The Leland's successful 1905 season caught the attention of the Philadelphia Giants and the Cuban X Giants who would both barnstorm the Midwest during the 1906 season. Leland would also benefit from the efforts of several entrepreneurs to form a semiprofessional baseball league.

Although the evidence is limited, the Leland Giants' 1906 season was a dismal one. Of the thirty-three games reported in the press, the Giants won only fourteen. A significant turnover in the Lelands' player force appears to be the reason for the team's unspectacular year. Leland lost captain Nate Harris, third baseman William Binga, and pitchers Billy Holland and Will Horn. Although the team acquired talented players like second baseman Danger Talbert, catcher Bruce Petway, and pitcher Bill Gatewood, the Lelands played poorly.

The one bright spot of the 1906 season was the Lelands' return engagement with the Cuban X Giants, billed as a colored championship series. The first game was a hard hitting affair, as the Cubans took a 10–0 lead into the sixth inning. The Lelands rebounded with two runs in the sixth, three in the seventh, and four in the ninth before bowing in defeat, 11–9. The second game was played in Dekalb, Illinois; the game was tied at three before the Lelands scored one run in the ninth inning to win, 4–3. In the final game, the Lelands took an 8–1 lead into the sixth inning before the Cubans rallied with three runs in the bottom of the sixth and three in the seventh before losing, 8–7. The Leland Giants got some satisfaction of avenging their 1904 series defeat from the team from New York.[11]

Prior to the Cuban X Giants series, the Leland Giants played two of the East's leading black clubs, the Philadelphia Giants and the Brooklyn Royal Giants. These series were costly for Leland because several of his former players ended up on the rosters of these clubs. Captain Nate Harris was a member of the Philadelphia Giants and Billy Holland played third base for the Royal Giants. By the latter half of the season, Leland lost pitcher Bill Gatewood and outfielder Sherman Barton to the Cuban X Giants. This could possibly explain why the Leland Giants performed poorly during the 1906 season.[12]

White semipros in Chicago evidently had trouble with players jumping from one team to another. On September 27, the *Chicago Tribune* reported that several club managers of the leading small parks would form an organization with the purpose of imposing salary limits. These clubs would reserve the current players on their rosters until April 1, 1907, rather than give them their release, which had been the standard practice. Each club would post $1,000 "to insure good faith," and they would not play any traveling teams the following season. The *Tribune* added that the action taken by these teams were independent of the Intercity Baseball Association which was expected to oppose the new organization.[13]

Although the evidence is limited, the new organization appeared to be the Park Owners Association (POA). The POA consisted of ten teams: Anson's Colts, Artesians, Gunthers, Lawndales, Leland Giants, Logan Squares, Normals, Rogers Park, South Chicagos, and West Ends. These clubs represented the top independents in the Windy City. The Gunthers were organized in 1899 by Charles F. Gunther, a businessman and alderman in Chicago's Second Ward. Jimmy Callahan, a former major league pitcher and manager, formed the Logan Squares. Callahan secured enough capital to build a new enclosed ballpark at the corner of Diversey and Milwaukee on the North Side. In 1907, Jake Stahl formed the South Chicagos. Like Callahan, Stahl was a former major league player and manager of the American League Washington Senators. Former major league star Adrian Constantine "Cap" Anson formed Anson's Colts. Out of baseball since 1898, Anson was pressured out of his job as the city clerk of Chicago during an employee payroll scandal. In 1907, he formed the club and after watching from the bench the first season, he returned the following year at age 57.[14]

As the 1907 season approached, Chicago's semiprofessional baseball infrastructure was significantly altered. Both the Intercity Baseball Association and the Amateur Manager's Baseball League served as official schedulers of weekend semiprofessional games. Semipro clubs who either owned or leased their own parks used either the IBA or the AMB to publicize the games they booked for a particular weekend. Teams without ballparks scheduled their games through the Traveling Managers Association who would then submit these games to either the IBA or AMB for publication. Weekend leagues like the Lake Shore League, Columbia League, or Royal League also used the IBA to announce upcoming games. Finally, the AMB created a commission to serve as an arbitrator for disputes among semipro teams or leagues.[15]

While the POA prepared for its first season, Frank Leland made efforts to strengthen his ball club. This move to rebound from the dismal 1906 season occurred simultaneously with the leading black club of the East, the Philadelphia Giants, losing several of its key players. Despite their phenomenal success on the field, several Giants' players were unhappy with the salaries they made. Their unhappiness resulted in Rube Foster leading a player exodus to the Midwest. Foster, along with Harry Moore, Pete Booker, Nate Harris, and Brooklyn Royal Giants shortstop George Wright traveled to Chicago to play for the Leland Giants.

Rube Foster was primarily responsible for the Leland Giants' rise to prominence. His ascendancy as both their player-manager and booking agent marked the start of his dominance of Midwestern black baseball. Foster was born in Calvert, Texas in 1879, the son of a presiding elder of Calvert's Methodist Church. Devoutly religious, Foster neither drank nor allowed anyone in his household to consume spirits, but he did tolerate it from others. Foster exhibited his organizational skills at a young age, operating a baseball team while in grade school. He left school in the eighth grade to pursue a career in baseball. By 1897, Foster was pitching for the Waco Yellow Jackets, a traveling team that toured Texas and the bordering states. In the spring of 1902, William Peters invited him to join the Chicago Unions, but since he sent no travel money Foster remained in Texas. At the same time, Leland invited Foster to join the Chicago Union Giants, which initiated a stormy relationship between the two men. By midsummer, Foster quit the Union Giants to join a white semipro team in Michigan. When its season ended, he headed east to play for the Cuban X Giants. From 1904 to 1906, Foster played for the Philadelphia Giants, and was instrumental in the team's phenomenal success. Before the start of the 1907 season, Foster traveled to Cuba to play for the Fe club. Upon his return to the US, he led a player's revolt that resulted in four players leaving the Philadelphia Giants.[16]

Frank Leland restructured the Leland Giants' management team after Foster accepted his offer. Leland served as general manager, but due to his failing health and his responsibilities as a newly elected Cook County Commissioner, Foster assumed control of booking Giants' games. From that time on, Foster established a business arrangement whereby gate receipts would be either divided in half with the visiting team, or he would offer a substantial guarantee to attract the top teams.

Foster's first act as field manager was to release the players of the 1906 squad despite Leland's opposition. Foster wanted his own players and he had just brought five players from the East to serve as the club's nucleus. Moreover, given the Leland's poor 1906 season, the move was understandable. Foster did re-sign Danger Talbert from the previous year to play third base. Nicknamed "Old Reliable," Talbert was considered one of the best defensive third baseman in the opening decade of the twentieth century. In addition to bringing Harry Moore, Nate Harris, Pete Booker, and George Wright from the East, Foster also lured pitchers Bill Gatewood and Walter Ball from the Cuban X Giants and the Quaker Giants respectively. Finally, Foster signed Andrew "Jap" Payne from the Brooklyn Royal Giants to play centerfield, and Haywood Rose to serve as the backup catcher. The club Foster assembled in his first year as player-manager was impressive.[17]

The 1907 season marked the beginning of Rube Foster perfecting the barnstorming schedule that would be his trademark for the next decade. On February 20, the Indianapolis *Freeman* reported the Leland Giants would embark on a spring training tour. The proposed tour was in response to white semipro clubs in Milwaukee, Chicago, and Joliet, Illinois organizing into a league, and supposedly receiving "protection" from the National and American Leagues. Apparently, this agreement was for each league to respect each other's players under contract. This proposed league led the *Freeman* to speculate that the Lelands were "about to break that strong barrier of race prejudice." Therefore, the Leland Giants would have to be in top form. More important, the proposed tour indicated for the first time a semiprofessional club that was black owned and operated had accomplished this feat.[18]

The Leland Giants would also have to be in top form to begin their first season in the Park Owners Association. The POA did not operate as a league in the traditional sense—the pursuit of a pennant and a season ending championship series. The association did not publish league standings in the press, nor maintain statistics for the players. The POA functioned essentially to formalize a scheduling system among the member clubs to maintain their rivalries and generate gate receipts. Rivalries currently existed between the Leland Giants, Logan Squares, and the Gunthers. With Jake Stahl's South Chicagos and Anson's Colts composed of top semipro and former major league players, the POA was the cream of the Windy City's semiprofessional crop.

On August 6, the Leland Giants began the first of two three-game series with Mike Donlin's All-Stars. Also known as "Turkey Mike," Donlin was a former major league player who began his career in 1899 with the National League St. Louis Cardinals. In 1901, he played with the American League Baltimore Orioles, who later became the New York Highlanders. Donlin's best season in the major leagues was in 1904 with the Cincinnati Reds, when he lead the club in hitting (.351), runs scored (110), and triples (18). He later appeared on the vaudeville stage, and would marry Mabel Hite, a well-known actress and vaudeville performer.[19]

Donlin organized a team composed of former major league, semipro, and college players. Logan Squares manager Jimmy Callahan and South Chicagos skipper Jake Stahl played left field and first base respectively. Centerfielder Jimmy Ryan began his major league career in 1885 with Cap Anson's Chicago White Stockings. After a brief stint with the Chicago club in the Players League, Ryan returned to the White Stockings and played for the team throughout the 1890s. He finished his major league career in 1903 with the Washington Senators, compiling a .309 lifetime batting average. Arthur "Doc" Hillebrand was the team's rightfielder who also pitched. From 1903 to 1905, Hillebrand coached the Princeton baseball club, amassing a 27–4 won-lost record. Former Dartmouth pitcher Percy Skillem and local semipro star hurler Gus Munch rounded out Donlin's All-Star team. Prior to the series on July 11, Donlin's All-Stars demolished the Leland Giants, 11–1, at Logan Square Park.[20]

The series began on August 6 at Charles Comiskey's American League Park. A side bet of $1,500 was riding on the first three-game series between the two clubs which turned out to be the Rube Foster show. In the first game, Foster engaged Percy Skillem in a pitcher's duel. The game was tied at two when the Lelands scored one run in the top of the seventh inning to win, 3–2. The All-Stars rebounded in the second game with a 6–2 victory behind the excellent pitching of Gus Munch. In the final game, six thousand fans watched Foster scatter five hits and shutout the All-Stars, 1–0. The Giants won the series and the side bet.[21]

The second three-game series began on August 27 at Comiskey's American League Park. Five thousand fans watched Rube Foster in top form, as he held the All-Stars to five hits in a 3–1 victory. Once again, Gus Munch held the Giants in check in the second game, holding the Lelands to two hits and striking out seven batters in a 3–1 win. Controversy surrounded the final game. According to the *Chicago Tribune*, Jap Payne disputed a call that resulted in the centerfielder punching the umpire. Payne was ejected from the game but he refused to leave the field, resulting in a ten-minute delay. When play resumed, the Lelands coasted to an 8–4 victory. Rube Foster had won four of the six games between the two clubs![22]

The black press applauded the Leland Giants' spectacular performance against Donlin's All-Stars. Understandably, the spotlight shined bright on Rube Foster. The *Broad Ax* proclaimed Foster as "one of the greatest [baseball] players in this country..." Under the pseudonym "Frederick North Shorey," a black sportswriter for the *Freeman* stated: "As for Rube Foster, well, if it were in the power of the colored people to honor politically or to raise him to the station to which they believe he is entitled, Booker T. Washington would have to be content with second place."[23]

The Leland Giants' series victories were also touted as a symbol of race pride through self-help. In the race rhetoric that epitomized the era of Booker T. Washington, black sportswriter and former Union Giants player Dave Wyatt stated the series showed how baseball was a "common leveler" in regards to race relations. "There was no color line drawn anywhere," Wyatt added, "our white brethren outnumbered [blacks] by a few hundred, and all bumped elbows in the grand stand, the box seats, and bleachers." Interracial spectatorship had always been the norm at black baseball games, however. The early black baseball entrepreneurs promoted their teams to cater to a white clientele. Economic factors made this strategy a necessity and not a luxury. Wyatt's comments did reveal the impact of early black migration on northern cities in the early twentieth century. Migration would not expand the black consumer market significantly until the war years. Yet in Chicago migration had expanded the Windy City's black consumer market to the point that baseball magnates could no longer ignore it. Chicago's black population grew continuously between 1900 (30,150) and 1920 (109,455). Thus Wyatt promoting the supposed racial harmony among blacks and whites could have possibly served to advance the economic interests of the black baseball entrepreneurs. In any event, the series victories over Donlin's All-Stars marked the beginning of the Leland Giants' dominance in the Midwest, and heighten Rube Foster's status to almost legendary dimensions.[24]

Wyatt's editorial illustrated the willingness of African American businessmen to work within the parameters of a biracial institutional structure to advance their economic interests. His rhetoric was consistent with the self-help economic initiatives commonly attributed to Booker T. Washington and W. E. B. DuBois. Black businessmen were not to isolate themselves from the larger society selling only to blacks, nor were black fans expected to patronize black baseball games only because they were black. African Americans were to advance themselves by free competition on the open market. Much like Washington, Leland and Foster's ultimate goal was not to build a black counterculture. Even in the nineteenth century, Frederick Douglass recognized that "A nation within a nation is an anomaly." The purpose of self-help and racial solidarity was to encourage black unity and self-assertion on a political level, while encouraging cultural and economic assimilation. This would, theoretically, result in the integration of blacks into mainstream American society. In the case for black baseball, this meant white Organized Baseball.[25]

In a short period of time, Rube Foster transformed the Leland Giants into one of the top black baseball teams in the United States. He displayed an ability to attract the top black players to the Windy City to accomplish this task. The Leland's spring training tour would be the first of many barnstorming tours to create a demand for the Giants in several locales. As a member of the POA, the Lelands were able to maintain their symbiotic business relationship with white semipros, and continue to operate within the parameters of a biracial institutional structure. While Foster ran the baseball operations, Frank Leland made civic ties with black Chicago's business leaders, and at the same time laid the groundwork to organize a black professional league.

The Leland Giants Baseball and Amusement Association

Frank Leland's alliance with Chicago's new black leadership resulted in an effort by these men to gain control of the Windy City's growing African American market. The expansion of northern communities—a direct result of migration—facilitated a new market that black baseball entrepreneurs attempted to exploit. These African American entrepreneurs, or "Race men," typified the business leaders who de-emphasized the fight for integration, and dealt with discrimination by creating black institutions. They left their imprint on black community development not by writing or speaking, but in business ventures, institutions, and organizational politics. They contributed to the development of a separate institutional life for Chicago's blacks by establishing black businesses, building a black political machine, and participating in the organization of black social agencies. The extent to which they were involved in the ideological battles of their era, they lean towards Booker T. Washington's philosophy of self-help. But, as historian Allan Spear points out, the Tuskegee ideology did not determine their action. It merely validated what they were already doing.[26]

The widening discrimination in Chicago and other northern cities resulted in the emergence of the physical ghetto. Chicago's African Americans, for example, were excluded from most white owned recreation and leisure venues. Many theaters seated blacks in the balcony, and bartenders frequently refused to serve black patrons. Illinois state law prohibited racial discrimination in public accommodations and municipal services. However, it was difficult to obtain a conviction under it. In 1905, a jury refused to award damages to a black politician who was denied service at a bar. In 1910, a jury decided in favor of a theater that had turned down an African American who was trying to buy tickets for the main floor. The plight of Chicago's African Americans forced them to make decisions confined by their exclusion from a host of social and economic institutions. Increased separation, however, did open new opportunities for entrepreneurship.[27]

It was within this context that Robert R. Jackson and Beauregard F. Moseley were prominent in consolidating Leland's ball club into a commercial amusement and recreation enterprise. Robert Jackson was born on September 1, 1869, in Malta, Illinois. He left school at age twelve and began working in various jobs that included a department store, dental laboratory, and an errand boy in a retail store. In 1888, Jackson became a clerk in the U.S. postal service, and maintained one of the highest efficiency ratings during his fourteen years on the job. Jackson was a member of several fraternal orders like the Pythias Lodge, Prince Hall Lodge, and the Grand Lodge. He also established his own printing and publishing business.[28]

Beauregard Moseley was born in Georgia, and move to Chicago in the early 1890s. Upon his arrival, Moseley established the *Chicago Republic* newspaper. He left the newspaper business in 1896 to pursue a career in law. Moseley was admitted to the bar that same year, and within six years he had built a lucrative practice worth approximately $8,000 a year. According to the *Broad Ax*, Moseley represented some of Chicago's foremost businessmen, and he was chief counsel of the Olivet Baptist Church, Chicago's largest African American congregation. When asked what attributed to his success, Moseley replied: "close attention to business and the happy faculty of knowing no one except my client in a lawsuit."[29]

Leland, Moseley, and Jackson combined to form the Leland Giants Baseball and Amusement Association (LGBBA). Incorporated in 1907, the LGBBA was more than just a baseball team, it was also a summer resort, skating rink, bowling alley, and restaurant, and the venture represented the black response to white discrimination in amusement venues and public accommodations. On October 19, the Indianapolis *Freeman* reported the LGBBA had increased their capital to $100,000 and secured a lease on the Columbia Dance Hall, an old building located on Fifty-third and State Street. Stock options were offered to the public at $10 a share to undoubtedly raise funds to remodel the old building. The *Broad Ax* reported the LGBBA would open a roller-skating rink under the management of Robert Jackson, Frank Leland, and Rube Foster. They also planned to open a "Dance Pavilion," a restaurant—known as the Grill Room—and a bowling alley called the Bowling Emporium. A contest was proposed to determine a name for the amusement hall. The first three persons to send in the most appropriate name would receive the following prizes: first prize, five dollars in gold; second prize, a pair of roller skates; and third prize, a season pass to Auburn Park and the skating rink. The amusement hall was named the Chateau De La Plaisance—the House of Pleasure.[30]

The Leland Giants Baseball and Amusement Association was formed around the business strategy of economic cooperation. Cooperative enterprises had its roots in the black community in the late eighteenth century. Early black entrepreneurs recognized that if they were to attain any success in developing black business to an appreciable level in the black community, it would come only through economic cooperation. It was evident to them that no concrete help in obtaining capital and credit could be expected from white America. Therefore, African American entrepreneurs would pool their resources together in an effort to create a successful business enterprise.[31]

On November 2, the Chateau De La Plaisance opened it doors to the public. From the outset, the Chateau was promoted to cater to Chicago's black elite. The *Broad Ax* listed several members of black Chicago's professional and business class like County Commissioner Edward H. Wright, Dr. Bert Anderson, and *Broad Ax* editor Julius Taylor who attended the opening day festivities. More important, the Chateau De La Plaisance served as an expression of racial uplift, an ideology that became the mantra of the African American elite in the early twentieth century. The amusement hall was a race enterprise created by blacks that sought to fulfill the wants and needs of a black consumer market. As Taylor explained: "Every enterprise which is not intended to degrade the Negro conducted by Afro-Americans, tends to raise every worthy member of the race up in the business world." Taylor concluded that as long as the Chateau was managed in a first class manner, "it should receive the patronage of the decent amusement loving public."[32]

Concurrently, Frank Leland made his only attempt to organize a black professional league. On November 9, 1907, the *Freeman* reported that a movement was put forth to form the National Colored League of Professional Ball Clubs. The proposed league was a clear exposition of the cooperative business philosophy. Leland along with *Freeman* editor Elwood C. Knox and Indianapolis ABCs club owner Randolph "Ran" Butler were the prime movers behind the enterprise.[33]

The primary focus in early league formation was raising enough capital for the venture and scheduling the first organizational meeting. League organizers encouraged Race men and "white capitalists" to form a stock company as a means of consolidation. The circuit was to be an eight-team league with prospective cities to include: Cincinnati, Cleveland, Louisville, Pittsburgh, Chicago, Indianapolis, Kansas City, Toledo, Detroit, Milwaukee, Memphis, Nashville, and Columbus, Ohio. The cities would be chosen according "to what showing they [would] make after a trial contest." It was unclear what constituted this trial contest, however. On December 18, preliminary plans were made to form the National Colored League. According to the *Freeman*, a "large body of representatives" met in Elwood Knox's office and elected the following officers: Frank Leland, President; Edward Lancaster of the Louisville Giants, Vice President; Edward S. Gaillard of the Indianapolis ABCs, corresponding secretary; Cary B. Lewis of the Louisville Giants, secretary; William Roberts of the ABCs, treasurer; and Charles Marshall, a *Freeman* sportswriter, organizer. A committee was selected to draft a constitution for the next meeting; however, the *Freeman* did not indicate who would serve on it.[34]

From December 28, 1907 to January 25, 1908, the league directors established guidelines for league entry. For a club to be considered for admission it had to (1) be represented by a stock company fully organized and incorporated under state law; (2) secure a bond (the amount was not specified) determined by the league's board of directors; (3) pay $50 into the league treasury to cover the expenses for league operations; and (4) secure a suitable ballpark and have full support of the press. A small percentage of the gate receipts from each city would be placed in the treasury, and the season would run from May to September.[35]

Despite these organizers' efforts, the league died stillborn. From the beginning, there was no clear direction on how the league would be placed on a sound economic footing. There was no indication that these organizers would pattern their circuit after the white major leagues. Throughout their organizational phase, the league directors asked for suggestions "from every person interested under the sun" on how the league should function. This lack of direction could possibly explain why prospective entrepreneurs were slow to commit to the enterprise. According to the *Freeman*, only Chicago and Indianapolis made commitments to the proposed league.[36]

There were also no indications that there were enough clubs to compete with the Leland Giants in the Midwest. From 1902 to 1907, press reports indicated that of the cities under consideration for league entry, only two—the Indianapolis ABCs and the Louisville Giants—made barnstorming tours to the Windy City. A third club, the Topeka Giants, played the Lelands in 1906, but they were not under consideration. Moreover, according to the *Freeman*, there were several black baseball magnates who were against league formation, fearing it would damage their business. Evidently several of the club managers felt that operating in a league format could lead to losing lucrative games with black and white semipro teams within their respective regions of the country. It could also lead to making extended barnstorming tours outside their respective regions. If, for example, clubs from Pittsburgh and Nashville were members of the league, it would increase the travel and overhead expenses of the Midwestern clubs to journey there. It would also create an unworkable format since most of the prospective cities were in the Midwest.[37]

A final factor dealt with Frank Leland's poor health. On February 15, 1908, the *Freeman* reported that Leland had suffered from heart failure. He did not attend the league meeting in Indianapolis on February 16, but he did send a letter stating that he would abide by any steps the league might propose. Leland seemingly spread himself too thin, fulfilling his duties as Cook County Commissioner, managing a skating rink, serving as general manager of the Giants, and organizing a black professional league. It was evident the league lost what little direction it had when Leland's health turned for the worst.[38]

The resurgence of the Leland Giants in Chicago was a combination of Frank Leland's efforts to strengthen his ball club, and simultaneously exploit Chicago's growing black consumer market. He accomplished this by hiring Rube Foster to run the baseball operations, and establishing an alliance with the Windy City's new black leadership. The Giants' successful 1907 season became the cornerstone of maintaining their symbiotic business relationship with white semipros, and starting a recreation enterprise to cater to Chicago's growing black consumer market. The baseball team, skating rink, restaurant, and bowling alley were promoted by the black press as a clear expression of racial uplift through self-help. Leland's endeavor to expand his influence in the Midwest through the creation of a black professional league ended in failure, however. The failed league, nonetheless, did not diminish the success the LGBBA achieved in a short period of time.

At the Peak of Its Prestige

Despite the failure to launch a black professional league, the Leland Giants continued their spectacular success on the diamond. The Giants became members of the newly created Chicago City League, and finished their excellent 1908 season with a six-game series with the American Association Minneapolis Millers. At the same time, LGBBA organizers expanded the Chateau De La Plaisance to include a "Moving Picture Show," a dance hall called the Terpsichorean Parlors, and a restaurant. The LGBBA sponsored several promotional events including a potato race, a "One Mile Handicap" race, and a skating contest in which contestants had to skate the entire rink backwards in ten minutes to win a prize. They made plans to open a summer amusement park called the "Summer Garden and Peruvian Gallery" that included a restaurant and an "Out Door Music Emporium." The LGBBA revised its management structure by electing the following members to hold office: Frank Leland, President; Robert Jackson, Vice President; Beauregard Moseley, Secretary and Treasurer; and Rube Foster, Manager and Captain of the team. Whereas the LGBBA expanded its recreation enterprise to include a movie theater, dance hall, and summer garden, the Leland Giants baseball team continued to be the foundation on which the venture was built.[39]

The Lelands began the 1908 season as a member of the newly created Chicago City League. Although the evidence is limited, a war over players occurred during the City League's organizational phase with the Park Owners Association. Forming the new league was further complicated when the stockholders of one of its member clubs, the West Ends, were split into two factions. Some of its stockholders favored joining the City League, while the others preferred remaining in the POA. Tensions between the leagues heightened when two POA clubs—the Logan Squares and the South Chicagos—defected to the new league. In any event, the Chicago City League began the season with eight teams: Leland Giants, Logan Squares, West Ends, South Chicagos, Riverviews, Marquettes, Athletics, and Spaldings.[40]

The Chicago City League began the season with high aspirations; however, it would collapsed by the middle of the season. The City League operated as a weekend league; this enabled the Lelands to continue their barnstorming pattern of playing weekday games throughout the Midwest, and returning to Chicago for Sunday games. Unlike the POA, the Chicago City League published league standings, but there were no indications that they would sponsor a season ending championship series. By the end of June, the Leland Giants had won all of their league games. Trouble surfaced within the league, however, when the Riverviews failed to play the Marquettes in a scheduled league game. According to the *Chicago InterOcean*, the gates at the ballpark were locked when the Marquettes arrived. The Riverviews were dropped from the circuit, and the City League operated with seven clubs. On August 1, 1908, the *Indianapolis Freeman* reported the Chicago City League disbanded.[41]

By the end of September, the Leland Giants concluded their regular season with a six-game series with the American Association Minneapolis Millers. The American Association was a double A minor league in Organized Baseball. After losing the first game of the series, the Lelands rebounded in the second game by scoring three runs in the eighth and two in the ninth on the way to a 6–4 victory. The Millers took a 3–1 lead into the sixth inning in game three, before the Giants erupted with four runs in the seventh inning and one in the ninth to win, 6–3. In game four, Giants pitcher Emmett Bowman gave up only five hits and shut out the Millers, 4–0. Unfortunately, the final games were not reported in the press. Nevertheless, the Giants' performance against the Millers was impressive.[42]

The Leland Giants excellent showing in the Chicago City League and their season ending series with the Minneapolis Millers served to heighten the club's prestige within the Windy City's black community. On October 15, several members of Chicago's black middle class sponsored a banquet on behalf of the Lelands. Nothing illustrated the rhetoric of racial uplift better than the praise bestowed on the Leland Giants on the pages of the *Broad Ax*:

> This team of Colored ball players have by their abilities won a place in the forefront of America's greatest past time baseball and have taken the whole race with them[;] nothing has contributed to the lessening of race prejudices in this community more than this gallant manly scientific gentlemanly aggregation of ball players, who have wrung from the throats of our enemies more praise than was ever showered upon us and have thereby served as a deterrent to the avalanche of hate that oftentimes comes our way.

Such praise illustrated the significance the Windy City's black middle class citizenry placed upon the Leland Giants' spectacular success on the diamond, in a sport that most Chicagoans respected and glorified.[43]

The Leland Giants continued their phenomenal success throughout the 1909 baseball season. On May 15, 1909, the Indianapolis *Freeman* reported the Leland Giants had traveled 4,465 miles playing black and white teams in Memphis, Birmingham, Fort Worth, Austin, San Antonio, Prairie View State, and Houston. Foster supposedly received a hero's welcome upon his return to his home state of Texas. According to the *Freeman*, he received a welcome in Fort Worth that would "have done honor to the President of the United States." In Houston, the Lelands played to the "largest crowd ever at a baseball game" in that city, as the Giants swept the Texas club in three games. A large contingent from Foster's hometown in Calvert attended one of the games there. The Leland Giants traveled by Pullman car to illustrate their reputation as an elite black independent club. It also served as a response to the widening discrimination African Americans confronted in the early twentieth century. The Pullman car not only provided a means of transportation, it was also the team's living quarters. Black teams did not have to deal with white hotel managers and their prejudice when they traveled on the road, particularly in the South.[44]

The Windy City's semipro baseball season was notable for the Chicago City League completing its first regular season. Six teams formed the revised league that included the Logan Squares, Gunthers, Anson's Colts, West Ends, Milwaukee White Sox, and the Leland Giants. By July 4, the Logan Squares, Leland Giants, and the Gunthers were locked into a close pennant race. On September 4, the Lelands clinched the City League pennant with a 5–3 win over the Logan Squares. They finished the season with 31 wins and 9 losses. The Giants' pennant winning season led a *Chicago Tribune* sportswriter to state that "while undoubtedly it is galling to many persons to see a colored nine take honors from five white teams, the Leland Giants are entitled to a place in the league by their drawing powers." The writer went on to describe how the Lelands had such talent that "at least five of them would be in the major leagues if white."[45]

The Leland Giants culminated their 1909 season with a three-game series with the National League Chicago Cubs. The Chicago Cubs were the best team in the National League. They won the NL pennant three years in a row, finishing second in 1909. They won a National League record 116 games in 1906 only to lose to the Chicago White Sox in the World Series. In 1908, the Cubs defeated the Detroit Tigers for the World Series championship. From 1906 to 1909, the Chicago Cubs won 426 games. The Cubs possessed the legendary double play combination of Joe Tinker, Johnny Evers, and Frank Chance, and boasted an outstanding pitching staff that included Mordecai "Three Finger" Brown, Orvie Overall, and Ed Reulbach.

The Leland Giants and Chicago Cubs played three tightly contested games. In game one, 2,344 fans watched the Cubs defeat the Lelands, 4–1, behind the excellent pitching of Three Finger Brown. The game featured a courageous effort by Giants' centerfielder Joe Green, who tried to score from first base on a broken leg. He was thrown out at home plate and collapsed to the ground under excruciating pain. In the second game, the Lelands took a 5–2 lead into the ninth inning before the Cubs scored four runs and won 6–5. The game ended on a controversial play when Foster, trying to slow down the Cubs' momentum, left the mound to consult with pitcher Pat Dougherty to determine whether the latter should relieve the former. This obvious stalling tactic irritated the Cubs and the home plate umpire. When Dougherty approached the mound, the umpire refused to let him enter the game. Amid this confusion, Cubs' rightfielder Frank "Wildfire" Schulte stole home and was called safe by the umpire to the dismay of Foster and the Lelands. The final game was a pitcher's duel between Three Finger Brown and Pat Dougherty. The game was called in the seventh inning because of darkness, with the Cubs ahead, 1–0.[46]

Despite losing the series to the Chicago Cubs, the Leland Giants Baseball and Amusement Association had made tremendous progress. They expanded the Chateau De La Plaisance and made plans to open a summer resort. The Leland Giants' barnstorming tour of the South, and winning the Chicago City League pennant heightened the club's prestige. When it appeared the LGBBA was ready for bigger and better things, however, the enterprise crumbled at its foundation.

Decline and Fall of the LGBBA

Progress made by the Leland Giants Baseball and Amusement Association produced a conflict of interest among the team's management. Although Frank Leland was elected president of the LGBBA, its secretary and past president, Beauregard Moseley, was the driving force behind the enterprise. Acknowledging his diminished role within the organization, Leland attempted to wrestle control of the Giants away from Rube Foster. However, the Association's investors felt it was in the corporation's best interest to retain Foster as manager. As a result, in a hostile takeover Moseley and Foster united to force Leland out. Foster's alliance with Moseley made the split inevitable.

In response to being forced out, Leland formed the Chicago Leland Giants in partnership with former Association members, Robert Jackson and Alvin H. Garrett. His goal was to make his Giants a top touring team to compete against the Leland Giants, and simultaneously contend for the Chicago City League championship. To accomplish this, Leland raided his old club for players. He signed Nate Harris, Harry Moore, George Wright, Chappie Johnson, and Walter Ball. Leland also signed black players from several other clubs, like Bob Marshall, Felix Wallace, and James Taylor from the St. Paul Gophers, and Joe "Cyclone" Williams from the San Antonio Broncos. Williams would become one of the premier pitchers in black baseball in the early twentieth century.[47]

Despite the breakup of its management team, the LGBBA made plans to move into its new ballpark located on 69th and Halsted streets. The new park possessed a seating capacity of 5,000, with 400 box seats and 1,600 bleacher seats. The park was easily accessible via the trolley lines, or the South Side L. Since the LGBBA owned the enclosed park, it served as a symbol of racial advancement through self-help. The *Broad Ax* hailed the new grounds as "the prettiest and most comfortable park in the city." More important, the new park enabled the LGBBA to maintain its symbiotic business relationship with white semiprofessional clubs, and at the same time attempt to corner the black consumer market on the South Side.[48]

The LGBBA continued to make inroads into the Windy City's black community to tap into its growing black consumer market. To invoke community pride and team spirit, the LGBBA created the "Leland Giants Rooters Club," and elected former Chicago Unions co-owner Al Donigan president. The Association contributed annually to Provident Hospital, founded by Daniel Hale Williams, the country's best known African American physician and one of the outstanding surgeons of the day. According to Allan Spear, Provident Hospital was the first and most ambitious African American civic undertaking in Chicago. In 1891, Williams formed a coalition of black community leaders and several of his white medical colleagues with the intent of organizing the first interracial hospital in the United States. Unlike any other hospital in the city, Provident received blacks on an equal basis and provided opportunities for black doctors and nurses. Provident received its major financial support in its early years from wealthy white Chicagoans, like Philip

Armour and Florence Pullman. The hospital also solicited and received contributions from the black community. Exhibition baseball games represented one way these financial residuals were raised. On August 26, 1910, for example, the Leland Giants played a benefit game for the hospital at Comiskey Park. Whereas this gesture was based on a profit motive, it also served as a means for the LGBBA to make their imprint upon black community development.[49]

Raising funds for Provident Hospital illustrated the use of public relations as an integral part of the LGBBA's strategy to maximize revenues. Sport management scholar Bill Sutton argues that public relations play an essential role in the marketing mix because of its long-term focus and direction and due to its limited organizational control and reliance on public perception and interpretation. Thus a public relations campaign is critical in positioning the product in the consumer's mind through an image-building/enhancement program. There is, nevertheless, no guarantee a consumer will accept the positioning of the product a marketer may present. The LGBBA used PR to sway public opinion in their favor to promote the Leland Giants baseball club, and serve the needs and wants of black Chicagoans through their various recreation enterprises.[50]

Public relations was used to wage another more subtle kind of battle. Through the creation of the LGBBA, Chicago's African Americans attempted to prove to the white world (and no doubt to their doubting brothers and sisters) that they were worthy of all the things they fought for. As Vincent Harding points out, blacks sought to "bind up the wounds of their own community, to improve the quality of its life, to serve its needy, to demonstrate their capacity for self-determination, self-improvement, and freedom." More important, they built the black community from within, preparing it for the continuing stages of its struggle towards a new humanity.[51]

On April 23, 1910, the *Broad Ax* reported the Leland Giants Baseball and Amusement Association took Frank Leland to court to prohibit him from the using the name Leland Giants. The court ruled in favor of the LGBBA, and stated, "no person or persons acting for Frank Leland shall in any way use the name Leland Giants, as it rightfully belongs to the Leland Giants Baseball and Amusement Association." The other persons were in obvious reference to Leland's business partners, Robert Jackson and Alvin Garrett. From that time on, the Chicago Leland Giants became the Chicago Giants.[52]

To further complicate matters, internal dissension emerged within the ranks of the Chicago City League. The Gunthers withdrew from the league over a dispute with the other semipro club owners. The City League was also involved in the lawsuit between the Leland Giants and Chicago Giants. The City League sided with the Chicago Giants and they replaced the Leland Giants in the circuit. The City League began the season with the Chicago

Giants, Rogers Park, Logan Squares, Spauldings, West Ends, and Donohue's Red Sox. The Gunthers and Lelands rejoined the Park Owners Association. The revised POA consisted of twenty-two clubs that included notable teams like the Cubans, Auburn Park, Mutuals, and the Normals. Eight clubs in the POA possessed their own parks while the remaining teams functioned as traveling teams. Despite the disparity, the Chicago *Defender* claimed the clubs with enclosed grounds made the POA "twice as strong as the City League."[53]

With the lawsuit settled between Leland and his former Association members, and the Leland Giants rejoining the POA, Beauregard Moseley had higher ambitions in mind for the LGBBA. Despite Leland's raiding his old club for players, the Leland Giants remained a competitive club. Foster secured the services of top players like Pete Hill, John Henry Lloyd, Pete Booker, Bruce Petway, and Andrew "Jap" Payne. Frank Wickware, Pat Dougherty, and Foster made the Giants' pitching staff awesome. In October 1910, after winning twenty straight games in the East and West, the Leland Giants made their first trip to Cuba. Along with the American League Detroit Tigers, the Lelands played the top Cuban clubs including the Havanas and the Alemendares. While the Giants won the majority of their games, they lost a tough series to the Alemendares.[54]

At the same time, Moseley advocated the need for blacks to organize their own professional league. He recognized that the raiding of player rosters was a destructive force that had to be eliminated. The proliferation of black teams from the South and Midwest, however, made it feasible, in Moseley's view, to form a black professional league. The proposed league was another exposition of the doctrine of self-help. In his statement of purpose, Moseley indicated that blacks "are already forced out of the game from a national standpoint" and find it increasingly difficult to play white semiprofessional teams locally. This "presages the day when there will be [no opportunities for black baseball players], except the Negro comes to his own rescue by organizing and patronizing the game successfully, which would of itself force recognition from white minor leagues to play us and share in the receipts." Moseley added, "let those who would serve the Race assist it in holding its back up ... organizing an effort to secure ... the best club of ball players possible."[55]

The prospective owners first met on December 30, 1910. Moseley was elected temporary chairman and Felix H. Payne of Kansas City temporary secretary. Eight cities were represented: Chicago, New Orleans, Mobile, Louisville, St. Louis, Columbus (Ohio), Kansas City (Missouri), and Kansas City (Kansas). Unlike Leland, Moseley had devised a twenty-point plan, explaining how the league should operate. Using the cooperative business philosophy, Moseley suggested that eight race men in each city pool their resources and form a stock company. The league projected an operating capital of $2,500 with each club paying roughly $300. Half the league's umpires would be black and paid five dollars a game. A reserve list would be developed and players who jumped their contracts would be banned from the league. Finally, an effort would be made to limit the league to one franchise per city.[56]

The league generated a lot of enthusiasm the following year and rumors persisted of other cities joining the loop, but it still died stillborn. Like the previous organizational effort, there was an unwillingness of investors to come forth. At its inaugural meeting only Chicago, New Orleans, and Kansas City (Kansas) were represented by investors, with the remaining five being represented by fans and no evidence to indicate that possible financiers existed in these cities. Second, although the evidence is limited, there was no semiprofessional baseball infrastructure in the aforementioned cities comparable to Chicago's. In addition to the City League and the POA, Chicago also had several other leagues and associations, like the Suburban League and the Inter-City League. Several independent clubs who did not belong to any league operated in the Windy City. This infrastructure was pivotal to black baseball teams functioning competitively and economically. Finally, Chicago's population (2,185,283) was exponentially larger than any city in the proposed league. The next closet city was St. Louis with a population of 687,029. This market imbalance could possibly explain why no comparable semiprofessional baseball infrastructure existed in these cities prior to World War I. Attempting to maintain a symbiotic business relationship with white semipros, and simultaneously to exploit the black consumer market also proved problematic. For example, Kansas City, Kansas' total population in 1910 was 82,331. Its black population was 9,286, hardly comparable to Chicago's African American population of 44,103. The unwillingness of black baseball entrepreneurs to venture too far outside their respective territorial regions was understandable.[57]

In 1911, Foster split with Moseley and formed the Chicago American Giants. It was not clear what led Foster to make the break with the LGBBA. Baseball was taking too much time from Beauregard Moseley's law practice. In a conference with Foster, Moseley supposedly said to the Giants' field manager, "You know baseball, I know law[;] you take the team and do whatever you see fit, and I will go back to my law practice." However, this assertion is somewhat problematic. As will be shown, Moseley would form a coalition of businessmen and professionals to run the LGBBA and compete against Foster's American Giants and Leland's Chicago Giants. A more plausible explanation would be the internal division within the LGBBA's leadership, and attempts to form two black professional leagues ending in failure led to Foster leaving the organization. The men that made the Leland Giants a successful baseball team, Frank Leland and Rube Foster, were no longer within the ranks of the

LGBBA leadership. Despite losing these baseball men, Moseley made efforts to keep this shaky organization together.[58]

Following the break with Foster, Moseley organized a booster coalition from the black community. The Leland Giant Booster Club (LGBC) was an aggregate of black middle class businessmen and professionals. For example, the LGBC president, Jesse Bolling, was a restaurant owner who donated his Burlington Buffet as the club's official headquarters. Thomas W. Allen, the club's secretary, was a city inspector. Other members of the coalition included the editors of Chicago's two leading black newspapers, Robert Abbott of the Chicago *Defender* and Julius Taylor of the *Broad Ax*.[59]

The formation of the LGBC exemplified the cooperative business philosophy and race rhetoric prevalent among the new black leadership that emerged in the early twentieth century. The venture served to promote one another's businesses. Their race rhetoric advocated a philosophy that combined self-help and racial solidarity with an economic ideology that emphasized the acquisition of middle class virtues and African American support of black businesses. They insisted on the necessity of African Americans "buying black" if black businesses were to develop in the face of declining white support for barbers, artisans, and to a lesser degree of black independent teams. If African Americans acquired wealth and middle class respectability, the race would earn acceptance into the mainstream of American society and prejudice would be eliminated. This compilation of ideologies functioned as an accommodation to the system of segregation and discrimination. This viewpoint also operated to inculcate group pride and self-respect.[60]

The LGBC was responsible for organizing several activities surrounding the Leland Giants' local season that had become ritualized in the prewar years. At the opening of each season, for example, the Giants had an opening day festivity known as "Flag Raising Day." Flag Raising Day was similar to the opening day activities that occurred at major league baseball games. As Harold Seymour explained: "there was always the march of the two teams across the field to the flagpole in centerfield, where the opposing captains hoisted the flag, then the return march to the dugouts, followed by the throwing out of the first ball by some dignitary." Another event the LGBC staged consisted of a touring car, known as the Red Devil, parading through the streets to the ballpark. These activities served to stimulate group pride among Chicago's black citizenry and increase spectatorship at Leland Giants games.[61]

The LGBC brought more attention to the members of the booster coalition than to the baseball club, however. Throughout the pages of the *Broad Ax* and the *Defender*, a particular focus was on who attended the game among Chicago's black elite. The *Broad Ax*, for example, stated: "Race present were

Dr. A. W. Williams, R. T. Motts of the Peking [restaurant], Thomas W. Allen, City Inspector [and] Jesse Bolling." The *Broad Ax* also pointed out that the "ladies were also present and looked as cute as ever," and encouraged its readership to attend the game the following Sunday. The *Defender* repeatedly stated the LGBC were the "fun makers of the baseball world..." The race rhetoric prevalent in the early twentieth century was used to promote the enterprise. The *Defender* indicated that Professor William Emanuel and Artist Johnson "were among the race building characters at Sunday's game who believed in patronizing [a] race enterprise." Press coverage on Leland Giants games was sporadic in both papers.[62]

Press coverage in the white dailies—most notably the *Chicago Tribune*— also began to decline. Nineteen games were reported in the press and the Lelands won eight of them. It appeared the Giants were still a competitive team on the field. Veteran players Nate Harris—who also served as team captain—Danger Talbert, Harry Moore, and Sherman Barton formed a solid nucleus for the club. Frank Wickware was the Leland's leading hurler until he jumped to the Chicago American Giants late in the season. Although the evidence is limited, Moseley failed to recognize the importance of maintaining a symbiotic business relationship with white semiprofessional teams. Of the games reported in the press, only three were with Chicago's leading white semipro clubs (two with the Gunthers and one with the West Ends). The Lelands played the Chicago Giants only twice during the season, losing both games, and there was no evidence of games with Rube Foster's Chicago American Giants. More important, consistent press coverage was the lifeblood of baseball promotions in the early twentieth century. Maintaining rivalries throughout the year was one way to ensure consistent press coverage. The lack of games with the leading black and white clubs in the Windy City made this difficult for Moseley's Leland Giants to achieve.[63]

Moseley had other obstacles confronting him and the LGBBA began to unravel. He was engaged in several business endeavors at once besides organizing a baseball league and booking games for the Lelands, and he probably did not delegate authority to booster club members or have an adequate management team to supervise his many operations. When the LGBBA began operations in 1907, the majority of its facilities were located outside the black belt, where increased white hostility made venturing unpleasant for Chicago's African Americans. In 1910, when the Leland Giants moved into their new ballpark on 69th and Halstead, Moseley had just renovated it no doubt at large expense. The obstacles were more than the LGBBA could withstand. By 1911, the skating rink closed for good and the Leland Giants were relegated to a local club for the remainder of the decade.

Conclusion

From 1907 to 1911, the Leland Giants Baseball and Amusement Association represented the continued efforts of African American entrepreneurs to create a commercial enterprise to advance their own economic interests. The Leland Giants' success enabled them to maintain a symbiotic business relationship with Chicago's white semiprofessional teams. Simultaneously, the Windy City's leading black businessmen created a recreation enterprise to cater to the wants and needs of a growing black consumer market. Merging these two commercial enterprises was both practical and ideological. On the one hand, given the expansion of Chicago's African American community, the Giants' association with the LGBBA served as a form of market promotion to attract black patronage to their games. On the other hand, the Chateau de la Plaisance benefited from the Leland's success on the field and it served to heighten the LGBBA's prestige.

The ideology of racial uplift was used as a source of market promotion for the LGBBA. The black press became an ally for the LGBBA organizers to win the favor of Chicago's black middle class. To accomplish this, the Association had to project an image that would reflect favorably on African Americans. The LGBBA tried to reach this objective by maintaining a competitive baseball team, sponsoring recreational activities to foster group pride, and engaging in philanthropic activities by making donations to institutions in the black community. In many ways, the LGBBA's efforts represented the modern day public relations campaigns used by professional sport organizations. What made the LGBBA's public relations endeavors unique was the need to emphasize race respectability and racial uplift through self-help.

Whereas the LGBBA was an innovative enterprise, it faced several obstacles that led to its demise. Although Chicago's black population grew tremendously in the early twentieth century—and attempting to tap into this growing market was a wise move on Leland and Moseley's part—it still for the most part was an economically depressed market. In other words, the black community exclusively did not have the disposable income necessary to support a commercialized amusement. In addition, when the LGBBA began operations in 1907, the majority of its facilities were located outside the black belt, where increased white hostility made venturing outside the black community unpleasant for Chicago's African Americans. This, undoubtedly, had a negative impact on black patronage of the LGBBA's recreation venues.

The mere fact that a segregated enterprise was created in the Windy City illustrated a lack of opportunity for African Americans. The rise of the LGBBA was but one reflection of a growing pattern of segregation and discrimination in early twentieth century Chicago. As the black community grew and opportunities for interracial conflict increased, a pattern of discrimination and seg-regation became more pervasive. Blacks were completely excluded from white-owned commercial amusements like skating rinks, dance halls, and movie the-aters. This was a fundamental reason why the LGBBA was created in the first place.

Finally, internal division among the LGBBA organizers led to its demise. Dissension among the leadership led to the expulsion of Frank Leland, and Rube Foster leaving the association. Losing these two men placed the LGBBA in jeopardy. The men who made the Leland Giants a success on the diamond were no longer with the association. Whereas Beauregard Moseley displayed a sharp business wit, he did not exhibit the acumen to run the baseball oper-ations. Moreover, it was Leland and Foster and not Moseley who developed the symbiotic business relationship with white semiprofessional teams, and maintained consistent press coverage—integral parts of the early black baseball business. Once the baseball team began to decline, the collapse of the LGBBA was inevitable. In the midst of the obstacles—both internal and external—these African Americans entrepreneurs confronted, it was a testament to these men's business acumen that the LGBBA functioned effectively in its brief his-tory.

Notes

1. Research regarding the Leland Giants Baseball and Amusement Association has been minimal. My article on baseball in black Chicago provided some insights on the LGBBA. See "Black Entrepreneurship in the National Pastime: The Rise of Semiprofessional Baseball in Black Chicago, 1890–1915," *Journal of Sport History* 25(Spring 1998): 43–64. The author would like to thank Larry Hogan for providing me with a photocopy of a baseball guide book published by the Chicago Giants in 1910. *Frank Leland's Chicago Giants Baseball Club* (n.p.) in Cooperstown, NY: Baseball Hall of Fame and Museum. (Chicago) *Defender*, November 21, 1914.

2. For a definitive discussion of both the Colored Championship and black baseball's busi-ness practices in the late nineteenth century, see Michael E. Lomax, *Black Baseball Entrepreneurs, 1860–1901: Operating by Any Means Necessary* (Syracuse, NY: Syracuse University Press, 2003).

3. Ibid.

4. *Chicago Tribune*, May 4, 1902. James A. Riley, *The Biographical Encyclopedia of the Negro Baseball Leagues* (New York: Carroll and Graf, 1994), 501.

5. *Chicago Tribune*, June 23, July 28, 1902.

6. For a secondary account on Chicago's semiprofessional baseball infrastructure, see Ray Schmidt, "The Golden Age of Chicago Baseball," *Chicago History* 29(Winter): 38–59; Lomax, *Black Baseball Entrepreneurs*.

7. *Chicago InterOcean*, April 7, 1903.

8. *Chicago Inter Ocean*, April 3, 1904; *Chicago Tribune*, May 17, 1904.

9. *Chicago Tribune*, June 7, 1904.

10. *Frank Leland's Chicago Giants Baseball*.

11. *Chicago Tribune*, June 4, 8, 11, 1906.

12. For games against the Brooklyn Royal Giants, see *Chicago Tribune*, May 7, 1906. For games against the Philadelphia Giants, see *Chicago Tribune*, May 21, 1906.

13. *Chicago Tribune*, September 27, 1906.

14. *Chicago Tribune*, June 13, 1904, May 5, 1907. Schmidt, "The Golden Age of Chicago Baseball," 49–50.

15. *Chicago Tribune*, April 14, 1907.

16. *Defender*, February 20, 1915. Secondary accounts on Rube Foster's career include: Robert Charles Cottrell, *The Best Pitcher in Baseball: The Life of Rube Foster, Negro League Giant* (New York: New York University Press, 2001); John Holway, *Blackball Stars: Negro League Pioneers* (New York: Avalon, 1988); Charles E. Whitehead, *A Man And His Diamonds* (New York: Vantage, 1980); Robert Peterson, *Only the Ball Was White* (New York: Oxford University Press, 1970).

17. Talbert's background in Riley, *The Biographical Encyclopedia*, 758–59. *Frank Leland's Chicago Giants Baseball Club.*

18. (Indianapolis) *Freeman*, February 20, 1907.

19. Donlin's statistics in David S. Neft, Richard M. Cohen, and Michael L. Neft, *The Sports Encyclopedia: Baseball*, 24th ed. (New York: St. Martin's Griffin, 2004). For Donlin's vaudeville career and marriage to Mabel Hite, see Harold Seymour, *Baseball: The Golden Age* (New York: Oxford University Press 1970), 118–19.

20. Neft et al., *The Sports Encyclopedia. Chicago Tribune*, July 11, 1907.

21. *Chicago Tribune,* August 7, 8, 9, 1907.

22. *Chicago Tribune*, August 28, 29, 31, 1907. *Chicago InterOcean*, August 28, 1907. *Freeman*, September 7, 1907.

23. *Broad Ax,* August 17, 1907. *Freeman*, September 7, 1907.

24. *Freeman*, September 21, 1907. For a secondary account regarding black baseball entrepreneurs catering their clubs to white consumer market in the late nineteenth century, see Lomax, *Black Baseball Entrepreneurs.* Chicago's black population in *Fifteenth Census of the United States: 1930* (Washington, D.C.: Government Printing Office, 1933), 67.

25. For an interpretation of Booker T. Washington and W. E. B. DuBois's economic philosophy, see Vishnu V. Oaks, *The Negro's Adventure In General Business* (Yellow Springs, OH: Antioch, 1949), 9–25; Wilson Jeremiah Moses, *The Golden Age of Black Nationalism 1850–1925* (Hamden, CT: Archon, 1978), 83–102.

26. Allan H. Spear, *Black Chicago: The Making of a Negro Ghetto 1890–1920* (Chicago, IL: University of Chicago Press, 1967), 71–72.

27. Ibid., 41–42.

28. Harold F. Gosnell, *Negro Politicians: The Rise of Negro Politics in Chicago* (Chicago. IL: University of Chicago Press, 1935), 67–68; *Broad Ax*, March 30, 1901, December 27, 1902, December 29, 1906.

29. Ibid.

30. *Freeman*, October 19, 1907. *Broad Ax*, October 12, November 2, 1907.

31. Lomax, *Black Baseball Entrepreneurs.*

32. *Broad Ax*, November 2, 1907.

33. *Freeman*, November 9, 1907.

34. *Freeman*, November 9, 16, 23, December 7, 28, 1907.

35. *Freeman*, December 28, 1907, January 11, 25, 1908.

36. *Freeman*, December 28, 1907, February 15, 1908.

37. *Chicago Tribune*, August 13, 1906, July 28, 29, 1907.

38. *Freeman*, February 15, 1908.

39. *Broad Ax*, October 12, 1907, June 13, December 5, 1908, January 30, March 13, May 1, May 15, 1909.

40. *Chicago InterOcean*, April 4, 18, 19, 26, May 3, 1908.

41. For league games and published league standings, see *Chicago InterOcean*, May 4, 11, 18, 25, June 1, 22, 1908. *Chicago Tribune*, May 4, 11, 18, 25, June 1, 29, 1908. For the Riverviews failing to play the Marquettes, see *Chicago InterOcean*, June 15, 1908. *Indianapolis Freeman*, August 1, 1908.

42. *Chicago Tribune*, September 22, 23, 24, 25, 1908.

43. *Broad Ax*, October 10, 1908.

44. *Freeman*, May 15, 1909.

45. Schmidt, "Golden Age of Chicago Baseball," 56. *Chicago Tribune*, May 2, July 6, July 19, September 5, October 4, 1909.

46. *Chicago Tribune*, October 18, 19, 22, 23, 1909.

47. *Defender*, January 22, July 23, 1910.

48. *Broad Ax*, March 12, 1910.

49. *Broad Ax*, May 7, 1910. For their yearly contributions to Provident Hospital, see *Defender*, May 14, 1910. For the benefit for the hospital, see *Broad Ax*, August 21, 1910; *Defender*, August 27, 1910. Spear, *Black Chicago*, 97–99.

50. William A. Sutton, "Marketing Principles Applied to Sport Management," in Lisa P. Masterlexis, Carol A. Barr, and Mary A. Hums, eds., *Principles and Practice of Sport Management* (Gaithersburg, MD, 1998), 51–52. See also Bernard J. Mullin, Stephen Hardy, and William A. Sutton, *Sport Marketing,* 2d ed. (Champaign, 2000).

51. Vincent Harding, *The Other American Revolution* (Los Angeles, CA: Center for Afro-American Studies, 1980), 30.

52. *Broad Ax*, April 23, 1910.

53. Schmidt, "Golden Age of Chicago Baseball," 57. *Defender*, February 5, 1910; *Chicago Tribune*, February 8, 1910.

54. *Broad Ax*, October 8, 1910; *Defender*, October 8, 1910; *New York Age,* December 8, 1910.

55. *Broad Ax*, January 21, 1911.

56. *Defender*, December 31, 1910; *Broad Ax*, December 31, 1910, January 21, 1911.

57. *Fifteenth Census Of The United States*, 67, 69, 71.

58. Moseley, quoted in "Rube Foster—The Master of Baseball," in the Rube Foster file, Ashland Collection, Baseball Hall of Fame, Cooperstown, New York.

59. For the activities and membership of the booster coalition, see any issue in either the Chicago *Defender* or the *Broad Ax* from May to June 1911.

60. J. H. Harmon, Arnett G. Lindsey and Carter G. Woodson, *The Negro as a Business Man* (College Park, MD: McGrath, 1929), 6–29; Abram L. Harris, *The Negro as Capitalist: A Study of Banking and Business Among American Negroes* (Philadelphia: American Academy of Political and Social Science, 1936), 49–54; Seth Scheiner, *Negro Mecca: A History of the Negro in New York City, 1865–1920* (New York: New York University Press, 1965), 70–81; August Meier and Elliot Rudwick, *From Plantation to Ghetto*, 3d ed., (New York: Hill and Wang, 1976), 212–18.

61. *Defender*, May 20, 27, 1911. Seymour, *Baseball: The Golden Age*, 63.

62. *Broad Ax*, June 3, 1911; *Defender*, May 13, June 3, 10, 1911.

63. *Chicago Tribune*, May 7, 8, June 5, 11, 12, 20, 26, July 10, 16, 17, 23, August 1, 20, 28, 31, September 3, 4, 10, 1911.

Bibliography

Manuscript Collections

Frank Leland's Chicago Giants Baseball Club. Baseball Hall of Fame and Museum, Cooperstown, New York.

Rube Foster File. Ashland Collection, Baseball Hall of Fame and Museum, Cooperstown, New York.

Articles

Lomax, Michael E. "Black Entrepreneurship in the National Pastime: The Rise of Semiprofessional Baseball in Black Chicago, 1890–1915." *Journal of Sport History* 25(Spring 1998): 43–64.

Schmidt, Ray. "The Golden Age of Chicago Baseball." *Chicago History* 29(Winter 2000): 38–59.

Sutton, William A. "Marketing Principles Applied to Sport Management," in Lisa P. Masterlexis, Carol A. Barr, and Mary A. Hums, eds. *Principles and Practice of Sport Management*. Gaithersburg, MD: Aspen, 1998.

Books

Cottrell, Robert Charles. *The Best Pitcher in Baseball: The Life of Rube Foster, Negro League Giant*. New York: New York University Press, 2001.

Fifteenth Census of the United States: 1930. Washington, D.C.: Government Printing Office, 1933.

Gosnell, Harold F. *Negro Politicians: The Rise of Negro Politics in Chicago*. Chicago: University of Chicago Press, 1935.

Harding, Vincent. *The Other American Revolution*. Los Angeles: Center for Afro-American Studies, 1980.

Harmon, J. H., Arnett G. Lindsey and Cater G. Woodson. *The Negro as Business Man*. College Park, MD: McGrath, 1929.

Harris, Abram L. *The Negro as Capitalist: A Study of Banking And Business Among American Negroes*. Philadelphia: The American Academy of Political and Social Science, 1936.

Holway, John. *Blackball Stars: Negro League Pioneers*. New York: Avalon, 1988.

Lomax, Michael E. *Black Baseball Entrepreneurs 1860–1901: Operating by any Means Necessary*. Syracuse, NY: Syracuse University Press, 2003.

Meier, August, and Elliott Rudwick. *From Plantation to Ghetto*, 3d ed. New York: Hill and Wang, 1976.

Moses, Wilson Jeremiah. *The Golden Age of Black Nationalism 1850–1925*. Hamden, CT: Archon, 1978.

Mullin, Bernard J., Stephen Hardy, and William A. Sutton. *Sport Marketing*, 2d ed. Champaign, IL: Human Kinetics, 2000.

Neft, David S., Richard M. Cohen, and Michael L. Neft. *The Sports Encyclopedia: Baseball*, 24th ed. New York: St. Martin's Griffin, 2004.

Oaks, Vishnu V. *The Negro's Adventure in General Business*. Yellow Springs: Antioch, 1949.

Peterson, Robert. *Only the Ball Was White*. New York: Oxford University Press, 1970.

Riley James A. *The Biographical Encyclopedia of the Negro Baseball Leagues*. New York: Carroll and Graf, 1994.

Scheiner, Seth M. *Negro Mecca: A History of the Negro in New York City, 1865–1920*. New York: New York University Press, 1965.

Seymour, Harold. *Baseball: The Golden Age*. New York: Oxford University Press, 1970.

Spear, Alan H. *Black Chicago: The Making of a Negro Ghetto*. Chicago: University of Chicago Press, 1967.

Whitehead, Charles E. *A Man and His Diamonds*. New York: Vantage, 1980.

Newspapers

Broad Ax, 1907–11.
(Chicago) *Defender*, 1905–14.
Chicago InterOcean, 1901–07.
Chicago Tribune, 1901–1911.
(Indianapolis) *Freeman*, 1907–11.

A Fantasy in the Garden, a Fantasy America Wants to Believe: Jeremy Lin, the NBA and Race Culture[1]

David J. Leonard

Shortly after the start of the 2012–2013 NBA season, and amid his on-the-court struggles, Marc Lamont Hill took to Huffington Post to serve as the ultimate "buzz kill" for the NBA's million-dollar story. "In all honesty, I'm sad that Linsanity turned out to be a sham. Like many people, I wanted to buy into the idea of a Cinderella hoops story. I wanted to believe that everyone—the coaches, the scouts, the executives, and even the cold hard statistics—were wrong. I wanted Jeremy Lin to be next big thing," noted Hill in "The Linsanity Sham: Why Jeremy Lin Really Can't Play." "But the truth is the truth. And in this case, the truth is that Jeremy Lin can't play. At least not at the highest levels. And no amount of 'Linsanity' can change that." To say that his article received a lot of responses would be an understatement. Hill's assessment of Lin's basketball skills and his argument that Linsanity resulted from a perfect storm that was more about social issues, cultural debates, and media structures than his jump shot and turnover-to-assist ration promoted both outrage and condemnation. From Twitter to the comment section, respondents criticized Hill, defending Lin and Linsanity with gusto and verve. While not interested in litigating the various arguments here, the reaction points to the investment in the Lin narrative, in Linsanity. His ascendance meant something not simply because it propelled the New York Knicks back into the playoffs, but because he represented or embodied a larger narrative; he signified larger debates and sources of tension.

Like many people, I was captivated by the Jeremy Lin story. His success on the court and the excitement generated by the emergence of the New York Knicks was amazing to watch unfold. While clearly a compelling basketball drama, the allure, spectacle and societal fascination had little to do with basketball. Part model minority discourse, part immigrant narrative, part American Dream, part anti-black racism, part American exceptionalism, and part Cinderella story, Linsanity offered a compelling story that allowed entry into a myriad of discursive fields. Whether talking race, culture, nation, or ethnicity, Lin offered a vehicle to rehash and recycle stereotypes galore.

Amid the endless articles about Lin, many reflected on the ways in which race and stereotypes about Asians limited the ability of scouts to recognize Lin's talent. Stereotypes not only about the lack of athletic ability of Asians as well as the stereotypes about African American success within basketball impacted the difficult roads traveled by Lin. "Lin was almost certainly underestimated, or misevaluated, because as an Asian American he does not look the way scouts and general managers expect an NBA player to look," wrote Touré. "If he'd walked into the gym and wowed everyone right away he would've stood out, but when he didn't, it confirmed the societal script that does not expect Asian Americans to be pro-level basketball players. That's the prejudice Lin had to fight through." This sentiment was commonplace throughout the public discussion, revealing a willingness to acknowledge that race does matter, that racism exists as an obstacle, and that stereotypes impact the ways that people interact on a daily basis. Acknowledging stereotypes and racism, the media discourse also deployed them with ubiquity, playing up model minority stereotype (Abelman & Lie 1997 Leonard 2003), those surrounding black athletes (Leonard 2006a; Leonard 2006b; Leonard 2004; Lapchick 2002) and countless other racial signifiers. Although couching these discussions in basketball terms, and denying the larger implications by framing around sports, the short-lived sanity provided a window into the arena of race, that which sits at the center of American sporting cultures and those on the outside. This chapter, thus, takes up the task of examining the racial meaning and implications of Linsanity, arguing that at its core are a tension between discourses of colorblindness/racial transcendence and the many narratives that elucidate the significance of race within contemporary America. Linsanity wasn't simply a frenzied moment but a window into the larger meaning of race within American society.

A Model Minority

Since Jeremy Lin emerged on the national scene during his playing days at Harvard, the media discourse has focused on his experiences as an immigrant; his Otherness within the NBA was imagined in relationship to his immigrant narrative. Lin's parents emigrated from Taiwan to the U.S. in the 1970s. According to an ESPN article, his Dad dreamed of coming to the U.S. to earn a Ph.D. and "watch the NBA."

In December 1966, *U.S. News and World Report* ("Success Story of One Minority in U.S.") promulgated the model minority stereotype, highlighting how this discourse relies upon the binary between Asians and African Americans. "At a time when it is being proposed that hundreds of billions be spent on uplifting Negroes and other minorities, the nation's 300,000 Chinese Americans are moving ahead on their own with no help from anyone else" (quoted in Perez, 2005, p. 226). Similarly, Joe Feagin and Rosalind Chou locate the emergence of model minority narratives as a counter to the radicalism, protest movements and identity politics that came about during the mid–1960s:

> Largely in response to African American and Mexican American protests against discrimination, white scholars, political leaders, and journalists developed the model minority myth in order to allege that all Americans of color could achieve the American dream—and not by protesting discrimination in the stores and streets as African Americans and Mexican Americans were doing, but by working as "hard and quietly" as Japanese and Chinese Americans supposedly did [2008, p. 13].

Commenting on the meaning and context of a model minority stereotype, Hiram Perez, in an essay about Tiger Woods, depicts the rhetoric surrounding a "model minority" discourse as simply homogenizing the Asian American by deploying stereotypes and celebrating Asian American accomplishments, but "disciplin[ing] the unruly black bodies threatening national stability during the post-civil rights era" (Perez, 2005, p. 226). Thus, the model minority discourse operates through the juxtaposition of homogenized identities, cultures, and experiences of Asian Americans with African Americans. According to Anita Mannur, "in recent years Asian Americans have been praised (in contrast to blacks and Latinos) for having 'assimilated" so well" (Mannur, 2005, p. 86). In other words, Asian Americans as a "model minority because they are hard workers they do not make a fuss, and are not loud" (Mannur, 2005, p. 86). Similarly Feagin and Chou conclude that, "Asian Americans serve as pawns in the racially oppressive system maintained at the top by whites" (2008, p. 17). Working in a "middling status," (Feagin and Chou, 2008, p. 17) or as "racial bourgeoisie" (Matsuda qtd. in Feagin and Chou, 2008, p. 17), Asians sit between whiteness and racial otherness within dominant racial discourse. "Whites' use of Asian Americans as a measuring stick for other Americans of color is highly divisive, for it pits groups of color against each other, as well as isolates Asian Americans from white Americans" (Feagin and Chou, 2008, pp. 17–18).

The Linsanity narrative was one right from the playbook of the Model minority meets American Exceptionalism meets American Dream meets Boot-straps narrative: Gie-Ming (his dad) dedicated himself to fostering their academic success (they would only get to play basketball after finishing their homework), along of their basketball prowess. Having studied the great players of the NBA, he passed this knowledge on to his children. According to Dana O'Neil, Lin's story is one of the "immigrant dream":

> All those years Gie-Ming Lin spent rewinding his tapes so he could teach himself how to play a game he never even saw until he was an adult? All those hours spent in the local Y with his boys, schooling them in fundamentals over and over, building muscle memory without even knowing what the term meant? That silly dream, the one in which his children would fall in love with basketball as much as he had?

The Bleacher Report's Jay Wierenga furthers emphasizes the role of Lin's family, celebrating the story as an example of fathers and sons and the beauty of sports within the immigrant experience. O'Neil describes it this way:

> Lin's father wasn't trying to make Jeremy his meal ticket. He was just bonding with his kids and playing the game he loves.
> He also was helping to integrate his American-born children into his new home.
> For immigrants, it is easy to retreat from your new land. It is a foreign place full of new and sometimes scary situations.
> Therefore, seeking shelter amongst those that came from the same culture can be tempting.
> But Lin's father realized early on that he wanted to integrate his children into his new country.

In a narrative historically unavailable to black athletes, given the media's emphasis on single mothers, poverty, and absentee fathers, the efforts to link Lin's success to his father is striking. This aspect of the model minority myth pits blacks against Asians. In focusing on values, on the emphasis on education, the Lin narrative reinforces an ideology of bootstrapism and the Protestant work ethic. That is, in celebrating Lin's success, one that because of racial ideologies requires explanation outside of the realm of hard work and athleticism, reinscribes both stereotypes about blackness and Asianness. From *Forbes Magazine*, which published a piece highlighting the lessons of hard work from Lin (Jackson 2012), to Sarah Palin, who described Lin as "an all–American story," the power and appeal in the offered Linsanity tale rests with its efforts to invoke meritocracy, colorblindness, and the Protestant work ethic. This line of discussion is clearly evident in Marc Ambinder's profile of Lin for *GQ:*

> Look again at Lin's own story: he faced discrimination as a kid playing on the courts of (even) Palo Alto, and slurs while at Harvard, but because of his

superior natural abilities, rose up through the most meritocratic institution in society. There is no affirmative action based on race or last name. If you can't play, you are not going to get on the court. That up-by-the-sneaker-laces narrative is a vital part of Lin's appeal—and the Republican deal.

Aside from the fact that Lin's basketball career points to the importance of affirmative action and the illusion of a meritocratic system, Ambinder encapsulates the popular appeal of the media-induced Lin fantasy that celebrates the American Dream and links its possibility to values, hard work, and determination. The "pull-yourself-up-by-the-sneaker laces" not only reifies a model minority myth but also blames those who have not found success on and off the court for their own nightmare.

Central to the efforts to explain Lin's success, a process that renders him as exceptional, has a focus on his parents. In the *New York Daily News*, Jeff Yang argues that, "the secret to Lin's success seems to have been a combination of high expectations and unconditional support—a kind of tiger-panda hybrid, if you will." Emphasizing his Dad's role as basketball tutor and coach extraordinaire who exposed Lin to the "signature moves from the likes of Dr. J, Moses Malone, Kareem Abdul-Jabbar, and, most of all, Michael Jordan," the media consistently depicts his father in the tradition of (white) American fathers who nurtured and encouraged athletic performance. His mom, on the other hand, is depicted as a "tiger mom" of sorts, as someone who balanced out the father by maintaining an emphasis on education. Requiring that Lin and his brothers complete their homework prior to basketball, the narrative describes Lin's athletic prowess as being the result of the perfect marriage of "Asian values" and "American" cultural norms.

While the media often links black athletic success to "God's gifts" or to physical "prowess," the efforts to chronicle Lin's rise as reflecting his cultural background reinforces dominant conceptions of both blackness and Asianness. Jenn Floyd Engel is evidence of this aspect of the narrative:

> Scared of offending, we instead act like there are no cultural differences. We ignore the truth in an attempt to be a color-blind society. This is offensive to me, mainly because it seems so patently wrong. His being Asian-American is exactly why I am not surprised by Lin's success in the NBA. And I am predicting more and more kids like Lin, raised to emphasize academics, to dominate athletics as already has happened in mathematics and engineering, law schools and medical schools, and almost every inch of an ever-tightening global job market.

Celebrating Chinese parenting and the values that emanate from this approach (the author does acknowledge the existence of black father Tiger Moms or single mom Tiger Moms), Floyd juxtaposes Lin's success to the dominant frame about sports and its relationship to black youth:

He is not starring in Linsanity simply because of God-given talent, or because his AAU coach told him how special he was, or because he called home and his dad told him he was getting run over by racist coaches in college or the NBA. Linsanity is a product of him learning the skills, work habits, and inner confidence that fueled him.

Similarly, Sam Borden and Keith Bradsher, with "Tight-Knit Family Shares Lin's Achievement," locate Lin's success on and off the court within the context of his family. "If Gie-Ming planted the basketball seed in Jeremy and his brothers (through frequent trips to the local Y.M.C.A. and repeated viewings of old N.B.A. games he taped on his VCR), then Shirley, now 55, is the one who cultivated it," they write in the *New York Times*. "As the Lins settled in Palo Alto, she quickly became a sort of hybrid 'tiger mom,' fiercely prodding her children to work tirelessly, but also advocating for them in whatever way she could." Providing the perfect balance, "Shirley embraced the duality of her role. She was strict with Jeremy about academics, calling his coaches to warn them that a poor grade meant Jeremy would not be going to practice without improvement."

The underdog, bootstraps, and stick-to-itness narrative ultimately depicts Lin as "overlooked." According to Howard Beck, the recent ascendance reflects a "continuing a long pattern of low expectations and surprising results." Noting his success in high school and at Harvard and the lack of attention from coaches, scouts and teams, Beck further argues: "At draft time, in June 2010, Lin was again overlooked. N.B.A. teams.... They were the kind of concerns scouts have every year about dozens of prospects, from all sorts of programs and all sorts of backgrounds. Yet there was no escaping Lin's unusual pedigree and the subtle sense that he did not fit a profile." His success is attributed to his intelligence, dedication, and his fundamentals. It is attributed to his hard work. Reflecting stereotypes, stories focusing on talent and athleticism are rare.

Part of the narrative of Lin exceptionalism has focused on how he has overcome racism and bigotry during his meteoric rise. His Harvard-to-riches story, his struggle to garner acceptance and an opportunity, reflects anti–Asian prejudice that led teams and fellow competitors to underestimate him. According to Pablo Tore, "the Kansases and Kentuckys, however, didn't exactly knock down.... Only four schools responded. Out of the Pac-10, Lin recalls, UCLA 'wasn't interested,' Stanford was 'fake interested,' and during a visit to Cal a staffer 'called me 'Ron.'" Lin specifically has cited racial stereotypes as an impediment to his recruitment: "I think in America, basketball is predominantly for, you know, black and white people. And so, I think it is just, yeah, I mean, I guess people aren't used to it and people don't expect it," he noted during an NPR interview. "In general Asian-Americans are seen or looked down upon on the basketball court."

Throughout his career, he has experienced prejudice from fans, who have yelled "wonton soup," "sweet and sour pork," "to play the orchestra," "beef and broccoli" and "sweet and sour chicken" in his direction. He has been called a "Chinese import" while others have demanded that he "Go back to China." The narrative of Lin exceptionalism, one that cites racism and prejudice, as yet another obstacle to overcome is emblematic of the power of the constructed narrative surrounding Lin.

The Jeremy Lin story is evident in the ways in which media narratives are used to convey racial and national meaning, the ways in which he has been ideologically marked, and the ways in which they have been used by the NBA and sport media to attract Asian and Asian American fans throughout the Diaspora. "In the era of globalization, the Phantom of race is articulated not through the body of the NBA's black (African-American) majority, but in the event of the minority athlete, who is not white but Asian," writes Grant Farred in his thoughtful discussion of Yao Ming, race, and the globalization of the NBA. "'Asian-ness' has often located Asian Americans outside of African-American blackness, which is to say, "above" African Americans in the racial economy.

Evident by ubiquitous media representations of Lin as "the very incarceration of humility" (Farred 2006) and a widely circulated narrative that consistently imagines him as "representative of the Asian immigrant who buys into the Puritan concept of hard work, self-sacrifice, and the honor in labor in order to secure a piece of the American Dream" (Farred 2006), his cultural power emanates from the perceived gulf between him and his black peers. According to Dave Zirin, "Athletes in the eyes of many fans are too spoiled, too loud, too 'hip-hop, too tattooed, too cornrowed—all of which translates to players are 'too black'" (Zirin 2004). In a post–Palace Brawl NBA, as noted by Norm Denzin in *Michael Jordan Inc.*, the black body functions as "a site of spectacle," as "a potential measure of evil, and menace," necessitating containment and control (Denzin, 2001, p. 7). Lin provides that needed containment. The media hype and the widespread celebration of Lin pivots on his Asianness and its relationship the meaning of blackness on and off the court.

In a world that imagines basketball as the purview of African Americans, the emergence of Jeremy Lin has sent many commentators to speculate and theorize about Lin's success. Focusing on religion, Eastern philosophy, his educational background, his intelligence, his parents, and his heritage, the dominant narrative has defined Lin's success through the accepted model minority myth.

In other words, while celebrating Lin's success as a challenge to dominant stereotypes regarding Asian Americans, the media has consistently invoked stereotypical representations of Asianness to explain his athletic success, as if his hard work, athleticism, and talents are not sufficient enough explanations.

Intentional or not, the story of Jeremy Lin is both an effort to chronicle his own success in comforting and accepted terms, and in doing so offer a commentary on blackness. "Discussions about the NBA are always unique because the NBA is one of the few spaces in American society where blackness, and specifically black masculinity, is always at the center of the conversation, even when it's not. Power is often defined by that which is assumed, as opposed to that which is stated," noted Todd Boyd in an email to me. "Because black masculinity is the norm in the NBA, it goes without saying. Concurrently any conversation about race in the NBA inevitably refers back to this norm. In other words, people seldom describe someone as a 'black basketball player' because the race of the player is assumed in this construction. So any current discussion about Jeremy Lin is taking place within the context of a league and its history where the dominant players have long been black men. Lin is 'the other' as it were, but here the standard is black, not white, as would normally be the case in most other environments." Not only does the constructed Lin narrative exist in opposition to the normative blackness of the NBA, but also the specific rhetorical utterances often play upon the dominant assumptions of today's black ballers.

The model minority myth, one that imagines Lin's family as easily integrating into society, as using dominant institutions like sport as part of this process, and in reducing success to cultural values, is ultimately not a celebration of Lin but of the American Dream, a story bound up in assumptions about race, class, and culture. Linsanity is not a story of Jeremy Lin or even basketball but a story that gains power from the deployment of ideologies of colorblindness and racial progress. Lin, like Tiger Woods when he first enters the national consciousness, symbolizes the possibilities and the purported exceptionalism of the United States. Interestingly, Woods, like Lin, was celebrated as "America's son" (Cole and Andrews 2001) not only because of his success in golf but because of the values and ethnics instilled in him by his parents. "Woods celebrity depends on a eugenical fantasy that stages a disciplining of the black male body through an infusion of Asian blood and an imagined Confucian upbringing," writes Hiram Perez. "Just as model minority rhetoric functions to discipline the unruly black bodies threatening national stability during the post-civil rights area, the infusion of Asian blood together with his imagined Confucian upbringing corrals and tames Tiger's otherwise brute physicality. Some variation of his father trained the body and his mother trained the mind is a recurring motif for sports commentators diagnosing Wood's success at golf." While Lin operates through a different point of reference, the dominant narrative continues to represent his success as the result of his father's ability to teach him about basketball, knowledge he learned from watching the NBA's black superstars, and his mother's emphasis on learning, school, and values. Whereas Asianness was depicted as the necessary disciplinarity to transform Tiger into a phenom, Lin, as product of family and culture, is imagined as antidote to the NBA's ills—its blackness.

Lin's place in the media sporting culture, and society at large, cannot be understood outside of its relationship to blackness. Whereas Lin has the "right" family culture, and values, blackness is often defined as being deficient in those arenas. "Constructions of deviant sexuality emerge as a primary location for the production of these race and class subjectivities," writes Micki Mcelya in *Our Monica Ourselves: The Clinton Affair and the National Interest.* "Policy debates and public perceptions on welfare and impoverished Americans have focused relentlessly on the black urban poor—blaming nonnormative family structures, sexual promiscuity, and aid-induced laziness as the root cause of poverty and mobilizing of welfare queens, teen mothers, and sexually predatory young men to sustain the dismantling of the welfare state." His middle-class professional "rags" to riches story, his story of immigrant parents teaching how to ball with humility, to breakdown opponents and equations, and to drop 3s and As is used to index his success all while marking the ways that players like Allen Iverson or LeBron James as something less than because they lack the requisite values and histories to be worthy of celebration, especially in those non-sporting spaces.

Pride and Prejudice: Jeremy Lin and the Persistence of Racial Stereotypes

The success and national visibility afforded to Jeremy Lin has both inspired Asian Americans and has been driven by the adoration and pride he elicits from some within the community. Whether on Twitter, Facebook, or in the stadiums, it is clear that Lin is not simply a national phenomenon but a treasure for the Asian American community.

According to Jamilah King, "regardless of how the rest of the season goes for Lin, and the Knicks, his moment in the spotlight is an important time to reflect on how the country views its Asian American athletes." Whereas past Asian athletes, whether Yao Ming or Ichiro captured the global Asian Diaspora's imagination, Lin is the most widely recognized Asian American athlete on the American team sport scene. Timothy Dalrymple highlights the appeal of Lin to Asian American males:

> He particularly has a following amongst Asian-Americans. And some Asian-American young men, long stereotyped as timid and unathletic, nerdy or effeminate or socially immature—have fought back tears (which may not help with the stereotype, but is understandable under the circumstances) as they

watched Jeremy Lin score 25 points, 7 assists and 5 rebounds for the New York Knicks.

In "Asian Americans energized in seeing Knicks' Jeremy Lin play," J. Michael Falgoust elucidates his cultural power within the Asian American community in quoting the thoughts of several different people:

> "I don't care about the outcome. I just want to see him in action. He's as good of an Asian American athlete as there is"—Rose Nguyen
> "I'm so proud. I don't care if he is Chinese or Korean. I had to see him ... my boyfriend has been talking about him so much"—Christine Lee
> "I'm really excited. He breaks so many stereotypes. And my friends are just as excited. If you go to my Facebook feed, it's all Jeremy Lin. I like that he plays smart. But then he's from Harvard. So that is expected. He is also humble. He reminds me a lot of Derrick Rose, who's always crediting teammates"—Andrew Pipathsouk

Andrew Leonard similarly argues that Lin's popularity amongst Asian Americans is emblematic of the power of social media and also the pride that athletic success garners for Asian Americans, otherwise seen as "nerds" not "jocks." While problematically invoking the language of "genetics" that erases Lin's tremendous athleticism/speed, Leonard concludes that Lin inspires Asian American kids who yearn for a masculine role model given persistent invisibility and anti–Asian racism within the public square. "He's a triumph of will over genetic endowment, a fact that makes him inspiring to an entire generation of Californian kids restless with their model minority shackles," he notes.

> On Monday, the social media world was also getting worked up about Michigan Republican Senate hopeful Pete Hoekstra's racist Super Bowl ad, featuring a Chinese woman (labeled "yellowgirl" in the HTML code for the Web version) gloating over all the jobs her country was taking from the U.S. Once thrown into the 24/7 crazy cultural mashup perpetual motion machine, it didn't take long before anger about that ad ran head on into Jeremy Lin pride. I have seen tweets urging Jeremy Lin to run for the Republican nomination for the Michigan senate seat, tweets warning that the only American jobs in danger from Asians are those belonging to New York Knick starting point guards, and even a tweet riffing off Kobe Bryant's self-identification as "black mamba"—Jeremy Lin is suddenly the "yellow mamba."

Lin trended #1 on twitter on three successive game days amid Linsanity; he was top–10 searched items on Sina Weibo and is all the talk of the sports world for several days during the height of his ascendance. For this moment, it was Jeremy Lin's world and we were all just living in it.

The pride and possibility reflects the broader erasure and invisibility of Asian Americans within popular culture. "Asians are nearly invisible on television/movies/music, so any time I see an Asian on TV or in the movies, I feel like I've just spotted a unicorn, even though usually, I see them being portrayed as kung-fu masters/socially awkward mathematical geniuses/broken-English-speaking-fresh-off-the-boat owner of Chinese restaurant/nail salon/dry cleaners," writes one blogger ("Jeremy Lin, the NBA, and Hegemonic Masculinity"). "Anyway, this phenomenon is 10× worse in sports. While there has been some notable progress with Asians in professional baseball, Asians are all but nonexistent in the big three sports in the U.S. (football, basketball, baseball)." Lin breaks down, or at least penetrates, the walls that have excluded Asian Americans from popular culture. The pride, adoration and celebration reflect this history of exclusion, a history of erasure, and invisibility. The efforts to link Lin to Nike's "Witness" campaign is illustrative in that we are all witness, maybe for the first, time in history, of an Asian American sports hero, someone who challenges and defies expectations and stereotypes.

Amid the invisibility is a history of feminization of Asian American males and the erasure of the Asian American athlete (King 2013; Wang 2012; Franks 2000). When present within media and popular culture, Asian American men have been represented as asexual, weak, physically challenged, and otherwise unmasculine. Sanctioning exclusion and denied citizenship, the white supremacist imagination has consistently depicted Asian male bodies as effeminate. The entry of Lin into the dominant imagination reflects a challenge to this historic practice given the power of sports as a space of masculine prowess. Whether shock or celebration, Lin's cultural power rests in his juxtaposition to the stereotyped Asian American male. According to Timothy Dalrymple, "their astonishment at the sight of Jeremy Lin outperforming the other players, their consistent references to how exhausted he must be, and how "magical" a night he's having (rather than a natural result of talent and hard work) suggests that they've bought into the stereotype of the physically inferior Asian-American male."

Lin's recent ascendance is not simply about success or dominance within the sports world, a place defined by masculine prowess. It reflects the cultural and gendered meaning of basketball. Lin is excelling in a world defined by black manhood, an identity the white racial frames construct through physicality, strength, speed and swagger. Unlike other players who burst onto the American scene (Yao Ming, Yi Jianlian, Wang ZhiZhi), Lin is a guard, who has found success because of his athleticism and skills as opposed to his presumed freakish stature. "The best part is how viscerally pleasurable it is to watch Lin play: His game is flashy, almost showoffy, and requires him to have guts, guile and flair in equal measure," writes Will Leich. "The drama of it is, it's obvious, what's most fun for him. It is all you could possibly want as a feel-good story. "

In other words, Lin's appeal comes from his ability to ball like a street player, to face off and dominate against black players at "their own game." The celebration of Lin as a challenge to the denied masculinity afforded to Asian American males reflects the ways in which black masculinity is defined in and through basketball culture. While surely offering fans the often-denied sporting masculinity within the Asian body, the power of Jeremy Lin rests with his ability to mimic a basketball style, swagger and skill associated with black ballers. Pride emanates from the sense of masculinity afforded by Lin, a fact that emanates from stereotypical constructions of black masculinity. "Through no fault of his own, Lin stands at a bombed-out intersection of expected narratives, bodies, perceived genes, the Church, the vocabulary of destinations and YouTube," wrote Jay Caspian Kang, who's Asian American, about Lin's electrifying play at Harvard. "What Jeremy Lin represents is a re-conception of our bodies, a visible measure of how the emasculated Asian-American body might measure up to the mythic legion of Big Black superman" (cited by King)

Fulfilling a fantasy for a "white American fantasy of an athletic prowess that can trump African-American hegemony in the league" (Farred, p. 56) and the appeal of a masculinity defined by its association with blackness, the celebrations, parties, and various public adoration are wrapped in these ideas of race, gender, and nation. Writing about Yao Ming, Grant Farred, reminds us about these issues:

> The body of the athlete, which has a long history of standing as the body of the nation, is simultaneously reduced and magnified in the Yao event, in its micro-articulation (Asian-American), it is asked to refute the myth of the feminized ethnic by challenging—and redressing the historic wrongs endured—those "American" bodies that have been dismissed the physicality of the Asian male. As representative of the Chinese nation, Yao is expected to remain a national subject even as his basketball heritage seems difficult to unlearn and continues to disadvantage him in the NBA.... In his representation of the "Chinese people," Yao will not become an NBA—which is to say "African American"—player. He will not trash talk, he will not develop an "offensive personality," in more senses than one, and to his detriment, he, will not become more "physical" [2006, p. 62].

Lin is confined by this trap, so his wagging tongue (that was blue during one game), his trash talk, his swagger, his reverse layups, his flashy speed, and his ability to dunk, all confirms that Lin isn't just a basketball player but a baller. The celebration is thus, wrapped up in the dominant configurations of blackness, and how hegemonic visions of black masculinity confer a certain amount power to Lin. According to Dave Zirin (2012a), Lin's power rests with his transgressive play: "Asian-Americans, in our stereotypical lens, are supposed to be studious and reserved. We would expect nothing less than that the first Asian-American player would be robotic and fundamentally sound; their face an unsmiling mask." While Lin is not the first Asian American to play professional basketball in the U.S. (Rex Walters, Wataru Misaka, and Raymond Townsend), Zirin's analysis points to the larger ways that race operates in this context. Lin's appeal comes because he defies people's expectations about Asian Americans because he is excelling and playing in a way that people expect from and authentically associate with black players. He goes further to argue, "Instead, we have Jeremy Lin threading no-look passes, throwing down dunks and, in the most respected mark of toughness, taking contact and finishing baskets." With this analysis we see how race not only defines Lin, but the NBA as a cultural space. His power rests with his ability to "become" black within the national imagination as baller, yet remain outside the prison/prism of the black-white binary. Or as Oliver Wang notes, the fanfare illustrates how "hegemonic masculinity is constructed whereupon whiteness hides behind a cloak of black desire."

Tongue-Tied: Jeremy Lin and the Dialogue of Race

The emergence of Jeremy Lin as international superstar, coupled by tweets from Jason Whitlock and Floyd Mayweather, has prompted widespread debate about whether or not race matters in both the media representation and in understanding the arch of his career. Without a doubt, race matters when talking about Lin given his path to the NBA, prejudice experienced while on the court, and the larger context of anti–Asian racism. Lin is not evidence of some post-racial fantasy, but instead a reminder of how race matters. It matters whether talking about sports, housing, education, foreign policy, economic inequality, media culture, and interpersonal relations.

Race matters when examining the media representations of black athletes, whether were talking about the demonization of Michael Vick, Barry Bonds, or LeBron James; it matters in the stories of redemption afforded to Ben Roethlisberger and Josh Hamilton, or the lack of media attention directed at Kevin Love after he stomped on another player's face. To deny the impact and significant of race with Lin is as absurd as deploying "the race denial card" in these contexts as well. To imagine Lin outside of the scope of race and racism, or to isolate race as something usual in this instance, especially given the ways that the NBA is associated with blackness (the subtext here feels as if the discussion is being reduced to anti–Asian prejudice from African Americans), represents an immense failure.

So race matters when thinking about Lin's recruitment (or lack thereof) out of high school and his path to the NBA. Race matters when talking about employment discrimination.

Racism holds people back in every industry, from higher education to the business world. Researchers at the Discrimination Research Center, in their study "Names Make a Difference" (Asthana 2007), argue that racial discrimination represents a significant obstacle for employees. Having sent out 6,200 resumes with similar qualifications to temporary employment agencies, the authors found that those with names associated with the Latino and white communities received callbacks more frequently than those presumed to be African American or South Asian/Arab American (called back the least frequently) (Miller 2004). Similarly, MIT professors Marianne Bertrand and Sendhil Mullainathan concluded that perspective applicants with "white sounding names" are 50 percent more likely to receive a callback after submitting a resume than were those with "black sounding names." They concluded that whiteness was as much an asset as 8 years of work experience, demonstrating that race has a significant impact on one's job future. In their study, "Are Emily and Greg More Employable than Lakisha and Jamal? A Field Experiment on Labor Market Discrimination," the authors conclude, "While one may have expected that improved credentials may alleviate employers' fear that African-American applicants are deficient in some unobservable skills, this is not the case in our data. Discrimination therefore appears to bite twice, making it harder not only for African-Americans to find a job but also to improve their employability" ("Employers' Replies to Racial Names" 2003). In a society where those with "black sounding" and "Muslim sounding" names receive call backs from perspective employments with 50 percent less frequency, this is an opportunity to talk about systemic racism.

Isolating or particularizing racism represents not only a failure to use Lin's experiences as teachable about persistent racism, but reinscribes model minority myth all while failing to see the ways in which racism operates throughout society. Writing about Lin, Ling Woo Liu, director of the Fred T. Korematsu Institute for Civil Rights and Education, notes, "Hopefully one day, Americans of Asian descent will no longer be seen as foreigners, economic competition or anything less than equal Americans. Until then, race matters, whether we like it or not." Likewise, until African Americans are no longer seen as criminals, welfare queens, and undesirable potential employees, until Latinos are no longer seen as exploitable labor, "illegals" and "unassimilable," race matters. Reflecting on persistent privilege and racism is a difficult process, and the media coverage of Jeremy Lin provides opportunity, one that shouldn't be missed, to expand rather than shrink that conversation.

Likewise, the belief that Lin is undermining, if not eliminating, stereotypes about Asian Americans, is optimistic to say the least. Timothy Yu, "Will Jeremy Lin's success end stereotypes?," embodies this hope: "American culture tells us, in short, that Lin shouldn't exist. Every time he drives to the basket, he upends stereotypes of Asians as short, weak and nerdy. Every time he talks to the media, he dispels the idea that all Asian-Americans are like foreigners speaking broken English." Jay Caspian Kang pushes this conversation further, arguing that it isn't simply Lin's presence on the court that undermines long-standing stereotypes but the style that he plays with. "I'm sure we'd all like to peg the humble Asian kid as unselfish. But Lin can be a bit of a black hole [with the ball]. Some of his most exciting baskets have come on drives that start around half court." Yet, that isn't the narrative in circulation. As noted by Picca and Feagin, stereotypes "act, like self-fulfilling prophecies tend to be reinforced when new information fits them, while information that negates a stereotype tends to be rejected." The stereotype, in itself, impairs our ability to see the reality. For example, in the aftermath of the Knicks loss to the New Jersey Nets, which was Lin's first game playing alongside Carmelo Anthony, the criticisms directed at Anthony focused on his selfishness and ball-hogging approach to the game despite the fact that Lin took 18 shots compared to Melo's 11. Understanding the desire to see Lin as a "game changer," as someone who is ushering in a new racial moment, the persistence of inequality and institutional racisms leaves me questioning the level of optimism, one that seemingly places stereotypes on the doorstep of those who have been confined within the prism of racial expectations.

One of the emergent narratives, especially in wake of tweets from Jason Whitlock and Floyd Mayweather, ESPN's headline and the MSG "fortune cookie" image has been the ways in which racism has been directed against Asian American communities. While illustrating the profound ways that racism guides both public discourse and material conditions impacting AAPI communities, the efforts to create a hierarchy whereupon anti–Asian prejudice (institutional racism is never figured) is tolerated whereas anti-black or anti–Latino racism is met with opposition and condemnation represents a significant failure. For example, Dave Zirin (2012b) argues that because of the absence of Asian American civil rights movement (although not true), America hasn't been forced to confront its own racism in this regard. "No one at ESPN would talk or write about a lesbian athlete and unconsciously put forth that the woman in question would have a 'finger in the dike,'" writes Zirin. "If an African-American player was thought of as stingy, it's doubtful that anyone at the World Wide Leader would describe that person as "niggardly." They would never brand a member of a football team as a 'Redskin' (wait, scratch that last one)." Similarly, Bill Plaschke (2012) asks, "Can you imagine a major American media company tolerating this sort of blatant racism if it were directed toward any of Lin's African American teammates?" While I don't need to imagine something I study each and every day, this illustrates a failed media narrative that seeks to divide rather than reflect on the links between anti-black and anti–Asian racism. Jason Whitlock's tweet, for example, didn't simply depict Asian men as having "small penises," but by extension played on longstanding racist mythologies regarding the black man's phallus. Likewise, when Robert Wright, with "The Secret of Jeremy Lin's Success?" plays into longstanding Orientalist fantasies to explain Jeremy Lin's success, he isn't simply recycling a long tradition of Asian stereotyping that gives legitimacy to the historic argument that black athletic success is the result of some biological or physical advantage. In absence of the "Asian heritage" that equips Lin "for success in basketball," the narrative reinforces stereotypes about black athletic success. The lack of sophistication in our language about racism, the efforts to create hierarchies and binaries, to pit one group against another, has been on full display, it points to the importance of media literacy that allows society to critically understand and unpack the narratives that are emanating here. Raising these questions is not "player hatin" but in fact wondering why we can't critically think about the game and the media story behind the game.

The God Squad: Tim Tebow, Jeremy Lin and Religiosity of Sports

Among the virtual saturation of Jeremy Lin online has been a poster of him with the words "We are all witness" emblazoned below. At one Knicks' game, fans donned "black T-shirts that read 'The Jeremy Lin Show' on the front" and "We Believe" painted on the back.

Encapsulating the hoopla and hype, while referencing the similar promise that LeBron James brought to Cleveland and the NBA (how'd that work out?), not to mention the spectacle of his meteoric rise, "the witness" iteration illustrates the religious overtones playing through the media coverage.

Since Lin emerged on the national scene while at Harvard, he has made his faith and religious identity quite clear. While refusing to abandon the "underdog" story, Cork Gaines focuses readers attention on his religious beliefs: "But there is more to Jeremy Lin than just being an undrafted Asian-American point guard out of Harvard. He is also a devout Christian that has previously declared that he plays for the glory of God and someday hopes to be a pastor" (Hughes 2010). Noting how post-game interviews often begin with Lin announcing his faith—"just very thankful to Jesus Christ, [his] Lord and savior"—Gaines uses this opportunity to deploy the often noted comparison that Jeremy Lin is the NBA's Tim Tebow.

While making the comparison through the Cinderella/overlooked narrative, the media celebration of their faith and evangelical beliefs serves as the anchor for the Lin as Tebow trope. "Tebowmania? That was so 2011. It's time for a new cult-hero phenomenon: Linsanity," writes Ben Cohen in "Meet Jeremy Lin, the new Tim Tebow."

> Then there's their shared religious values. "I'm just thankful to God for this opportunity," Lin said in an on-court interview Saturday before tweeting, "God is good during our ups and our downs!" His Twitter avatar is a Jesus cartoon. Tebow's, for the record, is his autobiography's cover.

Described as "Taiwanese Tim Tebow," (Beck 2012), as resembling "Denver Bronco's Quarterback, Tim Tebow" (Pan 2012) as filling the mold that Tebow "patented" (Zaldivar 2012) Lin's identity (meaning/significance) is ascribed by his connection to Tebow. Tebow defines him.

In "From Unknown to Phenom in 3 Games: Harvard Grad Jeremy Lin Saves the New York Knicks," Les Carpenter makes the comparison clear: "He is a Christian, vocal in his belief. And because of this and because he is a flawed player proving the experts wrong, people are comparing him to Tim Tebow." According to Gaines, "Lin and Tebow are not the first athletes to make their faith a key component of their athletic persona. But if Lin, another unconventional player fighting an uphill battle against haters and doubters, continues his spectacular play in The World's Most Famous Arena, the NBA may soon experience their own Tebowmania. And the fans are already calling it 'Linsanity.'" While dismissing the links beyond the uber-hype afforded to Tebow (and now Lin), Bethlehem Shoals furthers the comparison: "Tim Tebow, whose religious views are no secret, probably considers luck the pay-off for faith; Lin is also an enthusiastic Christian. Whether you feel like pushing things in that direction is your business. The bottom line is that, thus far, Lin has been a welcome surprise, a Cinderella story that no one wants to see end."

The comparison is instructive on multiple levels. Each exists in juxtaposition to blackness. The "underdog" narrative, the focus on hard work and intelligence, and the claims of being overlooked and discriminated against all elucidates the ways in which their bodies are rendered as different from the hegemonic black athletic body. Religion, thus, becomes another marker of difference, as a means to celebrate and differentiate Lin and Tebow. Whereas black athletes are seen within the national imagination to be guided by hip-hop values rather than religious values, Lin and Tebow practice an evangelical ethic on and off the field/court. Tebow and Lin operate as a "breath of fresh air." Writing about Tiger Woods, Cole and Andrews argue that Woods' emergence as a global icon reflected his power as a counter narrative. As "a breath of fresh of air," his cultural power emanated from his juxtaposition to "African American professional basketball players who are routinely depicted in the popular media as selfish, insufferable, and morally reprehensible" (Cole & Andrews 2001, p. 72).

The Tebow-Lin narrative reflects the centering of whiteness. In making the comparison, religion in sports and even Lin's ascendance becomes all about Tebow. While black athletes have long given "thanks," the efforts to construct Tebow as the source of a religious revival within America's sports world is a testament to the wages of whiteness. "Black athletes who give a shout out to God aren't seen as being evangelical but when someone like Tebow (i.e., white) does it, there's a different 'purpose' being read into it," notes Oliver Wang. "With Lin, I'd argue that because Asianness is coded as closer to white than black, the Tebow comparison becomes almost automatic." Wang highlights the profound impact of the comparison as it not only elevates Tebow as leader of the religious revolution of sports, but also furthers the coding of Lin as white body.

Through the comparison, we witness the profound ways that the media erases race by denying Tebow's whiteness (Leonard and Peterson 2012) while concretizing Lin's whiteness (of a different color). Represented through a dominant white racial frame despite his being subjected to racist taunts throughout his career, the comparison denies the power of race. It erases the ways in which whiteness serves as an anchor for the media sensationalism and celebration of Tebow; it erases the ways in which race and identity functions with the source of pride Lin's has delivered for Asian American community or the ways in which Lin operates in relationship to narratives of whiteness; and finally it ignores the profound ways in which the celebration of their religious ideals and practices is overdetermined by the meaning of blackness within contemporary sports culture.

So while the varied meaning of race, their experiences, and their identities render a Tebow comparison null and void, making one wonder why Lin isn't the new Avery Johnson or Hakeem Olajuwon, the ubiquitous conflation of Tebow and Lin illustrates its power and appeal. With Jeremy Lin we are all witness to a post-racial fantasy amid the racial spectacle of contemporary popular culture. Within American sports media, the God squad remains one defined and contained by race.

Conclusion

A "model minority"; "different from other NBA players"; someone with "swag"; someone who came out of nowhere—these descriptors and many others defined the rise of Linsanity. Noting his immigrant background, his IQ, and GPA, citing his humility and demeanor, praising his religiosity and otherwise praising him for his personality as much as his jump shot, the rise (and recent fall) of Jeremy Lin is a story of race. It is a tale of sports world defined by race and racial meaning; it is a narrative that disseminated racial meaning all while finding meaning within our racial landscape. Whereas some celebrated him as a game changer, as a breath of fresh air, he became a vehicle for more of the same. Lin did not break down stereotypes (maybe denting them), reinscribing them in many regards. Celebrated as "intelligent" and as "a hustler," his success has been attributed to his intelligence, his basketball IQ, and even his religious faith. His athleticism and the hours spent on the court are erased from the discussion. Moreover, in positioning him as the aberration, as someone worthy of celebration, the dominant media frame reinforces the longstanding stereotypes of Asians as unathletic nerds. Likewise, the juxtaposition of his identity, body, and basketball skills to the NBA's black bodies simultaneously reinforces the dominant inscriptions of both blackness and Asianness. While J-Lin brought something new to the table—an Asian American basketball role model; Knicks' victories—the narrative came without a lot of racial baggage that we cannot seem to shake in our purportedly postracial reality. While others have located Lin's rise as Linsanity, as a moment where people become some engrossed in all things Lin, the ultimate sign of insanity was the push and belief that race didn't matter.

NOTE

1. This essay includes and builds on several essays written by D.J. Leonard: "Jeremy Lin and the NBA's race problem" (2012, July 18), http://www.ebony.com/entertainment-culture/jeremy-lin-and-the-nbas-race-problem; "#LinSanity and the blackness of basketball" (2012, February 23), http://newblackman.blogspot.com/2012/02/linsanity-and-blackness-of-basketball.html; "Family ties: On Jeremy Lin, "Tiger Moms," and Tiger Woods" (2012, February 22), http://www.racialicious.com/2012/02/28/family-ties-on-jeremy-lin-tiger-moms-and-tiger-woods/; "Tongue-tied: Jeremy Lin and media dialogue on race matters" (2012, February 22), http://www.urbancusp.com/newspost/tongue-tied-jeremy-lin-and-media-dialogue-on-race-matters/; "When it comes to sports, race still matters" (2012, February 17), http://www.ebony.com/entertainment-culture/when-it-comes-to-sports-race-still-matters; "Going global: Jeremy Lin and the NBA" (2012, February 14), http://www.slamonline.com/online/nba/2012/02/going-global-jeremy-lin-and-the-nba/; "Pride and prejudice: Jeremy Lin and the persistence of racial stereotypes" (2012, February 10), http://www.slamonline.com/online/nba/2012/02/pride-and-prejudice/; "Linsanity! What Jeremy Lin means to the NBA" (2012, February 10), http://www.ebony.com/entertainment-culture/linsanity-what-jeremy-lin-means-to-the-nba; "The God squad: Tim Tebow, Jeremy Lin, and religiosity of sports" (2012, February 10), http://www.racialicious.com/2012/02/10/the-god-squad-tim-tebow-jeremy-lin-and-religiosity-of-sports/. Thanks to Mark Anthony Neal, Arturo Garcia, Rahiel Tesfamariam, Jamilah Lemieux and Ryne Nelson.

REFERENCES

Abelmann, N., and J. Lie (1995). *Blue dreams: Korean Americans and the Los Angeles riots.* Cambridge: Harvard University Press.

Ambinder, M. (2010, February 4). "Asian-American Ivy Leaguer has tall hoop dreams." Retrieved December 10, 2012, from http://www.npr.org/templates/story/story.php?storyId=123368990.

Ambinder, M. (2012, February 14). What the GOP can learn from Jeremy Lin. Retrieved December 10, 2012, from http://www.gq.com/news-politics/blogs/death-race/2012/02/what-the-gop-can-learn-from-jeremy-lin.html#ixzz2EfwW8ivL.

Asthana, A. (2007, April 28). Names really do make a difference. Retrieved December 10, 2012, from http://www.guardian.co.uk/science/2007/apr/29/theobserversuknewspages.uknews.

Beck, H. (2012, February 8). From ivy halls to the Garden, surprise star jolts the N.B.A. *New York Times.* Retrieved December 10, 2012, from http://www.nytimes.com/2012/02/08/sports/basketball/jeremy-lin-has-burst-from-nba-novelty-act-to-knicks-star.html?_r=2&hpw.

Bertrand, M., and S. Mullainathan (2003). Are Emily and Greg more employable than Lakisha and Jamal? A field experiment on labor market discrimination. Retrieved December 10, 2012, from http://www.nber.org/papers/w9873.

Borden, S., and K. Bradsher (2012, February 26). Tight-knit family shares Lin's achievement. *New York Times.* Retrieved December 10, 2012, from www.nytimes.com/2012/02/26/sports/basketball/tight-knit-family-shares-lins-achievement.html?pagewanted=3&_r=2&.

Carpenter, L. (2012). From unknown to phenom in 3 games: Harvard grad Jeremy Lin saves the New York Knicks. Retrieved December 10, 2012, from http://www.thepostgame.com/features/201202/jeremy-lin-nba-new-york-knicks-harvard-taiwan.

Chang, J. (1993). "Race, class, conflict, and empowerment: On Ice Cube's 'Black Korea.'" *Amerasia Journal* 19(2), 87–107.

Chou, R. S., and J. R. Feagin (2008). *The Myth of the model minority: Asian Americans facing racism.* Boulder, CO: Paradigm.

Cohen, B. (2012, February 8). Meet Jeremy Lin, the new Tim Tebow. Retrieved December 10, 2012, from http://online.wsj.com/article/SB10001424052970204136404577209274190816522.html.

Cole, C. L. (2001). Nike's America/America's Michael Jordan. In D.L. Andrews (Ed.), *Michael Jordan inc.: Corporate sport, media culture and late modern America* (pp. 65–71). Albany: State University of New York.

Cole, C. L., and D. L. Andrews (2001). America's new son: Tiger Woods and America's multiculturalism. In D. L. Andrews and S. J. Jackson (Eds.), *Sports stars: The cultural politics of sporting celebrity* (pp. 70–86). New York: Routledge.

Dalrymple, T. (2012, February 6). Jeremy Lin and the soft bigotry of low expectations. Retrieved December 10, 2012, from http://www.patheos.com/blogs/philosophicalfragments/2012/02/06/jeremy-lin-and-the-soft-bigotry-of-low-expectations/.

Denzin, N. (2001). Representing Michael. In D. L. Andrews (Ed.), *Michael Jordan inc.: Corporate sport, media culture and late modern America* (pp. 3–14). Albany: State University of New York.

Employers' replies to racial names. (2003, September). National Bureau of Economic Research. Retrieved May 18, 2007, from http://www.nber.org/digest/sep03/w9873.html.

Engel, J. F. (2012, February 16). Lin's success should be no surprise. Retrieved December 9, 2012, from http://msn.foxsports.com/nba/story/Jeremy-Lin-New-York-Knicks-success-based-on-foundation-of-hard-work-021612.

Falgoust, J. M. (2012, February 8). Asian Americans energized in seeing Knicks' Jeremy Lin play. Retrieved December 10, 2012, from http://usatoday30.usatoday.com/sports/basketball/nba/story/2012-02-08/Asian-Americans-flock-to-see-Jeremy-Lin-play/53017410/1.

Farred, G. (2006); *Phantom calls: Race and the globalization of the NBA.* Chicago: Prickly Paradigm.

Feagin, J. (2010). *The White racial frame: Centuries of racial framing and counter framing.* New York: Routledge.

Franks, J. (2000). *Crossing sidelines, crossing cultures: Sport and Asian Pacific American cultural citizenship.* New York: University Press of America.

Gaines, C. (2012, February 7). Faith and uphill battles could make Jeremy Lin: The NBA's Tim Tebow. Retrieved December 9, 2012, from http://www.businessinsider.com/faith-and-uphill-battles-could-make-jeremy-lin-the-nbas-tim-tebow-2012-2#ixzz2EgAE5pNT.

Hill, M. L. (2012, November 28). The Linsanity sham: Why Jeremy Lin really can't play. Retrieved

December 10, 2012, http://www.huffingtonpost.com/marc-lamont-hill/linsanity-jeremy-lin_b_2199606.html.

Hughes, F. (2010, July 26). Former Harvard standout Lin ready to prove himself with Warriors. Retrieved December 10, 2012, from http://sportsillustrated.cnn.com/2010/writers/frank_hughes/07/26/jeremy.lin.warriors/index.html#ixzz2Eg9iaV9e.

Jackson, E. (2012, February). Just Lin, baby! 10 lessons Jeremy Lin can teach us before we go to work Monday morning. Retrieved December 10, 2012, from http://www.forbes.com/sites/ericjackson/2012/02/11/9-lessons-jeremy-lin-can-teach-us-before-we-go-to-work-monday-morning/.

Jackson, E. (2012, February 7). Jeremy Lin, the NBA, and hegemonic masculinity. Retrieved December 10, 2012, from http://btg.bobngo.com/?p=206.

Kang, J. K. (2010, January 14). Jeremy Lin puts the ball in Asian Americans' court. *Los Angeles Times*. Retrieved December 10, 2012, from http://articles.latimes.com/2012/feb/21/entertainment/la-et-jeremy-lin-20120221.

Kang, J. K. (2010, January 14). The lives of others. Retrieved December 10, 2012, from http://freedarko.blogspot.com/2010/01/lives-of-others.html.

King, C. R., ed. (2010). *Asian Americans in Sport and Society*. New York: Routledge

King, J. (2012, February 8). The subtle bigotry that made Jeremy Lin the NBA's most surprising star. Retrieved December 10, 2012, from http://colorlines.com/archives/2012/02/jeremy_lin.html.

Lapchick, R. (2002). *Smashing barriers: Race and sport in the new millennium*. Lanham, MD: Madison.

Leitch, W. (2012, February 7). The Jeremy Lin show is just getting started, folks. Retrieved December 10, 2012, from http://nymag.com/daily/sports/2012/02/jeremy-lin-show-is-just-getting-started.html.

Leonard, A. (2012, February 8). Jeremy Lin's social media fast break. Retrieved December 10, 2012, from http://www.salon.com/2012/02/08/jeremy_lins_social_media_fast_break/singleton/.

Leonard, D. J. (2003, summer). Yo: Yao! What does the 'Ming Dynasty' tell us about race and transnational diplomacy in the NBA? *Colorlines*, pp. 34–36.

Leonard, D. J. (2004). The next M. J. or the next O. J.? Kobe Bryant, race, and the absurdity of colorblind rhetoric. *Journal of Sport and Social Issues*, 28 (3), 284–313.

Leonard, D. J. (2006a). The real color of money: Controlling black bodies in the NBA. *Journal of Sport and Social Issues*, 30 (2), 158–179.

Leonard, D. J. (2006b). A world of criminals or a media construction? Race, gender, celebrity and the athlete/criminal discourse. In A. Raney and J. Bryant (Eds.), *Handbook of Sports Media* (pp. 523–542). Mahwah, NJ: Lawrence Erlbaum Associates.

Leonard, D. J., and Peterson, J. B. (2012). The Tim Tebow effect or celebrating whiteness? Retrieved December 10, 2012, from http://loop21.com/life/op-ed-tim-tebow-affect-or-celebrating-whiteness?page=1.

Liu, L.W. (2012, February 14). Why Jeremy Lin's race matters. Retrieved December 10, 2012, from http://www.cnn.com/2012/02/13/opinion/jeremy-lin-race/index.html.

Manur, A. (2005). "Model minorities can cook: Fusion cuisine in Asian America." In S. Dave, L. Nishime and T.G Oden (Eds.), *East main street: Asian American popular culture* (pp. 72–94). New York: New York University Press.

McElya, M. Trashing the presidency: Race, class and the Clinton/Lewinsky affair. In L. Berlant and L. Dugan (Eds.), *Our Monica ourselves: The Clinton affair and the national interest* (pp. 156–174). New York: New York University Press, 2001.

Omi, M., and Takagi, D.Y (1996). Situating Asian Americans in the political discourse of affirmative action. *Representations* 55, 155–162.

O'Neil, D. (2009, December 10). "Immigrant dream plays out through son." Retrieved December 10, 2012, from http://sports.espn.go.com/ncb/columns/story?columnist=oneil_dana&id=4730385.

Pan, D.K.W (2012, February 7). Is Jeremy Lin the NBA's version of Tim Tebow? Retrieved December 10, 2012, from www.asianweek.com/2012/02/07/is-jeremy-lin-the-nba's-version-of-tim-tebow/.

Perez, H. (2005). "How to rehabilitate a mulatto: The iconography of Tiger Woods." In S. Dave, L. Nishime and T.G. Oden (Eds.), *East main street: Asian American popular culture* (pp. 222–245). New York: New York University Press

Picca, L.H., and Feagin, J.R. (2007). *Two-Faced Racism: Whites in the Backstage and Frontstage*. New York: Routledge.

Plaschke, B. (2012, February 20). Knicks' Jeremy Lin holds mirror up to America. *Los Angeles Times*. Retrieved December 10, 2012, from http://articles.latimes.com/2012/feb/20/sports/la-sp-plaschke-jeremy-lin-20120221.

Shoals, B. (2012, February 8). Jeremy Lin: Is the Knicks guard the NBA's Tim Tebow? Retrieved December 10, 2012, from http://bleacherreport.com/articles/1057850-jeremy-lin-is-the-knicks-guard-the-nbas-tim-tebow.

Torre, P.S. (2010, February 1). Harvard school of basketball. Retrieved December 10, 2012, from http://sportsillustrated.cnn.com/vault/article/magazine/MAG1165302/3/index.htm.

Toure (2012, February 28). "Jeremy Lin's triumph over stereotype threat." Retrieved December 10, 2012, from http://ideas.time.com/2012/02/28/jeremy-lins-triumph-over-stereotype-threat/#ixzz1oZCubOWe.

Wang, O. (2012, March 6). Living with Linsanity. Retrieved December 10, 2012, from http://blog.lareviewofbooks.org/post/18846363359/living-with-linsanity.

Wierenga, J. (2012, February 15). Jeremy Lin: Why every American should be rooting for Linsanity to last. Retrieved December 10, 2012, from http://bleacherreport.com/articles/1067330-jeremy-lin-why-every-american-should-be-rooting-for-lin-sanity-to-last.

Wright, R. (2012, February 14). The secret of Jeremy Lin's success? Retrieved December 10, 2012, from http://www.theatlantic.com/entertainment/archive/2012/02/the-secret-of-jeremy-lins-success/253051/.

Yang, J. (2012, February 15). Will Lin-sanity tame Tiger moms? *New York Daily News*. Retrieved December 10, 2012, from http://articles.nydailynews.com/2012-02-15/news/31064980_1_gie-ming-hoop-dreams-brother.

Yu, T. (2012, February 21). Will Jeremy Lin's success end stereotypes? Retrieved December 10, 2012, from http://www.cnn.com/2012/02/20/opinion/yu-jeremy-lin/index.htm.

Zaldivar, G. (2012, February). Jeremy Lin is modern-day hero America loves. Retrieved December 10, 2012, from http://bleacherreport.com/articles/1059364-jeremy-lin-is-modern-day-hero-america-loves.

Zirin, D. (2004, November 24). Fight night in the NBA. Retrieved November 24, 2004, from http://www.commondreams.org/views04/1122-30.htm.

Zirin, D. (2012, February 7). Feel the Lin-sanity: Why Jeremy Lin is more than a cultural curio. Retrieved December 10, 2012, from http://www.thenation.com/blog/166161/feel-lin-sanity-why-jeremy-lin-more-cultural-curio#.

Zirin, D. (2012, February 19). Jeremy Lin and ESPN's 'accidental' racism. Retrieved December 10, 2012, from http://www.thenation.com/blog/166382/jeremy-lin-and-espns-accidental-racism.

Institutional Barriers and Self-Handicapping Behaviors of Black Male Student-Athletes: Catalysts for Underperformance in the Classroom

Gary A. Sailes and *Rebecca Milton Allen*

Introduction

After having studied the experiences of black athletes in American college sports for over three decades, their story, we believe, is both alarming and disheartening. Black student athletes are among the poorest academic performers compared to all student athlete groups and have the lowest graduation percentages. Black athletes receive more attention from university officials and the media when they get into trouble, exacerbating the stereotype that black athletes are "gangstas" and emanate from undisciplined environments where few rules exist to restrict their behavior. Their celebrity status on campus does not insulate them from racial stereotyping, racist remarks, discrimination and higher expectations compared to their Caucasian counterparts. Black athletes feel the campus experience is different from anything they have ever experienced in life. Yet, the expectation for them to succeed is high and the actual social support they need to become successful rarely exists. Black student athletes, at best, call their experience on predominantly white university campuses "awkward."

In his highly controversial and much debated book *Darwin's Athletes: How Sport Has Damaged Black America and Preserved the Myth of Race*, (1997), John Hoberman argued that sport has damaged black America for the following reasons:

1. Many African Americans are so excessively focused on athletics that they fail to see the negative effects.
2. Institutions that are controlled by whites profit from this fixation.
3. These athletic over emphases and corresponding idealizations of black athletes among blacks have contributed to a growing and debilitating anti-intellectualism in black society.
4. Black intellectuals have failed to both articulate the negative consequences of this athletic fixation and to lead black youth to educational activities leading to conventional careers

[Hoberman, 1997; Curtis, 1998].

Hoberman's analysis of the struggles of black athletes introduced the societal issue currently taking place in American colleges and universities in which black male student-athletes are not academically succeeding at the same levels as their Caucasian peers. Across the nation, one of the issues that coaches and university administrators deal with is the lack of discipline and character of black student-athletes off the playing field and in the classroom (Tolliver, 2010). A constant debate occurs as to who should receive the blame when black student-athletes break the law or have trouble adjusting to collegiate life. While most fans cannot understand why a talented athlete would squander his athletic chances with drugs, fighting, guns or other unlawful behaviors, the black student athlete is not solely responsible for his poor choices. Often these athletes are placed in a new community where they are inundated with frustrations, obstacles and the lack of anyone to turn to for help off the playing field (Farrey, 1993). The issue cannot be broken down into right and wrong. Many young men are being put into an atmosphere where they are expected to conduct themselves in a cultural environment that is unfamiliar and totally foreign to them. Some of these individuals have been allowed to act in whatever way that they chose, believing that normal rules don't apply to them (Tolliver, 2010). When these individuals make it into a university or college, they are expected to change their behaviors to conform to the university environment with very little, if any, support from the school.

Many of the new intercollegiate "stars" have been raised in single parent homes and rough neighborhoods. Only 16 percent of African American households are made up of married couples with children. This is the lowest percentage for all racial groups (Coles & Green, 2009). In 2004, over 50 percent of black children lived in single parent households with their mothers (Coles

& Green, 2009). In 2000, 68 percent of all black women who gave birth were unmarried (Martin et al., 2003). A socioeconomic background of poverty can also influence an individual's achievement in higher education. Baltimore, a city known for its poor K-12 education and subsequent graduation rates, contains 15 percent of the state's children, and 87 percent of the state's children that live in extreme poverty (Bowler, 1998). And yet society expects black men to succeed in the collegiate atmosphere despite their meager upbringings and the drastic difference between their childhood experiences and their peers.

This essay will closely examine the factors which contribute to underachievement in the classroom for black male student-athletes. Using previous research and findings, we will analyze the institutional barriers introduced by the college and university as well as the cultural barriers that consequently lead to self-handicapping behaviors and decisions. By understanding all of the catalysts that lead to poor performance and understanding the causes of nonnormative behaviors and poor grades, societal and institutional improvements toward a better educational experience for this group are within reach.

Institutional Barriers

When black student-athletes transition to collegiate life they are expected to assimilate into a world completely different from their home communities. It is the role of the institution to ensure these student athletes have the ability to succeed both on the field and off. Unfortunately, research has shown that the institution itself is partly to blame for the lack of academic success of the African American student-athlete by not providing adequate transitional programs to better equip the black student athlete to succeed in the typical campus environment.

Professor and Peer Stereotypes

As represented in the documentary *Hoop Dreams*, colleges and universities do not scour the inner city to look for future scientists, doctors, teachers or the academically gifted. Inner city, athletically talented, black males are considered a commodity to these institutions (Jones, 1996). After being heavily recruited, the same individuals who were lured by institutional representatives through praise and worship are treated in a drastically different manner by their peers and professors. Research at the University of Georgia found that most black athletes are being exploited on the playing field, and neglected in the classroom (UGA News Service, 2010). Billy Hawkins, professor of sport management at the University of Georgia, wrote: "During sporting events, our racially and economically segregated community temporarily transcended its racial and class differences and forged a sense of unity, a communal identity and a common enemy—the opposing team" (UGA News Service, 2010). But while there is a commonality during a sporting event, there is drastic segregation in the classroom, and the worst culprits are white professors (Perlmutter, 2003). Black traditional students have reported that their relationship with professors was an important predictor of their academic success (Allen, 1998). Research has also proven that the relationship between male student-athletes and faculty members have far-reaching positive effects (Comeaux, 2005). Even though these relationships have proven beneficial, professors still hold negative stereotypes about black student-athletes that adversely affect the comfort level of facilitating such relationships and consequently the performance and success levels of the student.

Black male student-athletes experience the most damaging stereotyping and negative branding given to them by the campus community and professors (Edwards, 1984; Johnson, Hallinan & Westerfield, 1999; Sailes, 1993; Sellers, 2000; Comeaux, 2010). A 1993 study determined that white students at a Division I institution felt that their African American student-athlete peers were not academically prepared to attend college (Sailes, 1993). In the study conducted by Sailes, 80 percent of students felt that African American student-athletes received special privileges, 72 percent of students felt that African American student-athletes could not compete with them in the classroom, 54 percent of students felt that African American student-athletes received unearned grades, and 37 percent of students felt that African American student-athletes did not belong in school (Sailes, 1993). Stereotypes that seem to be resonating on campuses throughout the country also include a lack of intelligence and the earning of poor grades by black student-athletes. These findings were consistent with the "dumb jock" image and stereotype which insinuated that black athletes "have limited intellectual abilities, lack motivation, and do not perform well academically" (Benson, 2000; Edwards, 1984; Harrison, 1998; Lapchick, 1996; Simons, et al. 2007; Comeaux, 2010).

The "dumb jock" phenomenon can be found as early as 500 B.C. when Greek athletes were classified as useless and worthless citizens (Coakley, 1990). The media has helped to perpetuate the current "dumb jock" mentality by portraying athletes as inferiorly intelligent. The media also has an overwhelming effect on portraying significance in the values of black males, focusing on athletic prowess over educational gains (Beamon & Bell, 2006). Media portrayals play a large role in depicting the image that most of society, including professors and fellow student, accept as the typical black male athlete. It is detrimental for black male student-athletes to have to deal with these stereotypes from their peers, but it is even more disadvantageous for professors and faculty to typecast them in a negative way as well.

Student Involvement Theory states that academic success is drastically impacted by involvement in the campus community and involvement with faculty. Students often look up to faculty members and even idolize them in ways that create natural role models (Light, 2001). Gerdy (2002) stated the role and importance of bridging the gap for student-athletes between academics and athletics are as follows:

> For athletics to fulfill its purpose, coaches and athletic administrators must reconsider everything they do, and they must ponder what they will say and how they will say it to make sure they are contributing to the border goals of the institution. Similarly, faculty and academic leaders further education goals. The entire higher education community, athletic and academic leaders alike, are responsible for bridging the gap between the athletic and academic communities by reassessing how athletics can be used to contribute more directly to higher education's three-pronged mission of teaching, research, and service. To fulfill the New Standard, we must ensure that athletics is "a part of, rather than apart from," the university" [Harrison, 2006].

Unfortunately, while many campus officials realize the necessity of bridging this gap in order to ensure success of student-athletes, faculty members do not engage in behaviors which would facilitate its occurrence. One study determined that 60.3 percent of male student-athletes engage in interactions with faculty outside of the classroom occasionally or not at all (Comeaux & Harrison, 2001). In a study at a Division I institution, surveying 111 professors, findings determined that those surveyed felt that black male student-athletes were considered to be the lowest academic performers (Sailes, 1993). With no basis for this type of stereotyping, the beliefs and ensuing behaviors among white university professors conduct toward their black student-athletes are unjust and negatively impact black athlete during evaluation and grading by university faculty.

Qualitative research at the University of Georgia aimed to determine frequent behaviors among white professors and their black student-athletes (Perimutter, 2010). Professors often engaged in "overlooking" the student-athletes in their classes. Faculty felt that these individuals were on campus for the primary purpose of playing a sport and were ignoring their academic pursuits. This caused a feeling of transparency among the black student-athletes in the classroom summed up by one student that declared "you get the feeling that they don't think of you as a student. Or they don't see you at all" (Perimutter, 2010). Professors also tend to have lowered expectations of black athletes. The idea that these individuals don't have much to add to the classroom setting creates an atmosphere where C grades are praised and where black athletes tend to be ignored. Some black athletes report a starkly opposite situation in which they are overly scrutinized and punished for actions that their Caucasian peers engage in without consequence. One student reported that "during tests, whenever I looked up, the teacher was looking at me. I wasn't cheating. I know other guys, white frat guys, were; but it was like I was the most likely profile or something" (Perlmutter, 2010). Another student reported feeling like his professor was "working hard to fail him" (Perlmutter, 2010). One of the most unfathomable behaviors conducted by faculty members was the use of negative comments and racially charged statements. One professor told a student that "you people should be grateful to be here" (Perlmutter, 2010). The faculty in the study defended their behaviors by pointing out the negative behaviors of black student-athletes such as: missing classes, arriving late, sitting in the back and not participating and not acting interested in the class topic (Perlmutter, 2010). Using the negative behavior that a black student athlete may engage in against that student will not encourage them to achieve academically in class, and consequently cause higher engagement levels in the behaviors that are considered to be negative. This will lead to even greater instances of stereotyping and labeling among black student-athletes. It is the job of the faculty and professors to end the vicious cycle that occurs between stereotyping and negative behaviors in order to encourage the education of the student.

Under-Utilization of Support Services and Social Integration

College athletic programs, specifically basketball, are known to recruit academically challenged athletes (Knott, 2008). Jawanza Kunjufu, founder and president of African American Images, has written several books about raising and mentoring African American boys. He is often brought into school systems where blacks are doing poorly in order to "fix them" (Dodeson, 2012). But as Kunjufu teaches the schools and administrators who bring him in, it is not the black students that need to be fixed; it is the educational system (Kunjufu, 2007). Most institutions feel that there is nothing wrong with the school or the culture within the school. Kunjufu's research and findings have determined that poor academic results have more to do with the problems within the school, rather than the individual (Kunjufu, 2007).

Research usually cites the following institutional and educational causes for low academic success rates among black student athletes: questionable recruiting of student-athletes, the admission of individuals who are under-qualified and under prepared academically, the large time commitment required in order to be a student-athlete, and the reality that a growing number of young adults are leaving the K-12 educational system under-prepared for higher education or a career pursuit (Nikolaidis, Patsiaouras & Alexopoulos). Research on the persistence and efforts of students to reach graduation generally adopts one of several theoretical perspectives including economic, inter-actional, organizational, psychological, and societal models. Tinto's Longitudinal and Interactionalist model (1975, 1986) attempted to determine the causes for academic success and failures by understanding the importance of social and academic integration into the collegiate community (Meeuwisse, Severiens & Born, 2010).

Tinto's model determined that the greater the extent an individual socially and academically integrated oneself into the collegiate campus, the higher the chances for academic success (Meeuwisse et al., 2010). Individuals must achieve both socially and intellectually in order to fully integrate into their new atmosphere. In order to achieve this end, the individual must have programs and resources, as well as the capability of utilizing said programs and resources, to succeed. Prior research has determined that ethnic minority students have less contact with peers and professors and are less likely to utilize academic services than their Caucasian peers (Mangold, Bean & Adams, 1993). The importance of academic and social integration is such that "theoretically, student involvement inside and outside of the classroom facilitates the integration of students into the complex interdependent and overlapping academic and social spheres of educational organizations" (Mangold, Bean & Adams, 1993). Without full involvement in personal academic success, an individual will not fully integrate into the educational system. By not providing the tools and programs necessary to becoming fully involved, the school is disseminating a disadvantage to the student's integration. Consequently, black student athletes need to venture outside the athletic social environment and interact with more mainstream campus social, cultural and academic activities in order to have a complete positive campus experience.

Black male student-athletes are not getting support from their professors, nor are they utilizing the support services available to them through the campus. Tomlinson and Cope (1988) found that black students attending predominantly white campuses were not utilizing services that promote emotional health (Richardson, 1996). Implementing advising and academic programs and early warning system initiatives can help struggling students to succeed (Engle et al., 2010). These programs are not always offered by the institution and are not always utilized by the African American student-athlete for a multitude of reasons including: psychological barriers, lack of knowledge of how to use systems to one's advantage, limited resources that are available or accessible, using outdated delivery methods of information, ineffective communication by educators, counselors and administrators and lack of the student-athlete taking responsibility for his or her personal growth (Richardson, 1996). It is important for universities to advertise and promote the academic and support services available and make these programs welcoming experiences for all students, primarily the ones who are uncomfortable about utilizing them due to the fact that those are the individuals that need them the most.

Exploitation

Critics argue that 90 percent of the National Collegiate Athletic Association's revenue comes from black male athletes who participate in the Division I basketball tournament, more commonly referred to as March Madness (Steinbach, 2010). College sports are now referred to as an "edutainment industry" (Laforge & Hodge, 2011) and produce large sums of revenue for universities and the NCAA. University presidents cannot afford to miss out on large contracts from television deals nor other the revenues generated by college football and basketball. In 2011, the Southeastern Conference (SEC) brought in one billion dollars in athletic revenue and schools like Florida, Michigan, Penn State and Texas earned $40 million to $80 million in profits (Schroder, 2011). A recent publication from an athletes' advocacy group determined that if college sports divided their revenue in the same manner professional sports did, the average Bowl Championship Series (BCS) athlete would be worth $121,000 per year and the average basketball player would be worth $265,000 per year (Schroder, 2011). Ticket sales, post-season competition, NCAA and conference distributions, student activity fees, donations, concessions, radio and television rights, signage and sponsorships, sports camps, program sales and advertising bring in billions to collegiate campuses around the country (Grant, Leadley & Zygmont, 2008). However, student-athletes are not earning this revenue, the universities and NCAA are reaping the financial benefits of big time college athletes. Student athletes are expected to play for school spirit or for athletic scholarship and in those instances, many student athletes receive partial or no financial aid at all. Consequently, student-athletes are athletically exploited in order to make a profit for the university they attend. The time demands of athletics make it difficult to succeed academically. Resultantly, much of the focus on these individuals is geared toward their athletic commitments and not their academic responsibilities.

The increase in the importance of athletics to the income of universities is partially to blame for some of the resentment and negative attitudes held by faculty. In a study of college faculty members, one-third felt that academic standards had been lowered for student-athletes. Many also believed that the pressure placed on revenue producing sports also impacted the admission practices of the school, graduation rates and the overall academic reputation of the institution (Laforge & Hodge, 2011). While the increased importance and coverage of collegiate sports influences faculty opinions of student-athletes, it is the university as a whole that is exploiting these young men in order to make money. Billy Hawkins, a professor at the University of Georgia, compares the use of black student-athletes to slave ownership:

> If you look at the relationship initiated by a slave owner, it's purely economic. When we look at an institution's relationship with black student-athletes, and more specifically, black male athletes in the sports of football and basketball, it too is purely economic. They are generally selected or migrate from communities that are socially and culturally different and placed into this environment that is somewhat of a culture shock to them. No political power, whatsoever, when you talk about making decisions—even choosing a major [Steinbach, 2010; Hawkins, 2010].

Hawkins also points out that while society is inundated with public service announcements stating that more than 400,000 student-athletes are going pro in something other than sports, less than one percent of those 400,000 student-athletes generate more than 90 percent of NCAA revenue (Hawkins, 2010). An elevated level of African American participation in revenue producing sports leads to consequences such as lower academic achievement and higher expectations for futures in professional athletics (Beamon, 2010) both which serve as barriers to the black student athlete achieving academic success during their tenure on their respective college campuses.

The lack of male role models outside of sport and entertainment for many black males from lower economic classes inadvertently causes the focus on athletics to begin at a young age and provides a form of improbable success and achievement (Drummond et al., 1999; Harris, 1994; Sailes, 1998, Beamon, 2010). When the focus is on athletics from the very beginning, it is understandable why African American male student-athletes allow themselves to be exploited by the institution. Sailes (1991) found that the socialization patterns of African American student-athletes force them to be overrepresented in some sports while avoiding others due to lack of role models, absent facilities and institutionalized racism and discrimination. Not surprising, the sports that African Americans are over-represent in are the revenue producers for colleges and universities, football and basketball, leading to the students' exploitation for institutional financial gain.

Athletics Above Academics

It's a fact that athletic ability can lead to increased opportunity for education (Lucas & Lovaglia, 2002). With increased opportunity for these student-athletes, NCAA president-elect Mark Emmert's comment that "Everything we do in intercollegiate athletics must be driven by an overriding commitment to the academic success of our student-athletes" should be comforting

(Johnson, 2010). Unfortunately, the reality is that the education afforded to these individuals and the education they choose to acquire is drastically different. The focus on athletics from the beginning of an African American boy's life and the negative attitudes held by Caucasian peers and professors cause a drastic shift in priorities. It is understandable why so many male African American student-athletes place their focus on their sport instead of academics. The choice is predisposed for these individuals through societal pressures and norms. Unfortunately, the reality of the matter is that an oppositional relationship between sport and academic achievement exists and prioritizing athletics first can be detrimental to academic success (Beamon & Bell, 2006). The reverse is also true. Placing a priority on academics over athletics can lead to black student athletes underperforming on the athletic field placing their annually renewed athletic scholarship in jeopardy. Balancing both athletics and academics is the anticipated goal but is rarely achieved.

For decades, athletic programs have sacrificed the student part of student-athlete, to focus on the athlete. The accepted protocol and formula for revenue production in college athletics is to win. To do that, athletes must prepare and perform at a high level which takes time, more than likely, time taken away from academics. Black males are more eager to pursue higher education than in previous years, but many black student-athletes are arriving on campus under prepared academically and are unable to take on the challenges of balancing academics and athletics (Barbalias, 2002). Unable to put 100 percent effort into both academics and athletics, it is natural for the individual to place their focus on the area that has brought them the most success, athletics. Sailes (2010) conducted a study focusing on 1500 Division I student-athletes and the priority of the athlete in regard to balancing academics and athletics. Ninety-one percent of the individuals surveyed felt that athletics were more important and a higher priority than academics and their studies. The majority of those surveyed, 83 percent, reported studying the minimal amount of time necessary for them to remain eligible. Fifty-four percent of the student-athletes identified themselves more as an athlete than a student. Sixty percent of the individuals who took part in the study felt that peers at their institution held negative attitudes about athletes and their intelligence which is consistent with the research on beliefs held by non-student-athletes (Sailes, 2010). Studies like this give new meaning to the athlete-student mentality, they are majoring in eligibility instead of an academic major. The student-athlete needs to take a role in their academic success and institutions need to recognize the barriers that force student-athletes to feel alienated as intellectuals. It is vital to understand that the level of involvement and pursuit that many black male student athletes place on athletic excellence compromises the ability to mentally and physically apply equal effort toward academics (Simiyu, 2002).

Self-Handicapping

Black student-athletes arrive on campus with a disadvantage compared to their Caucasian peers due to institutional barriers beyond their control that prevent them from succeeding academically. Recognizing faults within the institution is important, however, the individual himself is also to blame for the lack of academic success during their collegiate tenure. While minimal research does exist on the topic of self-handicapping, further information needs to be gathered in regard to image perception and personal choices to understand why college students, and black student athletes in particular, choose to self-handicap themselves when they are already facing so many challenges to succeed academically. Student athletes stand to lose more from their self-handicapping behavior than the traditional university student. Student athletes could lose their financial aid and participation in athletics in addition to low grades or academic failure. It is not logical that students and student athletes self-handicap themselves with so much on the line, but the research is clear, it does happen.

Entitlement Mentality

Previous studies have determined that to understand and predict academic performance, demographic variables, family structure and socioeconomic status must be considered (Reynolds, L.M., 2007). The possibility of attending higher education institutions and the possibility of academic success are lowest among individuals from lower socioeconomic neighborhoods (Forsyth & Furlong, 2003). The poor upbringing of many African American males and the lack of father figures must be accounted for when understanding why they are performing so poorly in higher education. When black males are lucky enough to be large, fast and excel at a sport, they are told the same thing by classmates, teachers and society: "You've got it made, you'll get a college scholarship" (Wharton & Terry, 2002). The ability to succeed in sport, allows individuals from monetarily deficient families to attend institutions that otherwise wouldn't be affordable. Ten percent of black men enrolled in undergraduate education are there as scholarship athletes. In some cases, most students of color at some small private and public colleges are student athletes and generally outnumber the number of students of color who are not athletes. The research has determined that black males who have played their way into higher education and earned scholarships to campus are among the poorest performers academically (Wharton & Terry, 2002). So why does society emphasize athletics from the start to these individuals instead of academics? To understand this, it is also important to understand where the majority of African Americans are coming from.

African Americans are highly concentrated within blue-collar jobs and are commonly underpaid and fall below the poverty threshold (Coles & Green, 2009). There is a drastic discrepancy between incomes and poverty levels of black males and other ethnic groups in the United States today. This constant struggle leads to apathy of life and a feeling of insignificance. Adding to the financial burden at home is the fact that many African Americans are being born into single parent, matron lead, households. In a 2000 study, researchers determined that 68 percent of black women who gave birth during the year were doing so unmarried (Martin et al., 2003). While being unmarried doesn't always mean that a child is growing up without a father figure, further research determined that 37 percent of black unmarried fathers were not living with their children and their mother while in comparison 66 percent of white fathers and 59 percent of Hispanic fathers were living in the same household as their child (Carlson & McLanahan, 2008). When a child doesn't have the financial background to further his or her education, and the opportunity to do so can be gained through athletics, focus during youth naturally turns to the area where a future may be provided. Genethia Hudley Hayes, Los Angeles Unified School District board member, stated the problem in this succinct way: "Black teens are encouraged to develop their athletic skills but are rarely challenged academically, often placed in the easiest classes possible. We are not preparing them to be admitted or compete (in college)" (Wharton & Terry, 2002). Growing up in a lower socio-economic neighborhood tends to lead to the following difficulties for African American students and lower probability of academic success:

1. A lack of familiarity with higher education, which often results in enrollment in inappropriate courses or attending unsuitable institutions.
2. A lack of funds, which limits choices of courses or institutions and also the length of time which the individual is willing to remain at the institution.
3. A fear of debt, which plays a greater role on disadvantaged African American male athletes who are not receiving full scholarships or financial aid. This fear is also related to the individual's lack of confidence in their academic ability and their chances of finding a job after college.
4. Feelings of cultural isolation, particularly at more prestigious institutions which compromise the disadvantaged student's identity, lower their personal morale and lessen the commitment to study.

[Forsyth & Furlong, 2003].

Without sufficient financial income and lack of parental support, black males who excel at sports are prime targets for over-aggressive agents and single-minded coaches who embody a "win at all costs" mentality (Mereday,

2010). When examining these student-athletes, some coaches and agents see a cash cow that can provide them job security, a huge salary and money and fame if they are able to control their black student athletes to the point of getting them to perform on the athletic field and keeping them academically eligible. Often promises to under advantaged kids include houses, cars and wealth that surpass their meager upbringings (Mereday, 2010). Black parents who struggle with a lower income and often raise their children as a single parent, give up their roles in the lives of the development of their sons with the misguided understanding that the coaches, managers and agents have the child's best interest at heart (Mereday, 2010).

It is essential to note that not all African American males are being raised in single parent, poverty ridden houses and neighborhoods. Unfortunately, public opinion of the black family structure includes an overwhelming assumption that there is a high level of deficit between other ethnic groups and African Americans (Frazier, 1948). While many historians have pointed out the strengths of black families, the negative views of families living in poverty have been reinforced by research and led to the negative stereotyping of African American culture (Billinglsey, 1968; Hill, 1971). This can be just as detrimental to a child who is not living in poverty than the actual reality of living in poverty where opportunities are revoked and performance is undermined (Harry, B., Klingner, J.K., & Hart, J., 2005).

The community where an individual is raised, the family's financial situation and family structure cannot be considered self-handicapping behavior, but the subsequent entitlement mentality held by many star black male athletes can be. After growing up in a society where their athleticism provides the essentials they need, some black student-athletes arrive at a university feeling entitled to whatever they desire. High profile student athlete status on campus provides these individuals with access to gifts and services only allowed to them and others in similar positions (Snyder, 2011). The newfound fame and gifts are tempting and difficult to turn down by individuals who had very little growing up and consequently lead to feelings of empowerment and entitlement. Entitlement mentalities by student-athletes can subsequently lead to institutional barriers between athletes and professors. One professor wrote in the *Chronicle of Higher Education:*

> From the perspective of the small liberal-arts college where I teach, I suspect most of my faculty colleagues join me in seeing sports-particularly football-as a distraction at best. Many of our football players, and this is a Division III school, have a swaggering sense of entitlement that must have been engineered by too much deferential treatment in high school. It goes without saying that they tend to be among our weakest students. Seeking "power and standing over others" and having "the punch in the mouth" as "part of your repertoire"

are not commendable traits. If we must have sports at college, let's stick with cross country and ultimate Frisbee [The Case For and Against Sports, 2012].

The self-handicapping entitlement mentality that many black male athletes adopt when entering the college setting may lead them to beliefs of empowerment and provide material items that were not available during their youth, but ultimately lead to institutional criticism and negative expectations from faculty and students alike.

Unrealistic Hoop Dreams

A disproportionate percentage of young black males believe that the best and only option for social advancement in society is not through education and the acquirement of educational and vocational skills, but through participation and play in professional sports (*City Ball: A Documentary*). The entitlement mentality of many black male athletes is also driven by their unrealistic idea that they will one day play professionally. In a study by Gary A. Sailes, professor of sports sociology at Indiana University, Division I athletes were surveyed and subsequent findings determined that 95 percent of the student-athlete participants chose to attend the university they were enrolled in to increase their chances of being drafted into professional sports. Fifty-two percent of the athletes surveyed planned on pursuing a career in professional sports. Eighty-three percent of the participants said that they would enter the draft before graduating if they felt they could be drafted, which is clear evidence that athletics plays a top priority over athletics (Sailes, 2010).

While 50 percent of the study participants felt that their chances of playing at the professional level were good, the reality of the situation is much different. Table 1 identifies the probabilities of an individual going professional directly out of college as well as high school.

Table 1: Probabilities of Going Professional

Sport	Odds of Going Professional from College	Odds of Going Professional from High School
Football	68:1	1,222:1
Basketball	74:1	2,681:1
Baseball	55:1	1,001:1

Source: (Sailes, 2010)

The entitlement mentality held by many collegiate student-athletes leads to unrealistic goals and aspirations. These "hoop dreams" lead to higher emphasis on athletics and less focus on academics. It would be typecasting to say that all black male athletes placed all of their hopes and aspirations in professional sports. However, Sailes (2010) indicated that a black family is seven times more likely to push a child into sport than a white family. Moreover, his sample, black male athletes were more than twice as likely as their white counterparts to pursue a career in professional sports.

Image Portrayal: Dumbing Down and "Cool Pose"

While feelings of self-entitlement exists outside the realm of academics for black male athletes, inside the classroom is a much different situation. Many engage in what has become known as the "cool pose." Ethnic difference theories like cultural inversion, the cool pose, and stereotype threat-disidentification, encourage African American's to dumb themselves down in the classroom in order to fit into an environment where they do not feel comfortable (Wickline, 2003). The cool pose is a self-preservation tactic practiced by black males that enables an individual, who society has given up on, to make do (Malveaux, 2006). The implementation of the cool pose does not mean that black students correlate studying and doing well in school as "acting white," but it instead is a response of not caring about a society that doesn't care about them (Malveaux, 2006). In reality, the same young men who mock education and scholarships are the individuals at home studying behind closed doors in hopes of achievement and getting out of the lifestyle in which they currently live (Malveaux, 2006).

The cool pose, initially coined by psychologist Richard Majors, was created by African American hegemonic culture in response to the historical construct of white male dominance and white privilege. Utilization of this attitude and image creates and enforces stereotypes of delinquency and inferiority (Hall, 2009). Society has created a culture where black males gain acceptance of peers by dumbing down, acting out, and academically performing below what they are capable of (Hall, 2009). In a 1992 study, sixty African American teenagers in Boston were interviewed to better understand the usage of the cool pose. Self-reports found that the cool pose was utilized in order to establish male identity and to negotiate the perceived dangers and/or challenges black males encountered in their daily lives (Majors & Billson, 1992; Werner, 1993). While the cool pose is used primarily as a self-preservation technique, white peers and those in authoritative position do not realize the true reasoning behind the act. Instead they misread the actions and think that black males who demonstrate this trait are fearless, emotionless, macho, aloof, irresponsible, unconcerned, unmotivated and have attitude problems (Majors & Billson, 1992). The Boston study also found that the cool pose prevents black males from showing affection toward individuals in which they truly care about. This potentially leads to not only failure in the classroom, but failure within relationships as well as a lack of social integration. Utilization of the cool pose by young black men, who do not feel comfortable in their current situation, can lead to academic failure and reinforce already present negative stereotypes. A better understanding of the underlying motives for implementing the cool pose mentality can help professors, faculty and administrators to eliminate the need for its utilization and help the students achieve to their full potential.

Drinking, Drugs, and Promiscuity

Division I student-athletes experience the same stresses that normal students experience regarding social and academic adjustment to collegiate life. Student-athletes, also face the demands created by their participation in athletics, creating even greater challenges to the student experience (Howard-Hamilton & Watt, 2001; Jolly, 2008; Watt & Moore, 2001; Comeaux & Harrison, 2011). Student-athletes have an opportunity to engage in a variety of activities, some of them positive, others negative. Incoming freshman are the most susceptible to the pitfalls of collegiate life due to the drastic change in the campus cultural environment. When students are allowed freedoms without parental supervision, many engage in activities that were not previously considered acceptable. Black student-athletes are no different. Those individuals who come from lower socioeconomic backgrounds are being offered a multitude of gifts and opportunities that they did not have prior to their campus experience. Some of these may include chances to abuse alcohol, drugs, and to engage in promiscuous sexual behavior. Self-handicapping behavior refers to engaging in these activities to the point that they are detrimental to academic and personal success. Self-handicapping is officially defined as any action or choice of performance setting that enhances the opportunity to externalize (or excuse) failure and to internalize (reasonably accept credit for) success (Berglas & Jones, 1978).

Self-handicapping behavior is another form of self-preservation that an athlete may choose to engage in. Engaging in self-handicapping behaviors can blur the relationship between ability and performance. If an athlete performs poorly, he can blame his poor performance on other attributes rather than his personal ability and competency levels. For example, staying up late, drinking or partying can be used as an excuse for sub-par athletic performances. Subsequently, athletic successes are given greater significance because they were achieved despite outside negative self-handicapping behaviors and/or factors (Tice, 1991).

Self-handicapping activities may include; drinking, drug use, promiscuity, and illegal behaviors of other kinds. Other forms of claimed self-handicapping occur when an athlete blames anxiety or illness, or lack of self-esteem for lessened athletic abilities or failures (Coudevylle, Ginis & Famose, 2008). There is an important difference in behavioral self-handicapping and claimed self-handicapping. Behavioral self-handicapping is defined as any action that the individual takes part in (i.e. alcohol, drugs, promiscuity) that may lessen their chance of high performance. These types of self-handicaps tend to be more costly and riskier to the student-athlete in regard to athletic as well as academic performance. Claimed self-handicaps tend to transfer more into emotions, self-esteem and self-awareness.

Within the classroom setting, common strategies like sleeping through class, lack of participation, and failure to attend class are utilized frequently to manipulate the perceptions and opinions of others (Urdan & Midgley, 2001). In order to preserve ones appearance and not look less capable than others, individuals become motivated to use self-handicapping actions within the classroom. Self-handicapping can help preserve individual integrity in the event of failure and boost self-worth in the case of success (Covington, 2000; Feick & Rhodewalt, 1997; Higgins, Snyder & Berglas, 1990; Gadbois & Sturgeon, 2010). By engaging in self-handicapping within the classroom setting, the individual can blame poor performance and low grades on behaviors instead of personal ability levels.

Outside of the classroom, research has found that athletes are at a higher risk for alcohol abuse due to social standings and pressure (Olthuis, Zamboanga, Martens & Ham, 2011). While 45 percent of all college students are predicted to engage in risky drinking behavior, student-athletes are more likely to partake in heavy episodic drinking and experience a greater number of problems caused by alcohol usage and abuse (Martens, Dams, & Beck, 2006). Participation in the use of alcohol can be detrimental to the health of many student-athletes, but can also lead to poor academic performance and lower levels of success.

Drug use among student-athletes is another form of behavioral self-handicapping that can lead to detrimental outcomes both in academics and athletics. The research predicts that between three and twenty percent of student-athletes have used illegal drugs (Tricker, Cook & McGuire, 1989). Athletes often turn to drugs in order to overcome physical as well as psychological strains created by having to balance the time and physical demands of academic and athletic participation, often times as much as 80 hours per week during a sports competitive season. The effects of sports, stress, injury, frustration and exhaustion can lead to the use of illegal drugs as an escape (Ogilvie, 1981). As in the case of alcohol abuse, the use of illegal drugs can lead to failures both inside and outside of sports and can drastically decrease an individual's chances to succeed in either arena.

Previous research has determined a greater occurrence of risky sexual behavior among student-athletes compared to non-athletes. An association between alcohol and risky sexual behavior has also been found (Grossbard, Lee, Neighbors, Hendershot & Larimer, 2007). A study of 2,123 incoming college students, 221 reporting to be student-athletes at the university, found that athletes engaged in a greater weekly consumption of alcohol, reported a higher frequency of drinking before or during sex, and recounted a higher number of sexual partners than their non-athlete peers (Grossbard, Lee, Neighbors, Hendershot & Larimer, 2007). The opportunity to engage in risky behaviors allows black male student-athletes another opportunity for failure. Whether self-handicapping behavior exists in order to cope with the stress of balancing academic and athletic cultures, a method of self-preservation from perceived campus racial stereotypes, or any other factor relating to collegiate life, engagement in it, among black student athletes, acts as a catalyst for potential low academic success rates. With so many other barriers preventing black male student-athletes from succeeding, self-handicapping and negative personal actions need to be removed from the equation to ensure success in the classroom.

Conclusions

When the decision of Brown v. the Board of Education was handed down, Thurgood Marshall turned to Robert Carter and Constance Baker Motley (all three judges) and said, "In five years it will be all over boys, because there won't be a race problem. We will be integrated into American society" (*Frontline*: Interview with William Julius Wilson, 1997). According to William Julius Wilson, professor of Afro-America studies at Harvard University and an advisor to the Clinton administration on social and public policy issues, the problem is much deeper. The cause of continued racial segregation is "that a system of racial discrimination over a long period of time can create racial inequality, a system of racial inequality that will linger on even after racial barriers come down. That is because the most disadvantaged blacks victimized by decades and centuries of racial oppression do not have resources that allow them to compete effectively with other people. They are disadvantaged" (*Frontline*: Interview with William Julius Wilson, 1997).

Wilson's astute observations transfer directly to the ongoing problems within higher education and the low academic success rates of black male student-athletes. A varying array of institutional barriers and self-handicapping behaviors act as catalysts for African American's levels of underachievement in the classroom. Universities hold stereotypes that negatively affect classroom ability and success. Fellow peers hold stereotypes that perpetuate the "dumb jock" mentality and lead to engagement in the cool pose persona. Universities are not providing necessary support services and programs to help students acclimate to a new and unfamiliar culture. Even when these services are provided, many African American male student-athletes are not utilizing them to improve their academic standings. Colleges and Universities are looking at these" star" athletes as cash cows and exploiting their athletic abilities while ignoring their academic needs. Is it any wonder that many of these students are turning their priorities to the sports in which they are revered instead of the classrooms where they are ignored and viewed negatively by peers as well as professors?

Black male student-athletes are also sometimes engaging in behaviors that only hurt themselves academically. The self-preservation technique of the cool pose as well as the entitlement mentality that many of these individuals hold does nothing to help them academically or negate the negative stereotypes held by others. Pretending to not care in the classroom, while expecting preferential treatment outside of the classroom, does not help the individual succeed, and subsequently, helps to reinforce racial prejudices. The unrealistic expectation to make it into professional sports turns the focus of many black student-athletes from academics to athletics. When a future in professional sport seems more realistic than a future with an education, prioritizing athletics above academics seems only natural. African American's are not immune to the temptations of college and the lure to participate in self-handicapping behaviors. With research showing that student-athletes, as a subset, participate in higher levels of drinking and promiscuity, it is understandable that black student-athletes, who find themselves in entirely new surroundings and cultures, find the lure of these illicit behaviors even more appealing.

While research has determined that there are numerous causes for the underachievement of black male student-athletes at the undergraduate level, to effectively change the current problem, we must first stop playing the blame game. The athletes themselves, families, coaches, administrators, non-athlete peers, professors, scouts, and societal expectations all play a part in the academic under performance for this group. Until everyone involved takes responsibility for their role, a change cannot be made and the black student-athlete will continue to suffer educationally. There is a substantial amount of research present that determines the reasons behind underachievement, but very little research has been done to determine what incentives, plans and programs can be implemented to create change effectively. Understanding what can be done to address these issues can be the catalyst for a change that is in dire need in higher education. Tavis Smiley, talk show host and political analyst, once said on the *Tom Joyner Morning Show*, "When white American gets the sniffles, black American catches the flu!" What he was alluding to was that white privilege and black under privilege have different ways of reacting to the same social conditions in our country. Similarly, if self-handicapping is a problem on our college campus and potentially leads to under performance in the classroom for all students, it is a much more serious problem for individuals who come from already challenged social environments. In no way was it the intent of this paper to imply that institutional barriers and self-handicapping are problems exclusive to the black student athlete. Rather, it was the intent of this paper to identify the specific challenges faced by black student athletes in their attempt to navigate through the tough challenges which are a part of campus culture.

REFERENCES

Allen, W.R. (1988). Black students in U.S. higher education: Toward improved access, adjustment and achievement. *The Urban Review, 20,* 165–188.

Barbalias, P. (2002). Black student athletes: Improving their collegiate experience. *The Vermont Connection Journal.*

Beamon, K.K. (2010). Are sports overemphasized in the socialization process of African American males? A qualitative analysis of former collegiate athletes' perception of sport socialization. *Journal of Black Studies, 41.*

Beamon, K.K., and Bell, P.A. (2006). Academics versus athletics: An examination of the effects of background and socialization on African American male student athletes. *The Social Science Journal, 43,* 393–403.

Benson, K.F. (2000). Constructing academic inadequacy: African American athlete's stories of schooling. *The Journal of Higher Education, 71*(2), 223–246.

Berglas, S., and Jones, E. E. (1978). Drug choice as a self-handicapping strategy in response to noncontingent success. *Journal of Personality and Social Psychology, 36,* 405–417.

Billingsley, A. (1968). *Black families in white America.* Englewood Cliffs, NJ: Prentice Hall.

Bowler, M. (1998). Demographics are the downfall grades: "Quality Counts" findings put performance data in the context of census statistics and show how Baltimore schools pull down statewide averages. *Baltimore Sun.*

Carlson, M.J., and Marcia, J. (2008). Coparenting and nonresident fathers' involvement with young children after nonmarital birth. *Demography, 45*(2), 461–488.

The case for and against sports. (2012). *Chronicle of Higher Education, 58*(25), B18.

CityBall: A Documentary. http://kemetrosports.com/MetroSports-cityball.aspx. Retrieved June 9, 2012.

Coles, R.L., and Green, C. (2009). *The myth of the missing black father.* New York: Columbia University Press.

Comeaux, E. (2005). Environmental predictors of academic achievement among student-athletes in the revenue-producing sports of men's basketball and football. *The Sports Journal, 8*(3).

Comeaux, E., and Harrison, C.K. (2001). Gender, sport and higher education: The impact of student-faculty interactions on academic achievement. *The Academic Athletic Journal,* 38–54.

Comeaux, E., and Harrison, C.K. (2011). A conceptual model of academic success for student-athletes. *Educational Researcher, 40*(5), 235–245.

Coudevylle, G. R., Ginis, K. M., and Famose, J.P. (2008). Determinants of self-handicapping strategies in sport and their effects on athletic performance. *Social Behavior & Personality: An International Journal 36*(3), 391–398.

Covington, M. (2000). Goal theory, motivation, and school achievement: An integrative review. *Annual Review of Psychology, 51,* 171–200.

Curtis, R. L. (1998). Racism and rationales: A frame analysis of John Hoberman's Darwin's athletes. *Social Science Quarterly (University of Texas)*, *79*(4), 885–891.

Dodeson, A. P. (2012). Coming to the defense of black students. *Issues in Higher Education, 29*(6).

Drummond, R.J., H. Senterfill, and C. Fountain (1999). Role models of urban minority students. *Psychological Reports, 84*, 181–182.

Edwards, H. (1984). The black "dumb jock": An American sports tragedy. *The College Board Review, 131*, 8–13.

Engle, J., C. Theokas, and T. Education (2010). Top gainers: Some public four-year colleges and universities make big improvements in minority graduation rates. College Results Online: Education Trust.

Farrey, T. (1993). UW and its black athletes: A special report—The lonely struggle. *Seattle Times.*

Feick, D. L., and F. Rhodewalt (1997). The double-edged sword of self-handicapping: Discounting, augmentation, and the protection and enhancement of self-esteem. *Motivation and Emotion, 21* (2), 147–163.

Forsyth, A., and A. Furlong (2003). Socio-economic disadvantage and experience in higher education. York, England: Joseph Rowntree Foundation.

Frazier, E. F. (1948). *The Negro family in the United States.* New York: Citadel.

Frontline: Interview with William Julius Wilson. (1997). http://www.pbs.org/wgbh/pages/frontline/shows/race/interviews/wilson.html.

Gadbois, S. A., and R. D. Sturgeon (2011). Academic self-handicapping: Relationships with learning specific and general self-perceptions and academic performance over time. *British Journal of Educational Psychology, 81*(2), 207–222.

Gerdy, J. L. (1997, 2002). *The successful college athletic program.* Phoenix: American Council on Education and Oryx Press.

Grant, R. R., J. Leadley, and Z. Zygmont (2008). The economics of intercollegiate sports. New Jersey: World Scientific.

Grossbard, J. R., C. M. Lee, C. Neighbors, C. S. Hendershot, and M. E. Larimer (2007). Alcohol and risky sex in athletes and nonathletes: What roles do sex motives play? *Journal of Studies on Alcohol and Drugs, 68*(4), 566–574.

Hall, R.E. (2009). Cool pose, black manhood, and juvenile delinquency. *Journal of Human Behavior in the Social Environment, 19*(5), 531–539.

Harris, O. (1994). Race, sport, and social support. *Sociology of Sport Journal, 11*, 40–50.

Harrison, C. K. (1998). Themes that thread through society: Racism and athletic manifestation in the African American community. *Race, Ethnicity and Education, 1*(1), 63–74.

Harrison, K. (2006). Faculty and male football and basketball players on university campuses: An empirical investigation of the "intellectual as mentor" to the student-athlete. Unpublished manuscript.

Harry, B., J. K. Klingner, and J. Hart (2005). African American families under fire: Ethnographic views of family strengths. *Remedial and Special Education, 26*(2), 101–112.

Hawkins, B. (2010). *The new plantation: Black athletes, college sports, and predominantly white NCAA institutions.* New York: Palgrave Macmillan.

Higgins, R. C., C. R. Snyder, and S. Berglas (1990). *Self-handicapping: The paradox that isn't.* New York: Plenum.

Hill, R. B. (1971). *The strengths of black families.* New York: Emerson Hall.

Hoberman, J. (1997). *Darwin's athletes: How sport has damaged black America and preserved the myth of race.* Boston: Houghton Mifflin.

Howard-Hamilton, M., and S. Watt (2001). *Student services for athletes.* San Francisco: Jossey-Bass.

Johnson, D., C. Hallinan, and C. Westerfield (1998). Picturing success: Photographs and stereotyping in men's collegiate basketball. *Journal of Sport Behavior, 22*, 45–53.

Johnson, G. (2010). Emmert: Well-being of student-athletes the ultimate priority. *NCAA News, 2.*

Jolly, C. (2008). Raising the question #9: Is the student-athlete population unique? And why should we care? *Communication Education, 57*(1), 145–151.

Jones, L. (1996). *Hoop Dreams. Jump Cut: A Review of Contemporary Media, 40*, 8–14.

Knott, T. (2008). Graduation gap involves more than just race. *The Washington Times,* Gale Opposing Viewpoints in Context. Web. April 2012.

Kunjufu, J. (2007). *Raising black boys.* Chicago: African American Images.

Laforge, L., and J. Hodge (2011). NCAA academic performance metrics: Implications for intitutional policy and practice. *Journal of Higher Education, 82*(2), 217–235.

Lapchick, R. (1996). *Sport in society: Equal opportunity or business as usual.* Thousand Oaks, CA: Sage.

Light, R. (2001). *Making the most of college: Students speak their minds.* Cambridge: Harvard University Press.

Lucas, J. W., and M. J. Lovaglia (2002). Athletes' expectations for success in athletics compared to academic competition. *Sport Journal, 5*(2).

Majors, R., and J. M. Billson (1992). *Cool pose: The dilemmas of black manhood in America.* Lexington, VA: Lexington.

Malveaux, J. (2006). Culture and context: The plight of black male students. *Issues in Higher Education, 23*(5).

Mangold, W. D., L. Bean, and D. Adams (2003). The impact of intercollegiate athletics on graduation rates among major NCAA Division I universities. *The Journal of Higher Education, 74*(5).

Martens, M. P., K. Dams-O'Connor, and N. C. Beck (2006). A systematic review of college student-athlete drinking: Prevalence rates, sport-related factors, and interventions. *Journal of Substance Abuse Treatment, 31,* 105–116.

Martin, R., N. Rothrock, H. Leventhal, and E. Leventhal (2009). Common sense models of illness: Implications for symptom perception and health-related behaviors. *Social Psychological Foundations of Health and Illness,* 199–225.

Meeuwisse, M., S. E. Severiens, and M. P. Born (2010). Reasons for withdrawal from higher vocational education: A comparison of ethnic minority and majority non-completers. *Studies in Higher Education, 35*(1), 93–111.

Mereday, M. J. (2010). Encouraging black athletes: Remembering the mamas (and papas). *Regal Black Men's Magazine.*

Ogilvie, B. C. (1981). The emotionally disturbed athlete: A round table. *The Physician and Sportsmedicine, 9*(7), 68–74.

Olthuis, J. V., B. L. Zamboanga, M. P. Martens, and L. S. Ham (2011). Social influences, alcohol expectancies, and hazardous alcohol use among college athletes. *Journal of Clinical Sport Psychology, 5*(1), 24.

Papanikolaou, Z., D. Nikolaidis, A. Patsiaouras, and P. Alexopoulos. The freshman experience: High stress, low grades. *Athletic Insight: The Online Journal of Sport Psychology, 5*(4).

Perimutter, D. D. (2003). Black athletes and white professors: A twilight zone of uncertainty. *The Chronicle of Higher Education,* B7-B9.

Reynolds, L. M. (2007). The impact of selective demographics, psychological, and cognitive variables on the academic performance of student athletes. Texas Southern University: Dissertation.

Richardson, S. (1996). Black student athletes: Why they under-utilize traditional outreach programs and methods for increasing utilization of those programs. *Different Perspectives on Majority Rules.* http://digitalcommons.unl.edu/pocpwilst/9.

Sailes, G. (1991). The myth of black sports supremacy. *Journal of Black Studies, 21,* 480–487.

Sailes, G. (1993). An investigation of campus stereotypes: The myth of black athletic superiority and the dumb jock stereotypes. *Sociology of Sport Journal, 10,* 88–97.

Sailes, G. (1998). Betting against the odds: An overview of black sports participation. In G. Sailes (Ed.) *African American in sports.* New Brunswick, NJ: Transaction.

Schroder, E. (2011). Leaders failing college athletics. *From the Sidelines: The Official Publication of the Sports Turf Managers Association.*

Sellers, R. (2000). African American student athletes: Opportunity or exploitation? In D. Books and R. Althouse (Eds.) *Racism in college athletics: The African American athletes' experience* (133–154). Morgantown, WV: Fitness Information Technology.

Simiyu, N. W. W. (2002). Triple tragedy of the black student athlete. *United States Sports Academy American's Sports University.*

Simons, H.D., C. Bosworth, S. Fujita, and M. Jensen (2007). The athlete stigma in higher education. *College Student Journal, 19*(4), 464–479.

Snyder, D. (2011). Entitlement mentality isn't limited to college athletes. *The Washington Times.*

Steinbach, P. (2010). MoneyBall: Academics confront the exploitation of African-American male athletes. AthleticBusiness.com. http://athleticbusiness.com/articles /article.aspx?articleid=3555&zoneid=8.

Tice, D. M. (1991). Esteem protection or enhancement? Self-handicapping motives and attributions differ by trait self-esteem. *Journal of Personality and Social Psychology, 60,* 711–725.

Tolliver, A. (2010). Saturday thoughts: Struggles of black college athletes. Examiner.com. http://www.examiner.com/article/saturday-thoughts-struggles-of-black-college-athletes.

Tomlinson, S. M., and N. R. Cope (1988). Characteristics of black students seeking help at a university counseling center. *Journal of College Student Development, 29,* 65–69.

Tricker, R., D. L. Cook, and R. McGuire (1989). Issues related to drug abuse in college athletics: Athletes at risk. *Sport Psychologist, 3*(2), 155.

UGA News Service. (2010). UGA professor's research shows black athletes exploited physically, neglected academically.

Urdan, T., and C. Midgley (2001). Academic self-handicapping: What we know, what more there is to learn. *Educational Psychology Review, 13*(2), 115–138.

Watt, S. K., and J. L. Moore (2001). *Student services for athletes.* San Francisco: Jossey-Bass.

Werner, D. (1993). Cool pose: The dilemmas of black manhood in America. *Journal of Correctional Education, 44*(3), 144.

Wharton, D., and M. Terry (2002). The wrong message for black male athletes: NCAA report buttresses view that many youths are encouraged to neglect school for sports. *Los Angeles Times.*

Wickline, V. B. (2003). *Ethnic differences in the self-esteem/academic achievement relationship: A meta-analysis.* Presented at the American Psychological Association, August 7–10, 2003.

Why Do I Get Hit in the Face?
Boxing as an Expression
of Black Male Masculinity

Ray V. Robertson

Introduction

This study developed from a two and a half year ethnography and participant observation at an urban boxing gym in Southeast Texas. This case study focuses on myriad constructions of masculinity of a young African American professional boxer. The case study began with the overarching question, "Why did you start boxing?" Probing questions were derived from factors relevant to participation in the "sweet science" gleaned from relevant scholarship in this area with an emphasis on Wacquant's (1992) classic participation observation at a Chicago boxing gym. The interview responses were analyzed using latent-content analysis as outlined in Berg (2007) in order to identify emergent themes associated with why a young Black male participates in boxing, how he constructs and defines his masculinity, and negotiates the treacherous terrain of professional boxing.

Of myriad endeavors that black males can involve themselves in, arguably none says "I am a true man" more than the sport of boxing (Gems, 2004; Sammons, 1988; Wacquant, 1992, 2009, 2011; Woodward, 2004). The sport, most often referred to as the "sweet science," tests the masculinity of its adherents via the intense physical training, the possibility of death at any time, and the fact it is most often, women's boxing notwithstanding, man versus man (Anderson, 2007a; Bledsoe et al., 2005). So, the purpose of this case study was to explore how a young black male professional pugilist expresses his masculinity as he navigates the terrain of professional boxing.

Review of Literature

According to Martin et al. (2001), the bulk of scholarship on black masculinity has relied upon theoretical reviews that were Eurocentric in nature. Therefore, the agency of black men to engage in developing definitions of what masculinity means to them has not been a stalwart of scholarly discourse (Levant et al., 1998; Staples, 1978). Although the aforementioned dilemma is changing, for true African American liberation, scholars, particularly African American scholars, must continue to define what Black manhood means in its ever changing complexity (Martin et al., 2001).

Articulating a useful model of black masculinity entails an understanding of the European decimation of traditional African constructions of manhood (Ani, 1994; Karenga, 2010). An African-centered delineation of black masculinity is necessary as result of the dehumanization of men of African descent during the Maafa, i.e., the great disaster known as the transatlantic system of enslavement and European and Arab colonization of the continent of Africa (Anderson, 2007b; Karenga, 2010). The Maafa consisted of lynchings, murders, cultural decimation which contributed to multifarious definitions of black manhood (Ani, 1994; hooks, 1992; Karenga, 2010). hooks (1992) poignantly asserts "transplanted African men, even those who were coming from cultures where sex roles shaped the division of labor, where the status of men was different and most often higher than that of women, had imposed on them the white colonizer's notions of manhood and masculinity" (p. 90). Henceforth, we can assume at the very least that European constraints placed on African manhood have played a role in the formulation of contemporary definitions of black masculinity.

Akbar (1990) and Nobles (1980) assert that an Afrocentric model is in needed to delineate the exigencies placed on black men. Such a typology takes into consideration a racial identity shaped through a focus on community and collectivity (McClure, 2006). Furthermore, it eschews the emotional callousness and aggressiveness associated with the Eurocentric model and considers the effect of a unique history of subjugation faced by black men across the diaspora (Akbar, 1990; Nobles, 1980). The aforementioned historiography of black men elucidates that validating them using Eurocentric normative constructions would be reductionist at best (Connell, 2005).

The distinctive narrative of black men calls for a model of manhood that represents an amalgamation of Afrocentric and European models (Akbar, 1990; McClure, 2006; Nobles, 1980). The following themes are consistent with a typology of black male masculinity: (1) community needs and cooperation; (2) close relationships with men; and (3) an attenuated emphasis on the dichotomy between male and female (Akbar, 1990; Hunter & Davis, 2004;

Oliver, 1989). Interestingly enough, the literature shows that middle class black men are less likely to cultivate close relationships in line the African masculinity model and more likely to place importance on socioeconomic success which consistent with the European expression of manhood (Franklin, 1992; McClure, 2006).

The pressure to meet white prescribed definitions of masculinity for black men is wrought with challenges (Staples, 1982; Ture, 2007). One major obstacle to the aforementioned has been racism (Asante, 1998). Racism, and its exigencies, has resulted in a truncated portrayal of black manhood that has been defined within narrow Eurocentric parameters (Pierre et al., 2001). Such a limitation has contributed in to stressors and increased incidences of physical maladies such as hypertension, sleep disturbances, substance abuse, coronary heart disease, cancer, lung ailments, accidental injuries, cirrhosis of the liver, and suicide (Martin et al., 2001; Pierre et al., 2001). A European notion of manhood, which black men believe necessary to achieve social and economic success and opportunities, is based on individualism whereas the traditional African models of manhood were based on communalism and collectivity (Blackwell, 1995; Lazur & Majors, 1995).

Boxing is an intrinsically masculine endeavor due to the general lack of participation of women on a grand scale (Woodward, 2004). Despite the fact that women are participating in the sport in ever increasing numbers, your typical boxing gym contains very few women (Woodward, 2004). In Wacquant's (1992) ethnography on the sociology of boxing, women, be they wives, girlfriends, or relatives, were viewed primarily as distractions. The presence of these "non-men" could be deemed as de-masculinizing a manly sphere of social space. Further, Heiskanen (2012) can be surmised as asserting that boxing promotes hegemonic masculinity because the sport is masculine in the traditional sense, marginalizes the involvement of women, and systematically locks them out of the upper echelons of payment in the sport. Oates (1987, p. 92) contends "boxing is for men and about men, and is men." This idiom rings true from the lowest weight class to the heavy weights who are over 200 pounds (Woodward, 2004).

Heiskanen (2012) posits involvement in boxing can be perceived as an attempt to present oneself as a tough man. In other instances, boxing has served to save young men from the bad influences and dangers that are present in many blighted urban communities (Wacquant, 1992). In other situations, young men are often drawn to the sport via "hero-identification." This occurs when a young man is enticed to participate to the sport from identification with great boxers from the past (Woodward, 2004). For African American men, often these renowned pugilists are such luminaries as Muhammad Ali, Joe Frazier, Joe Louis, and Sugar Ray Leonard. Muhammad Ali, arguably one of the greatest boxers to every lace up a pair of gloves, engaged in a unique form of hero-worship that was one of his many inspirations to excel in the sport. Ali found inspiration in the many enslaved black men on plantations who were forced to put on boxing exhibitions for their slave masters (Remnick, 1999). Thus, his heroes were those who had their masculinity manipulated for the sadistic delight of others and did not have a choice in the matter. Consequently, perhaps it can be surmised that Ali's participation in the ultimate masculine sport, at least to some degree, was to honor his ancestors and fight against the cognitive memory of a perverse use of black male masculinity.

Working Class Assimilation

Boxing, prior to legalization, after legalization, and beyond, has been viewed as a means to escape a life of hopelessness and despair for many African Americans (Rhoden, 2005; Runstedler, 2009). Unbeknownst to many contemporary African American males, the National Football League, the National Basketball Association, along with Major League Baseball, excluded African Americans from their sports almost completely until the late 1940s and early1950s (Remnick, 1999; Sammons, 1988; Ward, 2004). Further, for an African American male of the early twentieth century, a way to improve his station in life when legitimate occupational, educational, and opportunities were scarce, was to become a pugilist (Aycock & Scott, 2008; Moore, 2010; Ward, 2004). This is not to suggest that prize fighting was not a rocky road to success. Early black fighters were often locked out of opportunities to win legitimate championships when their skills rendered them more than capable (e.g., Sam Langford). Black prizefighters were often robbed of substantial portions of their earnings from unscrupulous managers, promoters, and underworld figures, or denied access to fame in order to uphold white supremacy (Aycock & Scott, 2008; Runstedler, 2009; Ward, 2004).

Jack Johnson, born in Galveston, Texas, was crowned the first black heavyweight champion in 1908 by defeating Tommy Burns in Sydney, Australia (Rhoden, 2005; Ward, 2004). A product of humble beginnings, Johnson quit school at five or six and began boxing professionally at age twenty-four (Ward, 2004). Johnson often displayed his masculinity by playfully toying with white opponents as he beat them methodically in front of all white audiences (Dorinson, 1997; Sammons, 1988). The reaction to Johnson, and his taboo-like exploits (e.g., publicly dating white women), were so visceral that after his reign ended in a 1915 loss against Jess Willard, no other African American was allowed to even fight for the heavyweight championship until Joe Louis in 1937 (Rhoden, 2005, Ward, 2004). The reaction against Johnson and his antics were so visceral that noted historian Jeffrey T. Sammons states "Johnson's successes sparked a wholesale onslaught against boxing that subsided only with his defeat in 1915" (Sammons, 1988, p. 30). Additionally, after defeating white fighters in the ring, a display of black masculinity that challenged white notions of inherent superiority, whites would often kill innocent blacks in cities across the United States in attempt to ensure that no black man got of his place again (Sammons, 1988; Ward, 2004). Finally, perhaps as a sign of the inferior societal position of black males, when Joe Louis fought and defeated James Braddock for the heavyweight title in 1937, Braddock's manager was allowed to include a provision in the final contract to pay Braddock 10 percent of Louis' future earnings for a period of ten years (Remnick, 1999).

Working class men are typically reared in a contested social milieu (Gems, 2004). During the infancy of American boxing white ethnics, as a result of the discrimination they experienced when considered white ethnics as opposed to just white, participated heavily in the sport of boxing (Gems, 2004; Ward, 2004). Prizefighting was a way to escape the doldrums of economic and ethnic marginality. In contrast, black men had to deal with not only economic marginality, but also a vitriolic form of racism that stripped them of their self-worth and only allowed them to exert their manliness in way that affirmed their inferiority to the larger society by pummeling each other in a boxing ring (Runstedler, 2009; Ward, 2004).

As a result of the aforementioned, black sportsmen, including boxers, often ventured overseas to make more money (Rhoden, 2005; Runstedtler, 2009). In addition to hopes of greater fiduciary rewards from migrating to France, black fighters saw the trip as a way to escape Jim Crow and American racism (Aycock & Scott, 2008; Ward, 2004). To the contrary, the French, unlike white America, welcomed black boxers in order to complete their own racial narrative. This racial account insisted the French were more enlightened than the United States because in terms of modernity, providing American blacks with an athletic platform that was unavailable at home (Runstedtler, 2009).

In reality, France was only slightly more progressive than the United States in terms of race relations. Black males' masculinity was often pimped to legitimize the twisted racial logic of the French (Runstedtler, 2009). In America, black male inferiority was often maintained by not allowing black males to display their physical prowess alongside or in competition against whites. In France, ushering black men into the boxing ring, i.e., to beat themselves and others into submission, reaffirmed the idea that black men possessed a primal physicality to the French (Runstedtler, 2009).

Connell (2005) posited that genuine masculinity always emerges from black men's bodies. At first glance, such a statement may seem sanguine because of historical and many contemporary caricatures of black males. However, during the mid-nineteenth century the processes of urbanization and the American physical culture movement ushered in a dichotomous view of sports (Moore, 2010). On the one hand, prior to urbanization, participation in sports, including boxing, was viewed as anti-intellectual and uncivilized (Gems, 2004). Nevertheless, urbanization changed this perception. Urbanization brought lower class rural residents to cities. Due to the cramped living conditions, lack of education, jobs, etc., crime rates soared perceived that their way of life was threatened (Gems, 2004; Moore, 2010). Hence, beginning in the 1880s working class narratives of masculinity were enticing to middle-class men who transformed the meaning of boxing into a "manly art" (Moore, 2010). Middle-class men understood boxing as a way to stay physically fit, build character, and to defend themselves from the encroachment of working-class ruffians (Rotundo, 1993).

Black and white leaders viewed boxing a bit differently. In other words, prizefighting presented an interesting paradox for black and white men. Paradoxically, white men viewed boxing as cerebral in its characterization as a manly art, however, but only middle-class white men primarily partook in the sport to defend themselves against lower-class men if necessary. Black men, interestingly enough, participated in pugilism in order to earn a better living and to demonstrate to white men that they were fit for complete social and economic acceptance (Moore, 2010).

The perception of boxing as a worthy endeavor for middle-class white men intersected race and class lines (Moore, 2010). Black men often served as sparring professors or boxing teachers (Gorn, 1986). One of the noted sparring masters, Aaron Molineaux Hewlett, was the first black instructor at Harvard teaching physical culture at the college, from 1859 to 1871 (Moore, 2010). The class was attractive to many professors it was viewed as a way to recapture manhood that was fleeting as a result of rigors of the academy (Moore, 2010). Further, women were welcomed Hewlett's gym at Cambridge as well. Unfortunately, this movement of black sparring professors began to wane in 1880s because the majority of black men were trapped in menial dead-end jobs due to racism and discrimination and tried to ply their trade in the arena of professional prizefighting.

Method

The setting for this case study was an urban boxing gym. It was a tattered gym in an economically depressed, primarily African American community in Beaumont, Texas, which served as the backdrop for my two and half year exploration into the world of pugilism. While immersing myself in the research setting, I trained, sparred, discussed strategy, and "shot the breeze" with fighters (amateur and professional), coaches, and occasionally some small scale managers and promoters from January 2008 until approximately September 2011. In the next few paragraphs, I will delineate how I gained entry and acceptance in the boxing gym.

Sparring as a Means to Gain Entry

My interest in the sport of boxing is extensive. Personally, I have always had a great deal of respect for the way that boxers would literally "fight to the end" or, as insiders say, "go out on their shield" to achieve victory. So as the adage goes, "we often admire those who can do things that we cannot do ourselves." Thus, my love for boxing as a fan was based on the toughness one had to have to either take blows round after round, or render an opponent unconscious from a single punch. Nevertheless, in my eyes, boxers were hyper-masculine and very tough.

I have never characterized myself as a "tough guy" per se. I more aptly viewed myself as someone who was somewhat reserved, but will react aggressively if provoked. Now, did the aforementioned qualify me to attempt to be a fighter, or even spar? Heck no. But, I guess my own masculinity propelled me headfirst (literally and figurative) into the project.

At first glance, one may question the sanity of a tenured associate professor stepping into a boxing ring. I did not initially. Why? Because I always considered myself tad bit more athletically inclined than the average professor (which probably is not saying very much). I mean, in the world of professors, I considered myself a tough guy. So did that really amount to anything? To be a hyper-masculine professor in the world of fighters is similar to being a minimum wage worker in the company of billionaires. To be honest, several times during my study (especially when I was getting hit in the face) I questioned my own mental temerity frequently and consistently. I did not actually have a sanctioned amateur fight as Wacquant (1992) engaged in during his examination of a boxing gym, but my several rounds of sparring were more than sufficient for me.

Sparring is a necessary part of boxing in order to prepare a fighter for an opponent in terms of timing, conditioning, and implementation of strategy. So sense I was not actually trying to be a prizefighter, why would I be required to spar? It was simple; to gain a degree of acceptance in one of the most masculine spheres of social space required that I exhibit a willingness to display the type of masculinity that I desired to study.

I had been working out at the gym approximately two months before I was approached by K-Dub (subject of the case study). K-Dub considered the gym his. Therefore, as the baddest brother in the gym, it was his job to check-out all "newcomers." Thus, as I jumped rope K-Dub introduced himself with a simple "What's up?" He asked me what I was doing in the gym. I responded that I was trying to "get in better shape." Ostensibly, K-Dub was okay with my response and our friendship began.

Sparring for my acceptance and to gain entry into the world of aspiring pugilists began with K-Dub asking the question, "Would you like to spar?" My hyper-masculine side (yes, professors can be hyper-masculine) responded "yes" but inside I was less than masculine. I was downright nervous. K-Dub had a much decorated amateur career and was about to turn professional. To add to my utter fear, he was several inches taller than me and light years of me when it came to ring intelligence and speed and quickness.

I fought several rounds with K-Dub and different fighters ranging in weight from nearly three hundred pounds to one hundred and sixty pounds during my foray into the world of pugilism. I most frequently sparred with heavyweights (I ranged in weight from 210 to 220 during the study. I believe my sparring experience could most accurately be described as "instructional" than "competitive" although a few times my sparring did get intense. However, by "instructional sparring" I mean that the more experienced boxer was trying to show me how to throw certain punches properly (e.g., a jab, uppercut, hook) as opposed to trying to inflict physical pain. Nevertheless, I can say that nearly every blow the landed on my face or body was painful. Regardless, I believe that the sparring served a dual purpose. Sparring provided me with a small taste of what the sport is actually like and taught me to respect the sport and those who participate in it. All I can say was "mission accomplished."

In most of my sparring sessions, I got pummeled. Every now and then I would land a "blow for academia" but for the most part, I was introduced to how difficult participant observation can be. Therefore, even if I landed a punch, whomever I was sparring with at the time would land two in return just to remind who the pugilist was. But to me, it was an honor and an accomplishment to even share the ring with very good boxers. Seriously, how many college professors would be masculine enough to do this? I doubt that many would. Lastly, by the end of the sparring sessions I had learned enough to enable me to discern when my sparring partners were "taking it easy" and when they were "getting rough." Regardless, I had gained and a couple of boxers told me that I had "some power" and I believed that I gave a decent account of myself in the ring (all things considered of course).

K-Dub was a young pugilist who was the subject of the case study. He was in his late twenties, from a working class background, an African American, and had a successful amateur career. At the time of the study he had yet to be signed by a major promoter, but had begun to embark upon a pro boxing career. Consequently, without a major promoter or a "team" as boxers with a similar pedigree would have, at the very least K-Dub could be characterized as a tad bit frustrated. From my perception, K-Dub was the side of boxing that many casual fans rarely get a glimpse of.

Findings

K-Dub's construction of masculinity revealed themes that both corresponded to and differed from the traditional version of masculinity. Despite the fact that the traditional, i.e. Eurocentric or white middle-class construction of masculinity has went unnamed in scholarly discourse, it has been characterized as emphasizing toughness, emotional callousness, competitiveness, and a deviation from everything feminine (Connell, 1995; Speer, 1993). Furthermore, attention was given responses that fit into the Afrocentric masculinity schemata. The Afrocentric understanding of manhood involves an amalgam of the white middle-class model and traditional African expressions of manhood (Akbar, 1990; Asante, 1998). The Afrocentric model of manhood places primacy on community needs, cooperation among individuals, meaningful friendships among men, and holds disdain for the male-female dichotomy (Akbar, 1990; Asante, 1998; Hunter & Davis, 1994; Nobles, 1980).

The forms of masculinity expressed by K-Dub corresponded to and differed from the white middle-class model as previously mentioned. Moreover, there were some responses that could be perceived as consistent with Afrocentric typology. Nevertheless, the majority of the manifestations of masculinity were closer to the European model.

K-Dub provided several comments that can be perceived to most accurately fit into the Afrocentric model of masculinity. The African-centered model of masculinity places primacy on cooperation, togetherness, and close friendships among African American males. When queried about the importance of a trainer to a fighter, K-Dub opined on the numerous roles of a coach trainer while expounded on the importance of a coach to the success of a fighter. K-Dub opined:

> A trainer has several roles. A trainer can be like a father. The majority of the fighters come from broken homes and goes to the gym looking for a father figure. By teaching you how do things. Similar to how a Dad may teach you to fish or ride a bike.

K-Dub gave some additional responses that can be characterized as reflective of the Black masculine model. K-Dub comments:

> A good coach teaches you everything you need to know about boxing. Padwork, throwing a proper jab, teaching you balance how to slip punches. Coun-

selor: the coach teaches you life lessons. Forget everything that bothers you and train. In a fight, he keeps you motivated. Telling you what you are doing right and wrong. He is your eyes in the ring. Modifies the game plan in between rounds.

He continues:

A good coach can also act as a doctor. If my hand is hurting when preparing for a fight. He will tell you to stay off for a while and focus on the fight. Mentor: He will give you advice and lead in the right direction. A good trainer will give you advice about life as well as boxing. The trainer gets 10 percent.

In the provided responses, K-Dub expressed that the trainer/coach serves a myriad of vital functions. Particularly of note was the characterization of his coach as a father figure. In boxing, trainers, at least in a large proportion of cases, are not biologically related to their charges. Thus, the trainer-fighter relationship is close and more consistent with the Afrocentric/black model of masculinity which emphasizes the primacy of cultivating important connections among non-biologically related men. McClure (2006) suggests that the concept of "hegemonic masculinity is understood contemporarily as being white, straight, successful and competitive" (p. 58). Concordant with the aforementioned is that men are emotionally detached, callous, and competitive. However, K-Dub's construction of manhood entails the coach as serving as a counselor, giving advice, nursing injuries, and teaching important lessons. In essence, K-Dub's masculine frame eschews the exigencies of hegemonic masculinity in terms of the fighter-trainer relationship.

The Eurocentric masculinity construct differs from the Afrocentric one (Pierre et al., 2001; Akbar, 1990). This results in pressures on black men to meet mandates requiring them to serve as guardians, breadwinners, and authoritarians within a societal milieu that does not afford them the agency it does to their European counterparts (Asante, 1998; Staples, 1982). Hence, it should come as no surprise that masculine expression of black men takes a form representative of an amalgam of both European and Afrocentric ideals (Akbar, 1990). The aforementioned was asserted most succinctly when K-Dub was questioned about why he boxed and how he got started in pugilism:

That is a real good question. I box to keep myself motivated. I have a competitive nature. I feel that any other sport would be pointless right now because of my age. I started fighting growing up. It was in my nature. Fighting was a thrill to me. The idea of two guys thinking that they are better than each other. How do you find out who is the best? Well, you fight it out. Fighters have pride. It is like we are not going to turn down a fight. Because it is going to bother you later if you refuse a fight. If you are fighter you are going to have fear. We are not going to tell you and we are not going to show it. I do not want anyone to think I am weak especially being a fighter.

K-Dub's response to "why he started boxing" was interesting and informative. By insisting that his foray into boxing was facilitative of a belief that fighting was "in his nature" and enhanced a "feeling of pride," which is consistent with a Eurocentric expression of masculinity. Even though K-Dub is not racially white, his masculine ideology is more in line with the Eurocentric frame should not be surprising. Specifically, Pierre et al. (2001) posits black men often internalize white ideologies and normative expectations in an attempt to adapt and be accepted with a mainstream milieu that does not validate them or their existence. So, ascribing to a western masculine belief in an attempt to develop a psychological defense mechanism allows black men to cope with the demands of a white supremist society. Conversely, K-Dub speaks on the need to come to grips with and negotiate "fear" as part of being a fighter. The admission of fear involved acknowledging a degree of vulnerability reminiscent of the DuBoisian concept of the double consciousness (Majors & Billson, 1992). In other words, black men have to display some aspects of the white masculine frame in order to attempt to assimilate and survive. Further, the aforementioned must exist with a vacuum or truncated form, which is associated with Afrocentric version of masculinity, so as not to be perceived as a threat to the larger white society (Asante, 1998; Nobles, 1990).

When queried about how he got started in boxing, K-Dub responded:

> I first beat up a guy named Darius. I do not know why besides the fact that I was the new guy on the block. He picked a fight with me because I was the new guy. I was in the seventh grade. We fought two additional times. Then, his cousin said you "fight pretty good, you beat my cousin up. You should go to the boxing gym." So, I said let me go see. Initially, I went to the gym to see if I could learn some new skills. The coach told you to throw your own combinations. I was like I did not know how to box, so I stopped.

Here, K-Dub's retort falls with the contours of the European construct of masculinity. Particularly, his response corresponds with the masculine mandates of competitiveness and aggression. He delineates how his immersion into the world of boxing was spurred forward by a challenge to his manhood. After getting the better of a neighborhood tough guy, he goes on to discuss how beat the young man up two additional times to further cement his fistic superiority. Then he was asked by the young man's cousin, who liked his fighting style, to visit a boxing gym.

Moreover, two additional contrasts can be found in K-Dub's comments. First, he did not get into boxing as a means to leave a situation of socioeconomic despair which is often the reason young African American men become pugilists (Rhoden, 2005). The need to make money is a characteristic of the European model of masculinity and the version of manhood frequently adopted by African American men which represents an amalgam of Eurocentric and Afrocentric typologies (Franklin, 1992; Gems, 2004; Moore, 2010; Rhoden, 2005; Wacquant, 1992). Secondly, at the end of the comment, K-Dub initially stopped because he felt he already knew how to box. Accordingly, the fact that he was able to acknowledge that he first quit boxing shows his construction of masculinity allowed him to comfortably admit that he "quit" the sport. By revealing something that could be perceived as non-masculine, i.e., divulging that he stopped, he displayed a more versatile form of manhood which was is more consistent with the Afrocentric version (Akbar, 1990; Asante, 1998; Pierre et al., 2001).

A common reason that a large proportion of young men become boxers is hero identification (Remnick, 1999). Hero-identification basically posits that an identification that an aspiring pugilist has with a boxer whom he admires will serve as motivation to take up the sport (Gems, 2004). When questioned if there was a boxer whom he admired that drove him to the sport, K-Dub lamented:

> No, I did not watch boxing growing up. But one current boxer who inspires me is Shane Mosley. I like his energy that he brings to the ring.

Unlike many all-time great fighters, i.e., Muhammad Ali, K-Dub did not have a great boxer that he watched as a young person that inspired him to take up the sport. He only suggests that he became a fan of current boxing great Shane Mosley only after he became a boxer. Despite the fact this statement does not specifically fit with either Eurocentric or Afrocentric conceptualizations of masculinity. However, his sentiments are closest to the European manhood ideal because his decision to become a boxer was an individual one and the Eurocentric masculinity view stresses individualism (McClure, 2006).

The institution of slavery served to limit the ability of black men to construct their masculinity (Blackwell, 1975; hooks, 1992). Thus, black males had to create a version of manhood that involved certain African cultural residuals yet was truncated because expressions of indigenous African manhood were harmful to white supremacy (Pierre et al., 2001; Ture, 2007). So the interesting question was, "Do you view boxing as an expression of your masculinity/manhood?" So when K-Dub was asked this question K-Dub responded:

> No. Because you do not have to fight to prove that you are a man, a strong man. It takes a man to step into the ring. It takes a man go through the entire process of training.
> Why does one have to be a man to go through the process of training? It is hard. To go through the training you have to be a man. It is hard. The sacrifice is hard. You might have to work a job and go to the gym afterwards. A lot of men cannot do that. Your girlfriend may not like boxing, so you may have to quit your girlfriend.

Interestingly enough, K-Dub did not view boxing as a means to express his masculinity. This flies in the face of the stereotype of black boxers as big black brutes devoid of common sense and emotion (Rhoden, 2005; Woodward, 2004). More importantly, he saw fulfilling the responsibilities associated with being a successful boxer as more of an expression of manhood than actually physically beating someone up. Although he did believe that one has to be a man to step into the ring, he saw true masculinity as being expressed when one respects the sport, trains properly, and take care of one's financial responsibilities to themselves and their family. Unfortunately, he did suggest that a woman could serve as a distraction at times and if she does, a boxer needs to let her go. This idea that a woman could be a bother is associated with the Eurocentric version of masculinity which supports the male-female dichotomy (Hunter & Davis, 1994; McClure, 2006).

Conclusion

Black males will perpetually have to express their masculinity within a contested sphere of social space. The imposition of European normative standard along with cultural and racial subordination ensures that the meaning of black masculinity will always be fluid and tenuous. Thus, the growing need for black men to establish some agency over not only their masculinity, but also the social, political, and economic exigencies which define their struggle is necessary for their survival. Consequently, further exploration into constraints on black males and their myriad expressions of manhood via participation in sports is warranted.

REFERENCES

Akbar, N. (1990). *Visions for black men.* Tallahassee, FL: Mind Productions.
Anderson, J. (2007). *The legality of boxing: A punch drunk love?* New York: Routledge.
Anderson, S. E. (2007). *The black holocaust for beginners.* Danbury, CT: For Beginners.
Ani, M. (1994) *Yurugu: An African-centered critique of European cultural thought and behavior.* Lawrenceville: African World Press.
Asante, M. (1998) *The Afrocentric idea, revised and expanded edition.* Philadelphia: Temple University Press.
Aycock, C., and M. Scott (2008). *Joe Gans: A biography of the first African American world champion.* Jefferson, NC: McFarland.
Berg, B. (1998). *Qualitative research methods for the social sciences,* 3d ed. Boston: Allyn and Bacon.
Blackwell, J. E. (1975). *The black community: Diversity and unity.* New York: Dodd Mead.
Bledsoe, G., G. Li, and F. Levy (2005). Injury risk in professional boxing. *Southern Medical Journal,* 98, 994–998.
Carmichael, S. (2007). *Stokely speaks: From black power to pan–Africanism.* Chicago: Chicago Review Press.
Connell, R. W. (1995). *Masculinities.* Australia: Allen & Unwin.

Connell, R. W. (2005). *Masculinities*, 2d ed. Berkeley: University of California Press.

Dorinson, J. (1997). Black heroes from Jack Johnson to Muhammad Ali. *The Journal of Popular Culture*, 31, 115–135.

Engen, D. (1995). The making of a people's champion: An analysis of media representations of George Foreman. *Southern Journal of Communication*, 40, 141–151.

Franklin, C. W. (1992). Hey, home—yo, bro': Friendship among black men. In P.M. Nardi (Ed.), *Men's Friendships*. Newbury Park, CA: Sage.

Gems, G. (2004). The politics of boxing: Resistance, religion, and working class assimilation. *International Sports Journal*, 8, 89–103.

Gorn, E. (1986). *The manly art: Bare-knuckle prizefighting in America*. Ithaca: Cornell University Press.

Heiskanen, B. (2012). *The urban geography of boxing: Race, class, and gender in the ring*. New York: Routledge.

hooks, b., and C. West (1991). *Breaking bread: Insurgent black intellectual life*. Boston: South End.

Hunter, A. G., and J. E. Davis (1994). Hidden voices of black men: The meaning, structure, and complexity of manhood. *Journal of Black Studies*, 25, 20–40.

Karenga, M. (2010) *Introduction to Black Studies*, 4th ed. Los Angeles: University of Sankore Press.

Ladner, J. (Ed.). (1998). *The death of white sociology: Essays on race and culture*. Baltimore, MD: Black Classic.

Lazur, R. F., and R. Majors (1995). Men of color: Ethnocultural variations of male gender role strain. In R. F. Levant and W. Pollack (Eds.), *A new psychology of men* (pp. 337–358). New York, NY: Basic.

Levant, R. F., R. G. Majors, and M. L. Kelley (1998). Masculinity ideology among young African American and European American women and men in different regions of the United States. *Cultural Diversity & Ethnic Minority Psychology*, 4, 227–336.

Majors, R., and J. M. Billson (1992). *Cool pose: The dilemmas of black manhood in America*: New York: Lexington.

Martin, R., R. Mahalik, and W. Woodland (2001). The effects of racism, African self-consciousness and psychological functioning on black masculinity: A historical and social adaptation framework. *Journal of African American Men*, 6, 19–40.

McClure, S. (2006). Improvising masculinity: African American fraternity membership in the construction of a black masculinity, 10(1), 57–73.

Moore, L. (2010). Fine specimens of manhood: The black boxer's body and the avenue to equality, racial advancement, and manhood in the nineteenth century. *MELUS*, 35(4), 60–84.

Nobles, W. (1980). African philosophy: Foundations for black psychology. In H. McAdoo (Ed.), *Black Psychology*. New York: Harper and Row.

Oates, J. C. (1987). *On boxing*. New York: Doubleday.

Oliver, W. (1989). Black males and the tough guy image: A dysfunctional compensatory adaptation. *Journal of Black Studies*, 20, 15–39.

Pierre, M. R., J.R. Mahalik, and M. H. Woodland. (2001). The effects of racism, African self-consciousness and psychological functioning on black masculinity: A historical and social adaptation framework. *Journal of African American Men*, 6(2), 19–40.

Remnick, D. (1999). *King of the world: Muhammad Ali and the rise of an American hero*. New York: Vintage.

Rhoden, W. C. (2006). *Forty million dollar slaves: The rise, fall, and redemption of the black athlete*. New York: Three Rivers.

Rotundo, A. (1993). *American manhood: Transformations in masculinity from the revolution to the modern era*. New York: Basic.

Runstedtler, T. (2009). Visible men: African American boxers, the new Negro, and the global color line. *Radical History Review*, 103, 59–81.

Sammons, J. (1988). *Beyond the ring: The role of boxing in American society*. Urbana and Chicago: University of Illinois Press.

Staples, R. (1978). Masculinity and race: The dual dilemma of black men. *Journal of Social Issues*, 34, 169–183.

Staples, R. (1982). *Black masculinity: The black males' role in American society*. San Francisco: Black Scholar.

Ture, K. (2007). *Stokely speaks: From black power to pan–Africanism*. Chicago: Lawrence Hill.

Wacquant, L. (1992). The social logic of boxing in black Chicago: Toward a sociology of pugilism. *Sociology of Sport Journal*, 9, 221–254.

Wacquant, L. (2009). Chicago fade: Putting the researcher's body back into play. *City*, 13(4), 511–516.

Wacquant, L. (2011). Habitus as topic and tool: Reflections on becoming a prizefighter. *Qualitative Research in Psychology*, 8, 81–92.

Ward, G. C. (2004). *Unforgivable blackness: The rise and fall of Jack Johnson*. New York: Vintage.

Woodward, K. (2004). Rumbles in the Jungle: Boxing, Racialization and the Performance of Masculinity. *Leisure Studies*, vol. 23, no. 1, 5–17.

The Fritz Pollard Alliance, the Rooney Rule and the Quest to Level the Playing Field in the NFL

N. Jeremi Duru

Introduction

The National Football League, like the National Basketball Association and Major League Baseball, has a long history of racial exclusion.[1] And like these other long-standing American professional sports leagues, desegregation among players preceded desegregation among coaches.[2] As slowly increasing numbers of minorities assumed NBA head coaching positions and MLB managing positions toward the end of the twentieth century, however, minority NFL coaches were less likely to receive head coaching opportunities than their basketball and baseball counterparts.[3] Indeed, as of 2002, only two of the NFL's thirty-two head coaches were minorities, and only five, including those two, had held head coaching positions during the League's modem era.[4] Four years later, however, the NFL had more than tripled its number of minority head coaches and shone as a model for other athletic institutions seeking to provide head coaching candidates equal employment opportunities.[5]

This essay seeks to explore the history of racial exclusion in the NFL, the particular barriers minority coaches seeking NFL head coaching positions have faced, and the effort to level the playing field for such coaches. The first part of this essay traces the NFL's initial expulsion of African Americans, its eventual reintegration, and the patterns accompanying that reintegration. The second part explores the travails of the NFL's first three post-reintegration coaches of color as well as statistical evidence revealing that, as of 2002, NFL coaches of color generally suffered inferior opportunities despite exhibiting outstanding performance. The third part examines the campaign launched by attorneys Cyrus Mehri and Johnnie L. Cochran, Jr., to alter NFL teams' hiring practices, the creation of the Rooney Rule (the "Rule"), and the birth of the Fritz Pollard Alliance of minority coaches, scouts, and front office personnel in the NFL. The final part traces the Rooney Rule's success in creating equal opportunity for coaches of color in the NFL.

A History of Racial Exclusion

Fritz Pollard and the NFL's Initial Racial Expulsion

During the mid–1920s, the American Professional Football Association (APFA), now known as the NFL, began homogenizing, and by 1934, it had succeeded in expurgating all African Americans.[6] In doing so, it ended the APFA career of Frederick Douglas "Fritz" Pollard.[7]

Pollard entered the APFA in 1919 as a running back with the Akron Pros and was, by any estimate, a remarkable talent.[8] As elusive as he was fast, Pollard earned All-American Honors as a half-back at Brown University and led the Bruins to their first and only Rose Bowl appearance before graduating and pursing a professional football career.[9] For Pollard, often the only black player on the field, playing football was equal parts sport and survival, as opposing players, after he was tackled, routinely piled on him with intent to injure.[10] Still, Pollard was as effective with Akron as he was at Brown, and, in his second professional season, he led the Pros to the league championship title.[11]

Pollard's legacy, however, lies not on the actual playing field but on the sidelines: He became the APFA's first black coach, an extraordinary accomplishment considering the racial preconceptions of the day. Those preconceptions, which still endure to some degree, presupposed his physical fortitude just as they presupposed his intellectual frailty.[12] So while the accomplishments of the era's black players unsettled the American sporting community because blacks, despite their presumed brawn, were believed insufficiently sophisticated to excel in team sport,[13] Pollard's ascension to the coaching ranks shook sport to its core. Despite Pollard's accomplishments—or, perhaps, because of them and what they portended—the NFL teams' owners mutually agreed to force blacks out of the League, ending Pollard's APFA coaching career soon after it began.[14]

The NFL's Re-integration

Two decades later, the league began to re-integrate, but the stereotype of the physically superior yet intellectually inferior black would endure and impact opportunities for blacks in the league through the end of the twentieth century and beyond.

In 1946, the Los Angeles Rams became the first NFL team in twelve years to employ black players.[15] Interestingly, the Rams' decision to integrate its squad was not a bold repudiation of segregation, but rather a necessary consequence of the team's move from Cleveland to Los Angeles.[16] The commissioners of the Los Angeles Coliseum, in which the team would play, insisted as part of the stadium agreement that the Rams desegregate. The Rams agreed to do so,[17] and UCLA alums Kenny Washington and Woody Strode joined the Rams as the team's—and League's—only black players.[18] Notably, the positions Washington and Strode played, wide receiver and running back, are the paradigmatic football "workhorse positions"—positions viewed as demanding more physical ability than intellectual ability.[19] That a running back and a wide receiver were the first black players permitted to enter the league in twelve years is no coincidence. Indeed, as blacks slowly trickled into the league during the succeeding years, they trickled disproportionately into workhorse positions.[20]

"[F]ootball's thinking and control position," quarterback, on the other hand, remained reserved for whites.[21] As of the 1968 season's inception, twenty-two years after Washington's and Strode's debut, the NFL featured no black quarterbacks.[22] And during those twenty-two years, the league's only black quarterbacking presence was Willie Thrower, who, in 1953, entered just two games as a backup, completed three of eight pass attempts, and never played in the league again.[23] In 1969, James "Shack" Harris became the first black player to open an NFL regular season as a starting quarterback,[24] and he proceeded to have a productive twelve-year career, during which he was, in 1975, selected for the NFL Pro Bowl team and named the Pro Bowl game's Most Valuable Player.[25] Harris' success, however, did little to alter NFL teams' approaches to staffing the quarterback position, and black NFL quarterbacks remained a rarity. Doug Williams' extraordinary career, during which he quarterbacked the Washington Redskins to a 1987 Super Bowl victory and garnered Super Bowl Most Valuable Player honors,[26] did little more than Harris to eradicate the myth that blacks are not well-suited for the position.

In fact, as of 1998, in the history of the NFL's annual college draft, only three black quarterbacks had been selected in the draft's first round.[27] The following year seemed to portend a breakthrough, as the 1999 draft alone featured three teams selecting black quarterbacks with first round picks.[28] Nearly a decade later, however, black quarterbacks remain disproportionately rare. According to Dr. Richard Lapchick, director of the University of Central Florida's DeVos Sport Business Management Program, 67 percent of the NFL's players are black.[29] Of the thirty-two starting quarterbacks on NFL rosters at the beginning of the 2007 season, however, only six were black—just under 20 percent.[30]

As daunting as the barriers facing black quarterbacks have been, the barriers facing black coaches have been far more burdensome. The presumption of intellectual inferiority but physical superiority obviously hampers the black candidate seeking a quarterback position, for which both physical and intellectual ability are deemed necessary. The presumption, however, completely handicaps the black candidate pursuing a coaching position, a position for which physical ability is irrelevant and intellectual ability—the candidate's presumed weakness—is paramount. Saddled with a presumption of intellectual inferiority, therefore, blacks have struggled to find head coaching positions in the NFL.[31] Indeed, between 1946, when Strode and Washington re-integrated the NFL, and the beginning of the 1989 season, every head coach in the league was white,[32] despite an increase in the proportion of black NFL players during that period from zero to 67 percent.[33]

The Plight of the Black NFL Head Coach

During the 1989 season, the NFL's Los Angeles Raiders bucked a sixty-year tradition of maintaining Caucasian homogeneity among the league's head coaches by hiring Art Shell to lead the team.[34] Unfortunately, Shell's emergence would do little to increase equal employment opportunity for black coaches in the NFL. A survey of Shell's experience and the experiences of the black head coaches who followed him is revealing.

Shell took control of the Raiders midseason, when the team had a record of one win and three losses, following the organization's first two consecutive losing seasons in twenty-five years.[35] In his first full season as head coach, however, Shell transformed the team's fortunes, leading the Raiders to twelve wins and only four loses in route to the NFL's American Football Conference Championship game.[36] Despite amassing an impressive fifty-six wins against forty-one loses over the following four years and posting winning records during three of those four seasons, including the final two, Shell was fired after the 1994 season.[37] His firing was undeserved, as the Raiders' owner Al Davis would apologetically admit twelve years later.[38]

In 1992, two years before Shell's termination, Dennis Green became the second black coach in the NFL's modem era when he accepted the Minnesota

Vikings' head coaching position.[39] Green sparkled. During his ten years with the Vikings, the team won a remarkable 63 percent of its games, and in one year, 1998, won fifteen of its sixteen regular season games.[40] More impressive still, Green led his team to eight playoff appearances—a feat surpassed by only one NFL coach during the fifteen years between 1986 and 2001[41]—and two Conference championship games.[42] After the first losing season of his NFL career—a season doomed from the start by the tragic death of one of the team's best and most beloved players—Green was fired, despite being the most successful coach in the team's history.[43]

In 1996, the Tampa Bay Buccaneers, historically one of the worst teams in the NFL, hired Tony Dungy as its head coach.[44] During his six-year tenure, Dungy transformed the Buccaneers, a team that had enjoyed a mere two winning seasons in its twenty-two years of existence, into a powerhouse.[45] Dungy led the team to four playoff appearances and one conference championship appearance during those six years and lost more games than he won only once—in his first season.[46] Yet, after the 2001 season, he was fired.[47] The absurdity of his firing on the heels of such success is best understood in the context of the organization's previous head coach firings:

> Before Dungy, Sam Wyche coached the Buccaneers for four losing seasons before being fired. Before Wyche, Richard Williamson coached the Buccaneers for two losing seasons before being fired. Before Williamson, Ray Perkins coached the Buccaneers for four losing seasons before being fired.[48]

Dungy coached the Buccaneers for five straight non-losing seasons, established a tradition of excellence, and was fired.[49] While these anecdotal accounts certainly suggest inequitable employment opportunities for black head coaches in the NFL, statistical analysis offers confirmation. In 2002, civil rights attorneys Johnnie L. Cochran, Jr.,[50] and Cyrus Mehri[51] commissioned University of Pennsylvania economist Dr. Janice Madden to analyze the performance of NFL head coaches during the fifteen years between 1986 and 2001 and to compare the success of the five black head coaches who coached during that period against the success of the eighty-six white head coaches who coached during the same period.[52] Dr. Madden concluded that, by any standard, the black head coaches outperformed the white head coaches: "No matter how we look at success, black coaches are performing better. These data are consistent with blacks having to be better coaches than the whites in order to get a job as head coach in the NFL."[53] Indeed, in every category Dr. Madden studied, black coaches outperformed white coaches.[54] In terms of total wins per season—the primary category upon which a head coach's performance is assessed[55] -black coaches averaged over nine wins, while white coaches averaged eight wins.[56] While the 1.1 win differential might, at first blush, seem a minor matter, considering that NFL teams play only sixteen games during each regular season, one additional win is extremely significant.[57] Further, no win is more significant than the ninth, as, during the fifteen years studied, 60 percent of teams winning nine games advanced to the playoffs while only 10 percent of teams winning eight games advanced to the playoffs.[58]

The disparity in success is even more pronounced when considering coaches' success in their first seasons with a team.[59] In their first seasons, black coaches averaged 2.7 more wins than did white coaches in their first seasons and, accordingly, were far more likely to advance their teams to the playoffs than were white coaches.[60]

In addition, in their last seasons before being fired, black coaches outperformed their white counterparts.[61] Black coaches won an average of 1.3 more games in their terminal years than white coaches, and while twenty percent (20 percent) of the black coaches who were fired led their teams to the playoffs in the year of their firing, only eight percent (8 percent) of white coaches did the same.[62]

The Campaign to Change the NFL

Based on Madden's results, Cochran and Mehri authored a report entitled *Black Coaches in the National Football League: Superior Performances, Inferior Opportunities.* They concluded that black head coaches faced more exacting standards than white head coaches and were often dismissed under circumstances that would not have resulted in white head coaches' dismissals.[63] As stark as Madden's results were, Mehri and Cochran did not conclude that black head coaches were somehow inherently better than white head coaches. Rather, they concluded that because barriers to entry were more formidable for black coaches seeking head coaching positions than for white coaches, the black coaches able to surmount those barriers were exceedingly well equipped to succeed as head coaches. Additionally, as a consequence of those exceedingly high barriers, they argued that many black assistant coaches never received serious consideration for head coaching jobs.[64] Cochran and Mehri's report ultimately concluded that despite statistically "superior performance," black coaches have received "inferior opportunities": "In case after case, NFL owners have shown more interest in—and patience with—white coaches who don't win than black coaches who do."[65]

Armed with this conclusion and statistically significant analyses to support it, Cochran and Mehri possessed critical information in confronting employment discrimination: persuasive evidence that the discrimination actually exists. Over forty years after Congress issued broad-based anti-discriminatory legislative edicts, Americans are reluctant to acknowledge the discrimination still existing in their organizations.[66] Racial bias and discrimination in America are now more subtle than overt, and, according to some scholars, often subconscious.[67] Consequently, the suggestion that racial discrimination exists may, and often does, strike institutions' executives as inaccurate and offensive, prompting fierce denials and dampening the possibility of sincere and meaningful settlement negotiations. [68]

Statistically significant evidence of systemic discrimination buttressed by anecdotal evidence of that discrimination's impact-as opposed to anecdotal evidence alone-is often crucial in prompting institutions to honestly confront the existence of discrimination. Equipped with such statistical evidence, Cochran and Mehri were able to convince the NFL, which to its credit had previously expressed concern about the lack of diversity among its head coaches,[69] that some level of cooperation, as opposed to confrontation, was in order. Indeed, shortly after the report's publication, the League created a committee dedicated to increasing equal employment opportunities for coaching candidates.[70] Consisting of the owners of several teams and chaired by Pittsburgh Steelers' owner Dan Rooney, the Workplace Diversity Committee set out to consider the remedial recommendations Cochran and Mehri proffered.[71]

Crafting the Rooney Rule

The most notable of Cochran and Mehri's recommendations was the mandatory interview rule. Arguing that racial bias, whether conscious or unconscious, was steering teams away from minority head coaching candidates, Cochran and Mehri contended that NFL teams should be made to do what few had theretofore done-grant minority candidates meaningful head coach job interviews.[72] They believed that minority candidates would exhibit preparedness for head coaching jobs, and simply needed the opportunities to compete for the positions.[73] Cochran and Mehri, therefore, suggested that each NFL team searching for a head coach be required to interview at least one minority candidate before making its hire.[74] Crucial to the suggestion was that the interview actually be meaningful—that it be an in-person interview and that the interviewers be among the team's primary decision-makers.[75]

After some deliberation, the Workplace Diversity Committee recommended the rule to the broader group of NFL team owners, and the owners agreed by acclamation to implement it.[76] All parties agreed the rule should require nothing beyond a meaningful interview, and if after the interview the interviewing team chose to hire a non-minority coach, the choice was its to make.[77] In December of 2002, the NFL announced its mandatory interview rule, which would come to be known as the Rooney Rule (the "Rule") in honor of the Workplace Diversity Committee's chairman, Dan Rooney,[78] and which would prove to fundamentally change the NFL.[79]

From the start, the Rooney Rule was met with significant skepticism.[80] Indeed, criticism rained down from all quarters. NFL insiders questioned the League's decision to take its lead in pursuing diversity from two lawyers previously unaffiliated with the League and its internal mechanisms. If anyone should guide the League on these issues, they argued, he or she should be from the football community-from a group of NFL alums or from the league's, or one of its teams', front offices. Others, recognizing the Rule contained no accompanying penalty mechanism, wondered whether teams would bother to heed the Rule, and if they didn't, whether the league would do anything about their failures to do so.[81] Still others argued that even assuming teams followed the Rule, because the interviewing team had no obligation to hire a minority coach, the interview would prove merely ornamental.[82] Burdened with these criticisms, the Rooney Rule's early life was shaky.

The Birth of an Alliance

Those questioning the propriety of the NFL's reliance on outsiders to guide its equal employment opportunity efforts would soon be silenced.

Shortly after Cochran and Mehri issued their report, Floyd Keith, the executive director of the Black Coaches Association ("BCA"), an advocacy organization of black collegiate coaches,[83] suggested the lawyers consult with John Wooten, a former NFL All-Pro offensive lineman well-known throughout the league for his tenacity and intellectual acuity both on and off the field.[84] While Wooten was a remarkable player, he made his most lasting impact in NFL front offices, where he worked in various high-level capacities with the Dallas Cowboys, the Philadelphia Eagles, and the Baltimore Ravens over the course of almost thirty years.[85] More impressive than Wooten's success as a player or front office executive, however, was his unwavering and expressed commitment to racial equality in the NFL. For years, Wooten decried the homogenous composition of the NFL's head coaching ranks. Having played with and against scores of fellow black players who he knew would, if given the opportunity, excel as NFL head coaches, Wooten was incensed at their exclusion.

Cochran and Mehri's report offered quantitative support for what Wooten knew: with a fair chance to take the reigns of an NFL team, black head coaches would perform as well, if not better than, white head coaches. Wooten also knew that many black coaches in the league who had consistently been passed over for head coaching positions were anxious to meaningfully compete for those positions and would support the lawyers' efforts. Wooten committed to assisting Cochran and Mehri's work in any way he could and suggested they travel to Indianapolis, Indiana, in February of 2003 to meet with the NFL's black coaches during the NFL Scouting Combine (the "Combine"). The Combine, which serves as a nearly week-long tryout for collegiate players seeking NFL jobs,[86] is the one occasion when all of the league's teams and their staffs can be counted on to be in one place, and therefore presented the perfect opportunity for Cochran and Mehri to meet and share ideas with those they were hoping to help. The lawyers recognized that in order to initiate true reform in the NFL, the primary stakeholders would have to engage in the battle, and they hoped a meeting at the Combine would galvanize their interest in organizing as a unit.

Although Cochran was unable to attend, Mehri represented them both at the Combine. What Mehri imagined would be a gathering of a few dozen black coaches turned out to be a meeting of over one hundred black coaches, scouts, and front office personnel, all deeply concerned about equity in the NFL. The group, though, was not a monolith. Some in the room expressed reluctance to push the NFL and its teams too vociferously for fear of backlash. Others, exceedingly frustrated with lack of opportunity, felt no push could be hard enough. Still others staked out middle positions. Overwhelmingly, however, those in the room supported increased organization. They wanted to maintain a connection in order that there be a forum in which to engage issues that they shared. And they did so, forming an organization and naming it in honor of the individual who preceded and inspired them all. They became the Fritz Pollard Alliance (the FPA), an affinity group dedicated to equal opportunity of employment in the coaching, scouting, and front office ranks of the NFL.[87]

There was little doubt Wooten would serve as the fledging organization's chairman, guiding its vision and maintaining a strong relationship with the NFL, where he had over the years developed many close contacts and personal friendships. And when Wooten considered who might effectively manage the organization's affairs and serve as its public face, a few individuals came to mind, but none more compelling than Kellen Winslow, Sr.

Winslow, one of the NFL's all-time great players, was a tight end with the League's San Diego Chargers from 1979 to 1987, during which time he set numerous League records and revolutionized the position.[88] Whereas tight ends before Winslow were primarily utilized as blockers and rarely called upon to catch anything other than short passes, Winslow combined superior blocking skill with speed and pass-catching ability to rival even the best wide receivers.[89] Along with his physical abilities, Winslow mixed intelligence, dogged persistence, and compelling leadership ability to become a Hall of

Fame player,[90] the type of player capable of willing his team to win.[91] Because of these characteristics and his tremendous success as a player, Winslow naturally presumed he would, upon retirement, have opportunities to work in the NFL or in major conference collegiate football.[92] Retirement, however, brought with it a crushing realization when the opportunities he envisioned did not materialize. As Winslow described in his forward to *In Black and White: Race and Sports in America,* Kenneth Shropshire's incisive investigation of the intersection of race and sport:

> As long as I was on the field of play I was treated and viewed differently than most African-American men in this country. Because of my physical abilities, society accepted and even catered to me. Race was not an issue. Then reality came calling. After a nine-year career in the National Football League filled with honors and praises, I stepped into the real world and realized... I was just another nigger ... the images and stereotypes that applied to African-American men in this country attached to me.[93]

Winslow's revelation led him to channel his talents toward exposing inequity in the sports industry, and when he agreed to serve as the FPA's executive director, he carried that passion with him.

As a consequence of the FPA's support, the Rule, which was just a few months earlier decried as the brainchild of outside agitators, suddenly enjoyed endorsement from a body representing coaches, scouts, and front office personnel of color throughout the League. The Rooney Rule had gained instant credibility.

The Rooney Rule: Applied

Credibility, however, offered no guarantee of efficacy, and if the Rule were to be effective, it would need teeth. Detroit Lions' General Manager Matt Millen's approach to hiring a new head coach in 2003 would ensure that it had them. In January of that year, the Lions fired their head coach Marty Mornhinweg, after the team suffered through a lackluster season during which they lost thirteen games and won only three.[94] Three weeks earlier, the San Francisco 49ers had fired their longtime head coach, Steve Mariucci.[95] Millen wanted Mariucci to lead the Lions, and he expressed little interest in maintaining an open mind to other potential candidates. In his single-minded pursuit of Mariucci, Millen hired Mariucci without interviewing any candidates of color.[96] While such a hiring process would have been unobjectionable just a few months earlier, under the Rooney Rule it was facially non-compliant.

The NFL's then–Commissioner, Paul Tagliabue, had his test case, and his response would determine the Rule's fate. If Tagliabue responded with inaction or an empty condemnation, the Rule would be rendered useless as a change agent. It would exist as little more than a symbolic gesture, creating the impression of a League dedicated to equal employment opportunity for coaches of color in the NFL but having no actual impact. If, on the other hand, Tagliabue substantially punished the Lions, he would signal the NFL's commitment to the Rooney Rule and to the equity Cochran, Mehri, and the FPA sought to achieve.

Tagliabue's decision shocked even those hoping for a stout punishment. Explaining that Millen "did not take sufficient steps to satisfy the commitment that [the Lions] made" regarding the Rooney Rule, Tagliabue fined Millen $200,000, and explicated that Millen, not the team for which he worked, would have to pay the fine.[97] With the fine, Tagliabue made clear that as the Lions' principle decision-maker, Millen was responsible for following the league's mandatory interview guidelines, and he would have to pay account.

Notably, Tagliabue did not stop at issuing the fine. He went further still, moving away from the facts of the Lions' non-adherence and issuing broad-based notice as to the league's unwavering commitment to the Rule. The next principle decision-maker to flout the Rule would, Tagliabue promised, suffer a $500,000 fine.[98]

While the FPA celebrated Tagliabue's response to the Lions' head coach hiring process as revealing that the "'Rooney Rule' ha[d] finally arrived,"[99] Tagliabue's actions sparked outrage among Rooney Rule opponents and others who felt it was excessive.[100] After all, it did not appear Millen was seeking to exclude from consideration minority candidates to the benefit of a group of Caucasian candidates. He was, rather, committed to hiring a particular person—Steve Mariucci—and was uninterested in considering any other candidate, regardless of race.[101] If the Rule applied in this circumstance, they argued, future decision-makers interested in a particular candidate would offer an interview to a minority candidate simply to fulfill the Rule and for no other reason.[102] This criticism exposed an obvious potential weakness in the Rule. While the Rule requires a team to grant a minority candidate a meaningful interview, it is incapable of directing state of mind. The Rule, therefore, cannot require that a team grant a candidate meaningful consideration. Thus, the Rule is powerless to prevent the inconsequential interview—the interview with all the trappings of meaningfulness but whose outcome is predetermined.

The Rule's critics cited this reality as evidence the Rule would be ultimately ineffectual.[103] However, many commentators believe that, more often than one might initially intuit, a face-to-face, in-person, interview with an organization's primary decision-makers begets meaningful consideration—that sitting down together and discussing at length a common interest potentially melts away conscious or subconscious preconceptions and stereotypes that might otherwise color decision-makers' judgments.[104] As such, the Rule's supporters argued that despite being a process-oriented rule with no hiring mandate, the Rule carried the power to markedly increase diversity among NFL head coaches.[105]

The proponents' belief was borne out. Indeed, over the course of the several years following its implementation, the Rule has markedly increased diversity among NFL head coaches.[106] At the time of the Rule's implementation in 2002, two minorities held NFL head coaching positions.[107] Four years later, minority head coaches led seven of the NFL's thirty-two teams.[108] While this progress may not be entirely attributable to the Rule, the Rule has undoubtedly played a role despite critics' claims that a "meaningful" interview would not spark truly meaningful consideration.

Consider the Cincinnati Bengals' 2003 search for a head coach. Prior to that year, the Bengals had never, in franchise history, hired a person of color for its head coach position.[109] In fact, the Bengals had never even interviewed a person of color for one of its top three coaching positions (head coach, offensive coordinator, and defensive coordinator).[110] Under the Rooney Rule, the Bengals had to do something they had never done nor indicated desire in doing—they had to interview a minority candidate for their head coaching vacancy. With the opportunity to convince the Bengals of his merit, Marvin Lewis, a renowned defensive strategist and then the Washington Redskins defensive coordinator, interviewed for the position and became the Bengals' head coach.[111] In the year after his hire, Lewis transformed the Bengals, who were for years one of the NFL's worst teams, into a playoff contender,[112] a feat for which he narrowly missed receiving the NFL's Coach of the Year Award.[113]

Although Lewis has not yet guided his team to the Super Bowl, another Rooney Rule beneficiary has. In 2004, the Chicago Bears hired Lovie Smith, formerly the St. Louis Rams' defensive coordinator, as their new head coach.[114] Smith inherited a mediocre team, which had in the previous year gone 7–9.[115] In two seasons, however, Smith transformed the Bears' defense into, arguably, the best in the NFL, and in January 2007, Smith led his team to a victory in the National Football Conference championship game and to a consequent Super Bowl berth.[116] The 2007 Super Bowl would prove historic, as Smith would join Tony Dungy, coach of the Indianapolis Colts, as the first African American head coaches in Super Bowl history.[117]

By his own admission, without the opportunity the Rooney Rule produced, Smith may not have ascended to the NFL's head coaching ranks.[118] Given an equal opportunity, however, he did so ascend, and he proceeded to establish himself among the NFL's head coaching elite.

Conclusion

Five years after the Rooney Rule's emergence, the Rule is an established feature of NFL's teams' hiring processes. Indeed, although the NFL has stopped short of requiring such interviews, it has strongly encouraged its member teams to interview candidates of color for their highest-level front office positions.[119] And, just as diversity has increased among the League's head coaches, it has increased in the league's teams' front offices.[120]

In short, the Rooney Rule has succeeded. No team has flouted the Rule since Millen did so in 2003, it has increased diversity throughout the league, and its beneficiaries have met with substantial success. As such, the Rule is enjoying greater popularity than ever before–both among those affiliated with the NFL and among outsiders committed to ensuring equal employment opportunity in other contexts. Most notably, in October 2007, the NCAA's Division I Athletic Directors' Association, concerned that minorities are disproportionately scarce among the nation's Division I head football coaching positions, turned to a form of the Rooney Rule in hopes of increasing equal employment opportunities among minority head coaching candidates.[121] The organization's members have committed to including candidates of color among the interviewees for their universities' head football coaching vacancies.[122] Whether the athletic directors' commitment will translate into greater diversity among Division I head coaches is untold, but if the NFL's experience with the Rooney Rule is any indicator, prospects are bright.

As Cyrus Mehri and Johnnie L. Cochran, Jr., pressed the NFL to adopt the Rooney Rule, they insisted they had "provided the basis for meaningful change" and that it was the "obligation of the National Football League to see that change happen[ed]."[123] They were correct, and the league has, indeed, changed. Once an embarrassment among its peer leagues regarding equal employment opportunity for minority coaches, the NFL now stands as a model for other organizations seeking the change it has enjoyed.

NOTES

1. See Kenneth L. Shropshire, *In Black and White: Race and Sports in America,* 29–31 (1996) (discussing history of discrimination in all three sports). The NHL, America's fourth premier sports league, has had a discriminatory history as well, but in that athletes of color have historically played little hockey, discrimination in hockey has been rooted in national origin, dividing "French-Canadian and European players from their American and Anglo-Canadian counterparts." Kenneth L. Shropshire, *Minority Issues in Contemporary Sports,* 15; *Stan L. & Pol'y Rev.* 189, 191 n.9 (2004) (citing Lawrence M. Kahn, Discrimination in Professional Sports: A Survey of the Literature, 44 *Indus. & Lab. Rel. Rev.* 395 (1991)).

2. See Johnnie L. Cochran, Jr., and Cyrus Mehri, Black Coaches in the National Football League: Superior Performance, Inferior Opportunities 1. (2002), http://web2.customwebexpress. com/meska/UserFiles/File/Report_Superior_Performance_Inferior_Opportunities.pdf (last vis-

ited Apr. 9, 2008) (noting as of 2002, only 1.5 percent of the 400 coaches in NFL history were African American).

3. See Brian W. Collins, Tackling Unconscious Bias in Hiring Practices: The Plight of the Rooney Rule, 82 *N.Y.U. L. Rev.* 870, 877–884 (2007) (discussing coaching opportunities for African Americans in the NBA and NFL); Shropshire, *Minority Issues in Contemporary Sports*, supra note 1, at 203–05 (noting baseball was "impetus" for diversity initiatives creating opportunities for African Americans in managerial and coaching positions).

4. Tony Dungy and Herman Edwards were the NFL's only head coaches of color in 2002. Gary Myers, Sunday Morning QB: Black Coaches Try to Get in the Game, *New York Daily News*, Oct. 6, 2002, at 70. As of 2002, Art Shell, Dennis Green, and Ray Rhodes were the only other people of color to have held NFL head coaching positions in the league's modem era. Id.

5. Steve Wieberg, Division I-A Tackles Minority Hiring: Unlike NFL's Rooney Rule, ADs' Directive Will Only Encourage, Not Require, Action, *USA Today*, Oct. 3, 2007, at 1C.

6. Shropshire, *In Black and White: Race and Sports in America*, supra note 1, at 30 (citing Arthur R. Ashe, Jr., *A Hard Road to Glory: A History of the African-American Athlete Since 1946* 99 (1988)).

7. See Fritz Pollard Biography, http://www.profootballhof.conVhof/member.jsp?player_id=242 (last visited Mar. 30, 2008) (noting Pollard's last season).

8. See official site of the Pro Football Hall of Fame, supra note 7. (describing Pollard as one of the most feared running backs in the APFA).

9. Official site of the Pro Football Hall of Fame, supra note 7.

10. See Joe Burris, Forgotten Pioneer: Fritz Pollard was the NFL's First Black Coach (and the QB on a Champion Team) but Almost No One Knows His Name, *Boston Globe*, Feb. 18, 2004, at F1. (interviewing Fritz Pollard's grandson about his grandfather's football stories). Pollard met with such consistent brutality that he developed a mechanism of punishing those who sought to punish him after a tackle. Id. Upon hitting the ground, Pollard rolled on to his back, raised his feet into the air and waved them as if riding a bicycle while simultaneously propelling himself to an upright position. Id.

11. Id.

12. Richard Lapchick, *Sport in Society: Equal Opportunity or Business as Usual?* 9–10 (1995).

13. Timothy Davis, The Myth of the Superspade: The Persistence of Racism in College Athletics, 22 *Fordham Urb. L.J.* 615, 645 (1995) (citing Harry Edwards, *Sociology of Sport* 38 [1973]).

14. Shropshire, *In Black and White: Race and Sports in America*, supra note 1, at 30.

15. Id.

16. See Sports Business News, The Great One, McLean and Wirtz as Far from Lord Stanley as They'll Ever Be, http://sportsbiznews.blogspot.com/2007_04_I 5_archive.html (last visited Mar. 30, 2008).

17. Id.

18. Shropshire, *In Black and White: Race and Sports in America*, supra note 1, at 30. Bill Willis and Marion Motley joined the NFL's Cleveland Browns later that season. Id.

19. Richard E. Lapchick, *Smashing Barriers: Race and Sport in the New Millennium* 229 (2001).

20. See id. (suggesting African Americans have historically occupied brawny positions requiring less intelligence).

21. Id.

22. See Marlin Briscoe Biography, http://www.marlinbriscoefootball.com/biography.html (last visited Mar. 30, 2008) [hereinafter Marlin Briscoe].

23. Len Pasquarelli, Remembering Thrower's Contribution, ESPN, Feb. 21, 2002, http://espn.go.com/nfl/columns/pasquarelli-len/1338017.html (last visited Mar. 30, 2008).

24. See James Harris, http://jaguars.com/team/scout.aspx?id=2409 (last visited Mar. 30, 2008) (presenting James Harris's biography). During the previous year, Marlin Briscoe, a black quarterback, started a regular-season game for the Denver Broncos. However, at the time the Denver Broncos played in the American Football League rather than the NFL. Marlin Briscoe, supra note 22. The leagues merged two years later in 1970. *African American Sports Greats: A Biographical Dictionary* 305. (David L. Porter, ed., 1995) [hereinafter *African American Sports Greats*].

Ironically, Harris completed some of his 1969 passes to Briscoe, whom the Broncos traded to the Bills and the Bills converted to a wide receiver. Marlin Briscoe, supra note 22. Notably, generations of black college quarterbacks would suffer Briscoe's fate as they entered an NFL largely inhospitable to black quarterbacks. See Lapchick, supra note 19, at 228 (noting that as of 1998, 91 percent of all quarterbacks in the NFL were white). The trend continues even today. Indeed, two of the 2006 Super Bowl champion Pittsburgh Steelers' best wide receivers—Antwaan Randle-El and Hines Ward—played the quarterback position in college. About Antwaan, http://www.antwaanrandleel. com/about/ (last visited Mar. 30, 2008) [hereinafter Randle-El]; About Hines, http://hinesward. fsmgsports.com/main.html (last visited Mar. 30, 2008) [hereinafter Ward]. While Ward played quarterback, running back and wide receiver at the University of Georgia, Randel-El was strictly a quarterback at Indiana University and was one of the nation's best, placing sixth in balloting for the Heisman Trophy, an annual award given to college football's best player. Andrew Bagnato, Huskers' Crouch Proves Best Option; Nebraska QB Edges Grossman; Randle El 6th, *Chicago Tribune*, Dec. 9, 2001, at Cl; Randle-El, supra; Ward, supra.

25. James Harris, supra note 24.

26. See Shropshire, *In Black and White: Race and Sports in America*, supra note 1, at 45 (noting Doug Williams's Super Bowl MVP accomplishment).

27. Lapchick, supra note 19, at 228.

28. Id. The three black quarterbacks selected in the 1999 draft's first round were Daunte Culpepper, Akili Smith, and Donovan McNabb. Id.

29. Richard Lapchick, The 2006 Racial and Gender Report Card: National Football League 3 (2006), http://www.bus.ucf.edu/sport/public/downloads/2006-RGRC-NFL[I].pdf (last visited Mar. 30, 2008).

30. The names of these quarterbacks are Jason Campbell, David Garrard, Tarvaris Jackson, Donovan McNabb, Steve McNair, and Vince Young. Donovan McNabb tells HBO Black QBs Face Greater Scrutiny, ESPN, Sept. 18, 2007, http://sports.espn.go.com/espn/wire?section-nfl&id=3025563. (last visited Mar. 29, 2008).

31. See Cochran & Mehri, supra note 2, at 1 (documenting under-representation of African Americans among the NFL's coaching ranks).

32. Shropshire, *In Black and White: Race and Sports in America*, supra note 1, at 79.

33. Cochran, & Mehri, supra note 2, at 1.

34. Shropshire, *In Black and White: Race and Sports in America*, supra note 1, at 79.

35. *African American Sports Greats*, supra note 24, at 305.

36. Id.

37. Id.; Cochran, & Mehri, supra note 2, at 11.

38. Mark Purdy, Return to Team's Past Good Way to Forge Bright Future in Oakland, *San Jose Mercury News*, Feb. 12, 2006, at Sp. 1.

39. Cochran & Mehri, supra note 2, at 6–7.

40. Id. at 7.

41. Id. During that time period, Marty Schottenheimer led his team to nine playoff appearances and Marv Levy, like Green, led his team to eight. Id. at 7 and n.9.

42. Id. at 7.

43. Cochran & Mehri, supra note 2, at 12.

44. Id. at 7.

45. See id. at 7–8 (describing team's transformation under Dungy).

46. Id.at 7–8; see Tony Dungy Stats, http://sports.espn.go.com/nfl/players/coach?id=8. (last visited Mar. 30, 2008).

47. Id.at 12.

48. Id.

49. Id. at 12, Exhibit C at 7–8.

50. Johnnie L. Cochran, Jr., Biography, available at http://www.cochranfirm.com/pdf/ CochranBrochure.pdf, at 2 (last visited Apr. 9, 2008).

51. Cyrus Mehri Biography, http://www.findjustice.com/sub/cyrus-mehri.jsp (last visited Mar. 30, 2008).

52. Cochran & Mehri, supra note 2, at ii, 2.

53. Id. at Exhibit B at 3.

54. See id. at Exhibit B at 1–3 ("In each and every one of these comparisons, black coaches have a stronger record than white coaches.").

55. See id. at ii (noting that wins and losses are "the currency of football and all team sports").

56. Id. at 2.

57. See id. (recognizing a one-win difference often determines whether a team is successful in reaching the playoffs).

58. Id.

59. Id. at 3.

60. Id.

61. Id. at 4.

62. Id.

63. See id. at i–ii.

64. See id. at 8–10.

65. Id. at ii.

66. See Shropshire, *In Black and White: Race and Sports in America*, supra note 1, at 10 (discussing various methods individuals use to underplay their discriminatory hiring practices).

67. Charles R. Lawrence III, The Id, the Ego, and Equal Protection: Reckoning with Unconscious Racism, 39 *Stan. L. Rev.* 317, 323 (1987); R.A. Lenhardt, "Understanding the Mark: Race, Stigma, and Equality in Context," 79 *N.Y.U. L. Rev.* 803, 829 (2004).

68. See William L. Kandel, Practicing Law Institute: Litigation and Administrative Practice Course Handbook Series, 682 *Practical L. Inst.* 469, 483 (2002) (explaining that attacking the character of executives in negotiations as racist often hampers the ability to reach meaningful solutions).

69. See Collins, supra note 3, at 884 (noting ex-NFL commissioner Paul Tagliabue's efforts to increase minority hiring before the Rooney Rule's inception).

70. Id. at 886.

71. Id.

72. See Cochran & Mehri, supra note 65, at 15.

73. See id. at 14.

74. See id. at 15.

75. See Collins, supra note 3, at 901–04 (discussing problem of "sham" interviews with the Rooney Rule and difficulty of measuring franchises' good faith efforts in interviewing minority candidates during hiring processes).

76. See id. at 886 (noting that the NFL Committee on Workplace Diversity's suggestions were adopted by all 32 NFL owners).

77. Id.

78. Greg Garber, Thanks to the Rooney Rule, Doors Opened, ESPN, Feb. 9, 2007, http://sports.espn.go.com/nfl/playoffs06/news/story?id=2750645 (last visited Mar. 30, 2008).

79. See id. (discussing the effects of the Rooney Rule on the NFL).

80. E.g. Jay Nordinger, Color in Coaching, *National Review*, Sept. 1, 2003, available at http://www.nationalreview.com/flashback/nordlinger200504200048.asp (last visited Mar. 30, 2008).

81. See Collins supra note 3, at 871 (noting that the Rooney Rule appeared "vague and inefficient" at first).

82. Id. at 902.

83. In 2007, the Black Coaches Association changed its name to the Black Coaches and Administrators, and now encompasses black collegiate sports administrators as well. Erika P. Thompson, "Black Coaches Association Announces Name Change, Black Coaches & Administrators," Jul. 6, 2007, http://bcasports.cstv.com/genrel/072007aaa.html (last visited Mar. 30, 2008).

84. See John Wooten Bio, http://www.fpal.org/wooten.php (last visited Mar. 30, 2008) (noting Wooten's various work as a football player and front office executive).

85. Id.

86. NFL Scouting Combine, http://www.nflcombine.net/ (last visited Mar. 30, 2008).

87. Collins, supra note 3, at 887.

88. See Jay Paris, Browns' Winslow is the Mouth that Roars, *North County Times*, Nov. 2, 2006, available at http://www.nctimes.com/articles/2006/1 1/03/sports/professional/chargers/ 21–02_541 l2_06.txt (last visited Mar. 30, 2008) (claiming that Kellen Winslow revolutionized the tight end position).

89. See NFL 1980 League Leaders, http://www.pro-football-reference.com/years/leaders l980.htm (last visited Mar. 30, 2008) (showing Winslow second in the league in receiving yards).

90. The Pro Football Hall of Fame inducted Winslow in 1995. Kellen Winslow Biography, http://www.profootballhof.com/hof/member.jsp?player_id=233 (last visited Mar. 30, 2008).

91. Winslow's capability in this regard is perhaps best illustrated by his performance in a 1982 Chargers playoff victory over the Miami Dolphins, a performance ranking among the greatest individual performances in NFL history. See Page 2 Staff, The List: Best NFL Playoff Performances, ESPN, http://espn.go.com/page2/s/list/NFLplayoffperform.html (last visited Mar. 30, 2008) (ranking Winslow's performance the second greatest playoff performance of all time). During that game, Winslow refused to accept defeat. Despite being treated throughout the game for severe cramps, dehydration, a pinched nerve in his shoulder, and a gash in his lower lip requiring stitches, Winslow caught thirteen passes for 166 yards, scored a touchdown, and blocked a Miami Dolphin field goal that would have given the Dolphins the victory. Dan Ralph, *The Reluctant Superstar,* NFL Canada, Oct. 16, 2007, http://www.nflcanada.com/News/FeatureWriters/Ralph-Dan/2007/ l 0/16/4581021 .html (last visited Mar. 30, 2008).

92. Kellen Winslow, foreword to Shropshire, *In Black and White: Race and Sports in America*, supra note 1, at xii.

93. Id. at xi.

94. NFL Football Standings, ESPN, http://sports.espn.go.com/nfl/standings?season= 2002&breakdown=3&split=O (last visited Mar. 30, 2008).

95. Lions Hire Mariucci as Head Coach, Canadian Broadcasting Centre, Feb. 5, 2003, http://www.cbc.ca/sports/story/2003/02/03/mariucciO30203.html (last visited Mar. 30, 2008).

96. Collins, supra note 3, at 900–01. Ironically, Mariucci, the coach Millen pursued with such myopia, performed quite poorly as the Lions head coach. During his two-plus seasons with the team, Mariucci amassed a record of 15 wins and 28 losses and was ultimately terminated in the middle of the 2005 season. Skip Wood, After Digesting Turkey Day Debacle, Lions Fire Mariucci, *USA Today*, Nov. 28, 2005, available at http://www.usatoday.com/sports/footballlnfl/lions/2005- ll-28¬mariucci_x.htm (last visited Mar. 30, 2008).

97. Brain A. Maravent, Is the Rooney Rule Affirmative Action? Analyzing the NFL's Mandate to its Clubs Regarding Coaching and Front Office Hires,13 *Sports Law. J.* 233, 243 (2006).

98. Millen Fined for Not Interviewing Minority Candidates, ESPN, July 5, 2003, http:// espn.go.com/nfl/news/2003/O725/1585560.html (last visited Mar. 30, 2008).

99. Millen Fined $200K for not Interviewing Minority Candidates, CBS Sports, July 5, 2003, http://cbs.sportsline.com/nfl/story/6498949 (last visited Mar. 30, 2008).

100. Curt Sylvester, Detroit Lions Owner Lashes Out at NFL in Response to Diversity Fine, *Detroit Free Press*, July 29, 2003, at A1.

101. It merits noting that Millen did invite candidates of color to interview for the Lions' head coaching position, but recognizing that Millen had already decided to hire Mariucci and that the interviews to which they were being invited would be pro forma, and thus not meaningful, none of the invitees accepted. Collins, supra note 3, at 901.

102. See id. at 902 (discussing the possibility of "sham" interviews for minority coaching candidates).

103. Nordlinger, supra note 80.

104. See Shropshire, *In Black and White: Race and Sports in America*, supra note 1, at 37– 38 (discussing positive effect of Carol Moseley Braun's election to the United States Senate on the sensitivity to issues affecting minorities).

105. See Cochran & Mehri, supra note 2, at 17 (noting that their proposal for changes in NFL's hiring process had the capability to promote "meaningful change").

106. See Collins, supra note 3, at 907–11 (discussing statistical effect of Rooney Rule).

107. Maravent, supra note 97, at 245.

108. Collins, supra note 3, at 907.

109. Geoff Hobson, The Torch Has Been Passed, Cincinnati Bengals, http://www.bengals.com/news/news.asp?story-id= 639 (last visited Mar. 30, 2008).

110. Mark Curnutte, Coughlin, Lewis Come to Town, Cincinnati Enquirer, Jan. 10, 2003, at 1C.

111. Damon Hack, Bengals Draw Praise for Hiring of Lewis, *New York Times*, Jan. 17, 2003, at D3.

112. See Jim Corbett, Lewis Confident in Untested Palmer, *USA Today*, May 29, 2004.

113. Cincinnati Bengals, Marvin Lewis Biography, http://www.bengals.com/team/coach.asp?coach id=7 (last visited Mar. 30, 2008).

114. Bears Hire Smith to be Head Coach, *USA Today*, Jan. 14, 2004.

115. 2003 NFL Standings, ESPN, http://sports.espn.go.com/nfl/standings?season= 2003&breakdown=3&split=O (last visited Mar. 30, 2008).

116. John Mullin, Super Bowl Bound, *Chicago Tribune*, Jan. 21, 2007, available at http://www.chicagotribune.com/sports/football/bears/cs-07012 lbearsgamer,0, I88867.story?coll= chi¬homepagepromo440-fea (last visited Mar. 30, 2008).

117. Jarrett Bell, Coaches Chasing Super Bowl—And History, *USA Today*, Jan. 17, 2007.

118. Clifton Brown, NFL Roundup: Bears Hope Takeaways Lead Them to Title, *New York Times*, Jan. 30, 2007, at D2.

119. Mark Maske, Expansion of "Rooney Rule" Meets Resistance, *Washington Post*, Apr. 13, 2006, at D1. Indeed, the league's commitment to the Rooney Rule and its underlying principles is so complete that the league committed to interviewing candidates of color when seeking a replacement for former league commissioner Tagliabue. See Scott Brown, Rooney Rule Helping Minority Coaching Candidates, *Pittsburgh Tribune-Review*, Jan. 11, 2007, available at http://www.pittsburghlive.com/x/pittsburghtrib/sporis/steelers/s_488048.html (last visited Mar. 30, 2008) (noting that minority candidate Fred Nance was among the five finalists considered to replace Tagliabue).

120. See Brown, supra note 119. ("[T]he Rooney Rule, or the spirit of it, has led to more opportunities for minorities in NFL front offices.").

121. Steve Wieberg, Major-College ADs Tackle Minority Hiring, *USA Today*, Oct. 2, 2007.

122. id.

123. Cochran & Mehri, supra note 2, at 17.

BIBLIOGRAPHY

Bell, Jarrett. "Coaches Chasing Super Bowl—and History." *USA Today*, January 17, 2007.

"Biography of James Harris." Accessed March 30, 2008. http://jaguars.com/team/scout.aspx?id= 2409.

Brown, Clifton. "NFL Roundup: Bears Hope Takeaways Lead Them to Title." *New York Times*, January 30, 2007.

Burris, Joe. "Forgotten Pioneer: Fritz Pollard was the NFL's First Black Coach (and the QB on a Champion Team) but Almost No One Knows His Name." *Boston Globe*, February 18, 2005.

Canadian Broadcasting Centre. "Lions Hire Mariucci as Head Coach." *Canadian Broadcasting Centre*, February 5, 2003. http://www.cbc.ca/sports/story/2003/02/03/mariucci030203.html.

CBS. "Millen Fined $200K for not Interviewing Minority Candidates." CBS Sports, July 5, 2003. Accessed on March 30, 2008. http://cbs.sportsline.com/nfl/story/6498949.

Cincinnati Bengals. "Marvin Lewis Biography." Accessed on March 30, 2008. http://www.bengals.com/team/coach.asp?coach_id=7.

Cochran, Johnnie L., Jr., and Cyrus Mehri. "Black Coaches in the National Football League: Superior Performance, Inferior Opportunities." 2002. Accessed April 9, 2008. http://web2.customwebexpress.com/meska/userfiles/file/report__Superior_Performance_Inferior_Opportunities.pdf.

Collins, Brian W. "Tackling Unconscious Bias in Hiring Practices: The Plight of the Directive Will Only Encourage, Not Require Action." 82 *N.Y.U. L. REV.* 870, 877–884.

Corbett, Jim. "Lewis Confident in Untested Palmer." *USA Today*, May 29, 2004.

Curnutte, Mark. "Coughlin, Lewis Come to Town." *Cincinnati Enquirer*, January 10, 2003.

Cyrus Mehri. "Cyrus Mehri Biography." Accessed on March 30, 2008. http://findjustice.com/sub/cyrus-mehri.jsp.

Davis, Timothy. "The Myth of the Superspade: The Persistence of Racism in College Athletics." 22 *Fordham Urb. L.J. 615, 645*, 1995.

ESPN. "Millen Fined for Not Interviewing Minority Candidates." 2003. Accessed on March 30, 2008. http://espn.go.com/nfl/news/2003/0725/1585560/html.

ESPN. "2003 NFL Standings." Accessed on March 30, 2008. http://sports.espn.go.com/nfl/standings?season=2003&breakdown=3&split=0.

Garber, Greg. "Thanks to the Rooney Rule, Doors Opened." *ESPN*, 2007. Accessed on March 30, 2008. http://sports.espn.go.com/nfl/playoffs06/news/story?id=2750645.

Hack, Damon. "Bengals Draw Praise for Hiring of Lewis." *New York Times*, January 17, 2003.

Hobson, Geoff. "The Torch Has Been Passed, Cincinnati Bengals." Accessed on March 30, 2008. http://www.bengals.com/news/news.asp?story_id=1639.

"John Wooten Biography." Accessed on March 30, 2008. http://www.fpal.org/wooten.php.

"Johnnie L. Cochran, Jr., Biography." Accessed on April 9, 2008. http://www.cochranfirm.com/pdf/CochranBrochure.pdf.

Kandel, William L. "Practicing Law Institute: Litigation and Administrative Practice Course Handbook Series." 682 *Practical L. Inst. 469, 483*, 2002.

Lapchick, Richard. *Smashing Barriers: Race and Sport in the New Millennium*. New York: Madison Books, 2001.

Lapchick, Richard. *Sport in Society: Equal Opportunity or Business as Usual?* Thousand Oaks, CA: Sage, 1995.

Lapchick, Richard. "The 2006 Racial and Gender Report Card: National Football League." Accessed on March 30, 2008. http://www.bus.ucf.edu/sport/public/downloads/2006_RCRC_NFL[1].pdf.

Lawrence, Charles R., III, "The Id, the Ego, and Equal Protection: Reckoning with Unconscious Racism." 39 *Stan L. Rev. 317, 323*, 1987.

Lenhardt, R.A. "Understanding the Mark: Race, Stigma, and Equality in Context." 79 *N.Y.U. L. Rev. 803, 829*, 2004.

Maravent, Bram A. "Is the Rooney Rule Affirmative Action? Analyzing the NFL's Mandate to its Clubs Regarding Coaching and Front Office Hours." 13 *Sports Law. J. 233, 243*, 2006.

Marlin Briscoe Football. "Marlin Briscoe Biography." Accessed March 30, 2008. http://www.marlinbriscoefootball.com/biography.html.

Maske, Mark. "Expansion of 'Rooney Rule' Meets Resistance." *Washington Post*, 2007.

Mullin, John. "Super Bowl Bound." *Chicago Tribune*, 2007. Accessed on March 30, 2008. http://www.chicagotribune.com/sports/football/bears/cs070121bearsgamer,0,188867.stor?coll=chihomepagepromo440-fea.

NFL. "NFL Football Standings." *ESPN*. Accessed on March 30, 2008. http://sports.espn.go.com/nfl/standings?season=2002&breakdown=3&split=0.

NFL. "NFL 1980 League Leaders." Accessed on March 30, 2008. http://www.pro-football-reference.com/years/leaders1980.htm.

Nordinger, Jay. "Color in Coaching." *National Review*, 2003. Accessed on March 20, 2008. http://www.nationalreview.com/flashback/nordlinger200504200048.asp.

Paris, Jay. "Browns' Winslow Is the Mouth that Roars." *North County Times*, 2006. Accessed on March 30, 2008. http://www.nctimes.com/articles/2006/11/03/sports/professional/chargers/21_02_5411 _06.txt.

Pasquarelli, Len. "Remembering Thrower's Contribution." *ESPN*, 2002. Accessed March 30, 2008. http://espn.go.com/nfl/columns/pasquarelli_len/1338017.html.

Pro Football Hall of Fame. "The Pro Football Hall of Fame Inducted Winslow in 1995." Accessed on March 30, 2008. http://www.profootballhof.com/hof/member.jsp?player_id=233.

Pro Football Hall of Fame. "Fritz Pollard Biography." Accessed March 30, 2008. http://www.profootballhof.com.

Rooney Rule. *82 N.Y.U. L. Rev. 870*, 2007: 877–884.

Scouting Combine. "NFL Scouting Combine." Accessed on March 30, 2008. http://www.nflcombine.net/.

Shropshire, Kenneth L. *In Black and White: Race and Sports in America*. New York: New York University Press, 1996.

Sports Business News. "The Great One, McLean and Wirtz as Far from Lord Stanley as They'll Ever Be." Accessed March 30, 2008. http://sportsbiznews.blogspot.com/2007_04_15_archive.html.

Sylvester, Curt. "Detroit Lions Owner Lashes Out at NFL in Response to Diversity Fine." *Detroit Free Press*, 2003.

USA Today. "Bears Hire Smith to Be Head Coach." *USA Today*, 2004.

Wieberg, Steve. "Division I-A Tackles Minority Hiring: Unlike NFL's Rooney Rule, ADs' Directive Will Only Encourage, Not Require, Action." *USA Today*, October 3, 2007, 1C.

Wieberg, Steve. "Major-College Ads Tackle Minority Hiring." *USA Today*, October 2, 2007.

Wood, Skip. "After Digesting Turkey Day Debacle, Lions Fire Mariucci." *USA Today*, 2005. http://www.usatoday.com/sports/football/nfl/lions/2005-11-28-mariucci_x.htm.

Does Race Matter?
Core Character Matters

Edward "Will" Thomas

This essay is intended for those with a vested interest in promoting athletic careers that enhance individuals' lives to the greatest degree possible—mentally, physically, and financially. What are the benefits and rewards to be derived from athletic involvement? How is sustainability of these benefits and rewards accomplished? What do you want from sport? How much thought and effort have you expended on these questions? Who have you discussed this with?

The world of professional sports in America is a high stakes enterprise—one that has the potential to uplift you and set you up to enjoy a full and rewarding existence. Alternatively, involvement in sports has the potential to corrupt, twist, confuse, alienate, and fray the very fiber of your being. What I am talking about can easily be illustrated by comparing and contrasting the on- and off-field behaviors, and activities, of players like Ocho Cinco[1] and Calvin Johnson.[2]

Participation in professional sports is not recreation. Rather, it is participation in a billion-dollar business enterprise. And as such, it requires individuals to adopt a professional work ethic. A work ethic to excel in performing their individual and team-oriented jobs.

Furthermore, to fully benefit from bringing one's God-given talents requires foundational preparation beyond physicality. Yes, physicality is the ticket that grants entry, but it is not sufficient to sustain a career. Stories abound from college to the National Football League of individuals of supreme talent, bolstered by passion and intent, revered and mightily rewarded, who ultimately became discarded without fanfare when they in some way, egregiously contravened the bounds of what the machine could tolerate or when their transgressions could no longer be hidden or covered up. Cost-benefit analysis is quantitative in this economically driven enterprise, and results are final when the line in the sand is crossed. Consider Michael Vick[3] and his untimely and unfortunate exodus from football stardom to football obscurity. Or, consider the recent demise of young Tyrann Mathieu, finalist as All-American, and Heisman candidate, released three times for failing drug tests, finally suspended from the Louisiana State University football team.[4]

Registered from a common-sense approach, how do we assist up-and-coming athletes to avoid these pitfalls? How do we assist young athletes to benefit to the greatest extent possible from the opportunities available to them, regardless of what level of sport they pursue? In other words, how do we nurture future athletes, mind, body, and soul, to prepare them to fully embrace the joys and challenges that are inherent when one possesses out-of-the-ordinary athletic talent?

It is unfortunate to contemplate the tremendous talent and potential of those individuals (and countless others) not propelling them into lives of personal accomplishment and pride, but rather into situations of confusion and misguided behavior ultimately resulting in squandered potential.

What makes the difference between two highly athletically talented individuals such that one excels athletically and personally and the other loses the opportunity to bask in success and falls into personal turmoil? Over the years, as mounting incidences of athletes' lives, in various states of disarray, came to my attention, my curiosity peaked because these stories contradicted my relatively wholesome experience, and the stories that I had been nurtured with as a young athlete—stories about the lives and experiences of those who came before me, in which my predecessors were heroes and inspiration to me. They were accomplished men, role models strong enough in the culture of who they were as African American men to be dedicated and dignified to play for their people, for the greater good of the entire black community. Their actions were driven by a common goal—to uplift and nurture.

Additionally, my own experience also provided impetus for reflection. Between the extremes previously outlined reside the shades of grey where many, including myself, would place our experience ("If only I knew then what I know now"). I certainly would have leveraged my talent and super-stardom into valuable contribution to society and lucrative financial sustainability. While I don't have the economic freedom that "coulda... shoulda" followed my football career, I thankfully emerged morally intact, and over time, wiser about the process of fostering successful and life-enhancing athletic careers, including an understanding of the ramifications and pitfalls that lie therein. This in fact, has led to the development of Core Character Matters, a program designed to help young athletes and their parents maximize the potential of the educational, athletic, and financial opportunities at their disposal.

The principles embodied in Core Character Matters have been applied with tremendously positive results. Currently, a larger program is being implemented in New Orleans, Louisiana—my hometown—where I began and can now give back a valuable contribution to society.[5]

Theoretical Framework

The research question, the literature review, the data collection and analysis, and the conclusion for this essay derive from a narrative perspective based on personal experience.

The theoretical framework for Core Character Matters emerges from an examination and analysis of the cultural context in which I experienced my early life and sports nurturing, compared and contrasted to the experiences that began to unfold as I became more absorbed into the more structural business enterprise of the sport I loved and demonstrated great talent in. While this analysis is based on first-hand experience, parallels exist within the broader African American context as it relates to sport, thus bolstering the ideas presented herein. Consequently, I reveal my personal experience and cite parallels from the broader historical context to outline the underpinnings for Core Character Matters.

First, the constructs, cultural and structural, are defined, as is economics—the mechanism that predominantly determines structural practices. After the general definitions follows descriptions of these concepts as they relate to athletics. This background provides context through which to consider the subsequent stories of my personal experience and the larger historical story. The synthesis of these aids comprehension of how to better navigate the current dysfunctional quagmire that has unfortunately become all too common among talented, highly paid professional athletes. Understanding how the current state of affairs has developed provides the platform from which to start to make shifts to more positive action and results—the ultimate objective of Core Character Matters.

Cultural: Culture relates to the attitudes, beliefs, and values in which one is immersed—the paradigm, if you will. The cultural construct referred to in this essay belongs to and envelops the larger group. It consists of a sense of historical pride and belonging, and fundamental connection to a greater, bigger, wiser, purpose that is believed in, accepted, and adopted. Although it is not necessarily preached, what matters becomes known to all in the group through stories, lived experience, and modeling by the group. Consequently, it consists of the broader notions in which individuals in a particular community exist. And as such, it provides the underpinnings of values, attitude, and world view, in general, and with respect to specific situations or contexts. It is natural, almost absorbed by osmosis. And, its omnipresence results in its informing life lessons one encounters.

Structural: The structural is contrived and fickle and responds to the created "reality" that exists at any given time. It is artificial, and driven by economics on a powerful and complex level. It is maintained, molded, and manipulated by social conventions. It is acted upon, based on individual interpretation.

When operating from a structural perspective, one accepts the status quo as the ultimate reality and typically (1) conforms within and/or chooses to (2) adapt and excel, within that reality. Under both circumstances, that accepted reality becomes reinforced. Furthermore, when individuals creativity and competitively act upon that reality, additional twists, embellishments, or artificial benchmarks of superiority are established to which other individuals aspire, thus altering the structural conventions that guide subsequent behaviors of both those individuals and others. Structural is a reactive, contrived, man-made construct. The structural realm prescribes our actions in society. And, depending on the context within which we find ourselves, the range of actions spans the sublime (publish or perish—in academe) to the ridiculous (reality TV—of the rich and famous).

Society relies on structural conventions to guide behavior, and to create some semblance of order and cohesion to this complex entity we know as "reality." In a sense, the structural attempts to heuristically define reality. However, the structural realm is not sufficient to fully define reality. To use an analogy: information gleaned from social science research that relies solely on quantitative data is limited in its ability to make accurate conclusions. Social science research becomes much richer when supported with qualitative data. Likewise, structural conventions have their place, but they are weak and insufficient, even potentially inaccurate or detrimental, for guiding human behavior. To achieve a balanced existence cultural input is required.

Economics: Then, within the structural, resides economics. Economics drives everything. Economics, as it relates to this essay, is a tremendously powerful mechanism which in huge part controls the formation of what those in positions of power and influence present and cultivate as reality, and thus what the rest of us aspire to fit into, in turn reinforcing that reality. In this way, unchallenged by alternative notions, or unmitigated by values and ideas more in line with nurturing the human spirit (cultural influence—the natural state of being) this unreal reality flourishes. The fact is that this is the current way of the world. Consequently, it is critical that one understands this and learns to maneuver within this system. Furthermore, this is particularly true with respect to the management of one's finances. How does money work? What are the ways and means to ensure that our hard earned cash provides for our day-to-day needs and sustains us reasonably throughout our life? How can our money work for us? What are the principles with respect to money management that those in positions of power are using, and how can we take advantage of those principles to enhance our lives? These are life lessons generally sorely lacking in current society. We tend to fly by the seat of our pants, make relatively uninformed and/or naïve decisions, and hope that all works out okay.

Cultural, Structural, and Economics with Respect to Athletics

"Cultural" as it relates to sport is a pure adulterated joy in one's athleticism combined with a desire to take it to the highest level. Cultural in sport is immersion in a mutually understood purpose, communal spirit and cause, imbued with a deep-rooted sense of pride in that association with others of like mind. A nurturing cultural context that celebrates and honors athletic talent as something precious in its own right motivates great personal athletic accomplishments.

Cultural in sport, translates into legacy, a rich, moving, life-enhancing, fondly remembered experience that lives on in the hearts and minds of those who shared it. And, it continues to benefit and inspire others, through subsequent actions of those involved in the experience, as well as by the cultural history passed on.

The reference used to illustrate this is the history of the Grambling State College football team. That history reveals African American football players engaged in a game they loved, pushing themselves to attaining excellence, because they could, and because maximizing achievement was the expected norm of that cultural environment. It is cultural context which drove the pioneer black athletes to challenge the color barrier.

The "structural" as it relates to sport in the United States, with its general objective of providing entertainment for the masses, is fuelled by a frenzy of competition within a multi-billion dollar industry. It is molded and manipulated by society's current fascination with and reliance on television, computer, and social media as the purveyors of reality. And ultimately, this warped, morphed, artificial, contrived, and fickle reality is what those in professional sport must pay attention to. Individuals thus design their affairs based on their distinct and unique interpretations of how they can best survive and benefit in that reality.

This requires the athletically talented to contort from the joy derived from personally accomplishing masterful physical feats, to performing, to entertain the masses. In other words, tremendous external manipulation is wrought on athletes for the structural entertainment factor for the spectators. Sustainability of the multibillion-dollar enterprise requires the conformity and the collusion of all involved. What the structural demands of athletes is outside of them, their talent and their joy of their inherent talent.

And indeed, to support the highly financed enterprise that is professional sport in America, the stakes are extremely high. The conformity and collusion are motivated by the intoxicating allure of unfathomable (to the average person) amounts of money.

Tremendous naivety typically accompanies the "unfathomable" amounts of money that comes to professional athletes. As a result, inordinate numbers of players are bankrupt shortly after their careers end.[6] This is absurd and avoidable.

How do you even conceive of $50 million?[7] Then, how does one make it viable as an income for the present and into the future, because, that is the nature of involvement in sport. It is a relatively short-lived occupation, one that if managed well, has the potential of sustaining one into the future and replacing the norm of working 9 to 5 for 30 years.[8]

Armed with a frame of reference for the influences on athletes' lives, let us now consider stories that bring these concepts to life, so that we might consider alternate options, moving into the future, with up-and-coming athletes.

Personal and Cultural Influences

Athletically, I lived a charmed life. This began with my premature birth and my late uncle declaring to my mother, "This child will be a blessing. He is going to take care of you. Look at the size of his hands and feet. He is going to be a superstar athlete. He is *our* 'Will'" (making the connection to the superstar of the day, Wilt Chamberlain)—the name that my family has called me throughout my life, despite my birth name Edward.[8] Now, I didn't know this story until many years later but it existed in the fabric of my extended family, in the minds and hearts of those who regularly touched my life. And, from a very early age, as I began to develop, my uncanny athleticism was accepted, supported, and nurtured in subtle and natural ways. In other words, family members did not outwardly express awe at my talent, or make a big deal about my tendencies, but my time spent involved in sport, on the street, and in the park, oftentimes amongst much older kids, was accepted without question, despite my tender age. And, as time went on, my expressed desires were supported.

For instance, one very poignant memory for me is of my first "recruitment," at age seven, to a NOR (New Orleans Recreation) team. This came about, not through initiation of adults in my life, but through being "allowed" to be in the park. Someone outside of my family noticed me. Where the support for me came in, was when I went home and said I wanted to join this team, and announced that in order to do that, I needed my birth certificate. Unfortunately, my birth certificate was nowhere to be found. When, through my demands and behaviors, it became evident to those around me how important this was to me, an aunt secured the birth certificate and my football career began.

At this point in my life I was oblivious to the recruitment aspect of this scenario. I was merely steeped in my innate love of and desire to play sports, and an accompanying all round athletic talent that allowed me to be involved in sport. Additionally, I had this fierce competitive spirit, which propelled me to demonstrate determination and take on challenges in a way far beyond my biological years. However, again, this played out differently in the immediate circle of my extended family and the village within which I was immersed, and the broader, outside sports world. In the former, I was Will, allowed to play, and played with, but essentially left to my own devises to grapple with the God-given talent I was blessed with. I played in the "hood," and I wended my way into ever more challenging situations and with older kids. When I became defeated or daunted, that did not break my spirit, but rather reinforced my determination to get better. Losing was not an option for me. All of this came about naturally, from within, presumably linked to the tremendous talent I was blessed with, within the nurturing support and understanding of those around me.

By contrast, the outside world revealed to me (however unconsciously at this point) another side to sport. As already stated, at the early age of seven I was "recruited" by a NOR coach. Additionally, there are the recollections of school teachers challenging me to athletic feats such as foot races with far older children and requests on the basketball court to "make ten consecutive free throws." I always rallied. While I didn't yet consciously process or analyze these scenarios at that time, they obviously had some impact. Initially, my response can probably best be described as curiosity. I can vaguely remember having reactions like "Okay?! Sure. I can do that." And merely meeting (naturally) whatever challenge was placed before me. On the other hand, these incidents also provided me with glimmers of what was to come in terms of others, in some way, wanting to benefit from, participate in, and bask in, the glory of my talent. These incidents were the precursor, if you will, to my inauguration into the structural realm of sport, where my talent became a valuable and sought after commodity. Before that came into my consciousness, however, a likely positive benefit of these gentle, more structural experiences intersecting with my primarily cultural experience was the reinforcement of my winning spirit.

To reiterate, for me, failing was not an option. This came predominantly from within. In fact, it was a burning fire from within, which at times fueled discontent and angst. However, again, at an early age, and I believe, fostered by the unassuming, natural, loving acceptance of me by my family, I formulated the notion that anger and frustration leveled at myself, for not yet achieved athletic skills, goals, and accomplishments, was not in my best interest. I, very early on, came to realize that defeat was merely a platform from which to learn, and to, in subtle and natural ways, advance myself. In fact, this was the genesis of an attitude and work ethic that persisted and strengthened, and definitely factored into my consistently making all-star teams throughout my youth, into my professional sports career, and now, to my commitment to give back to the community.

At this juncture, I want to say a little bit more about "culture" as it relates to what I was immersed in, up to this point, in my family. We constituted a unit—a proverbial "village" responsible for uplifting, protecting, and nurturing one another. There were traditions and conventions within that village that did not require in-depth discussion or analysis. "They" made us come together for a reason. So, it was the culture of what we were as people that had us congregating as a group. It was an unspoken adherence that we lived by, driven by the principle that closeness of family should be known and understood. Consequently, when the call went out for example, that Fourth of July was going to be at Aunt Wileen's—that trickled down in some subtle and natural way, and everyone eventually showed up. It was a given. For some, it might be after a brief stop-in, out of obligation, to in-laws, but ultimately the destination was Aunt Wileen's to congregate with family. These gatherings were the venue in which anyone's and everyone's issues came to the floor, and discussion and resolution became community responsibility. In other words an uncle or a cousin was as readily available to me as a parent, in my times of need, at that particular event and beyond, as was the case for other members of the family as well.

It is also within this culture that universal family truths became absorbed and internalized. So, for instance, when I say that it wasn't until my late teens or twenties that I learned about my premature birth, the genesis of my name "Will" and most importantly, my uncle's prophecy about my super-stardom and taking care of my mother, that was the unspoken belief that the adults had and the underpinning of their nurturance of me. This is how it worked in our culture. These kinds of stories, family legacy, wholesome beliefs and values were the glue that held us together.

Within this culture of the family, everything was so good, even if it wasn't. We didn't know any different. We were protected by the whole, working for the good of everyone. This was the greater purpose. Consequently, we had everything we needed: all the food, all the clothes, all the love we needed, and the comaraderie, and the closeness, and the communications, everything! We didn't know anything about poverty, all our parents had good jobs and they all worked hard and they were all independently strong enough to take care of their families. Our grandma acted as the matriarch so if the parents were partying, she had all us kids together, which also fortified our grouping and bonding. It was unheard of for us to believe that we didn't have anything. And it was within this protective nest that I was able to pursue and exercise the wonder of the talent I was blessed with.

All of this promoted a solid foundation: development of a strong sense of self, and the opportunity to naturally hone the qualities, attitudes, and character that allowed me to become a superstar athlete. And ultimately (although I didn't know it at the time) it contributed to my fulfilling the understood prophecy for me, to excel in sport, and to truly "take care of my mother." All of this came about naturally. There was never a conversation in the family about "you have to make it." It wasn't about anybody pushing me. It was merely a commonly held and understood given.

Historical—Cultural Influences

I liken what was going on for me culturally, as described above, to the experiences of the early African American athletes in historically black colleges. They resided in environments where personal achievement was highly valued, expected, and nurtured. The historically black college experience provided a tremendous opportunity for African Americans to "celebrate that unique history"[9] and "to really, really know who you really, really are."[10]

These sentiments are poignant reflections of the broader cultural community. A community that, once able to step away from the bonds of slavery, immediately moved to educate and maximize the potential of its citizens. Grassroots schools sprang up everywhere, from abandoned buildings, to open fields, eventually to grow into full-fledged institutions.[11] These actions bear witness to the cultural underpinnings—pride, courageous spirit, and will of the African American people. Not only was education highly valued, but over-time, developing colleges developed their programs to include expanded agendas offering marching bands and sports teams. Furthermore, excellence was fostered and expected, in all realms, as is depicted in the 1968 documentary film *100 Yards to Glory* about Grambling State College.[12]

With this documentary and subsequent participation in the first Invitational Football Classic,[13] Grambling State became a well-deserved poster child for historically black colleges and specifically with respect to football. It is in large part the story of this history that informs my thesis about the contributing influence and importance of cultural context in creating foundational values, and ways of being in the world. And, specifically as it relates to football, the rich and valuable legacy that cultural context fostered.

The tradition of historically black colleges was a natural evolution borne out of the desire to uplift the community. The first Invitational Football Classic, Grambling versus Morgan State, played in New York's Yankee Stadium in 1968, was a direct descendant of that objective. These examples epitomize the essence of cultural influence in the African American community at this point in history, and particularly, on the African American athletic community. The Grambling State College football coach, Eddie Robinson, a staunch advocate for education, pledged the proceeds from this historic game to New York Urban League's Street Academy. The Street Academy was an organization that assisted individuals to earn their college degrees in non-traditional ways, thus making this achievement accessible to those for whom it would not otherwise be possible. Robinson was alarmed and concerned about the deteriorating conditions in Harlem in the '60s and particularly about the community's youth population. Consequently, when a number of variables converged (not the least of which was the untimely death of Dr. Martin Luther King, Jr.) during the negotiating stage for a proposed game at Yankee Stadium, Robinson seized the opportunity to give back to the community, an opportunity to potentially contribute to uplifting a segment of the population—this, despite him and his team being from a far distant part of the country. This fact, to a large extent, speaks to cultural strength and devotion. Those operating from more of a place of strength willingly gave of themselves to support others in the black community, others in need.

Considering the broader African American context, this was the Civil Rights era, and all things black were in the forefront of the nation's consciousness. One condition that existed during this time were the segregated black colleges of the South, which provided an opportunity for individuals to know and appreciate who they were as African Americans while pursuing knowledge, personal growth, and laying the foundation for future success.

This was the cultural context within which coach Eddie Robinson dwelt and devoted himself to. In addition to demanding that his players hone their athletic skills, he demanded that they also hone their intellectual skills. Furthermore, he strove to reveal to the rest of the country the high caliber of person and football player that those from Grambling represented—a reflection of the broader black community.

In line with this objective, and decisive in putting Grambling on the map, were the significant and effective efforts of Collie J. Nicholson. Tantamount among these efforts, Nicholson was instrumental in facilitating the occasion of the first Invitational Football Classic in the Bronx, at Yankee Stadium. This was a celebrated event that established pride and cohesion in the black community. In excess of 60,000 predominantly black people attended the game. And, it was an absolutely pivotal event in establishing a grand legacy. One that saw players from that game alone (from Grambling and Morgan combined) go on to play in the NFL, three of whom were eventually inducted in the Pro Football Hall of Fame. Of course, Grambling State's competitors in this game, Morgan State, are part of the overall legacy and must be acknowledged as well. They in fact won the game. They have their own distinct noble legacy. For the purpose of this essay, however, I focus on Grambling's legacy.

Clearly, these players, endowed with tremendous talent, immersed in supportive and nurturing environments, demonstrated that they could indeed, "collectively, as a family, prove that black college football was as good as any." The young men involved in this epic game,[14] glow with pride, to this day, in the retelling of their experience.[15] In that game and for years to follow, African American players played for powerful motivating reasons beyond their self-interest. They played for justice and equality. The groundbreakers fought through sport, for social change, to challenge disparity, inequality, abuse and misuse. That was the collective cultural consciousness amongst the athletes.

This cultural foundation spawned countless other positive developments and success stories. One direct spin-off was the establishment of the Invitational Football Classic as an annual event that ran for subsequent years. This in turn had a significant impact on American history. It brought to the entire country the exhilarating class of football being played in the historically black colleges since the turn of the century. And, ultimately, it is exposure of this talent and caliber of play that broke down the color barrier doors and allowed blacks to play professional football and to elevate the level of the game to what it is today. "Pro football owes them an enormous debt of gratitude."[16]

Specifically, the legacy produced at Gambling State by Coach Robinson lives on, not only in the numbers of players that went on to the NFL, but also the successful and high profile careers of many beyond football[17] and in the benevolent Grambling State Football Team Alumni Group that meets yearly to promote projects in the African American community.

Additionally, for the overall black community, then and now, historically black college football became woven into the cultural fabric as a time to come together to share and experience "part church ... part picnic ... part R&B concert ... and somewhere in there they'll play a football game."[18]

Unfortunately, the details and influence of this tremendous, noble legacy have largely become obscured from the general public and unfortunately from the current generation of ball players by the structural priorities of this time and age.

Personal—Structural Influences and Impacts

Back to my life, to begin to illuminate how the structural realm inserts itself into the lives of athletes. We have already established my love of sport, and my drive to excel, both of which merely strengthened with each passing day. I got a tremendous charge out of my successes and accomplishments in basketball, football, and track. The intrinsic rewards fuelled me. My charmed athletic life was very good. I was having amazing fun.

Ironically, over time, in secondary school, where athletic talent becomes sought after and revered, the charm began to fade. Indeed my talent was sought after, in fact, to the extent that I was investigated for allegedly receiving recruitment bribes/incentives/gifts. Despite no findings against me during the formal investigations, the school board disallowed me from playing football going from junior high to high school. This was somewhat of a discouraging and confusing time. Nonetheless, my talent and determination and my love of athletics were so strong that I turned my attention to track and basketball and made All American in both. Then, in senior high, when I was allowed to resume football, only playing for two years, I became one of the best in the state, and subsequently went to college on a football scholarship. In other words the passion and determination fostered in my formative years sustained me, immunized me against disappointments and hardships encountered relatively early on in my athletic career.

Furthermore, the above example represents a productive or positive manifestation of the confluence of cultural and structural constructs. It represents the mitigating power that culture can have in the face of structural challenges. Steeped in the solid foundation developed in the cultural nest of my family, I undauntedly rallied to the challenge of not being allowed to play football, to great success. My cultural foundation rendered me relatively immune to the external structure and its constraints. At the same time, it is important to note that cultural nurturance alone does not an all-round successful athletic career make. Rather, it is critical that one also understands, and knows how to maneuver within the structural context that exists. This will be expanded upon later.

The incidence of the structural realm entering my consciousness occurred gradually. Even though I had fleetingly recognized it, initially, I just went with it. I didn't have an agenda. I had wonderings, but those wonderings got really, really strong when I started hearing things about "politics" and how "it is not just about talent." When I started hearing those kinds of conversations I started to switch from a kid having fun to contemplating, "This has turned into some-

thing more than just having fun." With that happening, I got more conscious
about what was going on, and in some sense, what was going on took away
from what had been going on for me—the unadulterated joy I had previously
experienced.

Over time, it became revealed to me that, in addition to having natural
talent, I had to learn how to act and be around certain people, how to perform
around certain people, how to use certain words in certain groups. I started
getting instructions about who was watching me—"someone is always watching you." It all became like a script from a movie as opposed to being natural.

So, my high school years represented a transitional period, from a time
of cultural immersion to structural inauguration. During this time I began to
become aware that there was an element of external control capable of tam-
pering with this love that I naturally lived and breathed. There was another
dimension to all of this that I was not fully cognizant of, something outside
of me. From a time of being a kid having fun, to not having so much fun anymore, because my talent was not just natural, it was a commodity to somebody,
and they wanted more of my commodity than they were interested in my natural talent. Of course these are inextricably linked but they are also two distinct
entities, one cultural and the other structural as defined, and thus far outlined.

Historical—Structural Influences and Impacts

It's important here to review how structural influences entered into, and
began to shift the historical African American athletic tradition—specifically
football.

In segregated America no opportunity existed for African American athletes to participate in the NFL, despite their demonstrated superior talent and
skills. Talent and skills that in 1960, the newly formed, desegregated American
Football League (AFL) recognized and seized upon. In order to rival the NFL
the AFL started padding its roster with exceptional black players, to great success. Of course this further perpetuated the rising awareness of the tremendous
talent of African American players, but at what cost?

Other ramifications accompanied this shift. As the awareness of this
tremendous talent rose, colleges too sought to enhance their teams. And, in
their desire to do so, they started heavily recruiting from historically black
colleges.

Young enthusiastic men at these colleges, talented men who lived to play
football, became wooed by attractive incentives that these established institutions could offer them and the new frontier of possibly playing professional
ball.

On first blush this appears positive, however, the cultural tradition that produced these dedicated players was being tampered with. Most obviously, these young men were not among their peers, their people, steeped in the cultural nurturance and purpose that fostered their development in the first place. No longer was the experience so much for the community, but rather more individualistic.

Also, the academic requirements began to become less stringent than had been the tradition at the historically black colleges. Consequently, the nature of players' experiences shifted. Many naïve, ambitious men unthinkingly pursued this simpler road (as had I in high school). These are representations of the previously culturally nurtured African American football players' initiation/introduction to a structural perspective.

Structural Superseding Cultural (Personal)

The need for structural knowledge/education/ intelligence is now illustrated by the story of my naiveté in this realm.

My cultural experience was provided by my family and community who supported and allowed me to naturally experience and hone my God-given talent and intuitively learn to manage and understand the secondary impacts this had on my life. For instance, as already mentioned, learning to turn the frustration and anger that, when I was younger, often arose from my passion, into determination to improve. All of this led to the development of a solid foundation, self-assured, knowledgeable, and wise about my physical, and mental abilities and strategies as they related to athletics. I had been afforded the opportunity to explore all of that, to be acquainted with that, to the fullest extent possible, within a community that observed and appreciated my talent, one that expected that I would ride that talent into adulthood. And, one that nurtured me toward that end. But it was not that I was pushed and prodded into this. It was more like I was watched over and protected, and in this way I was provided the support that allowed me to work it out for myself, because ultimately, I was the one who was going to have to enact it.

By contrast, my structural experience, the experience wherein my talent was treated as a commodity, wherein others sought to "groom" me, mold me into "desirable, suitable" for the professional sports world, began to influence me concurrently. It began to seep into my life and impact my actions and decisions. In some ways, this intersection of the cultural with the structural started to mess with me, confuse me, and woo me, because within that context lurked the omnipresent lure of fame and fortune—two incredibly potent temptations.

Fame and fortune began to manifest for me within school. For instance, arriving in math class the day after a winning football game—in which I played a starring role—to my teacher's accolades, then subsequent declaration of "Oh, and forget about doing today's assignment," was sweet reward indeed! I also recall limiting my course load to the bare minimum in my final year of high school, because I could, and this afforded me freedom and status at the time. The sweetness of these rewards, at this time in my life, when I was being wooed, intoxicated by the elixir of "fame" (such as it was in high school), also superseded and led to my disregard of the passing advice of teachers: that I was going to need the forfeited knowledge and skills later in life.

My experience of the potential of the structural to corrupt, with the temptation of fame and fortune, resulted in me not thinking beyond immediate rewards, which ultimately lead to subsequent negative consequences. Related to the incidents above, when I entered college, it was like being back in kindergarten—I did not have the background, skills, nor required preparation to navigate this new experience.

In the grand scheme of things this was fairly minor and I was able to rally and recover and have a successful college career. It is my belief that this was possible because of my solid core developed in the cultural context from which I emerged. Although I was not immune to the distractions and distortions of reality prompted by the infusion of the structural context, any tremendously detrimental or permanent negative impacts were mitigated by my core character. And, ultimately I had my time in the limelight of the professional football world—a glorious and memorable time.

Structural Superseding Cultural (Historical)

Thus has not been the case for many collegiate and NFL players in recent history. Unfortunate stories abound. Following are some examples of careers gone awry.

Mike Tyson's incarceration lost him between $300 million and $400 million. The man who bit off Evander Holyfield's ear took on more than could chew, both in body parts and in life.

He was once known as the heavyweight champion of the world, but in 1992, he was convicted of sexual assault and served three years in prison. He attempted a comeback, but was disqualified during the high-profile match in which he bit off Holyfield's ear. The boxer earned between $300 and $400 million during his career but spent nearly all of it on pet tigers, mansions, and an expensive divorce.

Curt Schilling says he will lose all $50 million he saved playing baseball on a failed video game venture. The former Red Sox pitcher's video game company, 38 Studios, filed for bankruptcy after missing loan payments and the matter is proceeding in the courts. It currently owes $150 million and has just $21.7 million in assets.

Antoine Walker lost $110 million after taking out massive loans for his real estate ventures. Walker says he took out loans with eight different banks, but couldn't pay them all back at once. Here's what he said when asked if he blames his financial advisors: "No. I don't blame them. I blame more so myself. I think the one thing ... that is difficult to do is to do investments while playing basketball. I think if it was one thing I would tell any young guy or anyone who's playing and making money right now is to wait until the end of your career and start investing and start making money off the field or off the court."

Michael Vick's animal abuse lost him about $130 million. Michael Vick was once the highest-paid player in the NFL, signing a 10-year contract extension worth $130 million with the Atlanta Falcons. Everything changed in 2007, when he went to prison for participating in an illegal dog fighting ring. Vick lost his NFL salary and endorsement while incarcerated for two years.

He filed for Chapter 11 bankruptcy in 2008. All told, Vick lost about $130 million. However, he's making a bit of come back. After his release from prison, he was signed by the Philadelphia Eagles, was Comeback Player of the Year in 2010 and is backup quarterback.

Terrell Owens lost tens of millions that he said was "stolen and mismanaged." "I've been taken advantage of, financially," TO told Dr. Phil. Owens is suing two agents for breach of fiduciary duty, fraud and negligence, seeking to recover up to $6.5 million, according to legal filings obtained by Yahoo Sports.

Travis Henry lost about $20 million after paying for his many children. The 2002 Pro Bowl participant and former running back fathered nine children with nine different women, to whom he pays court-ordered expenses. Also, he was sentenced in 2009 to three years in a Florida prison for financing a cocaine trafficking operation. When all is said and done, Henry lost about $20 million of his fortune.

Tennis player Arantxa Sanchez Vicario says her parents took all of her $60 million in career earnings. She says her father handled her money and gave her a monthly allowance (of sorts). Later she claimed that her parents spent and mismanaged the money and left her with nothing.

Lenny Dykstra supposed business sense cost him about $50 million. Three-time All-Star player Lenny Dykstra, with his omnipresent wad of chewing tobacco, won the 1986 World Series. However, by 2011 he had lost about $50 million. In 2008, he began a high-end jet charter company and a magazine offering financial advice to athletes. In December 2012, he plead guilty to bankruptcy fraud and was sentenced to 6 months is federal prison, the *International Business Times* reported. He is currently serving time in state prison for grand theft auto, lewd conduct and assault with a deadly weapon.

Lawrence Taylor lost about $50 million after using drugs and prostitutes. Lawrence "L.T." Taylor won the NFL's MVP in 1986 and starred in two Super

Bowls. However, he used cocaine during his career and was jailed three times for attempted drug possession following his retirement.

He filed for bankruptcy in 1998, citing mortgage troubles. And in 2011, he pleaded guilty to sexual misconduct and patronizing a prostitute. He was ordered to serve six months of probation. The man considered one of the best defensive players in the league's history ultimately lost about $50 million.

Evander Holyfield lost about $250 million after failed business ventures. At the height of his popularity, boxing champion Evander Holyfield had sponsorships with international companies, a record label and a video game. However, his label witnessed only brief success and the father of 11 owed quite a bit in child support. His $10 million estate was auctioned off in 2008. All in all, he lost, in addition to his ear of course, about $250 million.

Chris McAlister lost $55 million amid $11,000-per-month child support payments. In court papers, the former Baltimore Ravens corner explained why he couldn't pay child support: "I live in my parent's home. My parents provide me with my basic living expenses as I do not have the funds to do so."

Marion Jones lost about $7 million after secretly using steroids. The former "fastest woman in the world" lost her title and her medals when the world found out she used performance-enhancing drugs. Steroid use, combined with multiple run-ins with the government, including committing perjury to the IRS, cost Marion Jones about $7 million. In 2008 she spent six months in jail resulting from her involvement in the check fraud case and her use of performance enhancing drugs.

Rollie Fingers thought a pistachio farm would be a good idea and lost about $8 million. The baseball star with the famous handlebar moustache was in 1992 the only second relief pitcher to be elected into the National Baseball Hall of Fame. He retired in 1985, after both Oakland and Milwaukee retired his jersey, and invested in pistachio farms, Arabian horses and wind turbines. In 1992, Fingers filed for bankruptcy. He paid his more-than-$4 million-debt by selling baseball cards and working and was eventually cleared in 2007 by the IRS. He still lost about $8 million though.

NFL QB Mark Brunnell lost all his savings in nine failed business ventures. The former Jaguar made around $50 million in his career, but a failed Whataburger, real estate venture, and other investments left him broke.

Jack Clark's penchant for fancy cars cost him about $20 million. "Jack the Ripper" played in the MLB from 1975 to 1992. However, the year 1992 brought some changes to Clark's life—to the tune of about a $20 million loss. He filed bankruptcy that year. At the time of his filing, he owned 18 luxury cars, including a Ferrari and three Mercedes Benzes. He also reportedly owes $500,000 in back taxes to Uncle Sam.

Muhsin Muhammad went on a spending spree that ultimately cost him about $20 million. Former Chicago Bear Muhsin Muhammad will always be remembered for his touchdown dance, featured in the opening credits of Madden NFL 2006. However, Wachovia Bank will remember him as the wide receiver sued for owing thousands of dollars in overdue credit card payments. The financial trouble ultimately prompted Muhammad, who lost about $20 million, to sell many of his assets, including a lakeside estate.

Latrell Sprewell lost between $50 million and $100 million after some violent outbursts. The man credited with leading both the New York Knicks and the Minnesota Timberwolves to the playoffs, couldn't calm his temper.

He assaulted P. J. Carlesimo, coach of the Golden State Warriors, twice during practice and was accused, but not charged, of strangling a woman on his yacht. In 2007, he was sued by his long-term companion for ending their relationship agreement, which called for him to support her and their children. According to Fox News he owed the state of Wisconsin $3.5 million in unpaid income taxes in 2011. His house was also reportedly foreclosed in 2008.

Kenny Anderson lost about $60 million to his ex-wives. Despite the fact that he earned about $60 million and played for nine different teams during his career, Kenny Anderson still lost a bunch of money. Anderson had three ex-wives, the first of whom challenged the couple's pre-nup and walked away with half of everything. In addition, he supports his other two ex-wives, his seven children, and helps his mother financially. In the end, he lost about $60 million.

Deuce McAllister lost about $70 million when his car dealership went bust. New Orleans Saint Deuce McAllister was a two-time Pro Bowl participant. However, off the field, his luck turned sour and he lost about $70 million. Nissan sued his car dealership in 2009 for nearly $7 million on a variety of items. In November 2013 Nissan Motor Acceptance Corporation filed suit against McAllister and the dealership. He is accused of still owing $1.5 million to the plaintiff following bankruptcy. He was named an honorary captain for the Saints in 2010, but retired at the end of the year.

Scottie Pippen's legal woes lost him about $120 million. One of the heroes of Chicago, Scott Pippen played an important role in Chicago Bulls' six NBA championships. However, his luck didn't hold off the court. He lost a lawsuit against his former law firm, in which he claimed they lost $27 million of his earnings in bad investments. And in 2007, he was ordered to pay more than $5 million to U.S. Bank. All told, Pippen lost about $120 million.

Conclusion

The time has come to candidly discuss and explore the idiocy of the state of affairs in the sports world, with respect to the imbalance between cultural and structural. This state of affairs is one driven by a highly financed and intricately structured apparatus, involving myriad hierarchical systems and political agendas. Cultural influences have become overwhelmed and superseded by structural influences. The result being ludicrous situations of players involved in activities far removed from the pursuit of athletic excellence.

The purpose of this essay is not to demean, blame or malign, but rather to acknowledge and examine the flaws that exist in order to deeply understand the disconnect that gave rise to less than optimal benefit, personally, athletically, and financially for too many professionally athletes. Too many to ignore. This phenomenon implores attention and means of resolution.

The structural perspective which is so prevalent and revered in the sports world is particularly detrimental when it is devoid of cultural perspective. The structural perspective that exists not only lacks cultural perspective, it also lacks the understanding of economics. A player steeped in the structural perspective, replete of the cultural perspective, runs the risk of moral bankruptcy complemented by financial ruin. On the other hand, it is also folly to consider relying solely on cultural perspective. In fact, the two need to work in tandem. Core character developed through cultural influence lessens the potential distorting disruptiveness rampant when structural influences are unfettered.

The pitfalls outlined are typical, even predictable, for aspiring athletes. At the youngest levels, aspirations of greatness are largely driven by the fantasy of "making it big." This sort of motivation is deficient, and as such prompts misguided values and actions. Core Character Matters contends that these pitfalls are avoidable with the right guidance. And, in fact, it proposes that a blending of cultural and structural components, and the respective understandings of each, is needed to foster the greatest potential of a successful, life-enhancing athletic experience.

Which begs the question: Does race matter? Core Character Matters. An African American cultural and historical perspective (the experience that I am privy to) has been presented to illustrate my points. However, race, in what I propose, is not what matters. It is the understanding of the concepts of cultural and structural and their intersections, illuminated in the stories presented herein, that matters.

Presumably, many people, regardless of race, color, or creed, can relate to factors which for them constitute their cultural underpinnings. My intent was to activate a sense of "cultural" regardless of their experience. To conjure up the powerful inner pride and strength that comes from values informed by common purpose and belonging, and history, and personal achievement and wholesome growth. Additionally, I wanted to prompt contemplation about how this can be appreciated and embraced in one's own situation and/or created in cases where it does not exist. This is a necessary first step in establishing a mitigating force against the distorted structural formulations that exist throughout sport currently. Furthermore, education with respect to structural necessities and temptations, and the pragmatics of economics, is critical to navigating athletic pursuit wisely and constructively.

NOTES

1. Ocho Cinco, aka Chad Johnson, an exceedingly successful and talented player in the NFL for years, underwent a colossal downward spiral. He gave over to a structural capitalistic intent. Johnson became invested in exposing his personal life to make himself a well-known actor/personality, at the expense of maintaining his integrity and talent as a football player. His outlandish actions and antics untimely led to an incident where he was charged with domestic violence and lost his football career, television career, and incurred incalculable other loses, personally, professionally, and financially.

2. Shak Harris, former quarterback from Grambling State, later to play in the NFL and eventually to be inducted into the Sports Hall of Fame, is currently a very successful, respected, high-ranking executive of the NFL organization.

3. In August 2007, hours after Vick pleaded guilty to federal charges in the Bad Newz Kennels dog fighting investigation, the NFL suspended him indefinitely without pay for violating its player conduct policy. In a letter to Vick, NFL commissioner Roger Goodell said the quarterback had admitted to conduct that was "not only illegal, but also cruel and reprehensible." While Vick was technically a first-time offender under the league's personal conduct policy, Goodell handed down a harsher suspension because Vick admitted he provided most of the money for the gambling side of the dog fighting operation.

4. In August 2012, LSU coach Les Miles announced that Mathieu would be dismissed from the football team due to a violation of team rules. Later than month, Mathieu withdrew from LSU and entered a drug rehabilitation program in Houston. He was drafted by the Arizona Cardinals in the third round of the 2013 NFL Draft.

5. Core Character Matters' program at the New Orleans Healing Center is working with potential 2014 draft picks and two former NFL players.

6. According to a 2009 *Sports Illustrated* article, 60 percent of former NBA players are broke within five years of retirement. By the time they have been retired for two years, 78 percent of former NFL players have gone bankrupt or are under financial stress.

7. *Broke*, part of ESPN's *30 for 30* documentary series, features the stories of dozens of pro athletes who wasted millions of dollars, including former NFL receiver Andre Rison, former NFL quarterback Bernie Kosar and former NFL linebacker Keith McCants. I watched an advance version of the documentary, and the basic answer to the question of how you can blow that much money is: Very easily. Kosar talks about how he trusted his father to take care of his money, and his father simply had no concept of how to properly invest millions of dollars. Rison boasts that he'd go to a club and spend tens of thousands of dollars, making sure everyone in the room knew that he was the rich guy. McCants says that when you're a drug addict like him, more money just means more problems.

8. The author was born Edward Lee Thomas, but is known by family members as "Wils" as that is how his grandmother pronounced "Wilt," as in Wilt Chamberlin. For that reason, and for most of his life, his family and friends have referred to him as Will.

9. Avra Rice, New York Urban League president and CEO.

10. Doug Williams, current Grambling head coach.

11. http://ripessna.wordpress.com/resources/solidarity-economy-in-north-america-a-history/.

12. In 1968, Howard Cosell and Izenberg produced the documentary *Grambling College: 100 Yards to Glory*.

13. *Sarasota Herald Tribune*, September 26, 1968.

14. Jerry Izenberg, *1st & Goal in the Bronx: Grambling vs. Morgan State, 1968.*

15. Ibid.
16. Ibid.
17. Eddie Robinson.
18. http://www.businessinsider.com/how-20-professional-athletes-went-flat-broke-2012-10?op=1.

BIBLIOGRAPHY

"Bad Newz Kennels Dog Fighting Indictment." *USA TODAY*, June 10, 2013.

"Ex-NFL Star Chad Johnson Gets 30 Days in Jail." *Yahoo! News*, June 10, 2013.

Helman, David. "Les Miles Discusses Tyrann Mathieu." *ESPN*, May 15, 2013.

Izenberg, Jerry. "1st & Goal in the Bronx: Grambling vs. Morgan State, 1968," *CBS Sports*, September 12, 2011.

Kleinpeter, Jim. "LSU's Tyrann Mathieu Dismissed for Failed Drug Test, Source Says." *The Times-Picayune*, August 12, 2012.

Manfred, Tony, and Abby Rogers. "How 20 Professional Athletes Went Flat Broke." Accessed October 4, 2012, http://www.businessinsider.com/how-20-professional-athletes-went-flat-broke-2012-10?op=1.

Poirier, Yvon, and Emily Kawano. "Solidarity Economy in North America: A History." Accessed July 2008, http://ripessna.wordpress.com/resources/solidarity-economy-in-north-america-a-history.html.

Robinson, Eddie, and Eric Deggans. "CBS Documentary Encapsulates Significance of 1968 Grambling vs. Morgan State Game, Impact on HBCU football." *University of Indiana*, accessed September 28, 2011, http://sportsjournalism.org/sportsmedia-news/cbs-documentary-encapsulates-significance-of-1968-grambling-vs-morgan-state-game-impact-on-hbcu-football.html.

Smith, Michael David. "Ex-NFL Millionaires Rison, Kosar, McCants Tell How They Went Broke." NBCSportswww, September 29, 2012.

Torre, Pablo S. "How (and Why) Athletes Go Broke." *Sports Illustrated*, March 23, 2009.

Sacrifice, Modality, Inspiration and Triumph: An Afrocentric Analysis of Race and Sport in America

James L. Conyers, Jr.

The concept of race and sport in America is vexing, however, it is also a paradox to define, describe, and evaluate. For some, the idea of sport and society are interwoven parcels, which reflect each other in myriad ways. Simply put, sport is a reflection of society, as we use metaphors, narratives, concepts of teamwork, and overcoming adversity as attributes to navigate transition and transcend struggle of life experiences. Kevin Hylton offers the following description of race and sport, writing:

> The problematic of "race" thinking for many in sport is its endemic omnipresent discourse. The popularity of "race" thinking is historically located in multifarious assumptions, and deeds that reinforce the legitimacy of "race" and therefore physical difference in sport. Assumptions that have endured are those that argue humans could be divided into a few biologically and phenotypically detached races; the similiarities within these groups could be reduced to ability, behavior and morality; these difference would be natu-rally passed from one generation to the next, and racial hierarchies exist with white people at the top and darker races at the opposite end.[1]

Reference then is registered at how equity, hard work, and evaluation are the moral fiber and ethics of Americanism. To the contrary, while living in a market culture, the components of dual labor economies, institutional racism, ethnocentrism, prejudice, and double standards press our understanding of race relations in America. Phrased another way, if you work hard, play fair, and evaluate your performance, the idea of disparity will be reduced, if not eliminated. Perhaps, as an optimist, one might engage in modifiers, metaphors, and existential ideas centering around disparity; nevertheless, social inequality is relevant and a reality. To discuss this issue further, Earl Smith defines the idea of African Americans in sociology of sport in the following manner:

> The sociological study of sport has always been dominated by concerns about African American athletes and their athletic prowess. Since racial and ethnic minorities are still systematically discriminated against in the United States, curiosity runs high when African Americans make inroads into territory that was once considered off-limits. If the socio-historical perspective on sport has even slightly shifted away from an almost exclusive concern with race and ethnicity, it is only since the implementation of Title IX in 1972, which focused serious attention on gender. As important as Title IX was in changing the institution of sport by opening up opportunities for women, this book will not specifically address women or the roles of whites, Asians, Hispanics, or Native Americans in American sport.[2]

On the other hand, an accommodations analysis of the thematic aspect of race and sport is pre-empted by Hasan Kwame Jeffries, espousing:

> Racial exclusion was the defining element in American sports during the Jim Crow era (from the end of Reconstruction to the Civil Rights Movement of the 1960s). Consequently, it is easy to understand why this period is often considered the "nadir" for black athletes. One hesitates to attach "nadir" to the sports experience of black athletes during the Jim Crow era, however, because highly developed alternative outlets for black athletic expression, created and sustained by the black community, existed alongside exclusionary white leagues.[3]

This study will provide a survey descriptive analysis of the continuing threads of disparity which exist in professional athletics. Whereas the topic of discussion could extend itself endlessly, a survey approach, by a review of the three major professional sports, is examined in a framework for discussion.

This essay will focus on four themes, with emphasis on race and sport: sacrifice, modality, inspiration, and triumph. Molefi Asante uses these themes as he describes and evaluates Afrocentric relationships.[4] Indeed, the four subject themes offer a working paradigm, which outline a meta-theory and triangulation, which curtails and examines race and sport in America.

The methodology is qualitative, but employs tools from alternate designs, which allow the collection of information and data. Table 1.0 is a survey description of the category descriptors.

Table 1.0: Research Approach to Race and Sport

Category	Approach
Sacrifice	Giving of one self to advance a general cause.
Modality	Principals used to describe and evaluate phenomena.
Inspiration	Uplift and incentive for completing a task.
Triumph	An individual's vision for seeking victory[5]

Methodology

The method of collecting data is qualitative, using content analysis and leasing tools from ethnography and historical analysis. This descriptive study will be located from a social science interdisciplinary cognate, using an Afro-centric cultural paradigm, postured within the Ujima theoretical framework. Hence, worldview and interpretation are critical instruments, when evaluating data, with emphasis on race, gender, and class. The use of mixed methods allows this researcher to have alternatives yet identify the limitations of the design, which lead the collection of data. Yet, a meta-analysis provides transport and exit, which sifts to the conclusion.

Using a historical perspective, Table 1.1 illustrates the themes of three major professional sports in America, baseball, football, and basketball. Furthermore, Table 1.2 shows when African Americans desegregated the professional sport. In short, the concept and continuous thread of disparity illustrates the removal and inequity when African Americans were prohibited from participation in professional sports. This denial also affected African Americans a chance to benefit socially, economically, and politically, from participation in professional sports.

Table 1.1: Historical Overview of Professional Sports

Sport	Year Established	Name(s)
Baseball	1869	Major League Baseball
Football	1920	American Football Conference (1920)
		American Professional Football Association
		National Football League
Basketball	1946	Basketball Association of America
		National Basketball Association

Definition of Race and Sport

With an imbalance of African American representation in college sports, there fails to exist this representation in the administration of athletic directors, head coaches of football, basketball, and baseball teams on the NCAA IA level. For some, collegiate leadership is the farm program, which can escalate to professional positions in the NFL, NBA, and MLB.[6] To extend this conversation further, regarding a survey and descriptive definition of the term race and sport, Eldon Snyder and Elmer Spreitzer note the following:

> The sociology of sport has yet to become a mainline specialty within the discipline, and some might questions whether it should ever become one. Given the proliferation of specializations within sociology, we might ask to what end is such elaboration of descriptive content directed. In other words, does a discipline grow by spinning off more and more content areas, or does it develop through the creation of paradigms that are generic in nature. The "hard" sciences did not develop by continually carving out new content areas; rather they developed through the creation of theoretical frameworks that transcended specific content.[7]

Harry Edwards provides a working description of race and sport sociology in the following:

> American's traditional relegation of sport to the "toy department" of human affairs conceals both its significant as an institution and the seriousness of its impact upon social relations and development. Nowhere is the validity of this assessment more evident than in the situation confronting Afro-Americans. Here, sport is revealed to be neither "fun-and-games," a citadel of interracial brotherhood and harmony, nor blacks' passport to the "good life." Rather, for blacks, it emerges as a fog shrouded, institutional minefield, even further obscured by naivete, ignorance, and decades of selectively accumulated myth.[8]

Lastly, Scott Brooks and Dexter Blackman offer another description of this phenomenon, writing:

> This importance of sports to American society is evident when watching television or reading popular magazines. Companies hire athletes to endorse their products and services, which masculinity and femininity are represented by athleticism, hard work and sweat, normative ideas of attractiveness, and fit bodies. While most people understand that the probability of a child becoming a professional athlete is remote, the dream of becoming a professional football, basketball, or baseball player is common for youth across race and class, particularly for males. Often, this dream is one of several youthful dreams that eventually fades, but for many African Americans, dreams of professional athletic stardom are not so easily abandoned. Black athletic achievement has often been excluded, downplayed, infantilized, or pathologized. Sadly, this has led to little scholarship historically on African Americans and sport. In 1939 Edwin B. Henderson's *The Negro in Sports* offered a mosaic of black athletic heroism, the strong work ethic and personal struggles, which he hoped would illuminate black success in sports and serve as evidence of black process and increased acceptance by whites. A.S. "Doc" Young's *Negro Firsts in Sports*, published in 1963, documented the pioneering efforts of black's sportswomen and

men and the ups and downs of black inclusion in sports in the United States. In both of these works, a wide range of sports is covered, rather than going into any depth to document the length of time African Americans had been involved, or their ability to master and excel as athletes.[9]

Edwards adds, "Only through a thorough understanding of the functions of sport as an institution and the dynamics of its disproportionately powerful influence upon Afro-American life can black people ever hope to extricate themselves from what can only be termed a political and cultural tragedy."[10]

Sacrifice

Sacrifice refers to an unwarranted giving of oneself, in order to advance the cause and trajectory of others. Modality refers to the paradigmatic shift in understanding structural and cultural imperatives, which examine wants and needs, and the indirect and direct correlations of market culture analysis. In short, the modality provides a contextual lens for examining a dual labor market and how Africana phenomena fit or do not fit in the overall framework of humans. In contemporary times, we are no longer addressing issues of a segregated America; instead, we are confronted with the perplexities of technology, information, systems and software, and disparity of Africana phenomena on a national and international level.[11]

Gary A. Sailes writes, "What accounts for the overwhelming success of the black athlete in American sport in the past few decades? This is very legitimate question to raise about the sports world today, in that black Americans constitute only 12 percent of the population in the United States yet are overrepresented in collegiate and professional sport. For example, black athletes represent 21 percent of professional baseball players."[12] While in contemporary times, few professional African American athletes have a knowledge of the history of blacks in their particular sports arena, or who invoke their names, or give credit to trailblazers. Without an understanding of sacrifice, it will be difficult for current-day athletes to advance, support, or develop legacy for participation in the games in the future. Yes, much of the sporting blogs discuss individual records, but few tabloids address politically salient issues, in which athletes can use their space, finance, and power to address issues of social disparity on a national and international basis.

Modality

The idea of reflective thought and action is not an attribute of substantive priority, within a market economy. What does this entail? Reference is drawn toward members of society playing a role in service and learning. But in a discussion of race and sport, our initial emphasis is on entertainment. However, the production of television, radio, or internet sportscasting involves tech support staff and reporters and also the athletes themselves in the gladiator competition. Therefore, modality takes shape and form for the purpose of those individuals who are considered in the masses as subordinate, having fifteen minutes of fame on a national level. This occurs at the collegiate and professional levels. Ironically, now, even high school athletes are getting this misconception of status and are cashed cows in the public sphere. Richard King expounds on this idea further, by writing, "Sports are only ubiquitous features of everyday life, but uniquely meaningful and powerful for countless individuals and institutions as well."[13]

Inspiration

Inspiration is relative to the paradigm of structural or cultural relevance whereas structural components identify how parts of a society work to produce labor and mechanical structure. However, a cultural analysis allows respondents a broader reference and resource pool to access in the interplay of subjects in our society. Lastly, triumph is the victory and results which are registered from a group's participation and deductive analysis. Michael Lomax describes African Americans' entry into professional football in the following manner:

> Because professional football has primarily been a post–World War II phenomenon, historical research efforts have been minimal. There have been a few investigations of the sport's prewar development. They have demonstrated that football teams in small towns like Pottsville, Pennsylvania provided a sense of community identification for its working-class residents. The Maroons also illustrated how these small town teams transformed from an amateur club, composed largely of local players, to a professional team recruiting players from outside the local arena. In contrast, clubs from Western Pennsylvania evolved from the efforts of upper class nouveau riche organizers, who sought to professionalize the game around the notion of a Victorian ideology. Research efforts have also examined the mythology that surrounded football stars, like Bronko Nagurski, and the meaning it gave for the lives of the people who made them their heroes.[14]

Additionally, Harry Edwards draws a critical analysis of the intersection of race and sport in America and draws attention to the shift in our market culture internationally and the decline of Africana participation in professional elite athletic sports.[15] As an aside, there are associations or caucuses within professional sports which place their emphasis on African American athletes. Unfortunately, many of these groups are structural in format, being less cultural, and do not offer correctives for disruptive behaviors such as substance abuse, fiscal mismanagement, or child support services. John Lucas II has been an example of delivering an alternative program of recovery for athletes, to position themselves for productive lives.

Table 1.2: Desegregation in Major League Baseball
National Football Association, National Basketball Association

Year	Team	Sport	Personnel
1946	Brooklyn Dodgers (National League)	Baseball (MLB)	Jackie Robinson
1947	Cleveland Indians (American League)	(MLB)	Larry Doby
1950	New York Knicks (NBA)	Basketball (NBA)	Nathaniel "Sweetwater" Clifton
1921	Akron Pros (APFA)	Football (NFL)	Frederick D. "Fritz" Pollard

Triumph and Conclusion

N. Jeremi Duru offers a provocative and stimulating study titled *Advancing the Ball,* eleven chapters plus Tony Dungy's foreword. Dungy renders an explanation of being a childhood fan of professional football, transitioning to a player on the collegiate and professional levels, and then becoming a coach in the NFL. He was one of two African American coaches who participated in the 2006 Super Bowl, and he describes the merit and value of the Fritz Pollard Alliance and the enforcement of the Rooney Rule, which impacted fair employment and diversity in the workplace. Furthermore, the author's use of sources exhibits a triangulation of historical methods, ethnography, secondary analysis, and oral histories. Coupled with a descriptive and evaluative study, Duru has presented a social science assessment of Africana phenomena in race and sport. Still, the interdisciplinary approach, use of a meta-theory, and mixed methods collection of data, sustains the author's central thesis and produces an exemplary analysis.[16]

In conclusion, there is an existing body of literature on the field and function of race and sport in America. Still, many of the collected interpretive studies, biographies, or critical race theory volumes are contextualized within a structural analysis. Structural analysis refers to how the parts of a system work and operate collectively. Yet, there is a continual pattern of contemporary athletes, having the perception of not being appreciative of the trailblazers, who provided paths and entry points for African Americans to participate in professional sports in contemporary times.

NOTES

1. Kevin Hylton, *"Race" and Sport: Critical Race Theory* (New York: Routledge, 2009), p. 3.
2. Earl Smith, *Race and Sport* (Durham, NC: Carolina Academic), p. 150.
3. Hassan Kwame Jeffries, "Fields of Play: The Medium Through Which Black Athletes Engaged in Sports in Jim Crow Georgia," *The Journal of Negro History*, vol. 86, no. 3 (Summer 2001), p. 264.
4. Molefi Kete Asante, *Afrocentricity: The Theory of Social Change* (Chicago: African American Images, 2003), p. 66.
5. Molefi Kete Asante, *Afrocentricity* (Chicago: African American Images, 1990).
6. "Black Teams, White Coaches: African Americans Are Making Almost No Progress in College Coaching Positions," *The Journal of Blacks in Higher Education*, no. 49 (Autumn 2005), pp. 32.
7. Eldon E. Snyder and Elmer Spreitzer, "Sociology of Sport: An Overview," *The Sociological Quarterly*, vol. 15, no. 4 (Autumn 1974), pp. 467.
8. Harry Edwards, "Sport Within the Veil: The Triumphs, Tragedies and Challenges of Afro-American Involvement," *Annals of the American Academy of Political and Social Science*, vol. 445, "Contemporary Issues in Sport" (September 1979), p. 116.
9. Scott N. Brooks and Dexter Blackman, "Introduction: African Americans and the History of Sport—New Perspectives," *The Journal of African American History*, vol. 96, no. 4, Special Issue: "African Americans and the History of Sport" (Fall 2011), p. 441.
10. Harry Edwards, "Sport within the Veil: The Triumphs, Tragedies and Challenges of Afro-American Involvement," *Annals of the American Academy of Political and Social Science*, vol. 445, "Contemporary Issues in Sport" (September 1979), p. 116.
11. http://fora.tv/2009/09/09/CONFLICT_Harry_Edwards_on_Race_Sport_and_Society.
12. Gary A. Sailes, "The Myth of Black Sports Supremacy," *Journal of Black Studies*, vol. 21, no. 4 (June 1991), pp. 480.
13. C. Richard King, "Preoccupations and Prejudices: Reflections on the Study of Sports Imagery," *Anthropologica*, vol. 46, no. 1 (2004), pp. 29–36.
14. Michael E. Lomax, "The African American Experience in Professional Football," *Journal of Social History*, vol. 33, no. 1 (Autumn 1999), pp. 163.
15. http://fora.tv/2009/09/09/CONFLICT_Harry_Edwards_on_Race_Sport_and_Society.
16. N. Jeremi Duru, *Advancing the Ball* (New York: Oxford University Press, 2012).

BIBLIOGRAPHY

Asante, Molefi Kete. *Afrocentricity: The Theory of Social Change.* Chicago: African American Images, 2003.
"Black Teams, White Coaches: African Americans Are Making Almost No Progress in College Coaching Positions." *The Journal of Blacks in Higher Education*, no. 49 (Autumn 2005), pp. 32–33.
Brooks, Scott N., and Dexter Blackman. "Introduction: African Americans and the History of Sport—New Perspectives." *The Journal of African American History*, vol. 96, no. 4, Special Issue: "African Americans and the History of Sport' (Fall 2011), pp. 441–447.
Duru, N. Jeremi. *Advancing the Ball.* New York: Oxford University Press, 2012.
Edwards, Harry. "Sport Within the Veil: The Triumphs, Tragedies and Challenges of Afro-American Involvement." *Annals of the American Academy of Political and Social Science,* vol. 445, "Contemporary Issues in Sport" (September 1979), pp. 116–127.
Hylton, Kevin. *"Race" and Sport: Critical Race Theory.* New York: Routledge, 2009.
Jeffries, Hassan Kwame. "Fields of Play: The Medium Through Which Black Athletes Engaged in Sports in Jim Crow Georgia." *The Journal of Negro History*, vol. 86, no. 3 (Summer 2001), pp. 264–275.

King, C. Richard. "Preoccupations and Prejudices: Reflections on the Study of Sports Imagery." *Anthropologica*, vol. 46, no. 1 (2004), pp. 29–36.

Lomax, Michael E. "The African American Experience in Professional Football." *Journal of Social History*, vol. 33, no. 1 (Autumn 1999), pp. 163–178.

Sailes, Gary A. "The Myth of Black Sports Supremacy." *Journal of Black Studies*, vol. 21, no. 4 (June 1991), pp. 480–487.

Smith, Earl. *Race and Sport*. Durham, NC: Carolina Academic, 2009.

Snyder, Eldon E., and Elmer Spreitzer. "Sociology of Sport: An Overview." *The Sociological Quarterly*, vol. 15, no. 4 (Autumn 1974), pp. 467–487.

Race, Colonization and the NFL Draft: A Fanonian Analysis of the Interviewing of Black NFL Prospects

Drew Brown

Introduction

Contemporary society is driven by the assumptions, dominance, and discrimination of white supremacy (Lewis, p. 46), and the NFL is no different. Scholars describe racism in two forms: overt and systemic (Feagin, 2000; Mills, 1997). While the Jim Crow era displayed overt forms of racism, contemporary society totes a heavier dose of systemic racism. Both forms are aligned with the practices of, and in fact originate from, colonization. The diminishment of overt forms of racism has allowed many people to remain ignorant to the systemic discrimination that continues to work with strength and persistence as a pillar of U.S. society. This is no more evident than in the sports industry. The sports industry in the United States is a perpetuator of racial hierarchy and a vehicle for widespread racism. The National Football League is a clear example of systemic racism that shrewdly attempts to further suppress blacks.

The NFL—most forms of entertainment, really—functions as a dimension of colonization that socializes black males, and more increasingly females, into subordinate social positions. Statistically, black players have dramatically dominated the NFL player population (almost 70 percent), yet they are barely represented in positions of leadership such as coaches, scouts, and general managers. Much like the *Social Contract*, the *Racial Contract* among whites causes white team leaders to unconsciously advance black-male stereotypes: intellectual inferior, brute, hypersexual, and violent and aggressive (Mills, 1997). They hire black players who display these stereotypical traits. Similar to the Europeans who colonized Africans and Native Americans, their descendants are now continuing the colonization process by systemically using the NFL to encourage social and cultural assimilation. NFL leaders are stacking the league with conforming, submissive, brute-like black players by qualifying them as such in evaluation interviews.

Every year, the NFL evaluates a new set of prospects in order to hire the best players. During this process, teams are given the opportunity to see players run, jump, throw and catch at what is called the NFL Combine. In addition to the playing-film and physical evaluations, teams are able to interview prospects for further evaluation. The evaluation interviews involve a timed meeting between a player and a panel of as many as five representatives from a team. NFL prospects are asked a variety of questions from dating preferences to favorite color. It is in these interviews where players and NFL team representatives (hiring agents) gather information about players by asking them a series of questions. Although labor laws restrict the hiring agents from asking discriminatory question, they are able to ask those which can be used to evaluate character, world-view, personality, and attitude. The major problem in this interview process that this essay seeks to explore is a racial one. The interviews function as an evolutional tool for hiring players into the most extreme industry for colonial exploitation since slavery. Many scholars liken it to a slave plantation, except, as some say, "the field hands get paid" (Rhoden, 2006).

Frantz Fanon is a Caribbean writer who has written on the impact of colonization. Fanon was once a talented soccer player. However, it is through his writings on colonization and race where his brilliance shines. In his book, *Black Skin White Mask* (1986), the Martinique writer and psychiatrist gives his analysis of a black man who attempts to find affirmation of his humanity in white-male acceptance. The black NFL prospects often seek similar acceptance into the white-male controlled colonial arena of the NFL. This is most evident in the evaluation interviews. Fanon discusses the antinomy of the colonized mind that causes blacks men to negate his own African identity. One major indication of antinomy in the colonized mind is the use of the colonizer's language. The second major characteristic is becoming submissive or childlike toward whites (Fanon, 1986). In addition to Fanon's characteristics, the third is an animalistic physical prowess that can be controlled by white leaders.

This essay traces the continuity of racial ideology as it manifests itself within contemporary U.S. sports society. More specifically, it will tie the NFL evaluation-interviews to the colonial project in order to highlight the pervasiveness of colonization. In the process, this essay will expose any racist orientation of NFL hiring agents. By using Fanon as a theoretical foundation to analyze the interview phase of the NFL drafting process, psychoanalysis and cultural politics of sports can appropriately applied to broaden the context of racial stereotyping. Therefore, this essay will examine the ways in which language, criminal stereotypes, and inferiority as characteristics of colonization exist in interviews during the NFL drafting process by NFL hiring agents and black NFL players, in order to further understand the pervasiveness of the colonial project in contemporary U.S. society.

In this essay many terms will be used which carry specific meanings determined by the author. The term "African" refers to all people of African descent living in or outside of Africa. The term is used as a broad identification of all people of African ancestry. "Black" is used to distinguish people of African diaspora and mostly of those living in America, and it is used interchangeably with "African American." Black and African American are used generally and without a defined criteria or required percentage of black ancestry or physical make-up—though both of those specifications are relevant. Black NFL Prospects (BNPs) are former college football players who have reached the required year of eligibility for entering the NFL draft. NFL teams owners and/or send coaches general managers, and other scouts are the team representatives who conduct interviews with NFL prospects. As their intent is to evaluate the players in order to select and hire them, the will be called "hiring agents" when referring to the evaluation process.

Race, Colonization and the NFL

Sport is not new to Africans. To best understand its centrality in black culture one must start with ancient Africa. Sport has always been a significant part of African societies. There is not much evidence of sports earlier than ancient Egypt, but many scholars believe this is no indication that sport was not present. Many sports competitions occurred in ancient Egyptian civilization. Tombs and wall drawings, written sources and miniatures display scenes of competition and evidence of sports. The temple of Ramesses III, from the twentieth dynasty, pictures of a sports contest between the Egyptians and another group; in it, the pharaoh participating in a sport with horses (Decker, p. 12). The gravesite of Prince Min of This shows him instructing Amenophis II in archery. The site also depicts scenes of fishing and bird hunting. Statues of wrestlers and female acrobats have been found and can be traced to Ancient Egypt (Decker, p. 12). Inscriptions were often found alongside visual representations of sports. Inscriptions accompanied the sports scenes in the tomb of Ramesses III. Also, written accounts of Ramesses II describe him as a great fighter (Decker, p. 14).

The types of sports present in ancient Egypt were similar to those of present day. The prevalence of visual representations and inscriptions would suggest that archery was the most illustrated sport. The bow predates the written history of Egypt (Decker, p. 34). It was used as a hunting tool and weapon and utilized by the Egyptian army in practicing their marksmanship. The master of archery was Amenophis II whose great athletic skills can be traced from his childhood. He may have possessed the greatest athletic abilities out of all the Egyptian kings and queens (Decker, p. 36). Egyptian chariots and equestrians arrived in the second millennium B.C. It re-emerges in the Greece mainly in the Olympic Games, but it was the Egyptians whom first made it an artistic sport (Decker, p. 47). The combat sports, such as wrestling, have also been significant and remain imbedded in most cultures of Africa. Egyptian wrestling is the most visually documented sport. While many believe that sports have been a recent popular activity of blacks, sport has been entrenched in African communities for as long as we could know. For BNP to not participate in the highest level of sport in America would be difficult given the long history of black sport.

Today, what attracts blacks to pursue a career in the NFL is a complex combination of things. First, the exclusion of blacks from other areas of employment has resulted in a malnourishment of black cultural heroes, while black images are paraded in the media. Second, sports are one of the few spaces where blacks feel superior and gifted (Hoberman, p. 5). Sports embody the stereotypes of black physical superiority. Third, the sports industry has produced hope, confidence and prosperity in the nihilistic black community (Hoberman, p. 9). These circumstances include the availability of opportunities that motivate young blacks to succeed. Sports offer substantial financial reward to a proportion of the population who often has limited social and economic opportunities.

The relationship between the African American community and African American sport is a reciprocal one defined by the heavy influence each has over the other. When asked, "Why are sports are so important to black males?" John Hoberman (1997) answers by suggesting that it is a ritual of survival (23). Many African Americans have seen sports as an opportunity of financial stability in an environment that does not afford event the basic opportunities for financial stability. It is the social-economic status of African Americans that drives many of them to participate in sports. In turn, it is the success of the well marketed and advertised African American athletes that makes them the models of success for the African American community. Sports sociologist Jay Coakley (2007) suggests that sports are connected to important ideas, beliefs and major fields of black social life such as the family, religion and education (p. 21).

Being drafted into the NFL is highly promoted in the black community for reasons of economic and social mobility. This often causes BNPs to face extreme pressure and desire to be drafted, not just from friends and family, but also from the glory given to successful athletes by the black community. Therefore BNPs make every attempt to be hired during NFL draft evaluation process. Even though they may be aware that they are being racially stereotyped by white scouts, they have described feeling as if leaving the interview because of poor treatment would not help their employment and might cost them considerably by causing them not to be drafted (Dufur & Feinberg, 2008).

Colonization is a continuous process that refuses to decelerate. The physical enslavement of Africans was only one, albeit major, dimension of the colonial project. The colonized —"every people in whose soul an inferiority complex has been created by the death and burial of its local cultural originality" according to Fanon (1986)—go through a physiological reorientation of the mind that causes a self-perpetuation of oppression. This has occurred in every race that has been subjected to colonization (Fanon). Slavery is still an operational form of colonization. It merely exists differently than the antebellum form. Dufur and Feinberg conducted a series of interviews of BNPs. Some of the BNPs admitted to feeling like "slaves." One BNP said, "It's prostitution, basically; the only thing is there's no sex. You know, buy you for as cheap as they can and use you to do as much as they can get you to do until they don't need you anymore, and then they drop you like used goods and you're never thought of again. You're just another number. Just another piece of the puzzle they can use for their history books" (Dufur & Feinberg, p. 65). Dufur and Fienberg (2008) reported in their study that all but one of the BNP referred to the combine as a "slave trade," while none of the white NFL prospects made the same reference.

The colonial project continues to assert everything white as superior to all other. The colonizer sets the conditions for manhood in order to create limitations and subjugation around it. They are also the gatekeepers of manhood. BNPs try desperately to impress hiring agents. It is not just a matter of being drafted or hired by the NFL; this is a matter of being accepted by white men into manhood. BNPs' colonized mind and cultural affinity to football has created conditions of self-destruction. They desire to be accepted in to the NFL is associated to being a man. To the BNP, to be a man is to be white (Fanon, 1986).

Being drafted into the NFL is highly promoted in the black community, causing BNPs to face extreme pressure and desire to be drafted. So much so that they pursue it even while it destroys and exploit them in the process. The successful images of the few materialistic black players who are brands are a marketing company's dream. The interests of the oligarchies (white male leaders of the financial sector who benefit from consumers spending money) lies in the obsession black NFL males have with material consumption. The commodified players become billboards for the products they fashion. Black NFL football players along with other entertainers influence the product consumption of many black males and lead to product sales. Therefore, the high salaries of a few NFL players benefit the white-controlled economic market more than it does the players.

There is often extreme pressure on the BNP to get hired by the NFL from family and friends. Therefore they make every attempt to be hired during interviews. Even though they may be aware that they are being racially stereotyped by white scouts, they have described feeling as if leaving the interview would not help their employment and might cost them considerably by causing them not to be drafted (Dufur & Feinberg, 2008).

Manhood has eluded the black man. The NFL draft is seemingly the threshold between the BNP and manhood. Fanon says, "He wants to prove to the others that he is a man, their equal." However, a history of racism has left a psychological castration of the black man (Majors & Billson, 1992). Scholars such as Richard Majors, author of *Cool Pose: The Dilemmas of Black Manhood in America,* would say that the white individualistic oligarchies of capitalism have traditionally excluded black men from acquiring power, in the basic philosophical sense, and even from the discussion of black-male exclusion from positions of power. Even though the investment of perseverance and hard work did not accrue the same rewards as whites, black men have still measured their manhood based on white concepts of manhood: provider, procreator, protector and patriarch. Unfortunately, black men have not had the same opportunities to successfully fulfill these ideas of masculinity. They therefore adopt what Majors calls the cool pose: a detachment from the unjust and unfair social structure and a self-defining look of success in order to maintain dignity (Majors & Billson, p. 2). Black men rationalize challenges to their dignity by asserting their own agency. They have constructed a new notion of black masculinity that allows them to ascend to their self-defined manhood (Dufur & Feinberg, 2008). Scholars have described black men using strategies of emotionlessness, fearlessness to protecting their self-esteem (Osborne, 1999). These survival skills are hyperactive when facing discrimination. This feeds into the need for an animalistic brute in the colonial project. In interviews, BNPs are provoked by scouts in hopes of generating some show of aggression. The BNP desires to be drafted in order be able to display their masculinity in addition to acquiring the resources and acceptance of whites. BNPs will continue to pursue manhood through NFL acceptance, while NFL leaders continue to use their pursuit to exploit them.

The goal of NFL leaders, like the colonizers, is to deplete blacks of healthy opportunities and promote dead-end opportunities by parading tokens of successful blacks in the NFL. According to Fanon, blacks want to be accepted because of the colonized mind (Fanon, 1986). Fanon explains how a black man, Jean Veneuse, was not satisfied with himself until he was accepted by white men. While BNPs hope for an NFL contract as an indicator of acceptance, Veneuse receives an "acceptance" letter into white manhood which says, "In fact you are like us—you are 'us.' Your thoughts are ours. You behave as we behave, as we would behave. You think of yourself—others think of you—as a Negro? Utterly mistaken! You merely look like one. As for everything else, you think as a European. And so it is natural that you love as a European" (Fanon, p. 49).

The BNPs, too, carry colonized minds and seek acceptance by white-male NFL leaders. So much so, the BNP will teach other BNPs to carry a similar mindset. The BNP's world-view and actions are one of a colonized person, imposing, perpetuating, and advancing the colonization process within his own community. Both Veneuse and the BNP live in "an ambiguity that is extraordinarily neurotic" (Fanon, p. 148). After being enslaved by whites, they enslave themselves by acting as whites have stereotyped them and subjecting themselves as whites have done.

NFL Evaluation Interviews

The hiring process of the NFL involves a set of evaluation periods. The interview process is an opportunity for scouts to evaluate the mental state of BNP's. Scouts may not admit to the attempt to marginalize and test how effective the seasoning process of college football has prepared black players for the NFL plantation. But C.W. Mills (1997) suggests that the Racial Contract is fully functional and colonization attempts to maintain a white dominated social system. This domination reaches into the function and structure of the NFL's hiring process.

In the interview portion of the NFL evaluation process, language is not only used to communicate, but also as a display of power through particular symbols and linguistic hierarchy. Pierre Bourdieu suggests that language is an economic exchange (Bourdieu, pp. 39, 44). The hiring agents often attempt to show power over the BNP through linguistic assumptions of power. The hiring agents often use a style of English that is socially regarded as being higher than the BNPs style of English. But, the colonized BNP will try to mimic the style of English that the hiring agents use in order to show an attempt of assimilation. Fanon argues that the black man carries two dimensions to his language. He says, he has "One with his fellows, the other with the White man. A Negro behaves differently with a white man and with another Negro" (Fanon, p. 8). This is a ritual of submission often seen by the colonized as a means of gaining acceptance. While trying to understand why the black man, when confronted by the French language, is so fond of speaking, in this case, French; Fanon suggests "To speak a language is to take on a world, a culture. The [colonized] who wants to be white will be the whiter as he gains greater mastery of the cultural tool that language is" (Fanon, p. 25). This is exactly the case for BNPS. Many of them want to either be white or prove they are equal to whites. It must be also understood that the BNPs have agency and not all of them function in this manner. Others are focused on gaining the economic wealth that awaits them if they are hired. Styling words to sound like the hiring agents' language may be his way of increasing the chances of gaining wealth. Fanon understands this motive as well. He says, "Historically, it must be understood that the Negro wants to speak French because it is the key that can open doors which were still barred to him fifty years ago" (Fanon, p. 25). When the BNP does not submit to speaking with the hiring agents' style of language, certain stereotypes take place based on the social linguistic hierarchy. If the BNP does not use the hiring agents' style of English perfectly, the BNP is seen as unintelligent (Fanon, p. 17). Stereotyping is an effect of power (Carrington, 2002). Stereotyping based on language denigrates and advances social hierarchies and inequalities. During interviews, language style associated with lower class can be stereotyped by hiring agents as coming from a BNP who is "unseasoned." When Fanon gives white patients a word association test, the stereotypes that are associated with black people emerge as biology, penis, strong, athletic, potent, boxer, Joe Louis, Jesse Owens, Senegalese troops, savage, animal, devil, and sin (Fanon, p. 128). In the vicious game of football, many of these terms are revered. Football is a space where the darkest side of people is on display in order to win at any cost. All the while, "the black man, whether physically or symbolically, represents the dark side of the personality" (Fanon, p. 147). Many of the names the white men listed were prominent black athletes of the period. Fanon argues that this shows the fear, desire, and fantasies whites carry *of* the black man and projected *on* him. Fanon states, "There is one expression that through time has become singularly eroticized: the black athlete" (Fanon, p. 122). For the hiring agents, this makes the BNP the ideal person to hire. For the BNP, he will come closer to being a real human being—in direct ratio to his mastery of the French language.

Like the enslaved Africans during of the seventeenth, eighteenth and nineteenth centuries, NFL team leaders, seemingly, want BNPs to submit to their authority and unquestionably follow their orders given the way they speak to them. During the NFL draft evaluation process, hiring agents are often white men, behaving like an adult with a child (Dufur & Feinberg, 2008). Fanon says whites in this situation will start smirking, whispering, patronizing, and cozening (Fanon, p. 19). Fanon's analysis suggests that not only are BNPs spoken to as children, but also their masculinity has been feminized (Carrington, p. 13). He says, "There is a fact: White men consider themselves superior to black men. There is another fact: Black men want to prove to white men, at all costs, the richness of their thought, the equal value of their intellect" (Fanon, p. 3). Given Fanon's analysis, BNPs are placed into a test of submission during interviews. The test: being their reaction to the hiring agents treating them like a child in order to see how submissive they will be to the authority of team leaders. This is important for the teams because of what they will experience if hired by a team. Historically, coaches have placed white players in decision-making, thinking positions (such as quarterback) and place blacks in positions where there is an emphasis on physical speed or strength (e.g., running back or cornerback) based on their assumption that blacks are physically talented. Scholars refer to this as "stacking" (Dufur & Feinberg, p. 56). Historically, whites have tried to justify such actions as "stacking" as good, not racist, by arguing that blacks have a deep desire for white rule (Fanon, 1986). Some scholar would suggest that the BNP, like most other black colonized black people, suffer from an inferiority complex that is intensified because of the submissive characteristics they have been forced to take on (Dufur & Feinberg, 2008; Fanon, 1986). The BNP feels as though he is a lower form of human than the white hiring agents, and other white NFL leaders, are far superior to him. As a result, the BNP submits to the authority of the white NFL leaders.

NFL hiring agents often look for a history of characteristics associated with criminal in BNPs in order to see the level of desired characteristics of criminals such as aggression and violence as well as the non-desired characteristics such as deviance. Dufur and Feinberg (2008) show that one of the primary areas where BNPs reported racist treatment by hiring agents was when questioned on their criminal behavior during interviews. The hiring agents ask questions based on the stereotypes of black criminals such as violent, aggressive and deviant (Feagin, 1991). White NFL prospects did not report such questioning.

Fanon makes this distinction while analyzing the black man who has reached a certain level of "acceptance" in white spaces. He says, "The Negro is a savage, whereas the student is civilized." This is to say that whites stereotype black men as uncivilized and not a student—in other words, not intelligent. Sociologist Joe Feagin (2000) agrees, "A majority of whites still stereotype black people as violence-prone ... and a substantial majority still stereotype black Americans as unintelligent" (p. 188).

Football is a violent and aggressive sport in nature. The stereotyping of black criminals as inherently violent and aggressive monsters causes hiring agent's desire these characteristics in BNPs because of the teams' need for aggressive players in the NFL. By Fanon arguing that whites look at "Negros" as both "savages" and intelligent, he is suggesting that, in the case of the BNP, hiring agents see increased intellectual gain as a decreased presence of aggression and violence (Fanon, p. 88).

While aggression and violence are desired traits of a BNP, as well as submission to NFL team authorities, the aspect of deviance and defiance is not a desirable trait to hiring agents. Fanon and Jean-Paul Sartre believe that the stereotypes of black men come from the white man's attempt create his own manhood. The whites man must demonize the black man in order to maintain his own manhood. Sartre explains by saying "there is nothing more consistent than a racist humanism since the European has only been able to become a man through creating slaves and monsters" (Sartre, 1963). The out-of-control image of BNPs has been largely advanced by the media's portrayal of black athletes (Welch, 2007).

In addition to the stereotypes of black men in general, there are specific stereotypes of black athletes. Over the past 20 years, the media has highlighted the legal encounters with major black athletes. Media studies have hypothesized that "the media focus on black athletes accused of committing crimes, such as Kobe Bryant, Mike Tyson, Ray Lewis, Jason Williams, and Allen Iverson, is serving to reinforce the perception that blacks are more menacing than criminals of other races" (Welch, p. 284). Patricia Hill Collins (2005) argues that in 1997 when Latrell Sprewell, a professional basketball player, choked his coach, the media coverage symbolized black masculinity as overly physical, out of control, prone to violence, driven by instinct (Ferber, 2007). The colonial discourse frames black masculinity as deviant and defiant, and they are labeled as animals and monsters (Carrington, 2002). "Athleticism" is often associated with "animalism" and therefore desire by hiring agents but only when BNPs do not display an uncontrollable level of deviance. This combination of violence and sexuality made black men inherently unsuitable for work until they were trained by white men and placed under their discipline and control. To explain these relations, white elites created the controlling image of the buck (Collins, p. 56).

However, the black male is also complicit in colonization, by mimicking and perpetuating the stereotype of aggression and violence. Majors (1992) suggests the cool pose is another display of African agency working to create a form of black masculinity that is distinct from Western masculinity. Cool pose is embraced and reshaped by the media and marketing groups to construct black masculinity in a negative way. The cool pose is a defense mechanism that allows oppressed African American males to protect their dignity and self-respect against social emasculation. More critically, cool pose renders the bravado of unemotional and unaffected carelessness toward their social degradation. This creativeness has constructed new characteristics of black masculinity and manhood including an unbreakable will, a violent, anti-intellectual stance, and actions that are tough and fearless. Majors explains how cool pose functions in the context of sports by saying, "Moreover, the demonstration of cool pose in sports enables black males to accentuate or display themselves (i.e., 'Here I am, world; watch me, see me, hear me, I'm alive'), obtain gratification, released pent-up aggression, gain prestige and recognition, exercise power and control, and express pride, dignity, and respect for themselves and for their race" (Majors, 1998, p. 21).

Conclusion

The U.S. sports industry, the NFL, and the drafting process are clear examples of the contemporary colonization. It shows the pervasiveness of the colonial project into the sports world. Through the analysis of Frantz Fanon and others, BNPs' willingness to go through a discriminatory process evaluation where they self-identify as a "slave market," indicates the antinomy of the colonized mind. Many blacks and other oppressed minorities in the general labor market, the political arena, education, etc. face similar experiences of subjected to inequities as the BNP (Feagin, 1991). They, too, cooperate with the colonial process for similar reasons as the BNP. Fanon attributes this to the black man/woman wanting to be white. Dufur and Feinberg (2008) conclude that BNPs' cooperation in this colonial project is directly to "the athletes' experiences as subordinates in predominantly white university settings, where coaches, academic counselors, athletic directors, media, professors, and NCAA administrators are overwhelmingly older white men" (Dufur & Feinberg, p. 69). The aggressive demeanor of the BNP is an attempt at defense symbolizing the trauma of colonization. The submission, aggressiveness, and childlike language are connected to how they are treated in life. Their experiences include poverty, harassment, self-hate and discrimination projected by negative media images and strategic representations of other BNPs (Dyer, 1993) . Therefore, language, criminal stereotypes, and inferiority as characteristics of colonization exist in interviews during the NFL drafting process by NFL hiring agents and black NFL players.

BIBLIOGRAPHY

Asante, Molefi. *The Afrocentric Idea*. Philadelphia: Temple University Press, 1987.

Bourdieu, Pierre. *Language and Symbolic Power: The Economy of Linguistic Exchanges*. Edited by John B Thompson. Cambridge, MA: Polity, 1981.

Carrington, Ben. "Fear of a Black Athlete: Masculinity, Politics." *new formations: A Journal of Culture, Theory, and Politics*, no. 45 (2002).

Coakley, Jay. *Sports in Society*. New York: McGraw-Hill, 2007.

Collins, P. H. *Black Sexual Politics: African Americans, Gender, and the New Racism*. New York : Routledge, 2005.

Decker, Wolfgang. *Sports and Games of Ancient Egypt*. Binghamton, NY: Vail-Ballou, 1992.

Dufur, Mikaela J., and Seth L. Feinberg. "Race and the NFL Draft: Views from the Auction Block." *Qual Sociol* 32 (December 2008): 53–73.

Dyer, Richard. *The Matter of Images: Essays on Representations*. London: Routledge, 1993.

Fanon, Frantz. *Black Skin White Masks*. Translated by Charles Lam Markmann. London: Pluto, 1986.

Feagin, Joe. "The Continuing Significance of Race: Antiblack Discrimination in Public Places." *American Sociological Review*, no. 56 (1991): 101–116.

Feagin, Joe. *Racist America: Roots, Current Realities, and Future Reparations*. New York: Routledge, 2000.

Ferber, Abby L. "The Construction of Black Masculinity: White Supremacy Now and Then." *Journal of Sport & Social Issues* (2007): 11–25.

Hall, Stuart. "Cultural Identity and Diaspora." In *Identity: Community, Culture, Difference*, edited by Jonathan Rutherford, 222–237. London: Lawrence And Wishart Ltd, 1993.

Hoberman, John. *Darwin's Athletes: How Sports Has Damaged Black America and Preserved the Myth of Race*. New York: Houghton Mifflin, 1997.

Lewis, Thabiti. *Ballers of the New School*. Chicago: Third World, 2010.

Majors, Richard. "Cool Pose: Black Masculinity and Sports." In *African Americans in Sports*, by Gary A. Sailes, 15–22. New Brunswick, NJ: Transaction, 1998.

Majors, Richard, and Janet Mancini Billson. *Cool Pose*. New York: Lexington, 1992.

Mazama, Ama. *The Afrocentric Paradigm*. Trenton, NJ: African World, 2003.

Mills, Charles W. *The Racial Contract*. Ithaca: Cornell University Press, 1997.

Osborne, J. W. "Unraveling Underachievement Among African American Boys From an Identification with Academics Perspective." *Journal of Negro Education*, no. 68 (1999): 555–565.

Sartre, Jean-Paul. "Preface." In *The Wretched of the Earth*, by Frantz Fanon, 7–31. London: Grove, 1963.

Welch, Kelly. "Black Criminal Stereotypes and Racial Profiling." *Journal of Contemporary Criminal Justice* (2007): 276–288.

About the Contributors

Rebecca Milton **Allen** is a doctoral candidate in kinesiology and an adjunct professor at Indiana University Bloomington. Her research interests deal with qualitative, longitudinal studies on the impact of collegiate athletic communities on academic success.

Ashley **Baker** is a doctoral student in the Department of Kinesiology, Sport Management and Policy at the University of Georgia. She was the director of student-athlete services at Bowling Green State University. Her research interests include race and sport, intercollegiate athletics and youth sport.

Drew **Brown** is a Ph.D. student in the Department of African American Studies at Temple University and a former professional football player in the Canadian Football League. He is the founder and chair of the annual conference, Passing the Ball: Race and Sports.

Akilah R. **Carter-Francique** is an assistant professor in the Department of Health and Kinesiology at Texas A&M University. Her focus is on race and ethnicity, gender, and sport and physical activity. She is also the co-founder and director of Sista to Sista, a leadership development program for black female athletes on predominantly white campuses.

J. Kenyatta **Cavil** is a visiting professor of health and kinesiology at Texas Southern University. He produces Dr. Cavil's HBCU Sports Top 10 Mid-Major and Major Polls (football, men's and women's basketball and baseball) and is a regular HBCU sport business and sports analyst on several radio programs with the *HBCU Sports Report*.

James L. **Conyers**, Jr., is the director of the African American Studies Program and the director of the Center for African American Culture at the University of Houston. He is the author or editor of more than 20 books.

Joseph N. **Cooper** is an assistant professor of sport management in the Department of Educational Leadership at the University of Connecticut. His research focuses on examining the impact of post-secondary institutional environments on the academic achievement and college experiences of black male student athletes.

N. Jeremi **Duru** is a professor of law at American University's Washington College of Law. He is a co-author of *Sports Law and Regulation: Cases and Materials,* 3d ed., has written numerous articles and book chapters exploring sports law, has been a legal analyst and commentator, and was the National Bar Association's Sports and Entertainment Lawyer of the Year in 2005.

Billy **Hawkins** is a professor in the University of Georgia's Department of Kinesiology's Sport Management and Policy. He is the author of *The New Plantation: Black Athletes, College Sports, and Predominantly White NCAA Institutions* and co-author of *Sport, Race, Activism, and Social Change: The Impact of Dr. Harry Edwards' Scholarship and Service.*

C. Richard **King** is a professor of comparative ethnic studies and former chair of the Department of Critical Culture, Gender, and Race Studies at Washington State University. He has written extensively on Native American mascots, race in post–civil rights America, the colonial legacies and postcolonial predicaments of American culture, and struggles over Indianness.

David J. **Leonard** is an associate professor and chair of the Department of Critical Culture, Gender and Race Studies at Washington State University, Pullman. He wrote *After Artest: Race and the Assault on Blackness* and co-edited *Visual Economies of/in Motion: Sport and Film* and *Commodified and Criminalized: New Racism and African Americans in Contemporary Sports.*

Rita **Liberti** is a professor in the Department of Kinesiology at California State University East Bay in Hayward, where she also serves as director of the University Center for Sport and Social Justice. Her research on gender, racial and ethnic identity, and sport appears in the *Journal of Sport History*, the *Journal of Sport and Social Issues*, and *Gender & Society*.

Michael E. **Lomax** is an associate professor of sport history in the Department of Health and Human Physiology at the University of Iowa. His primary research focus is on the African American experience in sport and the rise of sport entrepreneurs, and he is the author of *Black Baseball Entrepreneurs 1860–1901: Operating by Any Means Necessary.*

Demetrius W. **Pearson** is an associate professor and associate department chair in the Department of Health and Human Performance at the University of Houston. His teaching and research areas have been in professional preparation in sport and fitness administration, as well as socio-cultural and historical aspects of sport.

Ray V. **Robertson** is an associate professor of criminal justice at the University of Louisiana at Lafayette. He has written about critical race theory, police brutality, birthing options for African American women, boxing, the black Seminoles, and minority college students. He is on the editorial boards of the *Journal of Pan African Studies* and the *Journal of Public Management and Social Policy*.

Gary A. **Sailes** is an associate professor in the Department of Kinesiology and an adjunct professor in the Department of African American and African Diaspora Studies at Indiana University Bloomington. He is the author of seven books and more than 100 articles and book chapters. He received the 2011 Distinguished Service Award from the North American Society for the Sociology of Sport.

Earl **Smith** is a professor of sociology and the Rubin Distinguished Professor of American Ethnic Studies at Wake Forest University, where he is director of the American Ethnic Studies Program. He has published extensively on the sociology of sport and also on social stratification, family and urban sociology. He is the author of *Sociology of Sport and Social Theory*.

Edward "Will" **Thomas** attended the University of Houston, played football for the Tampa Bay Buccaneers and the Buffalo Bills and has two Super Bowl rings. He founded Original Gentlemen Enterprises, a footwear maintenance and repair company at hotels, and Moves Management, an event management and operations company.

Index

Numbers in **bold italics** indicate pages with tables.